Challenge Social Innovation

Hans-Werner Franz • Josef Hochgerner
Jürgen Howaldt
Editors

Challenge Social Innovation

Potentials for Business, Social
Entrepreneurship, Welfare and
Civil Society

Editors
Hans-Werner Franz
Jürgen Howaldt
Social Research Centre
TU Dortmund
Dortmund
Germany

Josef Hochgerner
Centre for Social Innovation
Vienna
Austria

ISBN 978-3-642-32878-7 ISBN 978-3-642-32879-4 (eBook)
DOI 10.1007/978-3-642-32879-4
Springer Heidelberg New York Dordrecht London

Library of Congress Control Number: 2012953561

© Springer-Verlag Berlin Heidelberg 2012
This work is subject to copyright. All rights are reserved by the Publisher, whether the whole or part of the material is concerned, specifically the rights of translation, reprinting, reuse of illustrations, recitation, broadcasting, reproduction on microfilms or in any other physical way, and transmission or information storage and retrieval, electronic adaptation, computer software, or by similar or dissimilar methodology now known or hereafter developed. Exempted from this legal reservation are brief excerpts in connection with reviews or scholarly analysis or material supplied specifically for the purpose of being entered and executed on a computer system, for exclusive use by the purchaser of the work. Duplication of this publication or parts thereof is permitted only under the provisions of the Copyright Law of the Publisher's location, in its current version, and permission for use must always be obtained from Springer. Permissions for use may be obtained through RightsLink at the Copyright Clearance Center. Violations are liable to prosecution under the respective Copyright Law.
The use of general descriptive names, registered names, trademarks, service marks, etc. in this publication does not imply, even in the absence of a specific statement, that such names are exempt from the relevant protective laws and regulations and therefore free for general use.
While the advice and information in this book are believed to be true and accurate at the date of publication, neither the authors nor the editors nor the publisher can accept any legal responsibility for any errors or omissions that may be made. The publisher makes no warranty, express or implied, with respect to the material contained herein.

Printed on acid-free paper

Springer is part of Springer Science+Business Media (www.springer.com)

 EUROPEAN COMMISSION

Bureau of European Policy Advisers

Foreword I

Challenge Social Innovation

Agnès Hubert[1]

The expression, the concept and hopefully some concrete social innovations have gained an immense popularity in the last few years, in the EU and beyond. "Social innovation is becoming a global phenomenon that concerns all countries. From Europe to the United States this new process has recruited politicians, entrepreneurs, civil talent and intellectuals. Social innovation is now gaining more attention in developing countries". These lines were recently published in an article on the "growing importance of social innovation" in *China Daily*, by Yu Keping, deputy director of the Communist Party of China's Central Compilation and Translation Bureau.[2] They would certainly not be contradicted by the growing movement witnessed in Europe, emerging both from grassroots movements and policy circles.

To say that a newly found passion for social innovation started in the wake of the current financial crisis would not fully reflect the reality. Not only the concept was born much earlier (some place its real beginning in the late nineteen's century in the wake of industrialisation and urbanisation) but it was revived on many occasions. What is interesting in the current situation is first to understand not necessarily the why but what social innovation means and can achieve and how it can help address, now and in the future, the challenges we are facing.

After having met stakeholders in a workshop organised in Brussels in January 2009, President Barroso concluded: "Social innovation is not a panacea but if encouraged and valued, it can bring immediate solutions to the pressing social

---

[1] *Agnès Hubert* is a member of the Bureau of European Policy Advisers (BEPA) of the European Commission. She was the responsible editor of the BEPA Report, the Commission's programmatic paper on Social Innovation, and she co-ordinates social innovation initiatives across the Commission's Directorates-General.

[2] http://www.chinadaily.com.cn/cndy/2012-02/08/content_14556022.htm

issues citizens are confronted with". He added: "In the long term, I see social innovation as part of a new culture of empowerment that we are trying to promote". This wide-ranging view of social innovation as a lever for societal change has ever since been underpinning initiatives promoted at EU level to boost social innovation in EU policies and on the ground in Member States. The first function of social innovation is to develop solutions to better answer the growing social demands which are further exacerbated by the crisis. It also challenges the traditional ways markets and public sectors have provided answers to social demands by making room for the engagement of society itself to generate social value. The culture of people's empowerment to create social change is central to the Commission's systemic approach to social innovation.

Following the workshop attended by the President, a networking collaborative exercise steered by the Bureau of European Policy Advisers started within the Commission to promote a new vision of social innovation. A report was produced[3] and BEPA has been given a light coordination mandate on social innovation initiatives in European policies. From a wealth of important but fragmented initiatives and programmes that were developed in the past (e.g. the EQUAL initiative), we moved to a situation where social innovation is a frontline issue for high-level decision makers in the institutions.

It is now firmly embedded into the two major EU policy documents to frame the next 10 years: The EU 2020 Strategy for smart, sustainable and inclusive growth and the Multiannual Financial Framework, that is the EU budget that will support European policies from 2014 to 2020. Also, the Single Market Act, a series of measures to boost the European economy and create jobs,[4] includes the promotion of social entrepreneurship.[5]

In the EU 2020 Programme with its five measurable targets (including poverty reduction) and its seven flagship initiatives (including in particular "Innovation Union" and the "European platform against poverty and social exclusion"), social innovation is an instrument to reach the objective of a smart, green and inclusive growth which Member States have agreed upon for 2020.

As for the Commission's proposals for the next seven years EU Budget (2014–2020), social innovation features explicitly in several of the draft financial regulations[6] by policy areas. In the European Social Funds for instance, social innovation will be promoted in all areas with the aim of testing and scaling up innovative solutions to address social needs; member states will be asked to identify themes for social innovation corresponding to their specific needs and the Commission will facilitate capacity building for social innovation, through mutual learning,

---

[3] "Empowering people, driving change: Social innovation in the European Union Publications Office ISBN 978-92-79-19275-3".

[4] http://ec.europa.eu/internal_market/smact/index_en.htm

[5] The social business initiative, adopted in November 2011 http://ec.europa.eu/internal_market/social_business/index_en.htm

[6] http://ec.europa.eu/budget/biblio/documents/regulations/regulations_en.cfm

the establishment of networks, the dissemination of good practices and methodologies. The same goes for the new research and innovation program, Horizon 2020, for which the Commission has proposed the largest budget increase of all EU policy areas (from €54.9 to €80 billion or 46 % increase). The programs presented for cohesion policy, agriculture, education, IT policies and the new digital agenda, and even Culture, contain either a mention and/or open opportunities for supporting social innovations.

So there are and there will be means at EU level (and hopefully at national, regional and local levels) to promote actions and initiatives to deepen our knowledge and practice of social innovation. The question is how we can best plan to use these resources to "empower people and drive change" to face upcoming challenges. This is where our knowledge about how social innovation works, grows and changes the way societies are driven is crucial.

In the BEPA report, we distinguish three complementary approaches to social innovation:

Social: The grassroots social innovations which respond to pressing social demands which are not addressed by the market and are directed towards vulnerable groups in society

Societal: The broader level which addresses societal challenges in which the boundaries between social and economic are blurred and which are directed towards society as a whole

Systemic: The systemic type which relates to fundamental changes in attitudes and values, strategies and policies, organisational structures and processes, delivery systems and services

The question is not which category should be nurtured, financed, made more visible and researched, but how we build on the complementarities of the three approaches to engage the systemic change which is necessary to effectively address poverty, ageing, unemployment, social justice, climate change, resource efficiency and growth in times of financial crisis. Empowering people and driving change are the twin key objectives, which we see as essential for innovation in general but also to allow the shift in attitudes, preferences and production for a sustainable, inclusive and smart economy of EU 2020.

By empowerment we mean education and knowledge plus governance and anticipation. Why do people need to be empowered? Because social innovations most often challenge conventional wisdom. As John Stuart Mill wrote when analysing the subjection of women, when the intentions and effect of an innovation is contrary to what is considered as "superior wisdom", one needs a disproportionate amount of conviction and perseverance to get it done.

Driving change: Should we rely on crisis to create change? After all, the post 1929 period is widely known as very fertile in social innovations and 9/11 has promoted a culture of solidarity and responsibility never seen in New York. Or should we try to shape change? As underlined by Josef Hochgerner in this volume, innovations do not develop in a vacuum but in a socially constructed environment. Where the dominant paradigm is hegemonic, innovation will not emerge; for example, where patriarchate is dominant, efforts to promote gender equality are doomed; the same is true for social innovation where the economic paradigm is too powerful.

How does this connect with our common future? Within our remit as an internal think tank for the European Commission, BEPA commissions research on dominant trends of the future. The most recent forward study, under the title "facing the future, time for the EU to meet global challenges",[7] identifies the main trends ahead and possible disruptive global challenges. It suggests how the EU could position itself to take an active role in shaping a response to them. Based on the criteria of urgency, tractability and impact, this research confronts quantified trends towards 2025 and beyond with experts' and policy makers' opinions on the likely consequences of these trends. It concurs with other future studies to point to three major challenges with a global scope which require action at the EU level:

- A green challenge: the need to change current ways in which essential natural resources are used – due to the non-sustainable human over-exploitation of natural resources. The most well-known effects are climate change, loss of biodiversity, increasing demand for food, deepening poverty and exclusion linked to continued exploitation of the natural resources, energy and water scarcity leading to competition and conflict, mass migration and threats in the form of radicalisation and terrorism.
- An inclusive challenge: the need to anticipate and adapt to societal changes including political, cultural, demographic and economic transformations in order for the EU to develop into a knowledge society. The main dimensions related to this challenge are economic growth mainly depending on increases in efficiency and productivity; ageing societies increasing pressures on pensions, social security and healthcare systems; flow of migrants from developing to developed countries; empowerment of citizens through enhanced education; barriers to the social acceptance of innovations due to lack of understanding of technological possibilities and related consequences; and inability to keep up with the speed and complexity of socio-economic changes.
- A smart challenge: the need for more effective and transparent governance for the EU and the world with the creation of accountable forms of governance able to anticipate and adapt to the future and thus address common challenges, and to spread democracy and transparency on the global level. Related to this challenge are the weakening of borders between nations with the problems of (especially neighbouring) developing countries increasingly affecting the EU, single policy governance approaches which can no longer cope with global issues and the lack of balance in representing nations in global fora.

Based on the above, the study presents a blueprint for policy makers at the EU level which includes detailed recommendations on policy alignment towards

---

[7] http://ftp.jrc.es/EURdoc/JRC55981.pdf

sustainability, social diversity and citizens' empowerment (including ICT) anticipation of future challenges to turn these into new opportunities.

My main message in mentioning these wide-ranging challenges is not to go beyond social innovation but to the heart of it, in its transformative power. The behavioural changes and innovative collective action triggered by social innovation on a large scale are *the* essential components to drive public policy reform to address these challenges.

To conclude: the commitments to Social Innovation made by the Commission as part of the EU2020 strategy and in the preparation of the new EU budget provide the elements of an agenda for change towards a smart, inclusive and sustainable growth. They range from the support to networking and access to funding for grassroots social innovations and social entrepreneurs to experiments of social policy instruments. They also include research in methodologies and changes in governance modes. It is now firmly embedded in the most important EU policies for the next decade and its contribution to the reform of social policies and to behavioural and systemic changes is promising. However, while the practical framework is ready to sustain a large development of social innovation, theoretical foundations are still insufficient to describe the potential scope and range of social innovation as a transformative concept. The "Challenge social innovation conference" contributed to highlight new theoretical insights and explored experiments in a large range of sectors and human activities. This is largely reflected in the rich contributions in this volume. Hopefully, as social innovation will be developing on a larger scale, so will the need to redefine value creation and the basis for growth and well-being. Reversely, social innovation will only make a difference where risk taking for the creation of social value by those most concerned becomes a respected activity. In this context, public debates on indicators of growth beyond GDP which was initiated by the Commission in 2007 may come to be seen as a great opportunity to complement the systemic changes which social innovation creates to address the challenges mentioned earlier. This is not only a debate for statisticians but it must engage social scientists, sociologists, anthropologists and economists. One of the elements of this debate is also about the slow transformation of what Durkheim called "the non-material social facts".

Foreword II

Antonella Noya[8]

In the last decade, social innovation has attracted particular attention from policy makers, academics, practitioners and the general public. The current unparalleled challenges at global, national and territorial levels call for innovative strategies and tools to successfully address them. Moreover, the recent financial and economic crisis, probably the worst we have seen in our lifetime, makes the shift to a new economic thinking urgent. Innovative models of growth and governance are needed to recreate trust among people, on the one side, and to allow economic and social sustainability and transparency in decision making, on the other side.

As the OECD (Organisation for Economic Cooperation and Development) Secretary General, Ángel Gurría, recently said "we must go social to give the people hope, confidence and perspectives".

Now, social innovation is key to giving people better perspectives. In fact, according to the definition that OECD provided in its Forum on Social Innovations (FSI), its final aim is to improve people's well-being and quality of life by promoting social change. Social innovation is, therefore, an important element of the new economic thinking, which is needed to put forward those fundamental changes in approaching economics and politics, thus avoiding a return to "business as usual". Social innovation should be central to the policy agendas of our Governments. Even if progress has been made in some countries to support social innovation, more remains to be done.

The role of research is important in furthering the knowledge around social innovation and the mechanisms and processes which are needed to implement it. Social sciences and humanities have clearly a role to play, as social innovations are vital in the field of social policies. The papers presented in this book underline the need for including social innovation in the paradigm shift of innovation. This is what the OECD Innovation strategy (2010) did, looking at innovation from a wide expanse of policy areas and acknowledging the rise of social innovation to

---

[8] Senior Policy Analyst at OECD, manager of the OECD LEED Forum on Social Innovations

tackle the global challenges such as climate change and the greening of the economy.

Indeed, the OECD has been an early player in the field of social innovation to increase policy awareness on its importance for more sustainable and inclusive public policies. In fact, through its LEED (Local Employment and Economic Development) Programme, the OECD established the Forum on Social Innovations, a multi-stakeholders platform, created in 2000 by a number of actors in the public, private and non-profit sectors, from different countries, which agreed to share knowledge and to help in shaping the policy agenda around social innovation. The Forum aims at facilitating exchanges of best practices and policies in social innovation, at providing a framework for a comparative assessment of social innovations and at reinforcing international networks of policy makers and practitioners in this field. The Forum on Social Innovations (FSI) is innovative and interesting for at least a couple of main reasons and could be, therefore, seen as a model for similar initiatives. More places, and even virtual places, of knowledge sharing and policy dialogue are, in fact, needed to increase awareness around social innovation and set up initiatives. What is interesting in the FSI and could also be inspiring is its multi-stakeholders approach, which is indispensable if social innovation is to be fostered and implemented.

Social innovation is not restricted to one sector. Rather, it can take place everywhere, but it does not simply "happen". It requires mechanisms and incentives to stimulate it. It is the result of joint efforts, creativity and of a shared vision of a more sustainable, fairer and people-oriented future. Some innovations appear in the public sector, some in the private and others in the non-profit sector. Bringing together different actors under the umbrella of the Forum on Social Innovations was a way to foster a creative dialogue between stakeholders around many different initiatives: conferences; capacity building seminars; study visits; and topics relevant for social innovation such as the social economy and the social entrepreneurship; important agents of social innovation, although not the only ones; corporate social responsibility, that is the role of private business in fostering social innovation; community capacity building, that is empowering people for them to be able to actively participate in their communities; demand-led innovation, that is bringing people in the innovation process; and, finally, innovative decision making processes.

The FSI is also interesting because of its balanced approach between a theoretical and a practical dimension: The FSI has put together "the theory and the practice", and in combining these two dimensions, it has set social innovation in motion. In fact, while providing a working definition of social innovation, the first ever provided by an international organisation, it has, over the years, explored a wide set of social innovations in different geographical contexts. Today, like yesterday, the theory of social innovation evolves and new definitions appear while many social innovations develop on the ground. Already 12 years ago the FSI wanted to capture the essence of social innovation through the analysis of social innovations appearing in different countries. This approach is still valid: while more research is needed to understand the boundaries of social innovation and to measure it, policy makers need to go beyond definitions and look at the realities which develop before their eyes to understand what is needed to foster social innovation and which mechanisms are the most appropriate and which leverages can be used.

Why was the decision to establish this Forum taken 12 years ago, at a time when social innovation was not yet high on the policy agendas of OECD member countries? Because many elements were already there to suggest that social innovation would have become an important factor of economic and social development. If the recent financial and economic crisis and the public budget constraints have now made this even clearer, we need to be aware that the factors that led to the creation of the OECD Forum on Social Innovations are still influencing the development of our societies and, in actual fact, represent triggers for social innovation to develop. This book analyses some of them, making clear that the time has now arrived to promote social innovation without any further hesitation.

Let us think, for instance, about the importance of the civil society and the social economy and social entrepreneurship. Their engagement in the social and economic development is central and they certainly cannot be considered, as they sometimes are, as residual actors. These actors have the willingness and often the capacity to act to transform the society and to provoke social change. Many initiatives undertaken by the social economy and by the civil society have proved to be innovative in dealing with social, environmental and societal problems, while contributing to the economic development. Not to mention that some entities, for instance social enterprises, are socially innovative devices themselves, thanks to their governance systems and their explicit mission of pursuing the general interest through an entrepreneurial approach.

The limits of the market and the state to address important social challenges (poverty, social exclusion, ageing population, rising inequalities, demographic change,) using conventional wisdom and traditional approaches are also factors that have played, and continue to play, an important role in the emergence of social innovation.

And obviously the global challenges that are first and foremost threats can also be considered as opportunities to "think out of the box" and implement social innovation. History confirms that the emergence of social innovation has always been linked to times of crisis.

Another trigger of social innovation, which started to be observed as a new phenomenon ten years ago, was the need of traditional business to reconnect with society and to adopt more socially accepted behaviours. This was, in turn, partially due to the increasing emergence of intangible assets, such as reputation, and trust. As the importance of intangible factors is even growing nowadays, social innovation can increase even more.

The emergence of new investors attracted by the social return on investment and therefore willing to invest in more socially responsible business and venture is also a factor that is having a positive impact on social innovation.

Social innovations are processes and outcomes which transform practices and policies of local and global economic and social development. Whenever social innovations appear, they always bring about new references and processes. The ingredients of social innovation are different and interconnected: individual, collective and institutional creativity are needed, together with the capacity to "think out of the box" and to walk off the beaten tracks. The capacity to work in partnership and to mobilise different kinds of human and financial resources is another important ingredient for social innovations.

But what is really needed is to have a systemic approach to social innovation, an enabling environment and eco-system providing the adequate incentives, finances, structures and drivers for social innovations to develop. The OECD has put forward in the last decade a number of policy recommendations on the measures and processes which can foster social innovation.

Social innovation is a challenge – one that cannot be missed. This book represents an excellent opportunity to "challenge social innovation" and to push thinking around it further.

Contents

Challenge Social Innovation: An Introduction 1
Hans-Werner Franz, Josef Hochgerner, and Jürgen Howaldt

Part I On Social Innovation Theory

Social Innovation Theories: Can Theory Catch Up
with Practice? 19
Geoff Mulgan

Shaping Social Innovation by Social Research 43
Jürgen Howaldt and Ralf Kopp

Do Non-humans Make a Difference? The Actor-Network-Theory
and the Social Innovation Paradigm 57
Alexander Degelsegger and Alexander Kesselring

Social Innovation: What Is Coming Apart and What Is
Being Rebuilt? 73
Denis Harrisson

New Combinations of Social Practices in the Knowledge Society 87
Josef Hochgerner

Part II Social Innovation in the Service Sector

What Is Social About Service Innovation? Contributions of Research
on Social Innovation to Understanding Service Innovation 107
Heike Jacobsen and Milena Jostmeier

Social Innovation and Service Innovation 119
Faridah Djellal and Faïz Gallouj

Innovators at Risk in the Public Service 139
Stuart Conger

Part III Social Innovation and Welfare

Social Innovations in Ageing Societies 153
Rolf G. Heinze and Gerhard Naegele

Social Innovation or Social Exclusion? Innovating Social Services in the Context of a Retrenching Welfare State 169
Flavia Martinelli

Part IV Social Innovation and Social Entrepreneurship

Social Innovation, Social Entrepreneurship and Development 183
György Széll

Social Innovations and Institutional Challenges in Microfinance 197
Anup Dash

Social Innovation and Social Enterprise: Evidence from Australia 215
Jo Barraket and Craig Furneaux

Part V Social Innovation at the Workplace

Social Innovation at Work: Workplace Innovation as a Social Process 241
Peter Totterdill, Peter Cressey, and Rosemary Exton

Social Innovation of Work and Employment 261
Frank Pot, Steven Dhondt, and Peter Oeij

Part VI Social Innovation, Open Innovation and Social Media

Challenges at the Intersection of Social Media and Social Innovation: A Manifesto 277
Christoph Kaletka, Karolin Eva Kappler, Bastian Pelka, and Ricard Ruiz de Querol

Coordination and Motivation of Customer Contribution as Social Innovation: The Case of Crytek 293
Daniel Kahnert, Raphael Menez, and Birgit Blättel-Mink

Part VII Measuring Social Innovation

Measuring Social Innovation and Monitoring Progress of EU Policies 309
Werner Wobbe

How to Measure the Intangibles? Towards a System of Indicators (S.A.V.E.) for the Measurement of the Performance of Social Enterprises 325
Andrea Bassi

Part VIII Social Innovation and the Social Sciences

Social Innovation and Action Research 353
Bjørn Gustavsen

Towards Advancing Understanding of Social Innovation 367
Anne de Bruin

Final Observations 379
Hans-Werner Franz, Josef Hochgerner, and Jürgen Howaldt

Challenge Social Innovation: An Introduction

Hans-Werner Franz, Josef Hochgerner, and Jürgen Howaldt

Abstract The introduction to the book provides information about the coordinates and intentions of the Challenge Social Innovation Conference that took place in September 2011 in Vienna. This conference was the principal background and framework of the book presented here. The introduction highlights the focal points of the authors invited to contribute to this book.

> *The tracks of international research on innovation demonstrate that the technology-oriented paradigm – shaped by the industrial society – does not cover the broad range of innovations indispensable in the transition from an industrial to a knowledge and services-based society: Such fundamental societal changes require the inclusion of social innovations in a **paradigm shift of the innovation system**.*
> *(Vienna Declaration)*

1 The Challenge of the Vienna Conference

When we started preparing the conference that took place in Vienna in September 2011 one hundred years after Schumpeter developed his economic theory of innovation it seemed to us a great opportunity to broaden the concept of innovation. Following the tracks of international research upon innovation it becomes more and

---

H.-W. Franz (✉) • J. Howaldt
Social Research Centre, Dortmund University of Technology, Evinger Platz 17, Dortmund 44339, Germany
e-mail: Franz@sfs-dortmund.de; howaldt@sfs-dortmund.de

J. Hochgerner
Centre for Social Innovation, Linke Wienzeile 246, Vienna 1150, Austria
e-mail: hochgerner@zsi.at

more obvious that the technology-oriented paradigm – shaped by the industrial society – is increasingly losing its explanatory and illustrative function.

That transition from an industrial to a knowledge and services-based society seems to correspond to a paradigm shift of the innovation system which implies an increasing importance of social innovation, as compared to technological innovation. This new innovation paradigm – as described e.g. by the experts of the OECD Study "New nature of innovation" – is essentially characterised by the opening of the innovation process to society. Alongside companies, universities and research institutes, citizens and customers become relevant actors within the innovation process. Terms and concepts such as "open innovation", customer integration and networks reflect aspects of this development. Based on these trends, innovation becomes a general social phenomenon that increasingly influences every aspect of our life.

However, the area of social innovation has been virtually ignored as an independent phenomenon in socio-economic research on innovation. Social innovation rarely appears as a specific and defined term with a clearly delineated scope but usually is used as a sort of descriptive metaphor in the context of social and technological change. We have to admit that "Social innovation is a term that almost everybody likes but nobody is quite sure of what it means" (Pol and Ville 2009). It was one of the objectives of the Vienna Conference to take care of this deficiency. When we called it Challenge Social Innovation we had in mind a triple challenge.

Firstly, it was the challenge to make this first world-wide scientific conference dealing with social innovation a success. It is easy to invite scientific experts; it is not so easy to get them all together and make them all move at the same time to the same place. Nevertheless, we managed to organise the hitherto largest scientific get together of nearly all those we knew already from their writings and not few we did not know yet. Key for the success was the very inspiring and fruitful co-operation with Net4Society, the network of National Contact Points for the Social Sciences and Humanities part of the Seventh EU Framework Programme for Research and a highly motivated organisation team. Few of those we really wanted to have in Vienna had to cancel their participation briefly before the event, e.g. Kriss Deiglmeier from the Center for Social Innovation at Stanford University (US) who was in the Steering Committee, and Frances Westley from the Institute for Social Innovation and Resilience (University of Waterloo, Canada). But most of those we had read and quoted before we had the pleasure to meet in Vienna. So we achieved what we had formulated as our target: *It is the objective of this conference to establish social innovation as a major theme of work and discourse in the scientific community.* This book is embedded in the same endeavour as is the publication of those contributions not selected for the book in the ZSI Discussion Papers 14–30 (www.zsi.at/dp).

Secondly, we had to deal with the challenge to make not only the scientific community meet, i.e. those who are interested in or working on social innovation. We also wanted them to meet a number of relevant people from the large agencies and institutions tuning in on social innovation such as the European Commission, the OECD Forum on Social Innovation and UNESCO. Science on and politics for social innovation need each other. If our motto "Innovating innovation by research – 100 years after Schumpeter" was to come true, also this challenge had to be met. This book will continue this idea of making the scientific community interested in the subject and providing support to those who in their political decision try to foster and focus on social innovation. This was and is not an easy task since the requirements of political definition and scientific analysis do not always go easily together. Here we could benefit from the very valuable and prolific work of the Young Foundation and the global network Social Innovation eXchange (SIX) who had published several books and in particular a study on social innovation (SIX 2010) for the European Commission that succeeded to conciliate scientific analysis with political need for handy definitions (see below). One of the outputs of the conference, the Vienna Declaration on "the most relevant topics in social innovation research" (cf. final chapter 23 of this book) provided a rich reservoir of desiderata vis-à-vis the programme makers of the European Commission, OECD and UNESCO who actively participated in the conference.

Thirdly, we had the aim to link the debate on social innovation closely to the discourse on innovation in general, following the heritage of ICICI, the international conferences on indicators and concepts of innovation. This is also one of the main objectives of this book. Social innovation is a challenge for all scientific disciplines that have dealt with innovation so far; but it is a particular challenge for the social sciences, since "social innovations are innovations that are social both in their ends and in their means" (SIX 2010: 17f; see also Mulgan in this book and BEPA 2010). This very helpful political definition of social innovation has the virtue to facilitate political decision making on what socially innovative projects to fund and to foster; it is an a priori definition making the distinction easier between what might be socially innovative and what not. It helps to solve the fundamental problem of any innovation (to become or not to be), i.e. the problem that we do not know whether it will be an innovation after all, since it is the success or failure of its diffusion, the eventual degree of generalisation which decides what can or cannot be considered an innovation. Political deciders face the problem that they have to take decisions on what should be considered as innovative before the innovative idea or invention can prove to become an innovation. Innovation in Schumpeterian terms is defined not only by its newness but by its acceptance, be it as a market success, be it by changing the way how a sufficient number of people do things together or alone. "Social in its ends and in its means" is a useful formula not only for deciding about social innovation, it could and should just as well be used as an additional criterion for decision making about technological inventions and prototypes, methods and processes just as the development of a new automobile nowadays includes asking the customers as well as the workers who will have to produce the car about how they conceive the plans for the new vehicle under their aspects and from their perspectives of using and producing it. It is useful because it conveys an idea of social as "good for many" or "socially desirable", as socially "valuable". Nevertheless, we have come to learn that not everything which is intended as good for many may eventually turn out to be considered as good from many.

From these few deliberations we can draw several conclusions. One is that for a scientific debate we have to aim higher and farther than at the needs of political decision making. Another one is that we should take into consideration that social innovation still is innovation and that the scientific basics of innovation are and must stay true for social innovation, too. And if they have to be reconsidered, social innovation must become an integral part of this reflective effort. So this book wants to be understood as a first global contribution to "embedding the concept of social innovation in a comprehensive theory of innovation" (Vienna Declaration, see "Final observations" in this book).

2 Towards a Handy and Useful Definition of Social Innovation

Testing the politically useful definition of "social in its end and in its means" against simple criteria of what can be considered as social innovation from a scientific point of view will prove it as (necessarily) imprecise and methodically doubtful. In strict scientific terms, defining 'social innovation' excludes using the terms social and innovation in the definition. Strictly speaking, the definition "social innovations are innovations that are social both in their ends and in their means" is tautological. What we can take from this definition is that social innovation is intentional, meant to change something in what people do alone or together to the better, at least as they perceive it. The intentionality of social innovation is what distinguishes it from social change. Social change just happens. But is all social innovation really intended as social and/or using social means?

Many a social innovation was not intended as social. McDonalds (and its imitators), the idea of a fast food restaurant – before, for many still a contradiction in terms – was and is a true social innovation by its results wherever it was and is introduced. It has succeeded to change the traditional idea of eating out alone or together dramatically for a very large proportion of the population, and in most of our societies it clearly co-exists as an established option for many along with other ideas of eating out together. But it was definitely not intended as being social, neither in its ends nor in its means, but most clearly as a for-profit mass consumption concept of highly rationalised food production and service organisation. It was developed to serve a specific market, and it was people who made it a specific part of our social life and culture. It is true, markets are also people and part of what in social sciences would be considered as social. Economy is in society! But it would stretch the concept of the social sphere as distinct from the economic sphere very far.

A similar observation can be made referring to the internet which is *the* major social innovation of the past 20 years. With billions of people participating, there can be no doubt that it is the largest and most rapidly generalised social innovation ever. It has radically changed the most essential features of mankind, i.e. our ways of communicating and our ways of working together. Here we could say that the ends of developing it were social, since it was originally developed to facilitate scientific collaboration. But the means are clearly technical developments and provisions, although, and here the social enters the scene, massively influenced in its evolution by the way how people have used and are using these technologies, for or not for profit, and undoubtedly based on the massive spread of a technological innovation, the 'personal computer'. This is true to the extent that we can put forward the assumption that the PC would be not such a widespread communication medium without the development of the internet. Under the definition of "social by its ends and by its means" we would have to start distinguishing between the social and the economic use of the internet in order to find out how much of it is only an innovation – but which sort of innovation: technological, economic, cultural? – and how much it is a social innovation. The internet clearly is a social innovation using technological means, as so many social innovations do. The mobile telephone stands for a very similar story. It has changed completely the communication behaviour or many people, certainly so of our younger generations.

What has changed in both these exemplary cases of innovation and what is the decisive characteristic of social innovation is the fact that people do things differently due to this innovation, alone or together. What changes with social innovation is social practice, the way how people decide, act and behave, alone or together (cf. Howaldt and Schwarz 2010: 26ff; also Howaldt/Kopp in this book). Or in sociological speak: when roles change or people interpret them differently; when relations between individuals or groups change regarding the expectations, achievements, rights and duties involved; when norms, i.e. rules of the most varied kinds from house rules to laws and international agreements, are changed or interpreted in a meaningfully new way; and when values change which are understood as general patterns of desirable modes of behaviour and attitudes (see Hochgerner in this book). It is extended social practice what has made McDonalds also a social innovation, and it is massive social practice what has transformed the internet from a scientific tool of co-operation into a worldwide tool of communication and exchange, first by electronically copying the old media, i.e. electronic mail instead of mail letters, then by stimulating further technological innovation empowering people to continuously develop today's social media (see Kaletka et al. in this book), online bartering, selling and buying as 'prosumers' (see Jacobsen/Jostmeier in this book), joint design and development as well as other forms of co-operation and even a change in managing innovation itself (see Blättel-Mink et al. in this book). The internet actually is a cluster of innovations, technological, social, economic, organisational, service etc., engendering continuously further innovation, a perfect example for the brightness of Schumpeter's original definition of innovation as a "new combination", both as a product and as a process (Swedberg and Knudsen 2010).

It is exactly this content, multitudinous individual or joint practice, what is missing in this handy definition of "innovation that is social both in its ends and in its means"; it defines the ends and means of such innovation as social, i.e. the extension of the concept, but it is missing content, the so-called intension of the concept. Defining social innovation only by its ends and means leaves the concept empty. "It needs to be complemented by a further articulation of what we mean by 'social' ... and of the scope of change" (BEPA 2011: 42). So a more complete handy definition for the purposes of making political choices proposed here is that social innovation consists in *new social practices with social ends and social means*. A slightly longer but more precise concept might lead to *new, more effective and/or more efficient social practices with social ends and social means*. It does not solve the problem of tautology. But is helps to delimitate the ground which separates social innovation from technological innovation. There are and, hopefully, will be lots of social scientists who offer considerably longer, more precise and more reliable definitions.

3 Distinguishing the Meanings of Social in Social Innovation

It is another great merit of the BEPA report that it differentiates social innovations according to their scope. The report distinguishes between *social*, *societal* and *systemic* (2011: 36ff; see also the foreword of Agnès Hubert in this book).

- Social is defined as "social demands that are traditionally not addressed by the market or existing institutions and are directed towards vulnerable groups in society" (ibid.: 43).
- Social meaning societal is defined as "societal challenges in which the boundary between 'social' and 'economic' blurs, and which are directed towards society as a whole" (ibid.: 43).
- Social understood as systemic is described as "reshaping society" (ibid.: 42) "in the direction of a more participative arena where empowerment and learning are sources and outcomes of well-being" (ibid.: 43).

While the differentiation into social, societal and systemic seems very useful, the definitions provided seem to be narrowing down the real importance of the three scopes. Here we see the limiting effect of the formula "social by its end and by its means" at work, at least from a social scientific point of view. How these three distinctions of scope can be made fruitful will need further research, theoretical and empirical, to develop them to the full richness of their distinction.

- Concerning *social*: Why should a new way of satisfying a social demand put forward by the market or by existing institutions not be considered as a social innovation? For political reasons of focusing funding, this may be acceptable, not from a scientific point of view.
- Social innovations of *societal* scope, i.e. concerning the society as a whole, will not only make boundaries between 'social' and 'economic' blur, in the context of society such boundaries may not even exist, since economy is part of the society (cf. Hochgerner in this book). When such a fundamental social innovation like old age retirement systems was introduced into our societies,

mostly in the nineteenth century, they affected the social as well as the economic spheres of society just as well as the individual citizen or employee, depending on the respective national system. And any fundamental change of such a system, for example from a labour-based funding scheme of retirement like the German one to a citizen-based funding system like the Swiss one, a fervent debate in Germany, will affect the whole of our societal balance. And such a change would be a top-down social innovation, by the way, politically induced, decided by parliament and implemented top down. And it would be a social, a societal and a systemic change at the same time.

- Finally, regarding social as *systemic*, the system need not necessarily be the whole society. All societal systems, e.g. organisations, be they for profit or not for profit, may undergo systemic social innovation. A good example across all social spheres is the ever wider spread of total quality management systems in organisations (Franz 2010) which indeed installs an ongoing process of reshaping these organisations towards more empowerment and learning, "leading to sustainable systemic change" which also in the BEPA report is considered as the "ultimate objective of social innovation" (2011: 38). Whether at the end of the day it will lead to more well-being, is a question of evidence and hence of research.

We remain with the final and decisive question of the social sciences. What is social? And in our context, what does 'social' mean when we talk about social innovation, social ends, social means, and social practice? We will have to reconsider the whole of theory on social action since social practice comes from social actors (see Hochgerner 2011a or 2011b). Geoff Mulgan has set the agenda by starting his contribution to this book with the following words:

> The field of social innovation has grown up primarily as a field of practice, made up of people doing things and then, sometimes, reflecting on what they do. There has been relatively little attention to theory, or to history, and although there has been much promising research work in recent years, there are no clearly defined schools of thought, no continuing theoretical arguments, and few major research programmes to test theories against the evidence. But to mature as a field social innovation needs to shore up its theoretical foundations, the frames with which it thinks and makes sense of the world.

This is exactly what all contributors to this book, to the ZSI Discussion Papers, and formerly to the conference intend to do. A quick review of the book's chapters and contributions may provide a first glance at what richness of thought we have collected and put together to meet the Challenge Social Innovation scientifically.

3.1 On Social Innovation Theory

It is Mulgan's contribution that surfs through a cosmos of literature presenting "ideas for an emerging field" at the beginning of the book's opening part *on social innovation theory*. It is the only contribution among those much longer ones than requested that we have left uncut as a bow to the immeasurable merits Mulgan, the late Diogo Vasconcelos and their organisations (cf. his CV) have accumulated in scaling up social innovation.

Why is social innovation coming up *now*? Howaldt and Kopp hold "the basic assumption" that "the transition from an industrial to a knowledge- and services-based society corresponds with a paradigm shift of the innovation system. This paradigm shift also implies an increasing importance of social innovation, as compared to technological innovation." This hypothesis would explain why social innovation is progressing in so many different areas of society of which we can only cover a few in this book, beyond the plain and commonplace observation that everything what humans do is social.

Degelsegger and Kesselring would extend this assertion to artefacts since they have 'translated' Bruno Latour's actor network theory for social innovation conciliating technological and non-technological innovation.

Harrisson argues that additionally to social innovation heading for more effective and efficient solutions to social problems, it is "based on moral and idealistic motivations with human beings searching for harmony and freedom" and that also along these lines "society is being rebuilt through the constituency of social innovation in three key facets: the public interest and common good, a new approach to the concept of service and the networks strengthening the bonds of trust between citizens."

Hochgerner maintains Schumpeter's denotation of innovation as new combinations of production factors can be adapted to social innovation as new combinations of social practices. A slightly longer, more analytical definition, and the adoption of some elements of action theory connect the Schumpeterian basics of innovation theory with social innovation and the main types of innovation addressed in standard frameworks of current innovation research. Four key terms to classify social innovations (roles, relations, norms, values) are advocated for inclusion in an extended concept of innovation, comprising innovations that may adhere to economic and social rationales alike, occurring in any sector of society. Looking forward, the relevance and need to re-position the economic system in society is highlighted, considering it might be most innovative – under social, societal *and* systemic perspectives – to introduce and implement 'management of abundance' as equally salient and urgent compared to the well established principle of managing scarcity.

3.2 Social Innovation in the Service Sector

It is not by chance that the book's second part deals with *social innovation in the service sector* since service is the largest economic sector, at least in the developed world, innovation of services and of their delivery probably are the largest but least perceived area of innovation. Moreover, service always consists in social interaction, be it immediate or mediated by technologies. Does this mean that all service innovation might be considered as social innovation? Both Jacobsen/Jostmeier and Djellal/Gallouj offer theoretical explanations for the "tertiarisation of innovation" (Jacobsen/Jostmeier) and regard the immateriality of services and the "intangibility of solutions" (Djellal/Gallouj) as a fundamental problem for hitherto presented innovation theories.

The first pair of authors asks "what is social about service innovation". They define service as an "act of mediation" between the social contexts "of generating or producing services and the context of using or consuming them"; the mediation consists in the application of competencies of people eventually leading to an act of co-creation. Intentional changes in the mode of providing this service (referring to Gershuny 1983) then might be considered as innovative from a viewpoint of the generating side. From the user side, "service innovation takes place when actors in the usage context are ready to change their expectations and their behaviour – in this sense it is a social innovation." This conclusion is flanked by the insight that the analysis of social aspects has to be developed further "carefully avoiding the traps of value rationality and hierarchical orders of technical/non-technical innovation."

It is exactly at this last point where the second pair of authors tunes in offering "a new typology of innovation" in order to bridge the "mutual ignorance" between the scientific perspectives on "the economics and socio-economics of services" and to meet the challenge of "making 'invisible innovation' visible" by stimulating "a dialogue between social innovation studies and service innovation studies." "The areas for dialogue raised in this exploratory contribution are the theoretical perspectives favoured, the nature of innovation and the question of its identification and measurement, its modes of organisation, its appropriation regimes and the evaluation of its impacts. However, other areas would also merit attention, in particular public policies to support social innovation and service innovation. A better understanding of social innovation in the light of service innovation and vice versa is likely to help reduce even further the hidden or invisible innovation gap in our economies and enable us to advance towards a new comprehensive innovation paradigm."

Stuart Conger, a veteran in social innovation thinking who wrote on "social inventions" as early as 1974, is the author of the third contribution to the part on social innovation and service innovation. He focuses on the risk of innovators in the public service coming to the case study-based conclusion that "innovation in government is not for the faint of heart or the risk-adverse person but rather for the dedicated professional who has a passion for making the system work in new ways".

3.3 Social Innovation and Welfare

"Social innovation and welfare" is the headline of the next part featuring two contributions, one focusing on "the challenges of population ageing" and "social innovations for ageing societies" (Heinze/Naegele), the other one concentrating on the changes of "publicly provided social services" and the "challenge of conjugating social innovation with universal social rights and citizenship, through a renewed role for the state" (Martinelli).

For Heinze and Naegele, population ageing is "a driver of social change and starting point for social innovations". They describe the magnitude of the task and the diversity of challenges for social as well as technological innovation in order to meet the overall challenge which is to allow independent living to the elderly. "There are many new products and services developed especially for the elderly, which support 'independent living' in old age." At the same time, the elderly "generate positive effects on economic growth and employment (market innovation) ... under the heading of 'Silver Economy'". "Networked living" is presented as a "special type of social innovation" at the interface between technology and social services. "Networked living is not only understood as integration of information and communication technologies but also as social cross-linking of different industries, technologies, services and other key players." Here is where the following contribution links in considering the changing role of public service for the social services.

Martinelli's controversial contribution titled "Social innovation or social exclusion?" is situated "at the crossroads of three partially overlapping streams of research: social services and social policy, social innovation, and social sustainability, addressed from a planner's perspective" and "provocatively challenges the broadly shared view of social innovation as inherently conducive to social inclusion." Her main plea is against the "retrenching of the welfare state" "to bring the state back into the picture", to "reinvent ... *the role of the state* in social innovation" "in order to ensure the sustainability of social innovation in social services ..., as a key topic for any new European research agenda on social innovation." "Social innovation in social services *cannot* be sustained *outside* or *in alternative to* the state, as is frequently implicitly or explicitly assumed, but must be promoted *within* and *with* the state" as "the ultimate guarantor of equity and the common good".

3.4 Social Innovation and Social Entrepreneurship

Three contributions are assembled under the headline of "social innovation and social entrepreneurship", another prominent field of the social innovation agenda. It is the subject dominating the OECD Forum on Social Innovation; and the most active Directorate-General of the European Commission in social innovation matters, DG Enterprise and Industry, funds a superbly active network concentrating on social entrepreneurship, the EUCLID network for third sector leaders (www.euclidnetwork.eu) which is also active in the Social Innovation Europe project and initiative (www.socialinnovationeurope.eu).

Széll proves to be a fervent advocate of social entrepreneurship and co-operativism as an answer to the cataclysm of the capitalist finance system and the spasms of the public debt crisis in their wake concluding that "today social innovation, social entrepreneurship and development with the aim to improve the quality of life and working life and to allow a sustainable development, have to build on the past, combining old and new in an innovative way."

Dash's paper on "social innovations and institutional challenges in microfinance" x-rays the weaknesses of the microfinance strategy where they have been abused by banks as "commercial finance" while the original intention was "development finance", i.e. "finance for the creation of longer-term social and developmental value (i.e., social profit)." According to the author, the field of microfinance that he has observed for many years in India "has grown through innovations flowing into the sector from both traditions. The first wave, with the most original fundamental social innovation in the form of a new social design for solidarity lending through groups, did create new economic and emancipatory space for the poor women. With the entry of commercial capital, microfinance grew with a new momentum driven by a new logic but with a 'change of heart', changing its focus from the clients to the institution and its sustainability, giving rise to a second wave of innovations in institutional development, market development, product development, and technology development. However, commercialization and its focus on institutional sustainability led to a mission drift. Driven by distorted market logic and a uni-dimensional narrow economism, it has run into a deep crisis today with a 'reputation risk'". "Microfinance is now disintegrating as a compelling tool for poverty alleviation. The present crisis creates an opportunity for a third wave of innovations for MFIs to grow to maturity as 'blended value' organizations, moving from efficiency to effectiveness, and to produce credible results in terms of social impact."

Barraket and Furneaux provide solid evidence from Australia on "social innovation and social enterprise" "drawing on Mulgan et al. (2007: 5) three dimensions of social innovation: new combinations or hybrids of existing elements; cutting across organisational, sectoral and disciplinary boundaries; and leaving behind compelling new relationships." Based on a detailed survey of 365 Australian social enterprises, the authors "examine their self-reported business and mission-related innovations, the ways in which they configure and access resources and the practices through which they diffuse innovation in support of their mission." Then they consider "how these findings inform our understanding of the social innovation capabilities and effects of social enterprise, and their implications for public policy development."

3.5 Social Innovation at the Workplace

Social innovation at the workplace has been one of the seed beds of the social innovation surge. Especially European social action programmes like EQUAL or the Lifelong Learning Programmes and numerous work organisation programmes on the national level in a considerable number of countries have made major contributions to this rise. For example, in Germany along with the continued existence of an industrial manufacturing structure, two major social innovations from this workplace-related context have greatly contributed to the relatively successful bridging of the world finance and economic crises of the last years.

One is 'Kurzarbeit', people receiving monthly payments of 68 % of their usual wage or salary from the semi-public redundancy fund fed by workers and employers at equal rates, for working time which is reduced to little or nothing, thus avoiding dismissals and allowing companies to maintain their skilled and experienced workforce. The instrument stems from the late 1950s when the structural change in coal mining started, and it was strongly used for a socially compatible reconversion of the coal and steel industries (cf. Franz 1994). The other one of relatively recent origin are flexible working time schemes with working time accounts introduced since the mid-nineties in many German companies with massive support from EU co-funded public programmes like ADAPT and EQUAL. They were usually introduced as a compromise of company and workforce interests and negotiated with the trade unions respectively with the works councils in German companies. These working time accounts were well filled with overwork when the crisis arrived and they were reduced, emptied or even used for 'deficit spending' of working time to be recovered in better times to come. It is in this range of social, societal and systemic innovations of workplace structures where the two contributions for this chapter have their background.

Totterdill, Cressey and Exton refer to the social learning and negotiation process and mutual trust record at the core of social innovation at the workplace. Based on an empirical study of the UK Work Organisation Network (UKWON) for the European Foundation in Dublin, screening and analysing the whole of the most recent European research on the subject, they detect workplace innovation as an "underused resource for European public policy at both EU and Member State levels" to the detriment of Europe's economic performance. Their plea is in favour of "embedded collective productive reflection", and they provide empirical analysis of the varying modes in which this social process is organised. As a conclusion the authors resume: "The concept and practice of productive reflection demonstrate the social nature of workplace innovation in two ways. Productive reflection, lying at the heart of workplace innovation, is an inherently social process which bridges formal and informal dialogue between different actors in the workplace. Secondly the win-win outcomes uniquely achieved through the participative nature of workplace innovation lead to profound social outcomes including enhanced health, active ageing, social cohesion and wealth creation. This is why the workplace should be at the heart of the EU's social innovation agenda."

Pot, Dhondt and Oeij argue that "social innovation of work and employment are prerequisites to achieve the EU 2020 objectives of smart, sustainable and inclusive growth". The research they analyse shows the possibility of convergence of organisational performance and quality of working life. They come to the conclusion "that, despite the use of broad concepts of social innovation in many of the EU policy documents and related studies, it can be discerned that the road is paved for workplace innovation as well. However, public and private organisations do not easily implement workplace innovation for the following reasons. There is only little research on the claim of a win-win situation. Quite a number of managers wait for others to find out how it works or prefer short-term results instead of long-term innovativeness. A lot of managers are not equipped for participatory approaches and/or are afraid to share power with their employees. Trust is a difficult asset to develop and to maintain. So, if we leave workplace innovation to the initiative of the market, we can only expect workplace innovation in a limited number of organisations with visionary governors and strong works councils. The majority of interventions will be just cost reduction strategies. EU and national campaigns are needed to support workplace innovation, in particular in those countries where there is little experience."

3.6 Social Innovation, Open Innovation and Social Media

As we have argued above already, the internet is one of the key innovations with profound structural consequences for our ways of communication and co-operation in all areas of life as well as for the management of any type of innovation itself. The two contributions of this part examine exactly these contexts.

Kaletka, Kappler, Pelka and Ruiz De Querol provide theoretical and empirical background to the Barcelona Manifesto *Social Media for Social Innovation*. "It promotes the possibility of using social media as a platform to effectively support the processes of social innovation, overcoming its limitations of speed and scale to become an alternative to currently established institutional mechanisms. Such social innovations comprise all new strategies, concepts, ideas and organizations that meet current social needs and strengthen civil society." "The new communication and coordination possibilities through social media are and could further be used for a societal evolution going much beyond the economics of leisure and consumption." The paradigm shift of communication challenges multiple layers of the knowledge society. The four most striking ones are: *change of labour:* "The potential of social media – not seen as a technology, but as a new communication paradigm – seems underexploited in labour processes"; *political participation:* In the U.S. as well as in Europe governments pursue the objective to "empower citizens and business by eGovernment services *designed around users' needs and developed in collaboration with third parties* [...]" (European Commission 2010); *eInclusion:* participation then needs an approach to overcome the "digital divide" of society and to support *digital* inclusion; *education and training:* The shift in modern learning environments from "teaching" to "learning" came along with pedagogical approaches and technological environments that enable learners to find their own way of acquiring needed knowledge, skills and competences. "The potential of social media for education and training seems underexploited by far."

Kahnert, Menez and Blättel-Mink focus on processes of open and user-driven innovation. Along with a critical analysis of the theoretical background of open innovation, the existing communities and the toolkits and motivations of such an approach, they present a case study of one of the largest German companies developing computer games (Crytek) "in order to find out how companies coordinate open resp. user innovation, and why users actively support companies in innovating.... Adopting the theoretical facets of user innovation to this case, among others game designers and community managers of Crytek have been surveyed as well as 'modders', kind of a new species of users who are deeply involved in generating new products." "In terms of user motivation, intrinsic, social as well as extrinsic motifs have a role. Extrinsic motifs of the modders correlate clearly with the intentions of Crytek itself, in that it every now and then recruits its employees out of this group."

3.7 Measuring Social Innovation

Measuring innovation cruises in the choppy seas of impact evaluation since innovation is measured according to the degree of its extent or intensity of application and with reference to the degree of change induced by it. By the pure nature of social innovation (e.g. immateriality and invisibility), this is a difficult task to tackle, though necessary in the context of developing a broader and more open paradigm of innovation beyond pure effectiveness and efficiency.

Wobbe offers a first overview of the existing instruments measuring innovation at large and develops a number of suggestions of how these instruments could be methodically guiding for social innovation, too. "Currently, innovation monitoring chiefly is applied with an economic focus although social data base developments have been funded by the European Commission research and development programmes over years. The paper presents selected EU research activities as well as the method and policy relevance of two innovation monitoring approaches targeting the economic dimension in the EU: the Innovation Union Scoreboard (IUS) and the Community Innovation Survey (CIS). The approaches shed some light on how monitoring instruments of social innovation may be developed." One of the conclusions is that "consensus needs to be reached on the point of view if and which targets for specific policies (innovation, security, health, social, environment, transport, etc.) shall be monitored to which social innovations are instrumental, or if social innovation is a subject in its own to be monitored."

Bassi presents the results of a research project the principal aim of which was to elaborate and test a measurement tool for non-profit organisations (NPOs) called SAVE (Social Added Value Evaluation) operating in the welfare area (social and health services). "The basic idea is to select a sample of 12 NPOs (six organizations of volunteers and six social cooperatives) dealing with services for disabled people, elderly, physical impaired, mental illness, youth, families with problems, etc., and to carry out an in-depth sociological analysis, using the case study model of social and organisational inquiry." NPOs are regarded as special organizations because they have a triple bottom line: an economic one, a social one (volunteers, workers, users, clients, etc.) and an environmental one (local community), reflecting their various stakeholders. The underlying hypothesis is that NPOs are characterized by two main features: the capacity to produce relational goods and their ability in generating social capital in the community.

3.8 Social Innovation and the Social Sciences

The final part asks for the role and contribution of the social sciences. First considerations on the subject could be found already in Howaldt/Kopp's paper in Part 2. The two papers of this final part draw on experience collected in Scandinavia and in New Zealand.

Gustavsen displays the vast experience gathered in Scandinavia. His contribution "traces the development of a research tradition where the point of departure was research-driven experiments with alternative forms of work organization but which has become subject to a communicative turn as well as a turn towards change that can involve many actors simultaneously." In its present shape the methodology starts to constitute a distributive set of activities with the idea of democratic dialogue as the core and a strong emphasis on notions like networks and regions. "This research tradition has played a major role in establishing Scandinavia as the leading area for 'learning organization' in Europe." The article concludes by discussing some of the challenges facing "bottom-up" change in working life today: "the increasing dominance of centrally managed systems thinking, a possible reduction in influence from the labour market parties and an associated breakdown of the strong links between the local and the central and, third, difficulties associated with integrating and giving a society level profile to a pattern of distributive research."

De Bruin's paper reflects the possible role of the social sciences on two distinct but interrelated levels. First it "reflects on the role and responsibility of researchers in advancing social innovation and traces the purpose and activities of the New Zealand Social Innovation and Entrepreneurship Research Centre to illustrate how academic institutes might catalyze social innovation." The second consideration regards "parallel discourses following either more micro- or macro-level leanings.... Bringing these two research streams closer and bridging dichotomous micro–macro perspectives, is necessary for a holistic view of innovation that recognizes social innovation as a crucial facet of innovation systems."

Last but not least, in "Final observations" the book keeps record of the Vienna Declaration which summarizes the results of the conference. "Further innovations in technology and business are imperative; yet in order to reap their full potential, and at the same time creating social development that is beneficial to cultures as inclusive as diverse, social innovations will make the difference: There is a lot of evidence that social innovation will become of growing importance not only with regard to social integration and equal opportunities but also with regard to preserving and expanding the innovative capacity of companies and society as a whole. The most urgent and important innovations in the twenty-first century will take place in the social field. This opens up the necessity as well as possibilities for Social Sciences and Humanities to find new roles and relevance by generating knowledge applicable to new dynamics and structures of contemporary and future societies."

References

BEPA (Bureau of European Policy Advisers). (2010). *Empowering people, driving change: Social innovation in the European Union*. Luxembourg: Publications Office of the European Union.

BEPA (Bureau of European Policy Advisers). (2011). *Empowering people, driving change: Social innovation in the European Union*. Luxembourg: Publications Office of the European Union.

Conger, S. (1974). *Social inventions*. Prince Albert: Saskatchewan Newstart.

European Commission (2010). *The European eGovernment Action Plan 2011–2015*, COM(2010) 743, December.

Franz, H. W. (1994). Manual social crisis management in the coal and steel industries. In: the Commission of the European Union, with a foreword by Padraig Flynn (Ed.), *European models and experiences*. Brussels/Luxembourg: Publications Office of the European Union (also available in French, German and Spanish).

Franz, H. W. (2010). Quality management is ongoing social innovation. In K. Müller, S. Roth, & M. Žák (Eds.), *Social dimension of innovation, 2010* (pp. 115–130). Prague: CES Centre for Economic Studies (College of Economics and Management).

Gershuny, J. (1983). *Social innovation and the division of labour*. Oxford: Oxford University Press.

Hochgerner, J. (2011a). Die Analyse sozialer Innovationen als gesellschaftliche Praxis. In: Zentrum für Soziale Innovation (Ed.), Pendeln zwischen Wissenschaft und Praxis. ZSI-Beiträge zu sozialen Innovationen (pp. 173–189). Vienna and Berlin: LIT.

Hochgerner, J. (2011b). The analysis of social innovations as social practice. In: bridges vol. 30, July 2011, http://www.ostina.org/content/view/5708/1505/. Accessed 25 July 2011.

Howaldt, J., Schwarz, M. (2010). Social innovation: Concepts, research fields and international trends, http://www.internationalmonitoring.com/research/trend_studies/social_innovation.html. Accessed 3 April 2012.

Mulgan, G., Tucker, S., Ali, R., & Sander, B. (2007). *Social innovation: What it is, why it matters and how can it be accelerated*. Oxford: Skoll Centre for Social Entrepreneurship.

Pol, E., & Ville, S. (2009). Social innovation: Buzz word or enduring term? *The Journal of Socio-Economics, 38*(2009), 878–885.

SIX (Social Innovation exChange at the Young Foundation) (2010). Study on social innovation, http://www.youngfoundation.org/files/images/tudy_on_Social_Innovation_22_-February_2010_0.pdf. Accessed 28 Feb 2012.

Swedberg, R., Knudsen, T. (2010). Schumpeter 2.0. In: The American (online Journal of the American Enterprise Institute). http://american.com/archive/2010/June-2010/schumpeter-2.0. Accessed 9 Feb 2012.

Part I
On Social Innovation Theory

Social Innovation Theories: Can Theory Catch Up with Practice?

Geoff Mulgan

Abstract The paper describes ten sets of theoretical sources that have either influenced social innovation or provide useful insights. It argues that although the field has been led by practice rather than theory it now needs stronger theoretical foundations in order to progress. The theoretical sources described include: theoretical perspectives on social plasticity and change; evolutionary theories; complexity theories; theories of entrepreneurship; theories of dialectical change; theories from innovation studies; theories of techno-economic paradigms; theories concerned with the ends of innovation, in particular well-being and capabilities; and epistemological approaches to social innovation. In each case I describe some of the main ideas and arguments, and their relevance to social innovation (and in some cases their key limitations). I then suggest ways in which these may be synthesized into an overall framework for social innovation that can generate useful and often testable hypotheses to guide practice.

1 Introduction

The physicist Wolfgang Pauli once commented on a theory proposed by a student that it was so bad it wasn't even wrong. By this he meant that it wasn't sufficiently precisely formulated to test its accuracy. He represented a view of scientific progress which sees it advancing through the constant generation of hypotheses which can be rigorously tested.

By this measure social innovation is a field very short of theories, let alone theories which can be shown to be either right or wrong. This reflects an evolution which poses challenges for academics. The field of social innovation has grown up primarily as a field of practice, made up of people doing things and then reflecting

---

G. Mulgan (✉)
National Endowment for Science Technology and the Arts, London, England
e-mail: geoff.mulgan@nesta.org.uk

on what they do. Practice has advanced well ahead of theory or research, mainly as a kind of craft knowledge. There has been relatively little attention to theory, or to history, and although there has been much promising research work in recent years, there are no clearly defined schools of thought, no continuing theoretical arguments, and few major research programmes to test theories against the evidence.

Much of my work in recent years has been concerned with advancing the practice of social innovation, and mapping systematically the methods being used globally. That seemed a more productive route to growing the field than attempting to deduce useful conclusions from theories. As the world experimented with a huge plurality of methods for doing social innovation, more was likely to be learned from attempting to spot the patterns than from abstract reasoning. That guided the creation of global networks, global scans of methods, and a series of publications identifying the key patterns.[1]

But it has become increasingly clear that we also needed theory to catch up and provide pointers to the future. Some encounters with theory were proving very productive. For example, many recent insights have come from anthropology and ethnography – and this has been a popular source of ideas for design-led and user-led innovation. There is also a strong interaction with theories of social movements. It's hard to understand some of the most important fields of recent innovation – such as the environmental movement or disability rights – without these insights. In my own work I have also drawn on some of the insights of theorists of technology such as Brian Arthur (discussed later), which provide important pointers to the importance of observation and simulation of natural social phenomena, and 'redomaining' in social innovation.

These few examples suggest that there is scope to link social innovation to broader theoretical discussions about innovation. Sharper theory will help to clarify what is and isn't known, the points of argument as well as agreement. It should help in the generation of testable hypotheses and to guide answers to questions: how much is social change driven by entrepreneurial individuals, by movements, teams or networks, or for that matter by political parties and governments? Why do some ideas travel well and others poorly? Should we expect any common patterns as to where the most influential ideas come from? Can the experimental methods of natural science be transplanted to accelerate social change? Do social innovations scale in the same way as business innovations? Is it possible to measure the innovative capacity of an organisation or a nation?

Sharper theory should also guide practice. Social theories, unlike theories in fields like physics, are inseparable from their purposes and their uses. Not all innovations are good, and nor are all social innovations. Here I map some of the main theoretical currents that are contributing to social innovation and that have

---

[1] SIX, the Social Innovation Exchange, remains the leading network for practitioners (and has recently run Social Innovation Europe). A first scan of global methods was done for 2010, *The Open Book of Social Innovation*. Other publications include: Mulgan (2006, 2007); Mulgan et al. (2007, 2010).

useful insights to offer. Some are theories to interpret the world, concerned with description and analysis; others are theories to change the world, more deliberately designed to encourage and advocate.

In what follows I aim to show:

First, that social innovation is a type of evolutionary change. In biology, culture and societies there are some common patterns of mutation, selection and growth, as well as important differences. Like any evolutionary process social innovation is not easy to plan or predict, but conscious action can help people and communities to self-organise, and shape the direction of evolution. The most successful innovation systems will be marked by strong capacities to mutate, select and grow.

Second, opportunities for social innovation are heavily shaped by historical circumstance: prevailing types of institution and industry; prevailing technologies; and the availability of freedom or spare capital. So it's important to understand the circumstances surrounding, for example, the diffusion of low carbon technologies or reactions against globalisation, with a wide peripheral vision and a sense of how the pieces fit together.

Third, the motivations for social innovation will usually come from tensions; contradictions; dissatisfactions; and the negation of what exists. We can draw from Hegel, Simmel and others the insight that these tensions are not unfortunate by-products of innovation; they are part of its nature, as is the disappointment and even alienation that innovation processes generate. The very act of innovation is also an act of rejection.

Fourth, social innovation as a field seems inseparable from its underlying ethic, which is one of collaboration, acting with rather than only to or for; a belief in rough equality; a cultural commitment to the idea of equality of communication (theorised in more depth by Jürgen Habermas) and perhaps an implicit idea that through collaboration we can discover our full humanity.

Fifth, the nature of the knowledge involved in social innovation is different from knowledge about physics or biology, or indeed the claims made for economic knowledge: it is more obviously contingent, temporary, and often context-bound. Measurement and testing have a big role to play: but the findings that result will not be eternally true.

Sixth, social innovation is not yet a fully defined domain. Other domains of technology (not just hardware domains such as aeronautics or structural engineering, but also others such as finance and software) are organised by domain experts who combine rich formal knowledge with the tacit knowledge of experience that enables them to put together multiple elements in ways that work, with a grasp of systems and sub-systems. It is plausible that within a decade or two social innovation could be more like these other domains.

Seventh, I suggest that the growing interest in wellbeing and capabilities could provide both the theoretical and practical glue to hold social innovation practice together, and provide some common measures of success.

These overviews of theory are attempts to make sense of a field that has fairly fuzzy boundaries. There are many, often lengthy definitions of social innovation in circulation (from sources including Stanford University, the OECD and NESTA), all describing the field of social innovation as concerned with ideas, products, services, that are for the public good (Dees and Anderson 2006). My preference is simple and short and defines the field as concerned with 'innovations that are social both in their ends and in their means' (The Young Foundation 2010). In other words, it covers new ideas (products, services and models) that simultaneously meet socially recognised social needs (more effectively than alternatives) *and* create new social relationships or collaborations, that are both good for society *and* enhance society's capacity to act. This definition helps to capture the dual quality of the practice, which is usually concerned with means as well as ends, and of much of the theoretical literature on which the field has drawn, which is concerned with notions of value as well as values. The definition also internalises within itself the conflict that is inevitable in the use of the word 'social': what counts as good, or a socially recognised need, is constantly contested, and this very contest provides some of the dynamic energy that drives the field.[2]

This definition hopefully clarifies what social innovation is not, as well as what it is. It is not just a subset of technological or economic innovation. It is not the same as, or a substitute for, larger scale political programmes for structural or systemic change, or programmes to extend rights, though there are clear complementarities between such programmes and the field of social innovation. If social innovation has any ideological bias it is towards deeper democracy and empowerment of society – but it does not of itself imply any view as to whether particular functions or services are best provided by public, private or non-profit organisations.

2 Innovation Studies

It should be obvious that social innovation has much to learn from the broader field of innovation studies. A significant group of academics have struggled for many decades with the challenges of theorising creativity, scaling and diffusion, incentives and ownership. Innovation was not a central concern for classical and neoclassical economists. Innovations were seen as exogenous; or as a black box that didn't need to be explained. But since the 1950s, as the importance of innovation has become ever more obvious, the field of innovation studies has slowly taken shape.

---

[2] This definition has emerged out of a series of research studies I've been involved in, cited above.

Some of this has addressed making innovation more endogenous to economics,[3] better understanding why markets work as innovation machines,[4] and patterns of diffusion.[5, 6] We lack comparable work to endogenise innovation in accounts of social change, but this may be a useful route to follow. Work that has been immediately useful for social innovation has studied the cognitive, economic as well as organisational barriers to diffusion and the importance of new kinds of behaviour (what Bart Nooteboom calls 'scripts') in business and social innovation.[7] Other relevant work includes Michael Piore's work on the decisive role played by interpretation[8] and Richard Nelson's work on the transformational impact of some technologies, and the dynamic of innovation systems.

The most sustained body of work in innovation studies was led over many years by Christopher Freeman, Giovanni Dosi, Luc Soete and Ian Miles, combining rigorous empirical analysis with theoretical creativity in mapping the larger 'techno-economic paradigms' within which innovation takes place. As I show later these provide a historical context for understanding the patterns of social innovation, as well as the interaction between societal shifts and adoption of technology.

I have already mentioned Brian Arthur's recent work on technology which arguably provides the clearest frame for understanding the nature of both technological and social innovation. He has shown how many innovations of all kinds begin with observation and the attempt to synthesise or replicate natural phenomena. This is as true of social innovations seeking to replicate friendship or monetary security, as it is of technological innovations seeking to replicate fire and light. There then evolve bodies of practice and knowledge with their own logics – such as microprocessors or the web, portals, paraprofessionals, tax credits and personal accounts, each forming a domain. Innovation then tends to advance through combinations and hybrids. The Ipod combined advances made in music compression (the MP3 technology supported by the Fraunhofer Institute), advances in music organization from Napster, in manufacturing from Foxconn and others, as well as the lessons learned by the first generation of MP3 players which failed in the market place. The elements themselves were not original: what was original was the design

---

[3] Helpman (2004). Following on from Solow's work Elhanan Helpman estimated that differences in knowledge and technology explain more than 60 % of the differences among countries in income and growth rates.

[4] Baumol (2003).

[5] Rogers (2003). Rogers defines an innovation as 'an idea, practice, or object that is perceived as new by an individual or other unit of adoption. It matters little, so far as human behaviour is concerned, whether or not an idea is objectively new as measured by the lapse of time since its first use or discovery. The perceived newness of the idea for the individual determines his or her reaction to it. If the idea seems new to the individual, it is an innovation.'

[6] Stoneman and Diederen (1994).

[7] Rogers (1995); Nutley et al. (2002); Nooteboom (2000).

[8] Lester and Piore (2004).

that brought them together. The same is true of new models of eldercare or digital education – all the successes combine a variety of elements.

Yet the most radical innovations tend to involve 'redomaining', applying a body of methods to a wholly new field. A good current example is the use of web platforms for collaborative consumption. Many of the features of these platforms were designed for logistics management within firms – but they turn out to be very helpful for aggregating citizens' own assets and capabilities.

Another related strand of work has focused on the tools used to advance innovation.[9] This has tended to challenge the claims made for radical 'out of the box' innovation made by business gurus and consultancies, showing how these are better understood as combinations of incremental steps, which may therefore be rather easier for others to emulate.[10]

A much more visible body of work has come from business studies. This has provided many metaphors for thinkers about social innovation, though it has suffered from the tendency of the field to follow fashions, and to present old ideas as new. Useful examples include Rosabeth Moss Kanter's work on businesses grappling with both social and commercial goals, and Clayton Christensen's writings on the role of disruption or the relatively poor performance of very successful innovations in their early phases of competition with more mature, and more optimised incumbents.[11] The recent surge of interest in open innovation, promoted amongst others by Henry Chesbrough[12] and user-driven innovation associated with Eric Von Hippel,[13] are both interesting examples of ideas with a long history in the social field being creatively adapted to business.

Some ideas can be quite readily adopted from business: performance management systems and the use of metrics; and, for social enterprises, the many tools for managing value. However, just as often it's evident how different social innovation is from innovation in business. Most social ventures draw on a wider range of resources – including volunteer labour, relational capital and commitment, that are hard to integrate into traditional business analyses. Specific examples also highlight the differences. For example franchising has encouraged great hopes – but not delivered them, mainly because of the practical challenges involved in sustaining both quality and an ethos through franchise contracts. Likewise, much writing in business assumes that value can be protected as IP: but in the social field most attempts to protect IP too vigorously impede the spread of the innovation (and rarely deliver much return to the innovator either).

---

[9] Markman and Wood (2009).

[10] I drew on some of this work to develop a framework of design tools for innovation, which shows how accessible methods for creative innovation can be used by anyone. See: http://www.google.co.uk/search?q=mulgan+creative+design+tools+%22social+design%22&hl=en&lr=&as_qdr=all &prmd=imvns&ei=4UmQT_y9KcTetAbT2MiSBA&start=10&sa=N&biw=1366&bih=487&surl=1

[11] For example, Christenson (2003).

[12] See for example, Chesbrough (2006).

[13] Von Hippel (1988).

3 Theories of Entrepreneurship Adapted to the Social Field

Joseph Schumpeter has enjoyed a great revival of interest over the last decade, partly thanks to the growing importance of innovation in the economy.[14] He believed that entrepreneurship could be found in every field, thought he peculiar circumstances of capitalist economies made it particularly relevant to business. These are his words on the spirit of social pioneers: 'In the breast of one who wishes to do something new, the forces of habit rise up and bear witness against the embryonic project. A new and another kind of effort of will is therefore necessary in order to wrest, amidst the work and care of the daily round, scope and time for conceiving and working out the new combination. This mental freedom presupposes a great surplus force over the everyday demand and is something peculiar and by nature rare.'

Schumpeter's decisive contribution to economic theory was his attention to the role of entrepreneurs in driving change, and pushing markets away from equilibrium. Schumpeter described 'stabilised capitalism is a contradiction in terms', and was interested in the dynamics of change. He was perhaps the greatest advocate for seeing capitalism through the lens of entrepreneurs and entrepreneurship, with the implication that the task for policy is to give them as much free rein as possible, so that they can hunt out undiscovered value.

The Schumpeterian view of how economies work has become much more widely accepted in recent decades. In his account the entrepreneur is the decisive actor, seeking out opportunities, spotting under-served markets or unused assets, taking risks (with investors' money) and reaping rewards. His attention to the vital role of credit in providing funds for entrepreneurs to take risks has also become main-stream.

This perspective is very different in spirit to most of mainstream economics. It emphasises the search for what's not known, what's uncertain and what's unmeasurable. In perfect markets with perfect information there is no room for entrepreneurs. Instead entrepreneurship highlights the difficultness of the world, its resistance to predictable plans, and how we learn by bumping into things, and then navigating around them. What entrepreneurs do is not wholly rational, indeed their success is presented as a kind of magic: in Schumpeter's words "the success of everything depends on intuition, the capacity of seeing things in a way which afterwards proves to be true, even though it cannot be established at the moment, and of grasping the essential fact, discarding the unessential, even though one can give no account of the principles by which this is done."[15]

A very different view of entrepreneurship (associated with the work of Israel Kirzner)[16] sees it not as the upsetter of equilibrium but as the creator of equilibrium, using information to take advantage of disequilibria and thus push the economy back

---

[14] McCraw (2007).
[15] Schumpeter (1934).
[16] Kirzner (1973).

into balance.[17] Like Schumpeter, Kirzner saw the entrepreneurial mind as distinct from rational management: it spots emerging patterns and 'weak signals' to use the current phrase: entrepreneurs demonstrate 'the ways in which the human agent can, by imaginative, bold leaps of faith, and determination, in fact create the future for which his present acts are designed'.[18] Entrepreneurship thrives in fields of uncertainty, on the edges of industries and disciplines; much less in stable contexts or where risk can be calculated.

In either light, entrepreneurship is not peculiar to business, and the Austrian school of economists and philosophers, concerned with action in conditions of uncertainty, recognised this from the start. Schumpeter wrote of entrepreneurship in politics as well as business (and was for a brief period a minister), and saw entrepreneurship as a universal phenomenon albeit one that was particularly dynamic in capitalist economies. Ludwig Von Mises wrote that entrepreneurship 'is not the particular feature of a special group or class of men; it is inherent in every action and burdens every actor'.[19] So it has been natural to extend Schumpeter to other fields: to see within universities some academics acting as entrepreneurs, assembling teams, spotting gaps, promoting the superiority of their ideas, and bringing together whatever resources they can find to win allegiance; or to see the founders and builders of great religions as great entrepreneurs, pulling together belief, attraction and money.

Social entrepreneurship adapts the same ideas to civil society, and social resources; it leads to an interest in the character of the entrepreneur; their motivations; the patterns of creating enterprises and then growing them; and, as with business entrepreneurs, the conflicts between them and the providers of capital on the one hand and the providers of labour on the other.[20]

Just as Schumpeter's account encouraged a heroic view of the business entrepreneur battling against the resistance of society, so has the same happened with social entrepreneurs. At one point there were even claims (from one of the leading US support organisations) of a formula – one social entrepreneur for every million in the population (though interestingly, it then went to the other extreme with the more inclusive slogan 'everyone a change maker').[21] According to the radical individualistic view, the more that exceptional individuals could be provided with resources, and the more that any constraints could be removed, the more likely they would be to solve social problems. This inevitably meant less attention to the other key actors in social innovation: the networks, teams, patrons and investors, though as in the case of natural science, the more particular cases are studied in detail the more it becomes apparent that individuals only achieve great things because of the complementary skills and institutions that surround them. It's interesting to note

---

[17] Shockley and Frank (2011).

[18] Kirzner (1982), pp. 150.

[19] Von Mises (1949/1996).

[20] Swedberg (2009).

[21] Drayton (2006).

that Schumpeter in his later years became increasingly interested in 'cooperative entrepreneurship' within large firms and the role of teams, and was convinced that this was a vital field for study.

The recent discussions of Schumpeter and Kirzner have provided a useful richness to the discussion of social entrepreneurship. They have, for example, opened up research on motivations. Schumpeter recognised that profit was unlikely to be the only or even the main motivation for business entrepreneurs, and clearly for social entrepreneurs a wide range of motives intermingle, from altruism to recognition, financial reward to the hunger for power. Their work also encourages attention to patterns of resistance from existing interests and ways of thought, and to the importance of there being sources of credit and investment for social entrepreneurs and innovators – why, for example, specialised banks (such as Banca Prossima and Banca Etica), or public investment funds for social entrepreneurs (such as the UK's UnLtd) matter so much.[22]

Neither Schumpeter nor Kirzner however addressed the broader question of value. Both treat economic value as an unproblematic concept. Yet one of the keys to their wider use may be to link them to parallel developments in the field of economic sociology, particularly the work of figures like Harrison White and David Stark. Drawing in creative ways on the work of Luc Boltanski,[23] they have shown how societies and economies are made up of systems of 'multiple worth', each with very different ways of thinking about value. Seen through this lens entrepreneurship isn't just about spotting new opportunities for profit. Instead, in David Stark's words, it involves 'the ability to keep multiple orders of worth in play and to exploit the resulting ambiguity'.[24] In other words it goes beyond the ability to exploit uncertainty rather than just calculable risk, but also entails arbitraging, or translating between, distinct fields. This is surely a good description of much social innovation and entrepreneurship, whose most successful practitioners are fluent across fields: medicine and business, voluntary action and education, law and politics, and able to juggle multiple orders of worth. It may also be one of the crucial reasons why attempts to distil social value into single metrics has been largely unsuccessful: by denying the plurality of value systems these attempt to bring certainty to actions that have to be ambiguous or multiple in nature.

How we think about entrepreneurship, and theorise it, has obvious practical implications. The idea of business entrepreneurship led in time to the idea that states should not only enable it through laws and (light) regulations, but should also support it, and many governments provide tax incentives, training courses and celebrations to encourage entrepreneurship. Social entrepreneurship too has encouraged various kinds of support from governments and foundations: prizes, funds and networks. In both cases however research has still not resolved some

---

[22] See for example Defourny and Nyssens (2008a, b).
[23] Boltanski and Laurent (2006).
    White (2001).
[24] Stark (2009).

fundamental questions: the balance to be struck between backing individuals, teams and organisations; whether to provide only knowledge and advice or also investment; what attitude to take to risk?

4 Evolution and Complexity: Frames for Thinking About the Processes of Innovation

Complexity theory is probably the body of ideas most favoured by leading practitioners in social innovation; it offers frames and metaphors that fit their experience of engaging with the world at multiple levels; it can combine the subjective and objective, the roles of culture and psychology as well as economics; and it points to the importance of non-linear as well as linear changes. The social innovation field is instinctively at home with organic development, trial and error; dispersed power, and with the ideas associated with the open source and open data movements which emphasise self-organising systems which use multiple horizontal links and complexity to solve problems.

Some of this theory can be traced back to the ideas of Charles Darwin and a century and a half of thinking about the nature of evolution as a self-organising complex system. Innovation is in large part a process of evolution that has direct parallels in the natural world. Evolutionary theory in particular helps us to focus on the three stages that are present in any process of innovation. One involves mutation – in evolutionary theory the random mutation of DNA that creates the potential for adaptation. Most mutations contribute little; and those that do contribute significant change generally fail. Then comes selection – in evolutionary theory the focus is on fitness for environments: occasional mutations outperform their predecessors and thus allow new types of organism to flourish. Finally there is replication – those mutations that pass the tests of selection will grow, displacing others and replicating their genes. Only the fit survive.

Evolutionary theory itself has coevolved with complexity theory, which has been much drawn on by people involved in social innovation.[25] Complexity theory is neither a single theory, nor wholly coherent and consistent. Rather it is a family of concepts and insights that have been applied in many fields, sometimes extending the earlier insights of systems thinking and sometimes pointing in different directions. Its key concepts include: the role of feedback loops, or more broadly, feedback processes to understand why change sometimes accelerates and more often is inhibited; the idea of 'strange attractors', and of social change as the shift from one to another; the idea that societies are made up of both tightly and loosely coupled systems which respond very differently to shocks; the idea of organisations operating at 'the edge of chaos'; the idea of emergence, of complex structures and

---

[25] See Westley et al. (2006).

institutions emerging from very simple principles; and the idea of non-linearity, that many social processes do not follow linear relationships.

The insights of figures such as Ilya Prigogine, Brian Arthur, Stuart Kauffman and others coming from very different backgrounds such as Niklas Luhmann, Humberto Maturana and Donald Schön, have made this a rich and stimulating field. It has certainly provided a useful antidote to the more simplistic currents of social innovation – anyone who has engaged with complexity theory is unlikely to talk glibly about 'solving social problems' or 'scaling' solutions. Instead they are more likely to recognise that the majority of issues that motivate innovation are complex, messy, interconnected and not amenable to one-dimensional solutions. Complexity theory tends to force attention to the connections between things, to feedback and feed forward processes; to path dependence and to the many ways in which initial conditions can radically change outcomes. It implies that policy should create generative rules rather than detailed top down prescription; that it should allow evolution and adaptation to local conditions; and that it should encourage the maximum feedback. In recent years these perspectives have been helped by improvements in modelling techniques which have made it easier to map and simulate social dynamics, or the patterns of linkages between social enterprises.

So far these theories have mainly been useful for providing a rich menu of metaphors, and a mind-set. Complexity theory has suffered from the weakness of all attempts to transplant theories from the natural sciences to social sciences: the inability to take account of reflexivity, the awareness of the people within systems. The same has been true in economics. Figures like Benoit Mandelbrot successfully used complexity theory to demolish the hubristic claims of financial forecasters – but offered little to replace them.[26] There are some promising attempts to apply these theories to more social phenomena, such as transport management or crowd control, and some interesting work on their applicability to development.[27] But for now as Gareth Morgan suggested nearly 30 years ago in his classic work on 'images of organisation', these ideas may be useful mainly as ideas and frames rather than as tools which can directly guide action.

5 Techno-economic Paradigms and the Historical Context for Social Innovation

Social innovation is powerfully shaped by historical context. What kinds of innovation will be possible at any point will be determined by prevailing technologies, institutions and mentalities. Wonderful ideas may simply be impossible at the wrong time. Some of the most influential and useful theories for making sense of historical contexts have

---

[26] Mandelbrot and Hudson (2008).

[27] A good review of literature and possible relevant to development is Ramalingam and Jones (2008).

come from a group of academics led by Christopher Freeman, Carlota Pérez and figures such as Luc Soete[28]. Their aim was to understand the long waves of technological and economic change, and to seek out common patterns and congruences between technologies, economics and social organisation. This has also been the concern of the work of figures such as Josef Hochgerner, who have synthesised perspectives from Weber to Schumpeter with more recent accounts of innovation systems.[29]

Perhaps the most influential current theorist of the connections between technological change and the economy is the Venezuelan economist Carlota Pérez who is a scholar of the successive techno-economic paradigms which define the shape of the economy. She has studied how these intersect with the financial cycles that have repeated themselves again and again during capitalism's relatively brief history. In Pérez' account, which builds on Kondratiev and Schumpeter, the cycles begin with the emergence of new technologies and infrastructures that promise great wealth. These then fuel frenzies of speculative investment, with dramatic rises in stock and other prices whether in the canal mania of the 1790s, the railway mania of the 1830s and 1840s, the surge of global infrastructures in the 1870s and 1880s,, or the booms that accompanied the car, electricity, telephone in the 1920s, and biotechnology and the internet in the 1990s and 2000s.

During these phases of technological exuberance finance is in the ascendant and laissez faire policies become the norm. Letting markets freely grow seems evidently wise when they are fuelling such visible explosions of wealth. During these periods some investors and entrepreneurs become very rich, very quickly. Exuberance in markets may be reflected in exuberance and laissez faire in personal morals – a glittering world of parties, celebrities, and gossip for the rest of the public to hang onto and experience vicariously. Entrepreneurs take wild risks and reap wild rewards. The economy appears to be a place for easy predation, offering rewards without too much work, and plenty of chances to siphon off surpluses.

The booms then turn out to be bubbles and are followed by dramatic crashes. 1797, 1847, 1893, 1929 or 2008 are a few of the decisive years when crashes took values tumbling. They are crashes of stock markets; and brought with them the dramatic bankruptcy of many of the most prominent companies of the booms, like so many railway companies in the later nineteenth century. Sometimes currencies collapse too.

After these crashes, and periods of turmoil, the potential of the new technologies and infrastructures is eventually realized. But that only happens once new social, political and economic institutions and regulations come into being which are better aligned with the characteristics of the new economy, and with the underlying desires of the society. Radical social innovation plays a key role in making possible much more widespread deployment of the key technologies. Once that has

---

[28] Freeman and Perez (1988).

[29] Hochgerner (2011). See also, Gerber (2006), Schwarz at al. (2010).

happened, economies then go through surges of growth as well as social progress, like the "belle epoque" or the post-war miracle.

These patterns can be seen clearly in the Great Depression and its aftermath. Before the crisis of 1929 the elements of a new economy and a new society were already available – and the promise of technologies like the car and telephone encouraged the speculative bubbles of the 1920s. But they were neither understood by the people in power, nor were they embedded in institutions. Then, during the 1930s, the economy transformed, in Perez's words, from one based on "steel, heavy electrical equipment, great engineering works (canals, bridges, dams, tunnels) and heavy chemistry, mainly geared towards big spenders ... into a mass production system catering to consumers and the massive defence markets. Radical demand management and income redistribution innovations had to be made, of which the directly economic role of the state is perhaps the most important." What resulted was the rise of mass-consumerism, and an economy supported by ubiquitous infrastructures for electricity, roads and telecommunications, and 'based on low cost oil and energy intensive materials (especially petrochemicals and synthetics), and led by giant oil, chemical and automobile and other mass durable goods producers. Its 'ideal' type of productive organization at the plant levels was the continuous flow assembly-line... the 'ideal' type of firm was the 'corporation'. Including in-house R&D and operating in oligopolistic markets in which advertising and marketing activities played a major role. It required large numbers of middle range skills in both blue and white collar areas... a vast infrastructural network of motorways, service stations, airports, oil and petrol distribution systems...' [30]

Seen in the light the great depression helped usher in new economic and welfare policies in countries like New Zealand and Sweden that later became the mainstream across the developed world. In the US it led to banking reform, the New Deal, social security and unemployment insurance (both backed by big business)[31] and later the GI Bill of Rights. In Britain it was the depression, as much as war that led to the creation of the welfare state and the National Health Service in the 1940s. Social innovation thrived in the wake of the depression, with a surge of energy in many societies as welfare states were created, along with new arrangements at work and in politics ... What emerged were more strongly bonded societies and new commitment devices – the large firm, the welfare state, as well as new and revitalised political parties, all of which were ways of getting people to pre-commit to actions and behaviours that then created value for them. Predatory extremes were reined in (in the USA, marginal income tax rates peaked at 91 % in the 1950s), and the dominant spirit in many countries emphasised fairness and fair chances.

---

[30] Freeman and Perez (1988).

[31] As in Europe big business could see advantages in the socialisation of risk: it ensured a more stable and efficient society, and tended to raise the relative costs more for small than for large firms.

Carlota Pérez suggests that we may be on the verge of another great period of institutional innovation and experiment that will lead to new compromises between the claims of capital and the claims of society and of nature. The rise of a low carbon economy, implying new kinds of arrangement for housing, transport, fuel; the maturing of a broadband economy, with ubiquitous social networks, open data are all part of this story, and they provide some of the context for social innovations. For example, the rise of the open source movement, and new forms of web-based collaboration; the rise of new types of green NGO and social enterprise, helping to push up recycling or push down energy usage.

Here Perez' work intersects with parallel theories have tried to make sense of the dynamics of societies based on information and communication, and their distinctive patterns of power which have made civic networked forms of organisation much more powerful. Manuel Castells' subtle and extensive accounts aim at a synthetic view that stretches from business to identity and social movements.[32] His work has shown the inter-relationships between technological innovation, social innovation and power. Others like Yann Moulier Boutang have tried to suggest a new phase of capitalism in which new kinds of enterprise (including ones based on common goods) are thriving.[33] Timo Hamalainen has linked these arguments to industrial strategy at the national and regional level,[34] and there has been a strong strand of research in Europe on the role of regions and places in the social economy.[35]

So for example, much contemporary social innovation is clearly linked to broader changes happening to the service economy: the rising importance of platforms; the ever more formal structuring of circles of support in ageing or childhood; and the many trends loosely summed up in the term 'personalisation'. Care, health and education are likely to rise significantly as shares of GDP, encouraging a proliferation of new social business models organised around intensive support.[36]

6 Plasticity and Progress and the Ethic of Social Innovation

The premise of any social innovation is that the world is imperfect; that our knowledge of the world is incomplete; that creative innovation can achieve improvement; and that the best way to discover improvements lies in experiment, rather than revelation or deduction. These premises may seem obvious. But right

---

[32] Castells (1996).

[33] Moulier-Boutang (2007).

[34] **Hamalainen** (2003).

[35] Hillier (2004); see, for example, Gerber (2006), Schwarz et al. (2010).

[36] Maxmin and Shoshanna (2002), was a good account of these issues that has been largely vindicated by subsequent events.

from the start they set social innovation at odds with many other traditions. They imply a view of society as engaged in its own self-creation. They see the invention of the future as a natural part of human action, and extend the enlightenment belief that the world is malleable, plastic and amenable to reform.

In all of these senses social innovation is a progressive approach (in the widest sense), clearly at odds with what Albert Hirschman called the 'rhetorics of reaction' (Hirschman 1991), the theories and arguments that present all attempts at conscious social progress as liable to futility (they simply won't work), jeopardy (if they have any effect at all it will be to destroy something we value) and perversity (the claim that if any attempts at improvement had effects these would not be the ones intended, so that, for example, wars on poverty leave behind a dependent underclass). Social innovation tends to ally itself, by contrast, with the mirror rhetorics of progress[37]: rhetorics of justice – the arguments for righting wrongs and meeting needs, whether these are for pensions or affordable housing, which draw on fundamental moral senses of fairness. Its practitioners draw on rhetorics of progress, the idea that change is cumulative and dynamic: new reforms are needed to reinforce old ones, or to prevent backsliding. So, for example, new rights to maternity leave are essential to make a reality of past laws outlawing gender discrimination. And they use rhetorics of tractability: the claims that social action works, and that whether the problem is unemployment or climate change, the right mix of actions can solve it.

These optimistic views about the potential for change, and their related claim that the future can be found in the present, in embryo, are highly political stances that are largely inconceivable outside the contexts of active democracy and civil society. They connect social innovation to a deep democratic belief in the virtue of empowering society to shape society; a view that the more broadly power is spread, the greater the capacity for good to prevail; and an enlightenment belief in the possibility of cumulative growth of knowledge and insight.[38] Such ideas also connect to the world view of science and technology, conceived as progressive in nature, and in impact, with technology having its own logics of evolution as one invention leads to another.

This progressive instinct is central to the liberal democratic view of the world, but alien to many strands of conservatism, rigid Marxism-Leninism, theocracy, and belief in autocratic rule. It also runs counter to many of the claims of the Austrian school of philosophy and economics which, as I show later, has contributed important insights to social innovation, but whose fundamental stance was much closer to the rhetorics of reaction than to those of progress.

One of the most interesting contemporary exponents of the connection between social innovation and progress is the Brazilian theorist, professor of law at Harvard,

---

[37] These rhetorics are described in my book Mulgan (2009).

[38] All three of these themes are very prominent in the life of Michael Young, who remains almost unique as an example of a successful social innovator who also reflected on the patterns which he exemplified. See, for example, Briggs (2001), and Young (1983).

and former minister, Roberto Mangabeira Unger, who in a series of works analysed the 'plasticity' of the world, and the role of law in processes of social change. His recent book 'The Self Awakened'[39] presents a bold attempt to provide a philosophical foundation for social innovation. In it Unger argues that individuals and communities are not contained by their present circumstance: 'the habitual settings for action and thought, especially as organised by the institutions of society and the conventions of culture, are incapable of containing us . . . this transcendence of self over its formative circumstances occurs in every department of human experience' From this Unger deduces a more fundamental argument about the potential for systemic change: 'we can do more than innovate in the content of our social and cultural contexts: we can innovate as well in the character of our relation to them: we can change the extent to which they imprison us.' Unger draws on the pragmatist traditions of Peirce and Dewey, but gives them a modern, political edge, advancing their arguments to advocate systematic experimentation, a model of social change as self-aware but also cautious about the hubris of grand plans and reforms. Its core is a belief in people as struggling with constraint and contingency, but able to create entirely new ideas and things; a belief in permanent innovation so that 'we rethink and redesign our productive tasks in the course of executing them' using 'the smaller variations that are at hand to produce the bigger variations that do not yet exist'; and a practical commitment to making change internal to social and political institutions, through permanent experimentation. In this, cooperation and innovation are seen as twins, but also in tension with each other since innovation will tend to disrupt.

The social sciences could play a central role in this story but instead are 'dominated by . . . rationalisation, humanisation and escapism..' which together 'disarm the transcending imagination'. His view is echoed by many practitioners: social science looks backwards and lacks the tools to look forwards. And so although we need evidence, we also need not to be imprisoned by it.

The solution, according to Unger, is to see the problem-solving mind as the bridge of 'is' and 'ought'. We become human 'only by resisting the constraints of all the established structures of life, organisation, thought and character'. That means teaching children from an early age with the 'means to resist the present' and not to see it as fixed, law-like and immutable. It also leads Unger to advocate systematic experimentation – a vision of society and government constantly trying new things, sometimes failing and sometimes succeeding, but with experiment as the only reliable path to progress.

This view of life accords with the implicit views of many innovators restlessly resisting the present and struggling to avoid being weighed down by the common sense of everyday reality, while also avoiding the risk of floating off into fantasy. It chimes with many of the most interesting innovations in innovation: the widespread experiment in new tools for crowd-sourcing, the mobilisation of mass social

---

[39] Managabeira Unger (2007).

entrepreneurship, or of users as shapers of innovation and design. It also leads to a strong commitment to pluralism.

Similar ideas to Unger's can be found in some of the work of Georg Simmel. After writing some of the definitive works of modern sociology, Simmel became increasingly interested in fundamental questions about the nature of life and its processes.[40] Life, he wrote, involves flux, freedom and the creative exploration of new combinations,[41] yet it constantly creates forms and it is through forms that action is organised. So genetic mutations lead to the form of the body and the cell; musical experiment leads to forms like the symphony or the 3 min pop song; and social action leads to the creation of new institutions. Yet it is the nature of forms that they are almost opposite to life: they are fixed, permanent, limited by rules. And so forms both express life and also stand against it.

Simmel used this insight to develop a remarkable set of ideas that went on to influence leading thinkers from Martin Heidegger to Jürgen Habermas. But his account also echoes the common experience of innovators themselves. Out of engagement with the world they come up with ideas, usually through messy processes of trial and error, 'kneading the dough' again and again until it takes the right form. Then ideas become formalised, codified and defined. Then in time they become new organisations and practices. But having become forms of this kind they also begin to become new orthodoxies. The greatest aspiration of the innovator is in this sense, paradoxically, to stop innovation, so that their idea can be scaled or mainstreamed. Not surprisingly many innovators experience ambivalence when they see their ideas translated into formal organisations. Some fall out with their creations; and some have to be moved to one side by their organisation as the necessary condition for it to grow (since growth usually involves further formalisation).

Philosophy also points to other similarly dialectical features of innovation in practice. In Hegel's account of change, like Simmel's, change is described as taking place through processes of differentiation: by becoming different from what exists, or even negating it, we create the new and define our own identity. These processes of dialectical change are sometimes summarised in the famous triad – thesis, antithesis and synthesis – which can be a rough description of some of the history of social innovation with its common patterns of inversion in which peasants become bankers or patients become doctors or readers become editors of encyclopaedias, usually on the way to new syntheses which combine elements of the old as well as the new. Dialectics can also (more accurately) be understood as a method for finding unity in opposites, ideas and practices that hold in balance apparently divergent forces, like the pressure to be simultaneously commercial and social.

But even more relevant to the experience of social innovation is Hegel's account of the dynamics of externalisation and internalisation. Often ideas have to be

---

[40] Simmel (2010).

[41] Kao (1991) and (1997), are both particularly good accounts of the creative dimension of innovation.

extracted from daily life, taken from tacit knowledge and turned into formal shape before they can become powerful. In this externalised form they can then be processed and adapted – for example, defined as a business model or a business plan. But they only become useful if they are then reinserted into the practice of everyday life and internalised into the thinking of providers or citizens. Hegel's apparently abstract ideas were used to guide innovation in Japanese firms, notably through the theories of Nonaka who paid particular attention to the need for processes that drew out the insights of tacit knowledge amongst shop floor workers, and then made them formal.

They also fit with what we know about the processes of scaling and growth of social innovations. These are sometimes portrayed simply as diffusion or spread, or in terms of the growth of enterprises. But without exception social innovations with the greatest impact achieve their effects by changing how people think and how they see the world: in other words they are re-internalised.

7 Pragmatism: The Epistemology of Social Innovation

What is the nature of the knowledge associated with social innovation? For some this is a field of science with cumulative experiments creating ever more knowledge about what works – ideally using randomised trials to weed out false knowledge.

A very different view, and one that has been more influential so far amongst social innovators, can be found in the pragmatist school of Charles Peirce, William James and John Dewey. They are of interest because they accurately describe the types of knowledge involved in social innovation, knowledge which is often rooted in practice, and which is not timeless or universal or abstract in the way that knowledge about physics would be.

This is a good summary by one author of the nature of their ideas: 'ideas are not out there waiting to be discovered but are tools that people devise to cope with the world in which they find themselves ... ideas are produced not by individuals but are social ... ideas do not develop according to some inner logic of their own but are entirely dependent, like germs, on human careers and environment ... and since ideas are provisional responses to particular situations their survival depends on not on their immutability but on their adaptability.'[42]

The pragmatists went out of fashion for a time. But it is striking how many of the most interesting contemporary thinkers have reengaged with them. I have already mentioned Roberto Mangabeira Unger's use of their ideas. Bruno Latour one of the world's leading thinkers on the place of science in society is another example of the creative reappropriation of this tradition, notably in his recent book on Walter Lippmann and the 'phantom public' which explores the point, fundamental to much of the work of social innovation, that in processes of social change it may

---

[42] Menand (2001).

be necessary to create the public that becomes the subject of action. In other words it is not enough to have a good idea, not enough to promote it or even to show its relevance. At each stage of social development a new kind of collective capacity may be needed which then calls forth the innovation.

On a more prosaic level, the growth of individual social innovations demonstrates a similar pattern. Innovations only grow if there is the right mix of effective supply – which means evidence that the innovation works – and effective demand, which means someone willing to pay for it. For innovators the implication may be that generating demand (for such things as drug treatment or eldercare) can often be more important than promoting supply; that in turn may require the creation of a new kind of public: a public that cares about cutting carbon emission; a public that consciously stands for humanitarian intervention to alleviate famine; a public that is willing to put its savings into social investment products.

The pragmatist view may appear to conflict with the scientism of randomised control trials. But there may be some overlap with what could be called 'experimentalism', the belief in constant experiment in social forms. This was of course the scientific method, and always intrigued social scientists as well as social reformers. Why couldn't society conduct experiments precisely analogous to those conducted by chemists or physicists? The economist Irving Fisher is generally credited as the inventor of randomised control trials, and used them first in agriculture. A couple of decades later Karl Popper suggested a grander philosophical account of experiment in his book the Open Society and its Enemies, advocating a vision of societies and science engaged in perpetual processes of experiment and disproof, with certainty always elusive, and openness to falsification as the true mark of freedom.

More recently experiments and RCTs have again fired the imagination of social innovators and reformers, notably in fields like criminal justice and economic development. The practice hasn't always been sophisticated, and not caught up with the debates in medicine where a rather more sceptical view of RCTs has been formed by experience. But experimentalism has a lot to offer; randomised trials can often show that apparently well-conceived programmes and policies do not work, or event cause harm. And they support a moral position for practitioners: 'know your impact'.

The pragmatist spirit is as alive as ever, and its philosophers continue to provide a vital set of theories that make sense of a field that has its roots in practice.

8 Theoretical Approaches to Purpose and Ends: Wellbeing and Happiness

A final set of sources concern the ends of social innovation: what it's for, and what counts as success. For social movements this was rarely problematic in the past: the goals of ending poverty or spreading rights seemed almost self-evident. But as innovation systems are built up with more significant flows of finance, it becomes ever more important to be specific about ends, to make it possible to judge what works and what doesn't. Hence the great interest in attempting to map and measure social value, including several hundred competing tools (I have written elsewhere about the practical and intellectual strengths and weaknesses of these tools, and why they are more described than used to guide decisions). In principle a rigorous mapping of social value provides an objective way to assess the ethical question of human advancement.

All of these different tools rest on either implicit or explicit views about what the ends of a society should be. Some treat these ends as unproblematic (and this has been a weakness of much of the work on social value). Others are beginning to link up to a very active debate about societal progress and its measurement.[43] This debate led in the past to the development of indices like the HDI – the Human Development Index – and assessment tools such as 'Blended Value'[44] and Social Returns on Investment (SROI), first developed by REDF in the United States.[45] But the pace has accelerated in the last decade partly thanks to the work of the OECD under Enrico Giovannini in the 'Beyond GDP' project,[46] which encouraged many statistical offices around the world to experiment with various combinations of indices and new measures of both economic prosperity and societal success. President Sarkozy's appointment of a commission under Joseph Stiglitz, Amartya Sen and Jean Fitoussi represented a major step forward, setting out a sophisticated critique of current measures of GDP and proposals for a more rounded approach.[47]

For some the central question is how to measure capabilities, the means for people to exercise freedom (with figures such as Sen arguing that there will inevitably be discussion and disagreement over which capabilities are critical). Many social entrepreneurs and innovators describe their own work in this way: realising otherwise wasted potential. This is the language used by figures such as Michael Young and Muhammad Yunus. Expanding capabilities is a good in itself, and allows people to decide on their ends for themselves.

But the important issue for social innovation is that rapid progress is being made in measurement of outcomes that until recently were thought to be unmeasurable. Many governments are now committed to regular statistical surveys, providing a test of impacts. There is, as a result, a real possibility of achieving more consistent and comprehensive assessments of the success of innovations, a comparator equivalent to profit or GDP in economic and business innovation.[48]

---

[43] Cho (2006).

[44] Emerson (2003).

[45] http://www.redf.org/

[46] http://www.oecd.org/pages/0,3417,en_40033426_40033828_1_1_1_1_1,00.html

[47] Stiglitz at al. (2009).

[48] Nussbaum and Sen (eds) (2010), is one of the best compilations of thought on the theory. Bacon at al. (2010).

What connects all of these arguments is a view of value. Antonio Damasio has argued persuasively that there is a fundamental concept of biological value which is analytically robust, and which is prior to either economic or social value.[49] This is the value of survival and flourishing. Survival depends on homeostasis, preserving the conditions for our bodies to live, with the right temperature, food and water and physical safety. But Damasio argues that we can also extend from this basic value to recognise the conditions under which we are fully alive, mentally stimulated, socially engaged, loved and cared for: in other words wellbeing is indeed a universal value and a solid foundation for constructing more specific measures in fields such as social innovation or action.

These theoretical perspectives can lead to radically different views of what matters – for example, implying a much greater priority to mental prosperity, rather than prioritising material factors, or focusing attention on psychosocial relationships and their cultivation. More controversially this turn is bringing the field of social innovation into the controversial debates about the relationship between wellbeing, economic growth, democracy and different forms of capitalism.

Perhaps the more interesting implications of this new field of theory and analysis is that it opens up novel questions: which kinds of consumption most contribute to happiness and which may diminish it? What kinds of work organisation are most conducive to wellbeing? Can philanthropy make up for the unhappiness of a very unequal society?

In an earlier phase of interest in social innovation and entrepreneurship these issues were largely excluded. It was assumed that if only social enterprises could become more like businesses, they would be more likely to succeed. Their priority was to grow, scale, and establish themselves as equivalent to big business brands. But the focus on wellbeing shifts the question. It implies that business may have as much to learn from the social sector, and that a field concerned primarily with wellbeing rather than either profit or GDP growth is bound to reach distinct conclusions. And it forces the field to attend to the quality of growth as well as its quantities.

9 Where Next

Clearly social innovation is not contained or monopolised by any of the traditions described above. It cuts across disciplines, fields and areas of knowledge. In many respects practice is ahead of theory – and the best role for theorists is to study practice and make sense of its patterns.

But my hope is that sharper theories will emerge in the years ahead, and that some will be amenable to assessment. We may be some way off the standards set by Wolfgang Pauli and physics – social theorems are rarely so easy to prove or

---

[49] Damasio (2010).

disprove. But we do need a stronger foundation from which to judge which fashions fit with reality, and which mislead, if only so that the efforts of social innovators themselves can stand more chances of success.

References

Bacon, N., Brophy, M., Mguni, N., Mulgan, G., & Shandro, A. (2010). *The state of happiness: Can public policy shape people's wellbeing and resilience?* London: The Young Foundation.
Baumol, W. J. (2003). *The free market innovation machine*. Princeton: Princeton University Press.
Boltanski, L., & Laurent, T. (2006). *On justification: Economies of worth*. Princeton: Princeton University Press.
Boutang, Y. M. (2007). *Le Capitalisme Cognitif: La Nouvelle Grande transformation*. Paris: Editions Amsterdam.
Briggs, A. (2001). *Michael Young: Social entrepreneur*. London: Palgrave Macmillan.
Castells, M. (1996). and later, *The rise of the network society. The information age: Economy, society and culture, Vol. 1, 2 and 3*. Oxford: Blackwell.
Chesbrough, H. (2006). *Innovation intermediaries, enabling open innovation*. Boston: Harvard Business School Press.
Cho, A. H. (2006). Politics, values and social entrepreneurship: A critical appraisal. In J. Mair, J. Robinson, & K. Hockerts (Eds.), *Social entrepreneurship* (pp. 35–56). London: Palgrave.
Christenson, C. (2003). *The innovators solution*. Cambridge, MA: Harvard Business School Press.
Damasio, A. (2010). *Self comes to mind: Constructing the conscious brain*. New York: Pantheon.
Dees, J. G., & Anderson, B. B. (2006). Framing a theory of social entrepreneurship: Building on two schools of practice and thought. In R. Mosher-Williams (Ed.), *Research on social entrepreneurship: Understanding and contributing to an emerging field* (ARNOVA occasional paper series, Vol. 1 (3), pp. 39–66). Indianapolis: Association for Research on Nonprofit Organizations and Voluntary Action.
Defourny, J., & Nyssens, M. (2008a). Social enterprise in Europe: Recent trends and developments. *Social Enterprise Journal, 4*(3), 202–228.
Defourny, J., & Nyssens, M. (2008). *Conceptions of social enterprise in Europe and the United States: Convergences and divergences*. Paper presented at the 8th ISTR International Conference and 2d EMES-ISTR European Conference, Barcelona, 9–12 July 2008.
Drayton, W. (2006). Everyone a changemaker: Social entrepreneurship's ultimate goal. *Innovations*, Winter, 1–32.
Emerson, J. (2003). *The blended value map: Tracking the intersects and opportunities of economic, social and environmental value creation*. Available online: http://www.blendedvalue.org/wp-content/uploads/2004/02/pdf-bv-map.pdf Accessed 10 June 2010
Freeman, C., & Perez, C. (1988). Structural crisis of adjustments, business, cycles and investment behaviour. In G. Dosi (Ed.), *Technical change and economic theory* (p. 60). London: Pinter Publishers.
Gerber, P. (2006). *Der lange Weg der sozialen Innovation – Wie Stiftungen zum sozialen Wandel im Feld der Bildungs-und Sozialpolitik beitragen können. Eine Fallstudie zur Innovationskraft der Freudenberg Stiftung*. Weinheim.
Hamalainen, T. J. (2003). *National competitiveness and economic growth: The changing determinants of economic performance in the world economy* (New Horizons in institutional and evolutionary economics series). Cheltenham: Edward Elgar.
Helpman, E. (2004). *The mystery of economic growth*. Cambridge, MA: Harvard University Press.
Hillier, J. (2004). Trois essais sur le rôle de l'innovation sociale dans le développement territorial. *Géographie, Économie, société, 02, 6.*
Hirschman, A. (1991). *The rhetoric of reaction*. Cambridge, MA: Harvard University Press.

Hochgerner, J. (2011). The analysis of social innovations as social practice, published in original German language under the title Die Analyse sozialer Innovationen als gesellschaftliche Praxis. In: Zentrum fur Soziale Innovation (Ed.), Pendeln zwischen Wissenschaft und Praxis. ZSI-Beitrage zu sozialen Innovationen (pp. 173–189). Vienna and Berlin: LIT.

Kao, J. (1991). *The entrepreneurial organisation*. New Jersey: Prentice Hall.

Kao, J. (1997). *Jamming: The art and discipline of business creativity*. New York: HarperBusiness.

Kirzner, I. (1973). *Competition and entrepreneurship*. Chicago: University of Chicago Press.

Kirzner, I. (1982). Uncertainty, Discovery, and Human Action: A Study of the Entrepreneurial Profile in the Misesian System. In Kirzner, I. (Ed.). *Method, Process, and Austrian Economics*. Lexington, Mass: D. C. Heath and Company.

Lester, R., & Piore, M. (2004). *Innovation: The missing dimension*. Cambridge, MA: Harvard University Press.

Managabeira Unger, R. (2007). *The self awakened: Pragmatism unbound*. Cambridge, MA: Harvard University Press.

Mandelbrot, B., & Hudson, R. (2008). *The (mis)behaviour of markets: A fractal view of risk, ruin and reward*. London: Profile Books.

Markman, A., & Wood, K. (Eds.). (2009). *Tools for innovation*. Oxford: Oxford University Press.

Maxmin, J., & Zuboff, S. (2002). *The support economy: Why corporations are failing individuals and the next episode of capitalism*. New York: Viking Press.

McCraw, T. K. (2007b). *Prophet of innovation: Joseph Schumpeter and creative destruction*. Cambridge, MA: Belknap Press.

Menand, L. (2001). *The metaphysical club: A story of ideas in America Farrar*. New York: Straus and Giroux Xi-xii.

Moulier-Boutang, Y. (2007). *Le Capitalisme Cognitif: La Nouvelle Grande transformation*. Paris: Editions Amsterdam.

Mulgan, G. (2006). *Social innovation: What it is, why it matters, how it can be accelerated*. London: Basingstoke Press.

Mulgan, G. (2007). *Ready or not? Taking innovation in the public sector seriously, NESTA Provocation 03*. London: NESTA.

Mulgan, G. (2009). *The art of public strategy*. Oxford: Oxford University Press.

Mulgan, G., Ali, R., Halkett, R., & Sanders, B. (2007). *In and out of sync: The challenge of growing social innovations*. London: NESTA/Young Foundation.

Murray, R., Caulier-Grice, J., & Mulgan, G. (2010). *The open book of social innovation*. London: NESTA/Young Foundation.

Nooteboom, B. (2000). *Learning and innovation in organisations and economies*. Oxford: Oxford University Press.

Nussbaum, M., & Sen, A. (Eds.). (2010). *The quality of life*. Oxford: Clarendon Press.

Nutley, S., Davies, H., & Walter, I. (2002). *Learning from the diffusion of innovations*. St. Andrews: University of St Andrews.

Ramalingam, B., & Jones, H. (2008). *Exploring the science of complexity: Ideas and implications for development and humanitarian efforts*. ODI Working paper 285.

Rogers, E. M. (1995). *Diffusion of innovations*. New York: Free Press.

Rogers, E. M. (2003). *Diffusion of innovations*. New York: Free Press.

Schumpeter, J. (1934b). *The theory of economic development: An inquiry into profits, capital, credit, interest and the business cycle*. New Brunswick: Transaction Publishers.

Schwarz, M., Birke, M., & Beerheide, E. (2010) *Die Bedeutung sozialer Innovationen für eine nachhaltige Entwicklung*. In: Jürgen Howaldt, Jacobsen H. (Eds.). Soziale Innovation. Auf dem Weg zu einem postindustriellen Innovationsparadigma. Wiesbaden: VS Verlag für Sozialwissenschaften.

Shockley, G., & Frank, P. (2011). Schumpeter, Kirzner, and the field of social entrepreneurship. *Journal of Social Entrepreneurship, 2*(1), 6–26. March 2011.

Simmel, G. (2010). *The view of life: Four metaphysical essays with journal aphorisms* (trans: Andrews, A. Y., Levine, D. J.). Chicago: University of Chicago Press.
Stark, D. (2009). *The sense of dissonance: Accounts of worth in economic life*. Princeton: Princeton University Press.
Stiglitz, J., Sen, A., & Fitoussi, J. (2009). *Report by the commission on the measurement of economic performance and social progress*. Paris: The Commission.
Stoneman, P., & Diederen, P. (1994). Technology diffusion and public policy. *The Economic Journal, 104*(July), 918–930. Oxford: Blackwell.
Swedberg, R. (2009). Schumpeter's full model of entrepreneurship: Economic, non-economic and social entrepreneurship. In R. Ziegler (Ed.), *An introduction to social entrepreneurship: Voices, preconditions, contexts* (pp. 77–106). Cheltenham: Edward Elgar.
Von Hippel, E. (1988). *Sources of innovation*. Oxford: Oxford University Press.
Von Mises, L. (1949/1996). *Human action: A treatise on economics* (pp. 252–253). San Francisco: Fox and Wilkes.
Westley, F., Zimmerman, B., & Patton, M. (2006). *Getting to maybe: How the world is changed*. Toronto: Random House Canada.
White, H. C. (2001). *Markets from networks: Socioeconomic models of production*. Princeton: Princeton University Press.
Young, M. (1983). *The social scientist as innovator*. Cambridge, MA: Harvard University Press.
Young Foundation/SIX report for the Bureau of European Policy Advisers, European Commission, (2010).

Shaping Social Innovation by Social Research

Jürgen Howaldt and Ralf Kopp

Abstract In light of the increasing importance of social innovation, this paper explores the question of what (new) roles social sciences can play in analyzing and shaping social innovation. The paper starts with an overview of the current situation and the perspectives of socio-scientific innovation research that have greatly contributed to the development and spread of an enlightened socio-scientific understanding of innovation. Against the backdrop of clear paradoxes and confusion in prevailing politics of innovation, the contours of a new innovation paradigm are becoming visible and causing social innovation to grow in importance. Consistently, the social sciences will be challenged to redefine their functions with regard to innovation. In the past, innovation research in the context of social sciences has contributed heavily to explain the social dimensions, the complexity and paradoxa of innovation processes. Henceforth, much will depend on realigning the range of competencies of social science and social scientists by contributing actively to the development and integration of innovations as well as by developing social innovation.

1 Introduction

Referring to the momentous implications of the current and constricted debate on innovation policy, we will describe the increasing importance of social innovation becoming apparent. This development is used to outline a sociologically founded, post-industrial innovation paradigm. The basic assumption is: The transition from an industrial to a knowledge- and services-based society corresponds with a paradigm shift of the innovation system. This paradigm shift also implies an increasing

---

J. Howaldt (✉) • R. Kopp
Social Research Centre, Dortmund University of Technology, Evinger Platz 17,
Dortmund 44339, Germany
e-mail: howaldt@sfs-dortmund.de

importance of social innovation, as compared to technological innovation. Whereas innovation used to focus primarily on natural and engineering sciences generating new products and processes, social innovation will become more and more pivotal. Consistently, the social sciences will be challenged to redefine their functions with regard to innovation. In the past, innovation research in the context of social sciences has contributed heavily to explain the social dimensions, the complexity and paradoxes of innovation processes. Henceforth, much will depend on realigning the range of competencies of social science as well as social scientists by contributing actively to the development and integration of innovations as well as by developing social innovation. The objective consists in understanding social science production not only as the production of social science but as the social production of science enhancing the self-reflective capacities of all individuals and social groups involved.

2 A New Innovation Paradigm: Current Status and Perspectives of International Innovation Research

Innovation research in the social sciences has made great contributions to the development and spread of an enlightened sociological understanding of innovation. Its interpretative possibilities have become widely and "successfully" practical. The central elements of a sociologically enlightened understanding of innovation could be summarized in the following way: the systematic and social character of innovation reduced to technical and organizational innovation; aspects of complexity, risk and reflexion; incompatibility with planning and limited manageability; an increasing variety and heterogeneity of involved agents; non-linear trajectory as well as a high degree of context and interaction contingency. Technical and social innovations are conceived as closely intertwined and can only be completely captured in their interaction with each other (cf. Braun-Thürmann 2005: 27 et seq.).

Against the background of the findings in innovation research in the social sciences and the clear emergence of paradoxes and confusion in prevailing innovation policies that have been described, the question arises whether the technology-oriented innovation paradigm that has been shaped by the industrial society is now becoming increasingly less functional. In light of the weaknesses of the German innovation system that are becoming recognizable, Rammert calls for an "innovation in innovation" in terms of a "post-Schumpeterian innovation regime" (2000: 2).

This sort of fundamental change process involving the entire institutional structure and the associated way of thinking and basic assumptions can be interpreted, in our opinion, in terms of the development of a new innovation paradigm.[1] This

---

[1] Paradigm means in this sense, borrowing from Kuhn (1996: 10), "a pattern of thought rooted in commonly held basic assumptions that can offer a community of experts considerable problems and solutions for a certain period of time" (cf. Kuhn 1996: 26).

approach opens up fundamentally new perspectives on recognized problems and thus simultaneously unlocks new possibilities for action. Especially in the light of the basic confusions and paradoxes in innovation policy in present times, this sort of interpretation of the current changes may open up new perspectives on innovation.[2]

International innovation research is providing numerous indications of a fundamental shift in the innovation paradigm. In his introduction to the "Oxford Handbook of Innovation", which compiles the key development trajectories of international innovation research, Fagerberg describes the variability of innovation as one of its central characteristics: "One of the striking facts about innovation is its variability over time and space. It seems, as Schumpeter (...) pointed out, to 'cluster' not only in certain sectors but also in certain areas and time periods" (Fagerberg 2005: 14). Individual analyses have led to descriptions of specific innovation systems in different *economic sectors and industries* (Malerba 2005). At the same time, a vast heterogeneity in innovation can be perceived in terms of the historical development of the process of innovation (Bruland and Mowery 2005: 374 et seq.).

The argument for the thesis of the emergence of a new innovation paradigm is supported by the work of Bruland and Mowery. The authors believe that fundamental changes occur in the structures of innovation systems in different time periods (Bruland and Mowery 2005: 374). These changes are described as an expression of different phases of the industrial revolution. When a new innovation system takes hold, it leads to far-reaching changes in the entire structure of the institution. "But both of these episodes highlight the importance of broad institutional change, rather than the 'strategic importance' of any single industry or technology" (Ibid.: 375). As such the "leading industries" (Ibid.: 374) have tremendous influence on the prevailing innovation modes.

In the face of the societal shift from an industrial society to a knowledge and service economy and the profound change this entails in the economic and social structures of modern society, there are many indications signaling a fundamental shift in the innovation paradigm that can be detected. New economic sectors and industries are increasingly determining the look of the economy and society and are changing the modes of production and innovation. As such, new forms of production and innovation cultures have developed on a global scale in the IT industry that centre on "partner management as a strategic function of the company" (Boes and Trinks 2007: 86). The new "leading industries" offer a good arena to investigate the central questions in modern innovation management for companies as well as the innovation policies in developed economies at a relatively early stage (cf. Ibid.).

The opening of the innovation process to society is a key characteristic of these changes (cf. Fora 2010: 15 et seq.). Other companies, technical schools and research institutes are not the only relevant agents in the process of innovation. Citizens and customers no longer serve as suppliers of information about their

---

[2] The authors of a current study relating to the OECD Committee for Industry, Innovation, and Entrepreneurship (CIIE) advance this thesis: "A new nature of innovation is emerging and reshaping public policy" (cf. Fora 2010).

needs (as in traditional innovation management); they make contributions to the process of developing new products to resolve problems. Terms and concepts such as "open innovation" (Chesbrough 2003), customer integration (Dunkel and Rieder 2007) and networks (Howaldt et al. 2001) reflect individual aspects of this development. This enables the discovery of clear parallels to fundamental changes in the production system, particularly in the area of the production of services, that have been discussed in this area for several years (cf. Greenhalgh et al. 2004), and gives them new momentum via the technological possibilities of the internet (cf. Hanekopp and Wittke 2008). At the same time, innovation – based on economic development – becomes a general social phenomenon that increasingly influences and permeates every aspect of life.

3 Social Innovation: Concepts, Dimensions, Topics

With the development of a new innovation paradigm, so too a change in the subject matter of innovation occurs. At the heart of the industrial society innovation paradigm are technical innovations relating to products and processes that are regarded as (almost) the only hope of societal development. Non-technical and social innovations, however, although they exist constantly and widely in social systems, are largely ignored as a topic and are a little recognized phenomenon (cf. Gillwald 2000), though this offers them no protection from enormous expectations of providing answers to problems given that issues such as massive unemployment, the erosion of the social security systems or the intensification of ecological risks cannot be overcome without implementing social innovation. And in light of the current and extensive financial and economic crisis, it is becoming increasingly clear that social innovations, as they relate to extensive change in both the leading cultures that influence behaviour and the social practices in economy and consumption, determine "in what sort of world the next generation of the citizens of free societies will be living" (Dahrendorf 2009).

This is why it is all the more amazing that social innovation as an independent phenomenon has garnered so little attention in research funding and research practice (cf. Zapf 1989; Gillwald 2000). "Innovation-related thinking is asymmetrical. The emphasis is on technical innovation" (Rammert 1997: 3).

The sociologist Ogburn is among the few authors who make an explicit distinction between technical and social innovation. "The use of the term invention does not apply merely to technical inventions in our context, but instead comprises social inventions such as the League of Nations; it is also used to denote innovations in other cultural areas, such as the invention of a religious ritual or an alphabet. In the following we understand invention as referring to the combination or modification of previously existing and known and/or intangible cultural elements to create a new element" (Ogburn 1969: 56). But even Ogburn proceeds from the assumption of primarily technical inventions. For him, technical advancement is a driver of social development. He connects this with the thesis of a "cultural lag" (Ogburn 1957), namely a distance between a culture and technical developments that creates a pressure to "catch up" in the material facets of life. "His reports on trends for the US government that started appearing on a regular basis starting in 1936 (...) laid out the conceptual and institutional foundation for assessing the effects of technology and evaluating it" (Rammert 2008: 11).

An initial conclusion can be made that phenomena of social change are consistently looked at in connection with technological innovation in techno-sociology and technical research in the prevailing paradigm of a social-technical system but not from the perspective of an independent type of innovation that can be demarcated from technical innovations. From the perspective of techno-sociology and its central field, this is not only possible but necessary. The conflation of innovation as a term becomes problematic when the concepts for innovation developed in techno-sociology and technical research are universalized into a comprehensive theory of innovation. This is inadequate in light of the declining functionality of the technology-oriented paradigm shaped by the industrial society.

While the changed and intensified social and economic problems identified in public discourse are increasingly prompting a call for extensive social innovation, the topic continues to remain a largely under-explored area in the social sciences as well as government innovation policies. "The field of social innovation remains relatively undeveloped" (Mulgan et al. 2007: 3).

3.1 What Makes an Innovation a Social Innovation?

The substantive distinction between social and technical innovations can be found in their immaterial intangible structure. Social innovation is not substantialised as technical artefacts but occurs at the level of social practice. A social innovation is a new combination[3] and/or new configuration of social practices in certain areas of action or social contexts prompted by certain actors or constellations of actors in an intentional, targeted manner with the goal of better satisfying or answering needs and problems than is possible on the basis of established practices. An innovation is therefore social to the extent that it, conveyed by the market or "non/without profit", is socially accepted and diffused widely throughout society or in certain societal sub-areas, transformed depending on circumstances and ultimately institutionalized as new social practice or made routine. As with every other innovation, "new" does not necessarily mean "good" but in this case it is "socially desirable" in an extensive and normative sense. According to the actors' practical rationale, social attributions for social innovations are generally uncertain.

---

[3] The term relates to the Schumpeterian definition of innovation as a new combination of production factors (cf. Schumpeter 1964).

In this sense, social innovation (borrowing from Crozier/Friedberg) can be interpreted as a process of collective creation in which the members of a certain collective unit learn, invent and lay out new rules for the social game of collaboration and of conflict or, in a word, a new social practice, and in this process they acquire the necessary cognitive, rational and organizational skills" (Crozier and Friedberg 1993: 19). Social innovations, understood as innovations of social practices, are (examined in terms of their substantive aspect) an elementary part of sociology, and therefore – in contrast to technical innovations – can be not only analysed, but also engendered and (co-)shaped; they are oriented toward social practice and require reflection on the social relationship structure.[4]

In the face of the depth and development of change in modern societies and the rising dysfunction in established practice, social innovations are gaining greater importance, also in terms of economic factors, over technical innovations. They are not only necessary, but also can contribute proactively with regard to anticipated developments, such as demographic developments or the effects of climate change "to modify, or even transform, existing ways of life should it become necessary so to do" (Giddens 2009: 163).

4 On the Role of the Social Sciences in Researching and Shaping Social Innovations

As we can see, criticism of a one-sided innovation paradigm limited to technology is the central starting point for the discussion of the topic of social innovation in the greater public as well as in the social sciences. In many concepts, this also connects to a critical look at the role of the social sciences in innovations. The 'division of labour' between natural and engineering science, on the one hand, and social sciences and the humanities, on the other hand, that is part of the current debate on innovation is described by Blättel-Mink (2006) as follows: "Natural and engineering sciences are different from social sciences and the arts primarily in that the former produce innovations or the prerequisites for innovations while the latter reflects on the emergence, the implementation and the success of innovation or also seek to explain the process (by means of comprehension)" (Ibid.: 31).

Specifically in its analytical function, research in the social sciences can contribute greatly to conceptually processing the social prerequisites for innovation and the social character of innovation processes. Its strengths rest in the analysis of innovation processes and their contextual circumstances. The findings picked up here have permeated social consciousness deeply, have determined the thinking and

---

[4] In our trend study "Social Innovation: Concepts, Research Fields and International Trends" we deliver an overview of the different concepts and research fields of social innovation in the international debate (cf. Howaldt and Schwarz 2010).

action of social actors and have contributed significantly to establishing a new "sociologically enlightened" innovation paradigm.

The social sciences have reinterpreted the process of innovation, but other disciplines continue to dominate this field, primarily technological natural sciences. Shifting the perspective on innovation from technical to social innovation as an independent type of innovation, the present self-limitation of the social sciences to the concomitant research associated with a reference to the complexity and paradoxically loaded nature of innovation proves to be insufficient. For it is here that the subject matter of innovation itself rests immediately in the disciplinary perspective of the social sciences and the affiliated capacity for action and formation.

Purely analytical concepts fall short precisely in relation to the specific content of social innovations. After all, as mentioned previously, social innovations (in contrast to technological innovations) are a natural subject of the social sciences (especially sociology) in terms of content, and as such social innovation can be not only analyzed and indicated from a level of comprehension, but also be engendered and (co)shaped in terms of its (social and societal) preconditions, repercussions, etc. Thus, it is hardly surprising that the role of the social sciences in examining *and* shaping social innovation is an important issue in the international scientific discussion on social innovation.

4.1 Social Innovation as the Topic and Subject Matter of the Social Sciences

Wolfgang Zapf connected the analysis of the meaning and specifics of social innovations with the question about the role and possibilities of the social sciences in researching social innovations (Zapf 1989: 182 et seq.). Up to now these ideas have not lead to increasing the social sciences' responsibility to play a role nor has it enhanced its capacity to do so (cf. Howaldt 2004). It is worth noting in this regard that the action research appreciated by Zapf as social innovation in German social sciences has become less influential. This can only be partially explained by the weaknesses of action research itself which aims at merging both the scientific demands and the problem-solving processes practiced on a day-to-day basis, which is quite problematic in light of the differentiation of societal sub-systems (cf. Howaldt 2004: 28). However, it is not a satisfactory solution to renounce of large portions of research in the social sciences to some sort of practical efficacy defined in whatever way and to return to a natural science-oriented self-conception as "pure" science with the function of scientific analysis and describing society (cf. for example Kühl 2003) in the light of society's changed demands.

To resolve the specific problems of sociology and to re-describe the specific roles of the social sciences beyond the science-centred understanding of the practice of science, the discussion on the topic of social innovation offers important inspiration. Key references to the specific potential of the social sciences can be found in Zapf. "Social scientists search for, develop and select new ways to do certain things and solve problems" (Zapf 1989: 183). In this sense, Zapf believes that they could be helpful in building new institutions. In the previously mentioned positive reference to action research, Zapf emphasizes that it is precisely the application-oriented "tools for making decisions [delivered by the social sciences] – forecasts, incremental planning, social experiments, evaluation, practices for mobilization and motivation – (...) that [can] indeed enhance the ability of modern societies to solve problems and direct themselves" (Ibid.: 183). Zapf distinguishes potential contributions the social sciences can make to social innovation:

- Decision-making support (survey research, personality tests, risk assessment and technology impact, human resources planning, etc.),
- Sources of social technologies (quality management, co-determination model, group therapy),
- Approaches to general theory in order to better understand innovation and productivity (Zapf 1989: 182 et seq.).

However, recognizing that social innovations are increasingly building on "the knowledge, skills and toughness of politicians, managers and professionals (...) and the day-to-day practices (pratiques) of subcultures and social movements from the bottom-up" (Ibid.: 182) as technical innovation is of great importance for developing appropriate concepts in a version of the social sciences that is oriented towards shaping social innovation.

This sort of understanding of innovation processes requires developing appropriate forms of co-operation between science and practice that are not centrally focused on the transfer of expert knowledge into social practice. In this context, contributions from the social sciences to shaping innovation cannot be exhausted in "consumer goods"; instead, forms of generating knowledge must be developed that do not conceive potential users or customers as final adopters of innovation only but are incorporate them into complex communication networks as equal co-producers (cf. Howaldt 2004). The aim of the conception of co-operation is to organize the process of change itself as a learning process that fosters the development and skills of every actor involved and enhances their ability to determine and reflect.

In this context, interest in the subject of consulting in the social sciences has been increasing since the mid-1990s. This interest is not only due to the growing importance of the consulting sector in the wake of establishing a knowledge-based society. It also involves the question regarding appropriate concepts that increase the practical efficacy of research in the social sciences in the context of organization-related or regional innovation processes and could arise in coming transfer models (Nowotny et al. 2001). Consultancy concepts inspired by systems theory are of particular interest in this regard. New formats for design-oriented social sciences thus emerged at the intersection of consulting and research.

4.2 Conceptual Design and Research in the Context of Social Innovation

The way how these new roles for the social sciences are perceived and the research designs and methods are applied vary across the different fields of research in social innovation.

The Zentrum für Soziale Innovationen (ZSI) founded in 1990 in Vienna with a consistent transdisciplinary approach has concentrated successfully on the research, development and dissemination of social innovations in different areas of activity for over two decades and thus affirms Zapf's assessment that tools in the social sciences are well-suited for this in a unique way. In this context, transdisciplinarity means both collaboration in the practical application and use of knowledge in non-scientific fields of work as well as the integration of findings from practical settings into the process of teaching, developing methods and constructing theories in the sciences (cf. Hochgerner 2008: 5). As such it combines the processes of research, consulting, network co-ordination and education into an integrated concept.

In a similar way, the Sozialforschungsstelle Dortmund (Social Research Centre) has been developing a new type of research in operational and regional innovation processes since the mid-1990s focusing on the production of scientific findings in connection with solving practical problems to master social innovation processes in companies, regions and politics (Howaldt 2004). For instance, this involves the development of new forms of working and organization in companies, the creation of inter-organizational co-operation and learning networks, the support of international transformation processes in regional networks as well as the interdisciplinary and transdisciplinary development and implementation of technical and social innovations with regard to proactively and dynamically adapting regions to the effects of climate change.

The work of Geoff Mulgan et al. also concerns practical matters. "Together, these would contribute to a more social innovation system, analogous to the many and diverse systems which exist around the world to promote technological innovation" (Mulgan et al. 2007: 5). In a collaborative research report by the Young Foundation 2009 and NESTA (National Endowment for Science, Technology and the Arts), the focus is on recommendations concerning social innovations for politics and financing as well as an action guideline for innovators.

With projects like ALMOLIN and SINGOCOM in the field of local and regional development, Moulaert et al. aim at promoting developments that propel social integration in different social spheres from the labour market to the educational system and socio-cultural developments (Moulaert et al. 2005: 1970).

As an interdisciplinary and inter-university research centre for social innovation, the Centre de recherche sur les innovations sociales (CRISES) also aims to examine and spread social innovation in the areas of regional development as well as life and job quality. It also collaborates systematically with partners in economy, politics and society (http://www.crises.uqam.ca/pages/en/).

An example of how politics and science can promote social innovations can be found at Sozialforschungsstelle Dortmund that commissioned by the Economic Ministry of North-Rhine Westphalia organised and evaluated a "service contest for the Ruhr region". The objective of the competition was to develop innovative, marketable services with the intention of unlocking new areas for growth and employment opportunities in the Ruhr region as one of the largest European service markets. Project ideas were awarded that were aiming to improve the housing conditions and quality of life for the elderly, integrate mentally ill migrants, establish daycare regimes, etc. These ideas involve social innovations that are translated into concrete business ideas and marketed as innovative services (cf. Kutzner 2010).

In conclusion, it can be maintained that the underlying field and area of application for social innovation can be separated from technical innovation and that it simultaneously seems to mark a relevant unique characteristic regarding the role and potential of the social sciences. The approaches described here are closely connected with scientific reflection and practical creative drive. As Kesselring and Leitner (2008: 14 et seq.) explain, social innovation is to be "regarded as the interface between sociological reflection and social action as it requires reflecting on social problems and intentional action."

5 Conclusion and Outlook

Innovation is not an end in itself. It is always a provisional result of complex socio-economic activities. The institutional prerequisites and their associated staff competencies are also integrated into this complex, open-ended process of change and are themselves under pressure to innovate. This observation is not new – it was summed up in a visionary style as far back as 1945 by V. Bush, an American engineer and analogue computer pioneer, in the book "Science, the endless frontier": "An 'endless frontier' means that these developments are constantly being pushed farther ahead, that little is ultimately known about them and that the related research from now on needs to be integrated into the research and innovation process. After the scientist and the engineer, now comes the person of the mediator, the interpreter, whose new and so far little codified task would have to consist in bringing into contact with each other the various actors of change within a society which has set itself objectives in the common interest that find widespread support (collective work and socio-technical testing)" (European Commission 1998: 143). Bush assigned this role to the state and to politics. Given his technical background one is led to suspect that the technical/natural science disciplines did not seem to him suited to generating multi-dimensional innovations and that he sought a social controlling authority. That social science was not explicitly taken into consideration as a further relevant actor in the role of mediator may be due, among other reasons, to the fact that at this time no corresponding organization-oriented competencies were available in the discipline.

Nevertheless, a need was named here that has been the productive concern of at least a part of the application-oriented discipline.

Social innovations in particular need successful communication, co-operation and knowledge integration between heterogeneous stakeholders. "Given this, the relevance of social science expertise for the analysis and organization of innovation processes is not obsolete but more current than ever" (Bienzeisler and Bullinger 2007). To this extent, both the occasion and the opportunity arise for the discipline to redefine its role in the modernization process and reposition itself where necessary. The requisite know-how is found in the sociology of technology, economic sociology, and organizational sociology. The network approach, in particular, offers tried-and-tested concepts and methods with high development potential. Concepts such as innovation and learning networks, learning communities (Senge and Scharmer 1997), communities of practice (Wenger and Snyder 2000) etc., but also the debate on interactive value creation and the hybridization of material products and services (cf. Reichwald and Piller 2005) are smoothing the way for a transformed understanding of innovation, for which close co-operation between practice, guidance, science and politics is essential. In researching, developing and testing social innovations, the social sciences do not have to limit themselves to critical accompaniment of and commentary on innovation processes. If they exploit and develop their potential to integrate heterogeneous high-grade knowledge, they may "be able to play a role similar to that played by the natural sciences for technical innovations" (Zapf 1989: 182). The social sciences have reinterpreted the innovation process. The important thing now is to make a contribution to the development and organization of innovation processes. They should not wait too long to do so, since it is true that the "loss of knowledge innovation monopolies also applies to the scientific disciplines. Not only business management studies but also the engineering sciences have now recognized the relevance of what are called 'soft' factors and have developed corresponding knowledge and know how" (Bienzeisler and Bullinger 2007: 57).

References

Bienzeisler, B., & Bullinger, H. J. (2007). Innovation und hybride Wertschöpfung. *Internationale Zeitschrift für Veränderung, Lernen, Dialog, 13 (1, 2007),* 54–58.
Blättel-Mink, B. (2006). *Kompendium der Innovationsforschung*. Wiesbaden: VS Verlag für Sozialwissenschaften.
Boes, A., & Trinks, K. (2007). Internationale Innovationspartnerschaften in der IT-Branche. In J. Ludwig, M. Moldaschl, M. Schmauder, K. Schmierl (Eds.), *Arbeitsforschung und Innovationsfähigkeit in Deutschland* (pp. 85–94), Vol. 9. in: Moldaschl, M., Arbeit, Innovation und Nachhaltigkeit, Munich, Mering: Hampp Verlag.
Braun-Thürmann, H. (2005). *Innovation*. Bielefeld: Transcript Verlag.
Bruland, K., & Mowery, D. C. (2005). Innovation through time. In J. Fagerberg, D. C. Mowery, & R. Nelson (Eds.), *The Oxford handbook of innovation* (pp. 349–379). Oxford, NY: Oxford University Press.
Chesbrough, H. W. (2003). *Open innovation: The new imperative for creating and profiting from technology*. Boston: Harvard Business School Press.

Crozier, M., & Friedberg, E. (1993). *Die Zwänge kollektiven Handelns: Über Macht und Organisation*. Frankfurt: Hain.
Dahrendorf, R. (2009). Nach der Krise: Zurück zur protestantischen Ethik? Sechs Anmerkungen. *Merkur, Deutsche Zeitschrift für europäisches Denken, 63 (720, 2009)*, 373–381.
Dunkel, W., & Rieder, K. (2007). Innovationspartnerschaften in neuen Unternehmen-Kunden-Beziehungen. In J. Ludwig, M. Moldaschl, M. Schmauder, K. Schmierl (Eds.), *Arbeitsforschung und Innovationsfähigkeit in Deutschland* (pp. 113–118), Vol. 9, in M. Moldaschl (Eds.), *Arbeit, Innovation und Nachhaltigkeit*, Munich, Mering: Hampp Verlag.
European Commission (1998). Die Gesellschaft, letzte Grenze. Eine europäische Vision der Forschungs- und Innovationspolitik im XXI. Jahrhundert, Brussels, Luxembourg: Amt für Amtl. Veröff. der Europ. Gemeinschaften.
Fagerberg, J. (2005). Innovation: A guide to literature. In J. Fagerberg, D. C. Mowery, & R. Nelson (Eds.), *The Oxford handbook of innovation* (pp. 1–26). Oxford, NY: Oxford University Press.
FORA (2010). New Nature of Innovation. Report to the OECD, Kopenhagen http://www.newnatureofinnovation.org/introduction.html. Accessed March 2010.
Giddens, A. (2009). *The politics of climate change*. Cambridge/Malden: Wiley.
Gillwald, K. (2000). Konzepte sozialer Innovation. *WZB paper: Querschnittsgruppe Arbeit und Ökologie*, Berlin. http://bibliothek.wzb.eu/pdf/2000/p00-519.pdf. Accessed Jan 2010.
Greenhalgh, T., Robert, G., Macfarlane, F., Bate, P., Kyriakidou, O. (2004). Diffusion of innovations in service organizations: Systematic review and recommendations. *The Milbank Quarterly, 82(4, 2004)*, 1–37. http://www.milbank.org/quarterly/8204feat.html. Accessed Nov 2009.
Hanekopp, H., & Wittke, V. (2008). Die neue Rolle der Anwender in internetbasierten Innovationsprozessen. *Arbeits- und Industriesoziologische Studien 1(1, 2008)*, 7–28.
Hochgerner, J. (2008). Auf dem Weg zur Transdisziplinarität. In Zentrum für Soziale Innovation (ZSI), *Impulse für die gesellschaftliche Entwicklung*. Vienna: ZSI, 5.
Howaldt, J. (2004). *Neue Formen sozialwissenschaftlicher Wissensproduktion in der Wissensgesellschaft: Forschung und Beratung in betrieblichen und regionalen Innovationsprozessen*. Münster: LIT Verlag.
Howaldt, J., & Schwarz, M. (2010). Social innovation: Concepts, research fields and international trends. http://www.internationalmonitoring.com/index.php?id=256&L=1. Accessed May 2011.
Howaldt, J., Kopp, R., & Flocken, P. (2001). *Kooperationsverbünde und regionale Modernisierung: Theorie und Praxis der Netzwerkarbeit*. Wiesbaden: Gabler.
Kesselring, A., & Leitner, M. (2008). Soziale Innovationen in Unternehmen. Prepared on behalf of Unruhe Stiftung, Wien: ZSI http://www.zsi.at/attach/Soziale_Innovation_in_Unternehmen_ENDBERICHT.pdf. Accessed May 2011.
Kühl, S. (2003). Wie verwendet man Wissen, das sich gegen die Verwendung sträubt? Eine professionssoziologische Neubetrachtung der Theorie-Praxis-Diskussion in der Soziologie. In H. W. Franz, J. Howaldt, H. Jacobsen, & R. Kopp (Eds.), *Forschen-lernen-beraten: Der Wandel von Wissensproduktion und -transfer in den Sozialwissenschaften* (pp. 71–92). Berlin: Edition Sigma.
Kuhn, T. S. (1996). *Die Struktur wissenschaftlicher Revolution*. Frankfurt: Suhrkamp Verlag.
Kutzner, E. (2010). Innovationsförderung als soziologisches Projekt – das Beispiel, Dienstleistungswettbewerb Ruhrgebiet. In J. Howaldt, H. Jacobsen (Eds.), *Soziale Innovation* (pp. 315–331). Auf dem Weg zu einem postindustriellen Innovationsparadigma. Wiesbaden: VS Verlag für Sozialwissenschaften.
Malerba, F. (2005). Sectoral systems: How and why innovation differs across sectors. In J. Fagerberg, D. C. Mowery, & R. Nelson (Eds.), *The Oxford handbook of innovation* (pp. 380–406). Oxford, NY: Oxford University Press.
Moulaert, F., Martinelli, F., Swyngedouw, E., Gonzalez, S. (2005). Towards alternative model(s) of local innovation. *Urban Studies 42(11, 2005)*: 1669–1990.

Mulgan, G., Ali, R., Halkett, R., Sanders, B. (2007). In and out of sync. The challenge of growing social innovations. Research report http://www.youngfoundation.org/files/images/In_and_Out_of_Sync_Final.pdf. Accessed January 2010.

Nowotny, H., Scott, P., & Gibbons, M. (2001). *Re-thinking science: Knowledge and the public in an age of uncertainty*. Cambridge: Polity Press.

Ogburn, W. F. (1957). Cultural lag as theory. *Sociology and Social Research 41(1, 1957)*: 167–174.

Ogburn, W. F. (1969). Erneute Betrachtung des Problems der sozialen Evolution. In H. Maus, F. Fürstenberg (Eds.), *Soziologische Texte,* Vol. 56, Ogburn, W. F., Kultur und sozialer Wandel, Ausgewählte Schriften, Neuwied, Berlin: Luchterhand.

Rammert, W. (1997). Innovation im Netz. Neue Zeiten für technische Innovationen: heterogen verteilt und interaktiv vernetzt. *Soziale Welt 48(4, 1997)*: 397–416.

Rammert, W. (2000). Innovationen – Prozesse, Produkte, Politik, Download from: TU Berlin (http://www.tu-berlin.de/~soziologie/Crew/rammert/articles/Innovationen-PPP.html). Accessed 01 Jan 2010.

Rammert, W. (2008). Technik und Innovation(TUTS-WP-1-2008). In Techniksoziologie (Eds.), *Technical University of Berlin*. Technical University Technical Studies Working papers. http://www.ssoar.info/ssoar/files/2008/330/tuts_wp_1_2008.pdf. Accessed April 2010.

Reichwald, R., & Piller, F. T. (2005). Open Innovation. Kunden als Partner im Innovationsprozess, Arbeitsbericht des Lehrstuhls für Allgemeine und Industrielle Betriebswirtschaftslehre der Technical University of Munich, http://www.impulse.de/downloads/open_innovation.pdf. Accessed September 2010.

Schumpeter, J. (1964). *Theorie der wirtschaftlichen Entwicklung*. Berlin: Duncker and Humblot.

Senge, P., & Scharmer, C. O. (1997). Von Learning Organizations zu Learning Communities. In H. von Pierer & B. von Oetinger (Eds.), *Wie kommt das Neue in die Welt?* (pp. 99–110). Munich/Vienna: C. Hanser Verlag.

The Young Foundation (2009). Social Innovation wins backing of President Obama and Barroso. http://www.youngfoundation.org/social-innovation/news/social-innovation-wins-backing-president-obama-and-barroso. Accessed April 2010.

Wenger, E. C., & Snyder, W. M. (2000). Communities of practice, Warum sie eine wachsende Rolle spielen. *Harvard Business Manager 22(4, 2000)*: 55–62.

Zapf, W. (1989). Über soziale Innovationen. *Soziale Welt 40(1&2, 1989)*: 170–183.

Do Non-humans Make a Difference? The Actor-Network-Theory and the Social Innovation Paradigm

Alexander Degelsegger and Alexander Kesselring

Abstract Social innovation is becoming a widely used term in international debates in the context of social challenges. Neither in political nor in social scientific discussion there seems to be a consensual definition or concept of social innovation. In search of a sociological understanding of social innovation this paper turns to Latour's Actor-Network-Theory (ANT).

Latour is known for his insistence on the role of non-humans (which usually refers to technological artefacts) in society and how the reference to non-humans changes our understanding of social action and structure. In his view, the "social" is nothing but a type of relation, it is the way human and non-human actors link to each other, are translated and form actor-networks in a "flat" world without a "context" or "macro-level". As a consequence, we cannot separate technological artefacts from the "social sphere" of humans anymore. Furthermore, Latour and Callon introduced a variety of general concepts that allow to empirically study this world of relations and translations.

This article discusses the potentials in applying Latour's version of ANT to social innovation following two main questions: Does ANT provide empirical tools appropriate for analyzing innovation processes that do not have technology as their main driver and output? Does ANT help us to conceptualise social innovation in a way that avoids the exclusion of technical artefacts per se?

A. Degelsegger (✉) • A. Kesselring
Centre for Social Innovation, Vienna, Austria
e-mail: degelsegger@zsi.at

1 Introduction

"Social innovation" is currently promoted by the European Commission, governments (in particular in the UK and US), umbrella organisations, research organisations and NGOs worldwide.[1] While the concept of social innovation (or similar concepts such as social invention) is not entirely new (Zapf 1994), there is still no broad consensus about its exact meaning and scope. Sociology is still trying to catch up in reflecting and situating the recent development. There is no established theoretical and empirical framework for the definition and study of social innovation. In this article we would like to contribute to this challenge in relating social innovation to a relatively new sociological theory – the actor-network-theory (ANT) – originally developed by the French sociologists Bruno Latour and Michel Callon (Callon and Latour 1981; Latour 1987). Establishing this connection has to be considered a theoretical experiment rather than an attempt to actually provide a framework theory for social innovation. The experiment, however, also offers insights to the study of innovation in general.

We are going to do two things: Firstly, we would like to show how concepts of ANT may be used to study innovation processes and in particular aspects of innovation that mainstream sociology would identify as the "social aspects" of innovation. It is clear that the initiatives which are commonly regarded as social innovations such as micro-finance, complementary currencies or alternative education programmes certainly include "technology" in a different way than R&D intensive business innovations aiming at developing a technological product. "Technology" in these examples of social innovation is used on a rather rudimentary level and is often not the main driver or output of the innovation process. We will see however that Latour – although coming from laboratory studies – is actually not primarily concerned with high-tech in his theory. High-tech is just one of the most visible manifestations of technology in innovations processes – but as we will show his theory clearly goes beyond that. It is rather concerned with the interrelatedness of human and non-human, primarily technological artefacts as a

---

[1] **European Union:** In 2009 the bureau of European policy advisers (BEPA) organised a workshop on social innovation with an expert meeting together with EU president Barroso: http://europa.eu/rapid/pressReleasesAction.do?reference=IP/09/81&format=HTML&aged=0&language=DE&guiLanguage=en

Great Britain: The National Endowment for Science, Technology and the Arts (NESTA) funds and implements different programmes for the support of national innovation capacity, among these are also programmes on social innovation: http://www.nesta.org.uk.

The Young Foundation is a social innovation incubator and research centre: http://www.youngfoundation.org.uk/.

Social Innovation Exchange (SIX) is a platform for social innovation in Europe: http://socialinnovationexchange.org/.

United States: Under President Obama the White House established an "Office of Social Innovation and Civic Participation" see: http://www.whitehouse.gov/administration/eop/.

Social innovation centres exist in Canada, Denmark, Australia, Austria, Spain and other countries.

fundamental characteristic of society or the collective, as Latour calls it, as a whole. This is exactly why we think that it makes sense to experiment with Latour's concepts when studying less technology-focused forms of innovations.

Secondly, in the course of this text, we develop the argument that Latour's perspective may prevent us from making a mistake in the definition and conceptualisation of social innovation. The "social" in social innovation suggests making a difference between technological or business innovations and social innovations and to look for the "social dimension" of innovation. In doing so, the sociological meaning of "social" in terms of interaction and communication becomes (often implicitly) linked with the colloquial use of the word: taking care. Social innovation may then be seen primarily as a human-to-human interaction, free from technological aspects and business motives, only focused on the common good. This not only seems to be a naive image of social innovation, it may also be a "strategic" mistake. It would separate social innovation from core areas of society, their resources and their problems. In reminding us that technology cannot be separated from the "social" Latour may help us to find a better conceptualisation of social innovation.

2 Introduction to Actor-Network-Theory

Initially, Latour came forward with two key insights which are simple and provocative (or provocative because they are simple) and stem from his field research on the production of scientific knowledge in labs in the 1970s and 1980s before and while he was working for the Centre de Sociologie de l'Innovation at the École des Mines in Paris. The first insight is that, according to his studies, scientific facts are constructed rather than discovered. The second insight, more relevant to us here, translates into a methodological premise: It is necessary to include non-human actors in sociological explanations and not to distinguish ex-ante between human and non-human actors. Both humans and non-human artefacts have the potential for agency. What Latour does here is, in his own words, to generalise and fully realise the symmetry principle of the "strong programme" of the Edinburgh school of science studies (Bloor 1991/1976) which stated, among other things, that both knowledge considered true and knowledge considered false needs explanation and that these explanations should be developed using the same set of methods.

Later in his career, Latour developed these assumptions further into a critique of modernity whose main argument is the following: To be modern would mean to simultaneously advance two "ensembles of practices" (Latour 2008, 19) without being aware of it: first, practices creating "hybrids" of nature and culture ('translation'); secondly, practices creating ontologically separate spheres of human and non-human beings ('purification'). One of Latour's hypotheses is that modernity forbids to think of hybrids while, at the same time and because of this prohibition, the pace of their generation is accelerated. As soon as we start to *look* at both practices – translation and purification – simultaneously, we stop being modern and we stop "having been modern", for we understand that both practices have never been separate in the development of society. In this new perspective, what we formerly referred to as the "human society" becomes a collective of humans and non-humans. The interrelation of human and non-humans and their "exchange of qualities" is for Latour a main driver of societal development (cf. Latour 1994).

To understand what a "hybrid" is, we need to follow Latour a bit further in his argumentation. As indicated, we are most interested in the methodological premises advocated by Latour, who states that we should include non-humans in sociological explanations and, what is more, free us from the habit of ontologically separating human actors and non-humans at the outset. In one of his key articles (1992), Latour presents the following example to illustrate what he aims at: He describes a hotel with guests and a manager. Upon leaving the hotel, the guests tend to take their keys with them, which leads to problems if, for instance, they lose the key. A sign at the reception stating that guests should leave their key as well as the hotel manager's verbal indications do not trigger the result of the guests leaving their key at the reception. Then there comes an innovation: a metal weight is attached to the keys. Suddenly, the guests do not want to carry their key along as they are heavy and do not fit well into pockets. They return the keys at the reception when leaving the hotel. "Where the sign, the inscription, the imperative, discipline, or moral obligation all failed, the hotel manager, the innovator, and the metal weight succeeded" (ibid.: 104).

With this example, Latour aims to demonstrate several things: First, the metal key weight is an actor in this constellation. Only its appearance in the network of other actors made a difference; Latour's definition of the actor is precisely: everything that "makes a difference" (Latour 2007, 71). Moreover, another key principle of Latour's approach becomes clear: an innovation never proceeds only because of its inherent qualities or some kind of essence. "[T]he force with which a speaker makes a statement is never enough, in the beginning, to predict the path that the statement will follow. This path depends on what successive listeners do with the statement" (Latour 1992, 104). In Latour's terms, the 'programmes' (or programmes of action) of the speaker and listeners must allow both sides to meet and carry on with the statement. All elements involved, the statement, the speaker and the listeners, are transformed along the process. The hotel manager is no longer the same after the key weight is introduced (he is no longer desperately reminding guests to leave the keys), the guests are transformed (they leave the hotel in different ways, feel the need to minimise the time spent with the key weight in their bags) and the key is transformed (has changed from an artefact disappearing in bags and pockets to a clumsy thing that one wants to get rid of). "[T]he order that is obeyed is no longer the same as the initial order. It has been translated, not transmitted" (ibid.). In these translations, humans and non-humans *associate* in chains of different kind and length (cf. ibid.: 105ff), chains whose elements co-constitute each other and form actor-networks. Chains are embedded in other larger chains, actors made up of actor-networks. It is rather a methodological necessity than an ontological possibility to define the limits of the chains of interest. Elements within the chain of associations can be substituted, modifying the chain and type of network. Thus, the "hybrid" is an assemblage of humans and non-humans, created through the exchange of qualities and programmes of action. The case of the key weight is obviously a very simple one, but we may also think, for instance, about hybrid assemblages comprising electric grids (including power plants, social and spatial configurations, etc.). We then can imagine the vast extension of hybrid actor-networks and the way they shape the collective.

3 Does ANT Make a Difference? ANT in the Context of the Sociology of Technology

What could have been a friendly reminder to sociology to re-integrate non-humans, completely changed Latour's understanding of sociology, the social and sociological explanations, which led him to emphasise the discontinuity between his approach, Actor-Network-Theory, and the "sociology of the social" by which he describes mainstream sociology before ANT. We will shortly explore how much continuity and discontinuity there actually is, trying to elaborate the main arguments that may set ANT apart from other positions, continuing with the question whether these assumptions may help us to study innovation processes.

The sociology of technology is a well established field of social scientific research with a considerable body of literature that poses the question of the role of technology in society the capacity for agency of non-human artefacts. When it comes to the German discussions in this field, Werner Rammert, in the anthology with the title "Do machines act?" (Rammert and Schulz-Schaeffer 2002), provides a systematic overview on theoretic positions in the field of the sociology of technology. As a result, Rammert classifies positions by cross-tabulating selected variables. The main differences between theoretic approaches are defined by (1) either a normative (capacity of agency is theoretically postulated) or descriptive (capacity of agency is empirically described) stance; (2) by choosing either an attributive (How do humans ascribe agency to non-humans?) or quality-related approach (In which ways are humans and non-humans capable of acting?) and (3) by the question whether agency is only attributed to advanced non-humans (artificial intelligence) or to all non-humans (including Latour's famous key weight). The diagram below only shows the categories of the resulting matrix and the positions attributed to ANT theorists.

Theoretical approach	Any technological artefact has the capacity for agency OR only advanced technological artefacts	*Agency of technological artefacts is a result of attribution*	*Agency of technological artefacts is an observable quality*
Descriptive	Any technology		"Actants" (Callon, Latour)
	Advanced technology		
Normative	Any technology	Generalised symmetry (Latour)	
	Advanced technology		

Source: Rammert and Schulz-Schaeffer (2002) (adaptation and translation by the authors)

Interestingly, Latour appears in two cells of the matrix: "Normative"/"Any technology"/"Agency as attribution" would mean that Latour theoretically postulates that all non-humans are actors (have the capacity for agency) and that this is the result of attribution (by the theorist?). "Descriptive"/"Any technology"/"Agency as quality" would mean that the capacity for agency can in general be empirically described for any non-human as an observable quality.

We think that this assignment, in being somewhat inconsistent, reveals relevant difficulties in understanding Latour's positions that may also be caused by his shifts in the use of ANT terms and different formulations of main assumptions. We think that Latour actually occupies many of the cells presented therein, although not without significantly changing the meaning of the descriptions used. According to Latour, the principle of "generalised symmetry" is not determining the capacity for agency of non-humans or humans (and is therefore not normative in Rammert's sense). It does not say that humans and non-humans act the same way or that non-humans would act intentionally. Latour is not interested in determining empirically whether the key weight or the artificial intelligence acts "causally", "contingently" or "intentionally" and to which degree, which is Rammert's own proposal for a "gradual theory of agency" (Rammert and Schulz-Schaeffer 2002, 39). Latour focuses instead on the interrelations between humans and non-humans, the exchange of non-human and human qualities and the way humans and non-humans co-constitute the collective (Latour 1994, 46ff). Humans can extend their intentionality to a key weight and in doing so they become part of actor-networks that will change themselves in transferring non-human qualities back to them (maybe also changing the structure of their intentionality). Thus, Latour definitively would not say that non-humans act in a specific way – only that they potentially may become actors anytime.

Latour is "descriptive" in making the assumption that we can observe or at least empirically trace the interrelation between actors, respectively the process of an actant, i.e. an actor who "has no figuration [as a specific character in a story] yet" (Latour 2007, 71), becoming an actor. This also means that the empirical description of the "capacity for agency" of humans and non-humans will change with the case at hand. We cannot validate the capacity for agency of non-humans once and for all – neither empirically nor theoretically. We actually never know what a non-human or human is capable of doing, because it depends on their figuration. The name "Actor-Network-Theory" is the best hint that Latour does not intend to describe isolated humans or non-humans: Action is distributed among actors, across space and over time (Latour 1994, 40ff). Action is only manifested as an actor-network.

Latour is furthermore concerned with attribution, because in his ethnomethodological approach (cf. Latour 1999a, 19) he often depends on the account of humans who tell the researcher to which non-humans they are related in which ways. The researcher then can use the meta-language of ANT to trace these interrelations. This means that Latour is interested in attribution as a methodological necessity, but not in the sense that he would only be concerned about how humans attribute agency to non-humans – he goes beyond that in describing the actor-network itself and not just the attribution.

4 Deploying Selected Concepts of ANT for the Analysis of Social Innovations

In the preceding chapter, we have introduced the theoretical framework of ANT and contextualised it by presenting limited parts of the discussions surrounding it. Now we would like to pick a series of concepts developed within ANT that we consider useful for the analysis of innovation processes. One of their major advantages seems to be that no ex-ante discrimination is necessary between those forms of innovation involving (or focussing on) technological artefacts and those forms not involving or not primarily aiming at artefacts. This allows us to look at innovation from a formal perspective as the creation of new actor-networks that are, in the accounts of the human actors, linked to intentional change.

One of the general and key characteristics of innovation processes is that they involve new entities or new combinations of entities, that is, in ANT terms, evolving associations of mediators to chains and actor-networks. The overarching term for describing these processes is "translation". Translation is understood as "[a] relation that does not transport causality but induces two mediators into coexisting" (Latour 2007, 108). The mediators induced into coexistence can be human or non-human. Again, this distinction does not matter to Latour. More important is that the associated mediators exchange qualities and change in the process. The result is a new actor, an actor-network which is somehow more than the sum of the components. It's not "only" a network of actors, but an actor-network. Latour (1999b) offers the example of the gun and the man. It is not very useful to think about the actor quality of a "gun" and the actor quality of a "human" per se, when the actor of interest is the "human with a gun" – a non-human and human hybrid that transformed the action programme of the "human" and the "gun" into something different (different aims, different means, different effects). This process does not start with the "human" taking up the "gun", but starts with the problem of "how to kill people" and with substituting step-by-step bare hands with technology. The "human with a gun" is only the last manifestation of this far-reaching process of human and non-human interrelation and exchange which Latour calls "translation".

Michel Callon, in his elaboration of the Sociology of Translation (1986), defines four overlapping phases or "moments" of the process of translation which involves the negotiation and demarcation of the actors' identity as well as the possibilities for interaction and agency.

The first moment is called *problematisation* and involves, as a part of it, the definition of a so called "obligatory passage point": Our sociological observations always start by looking at given actors (there is no moment in time "before" any actors are in place) and their construction and deconstruction of nature and society. Accepting this as given, we can look at a set of actors (e.g. scientists working on a specific topic) and will see that they, in tackling a problem of relevance to them, define (in written documents, verbal exclamations, gestures) a set of other actors (colleagues, study objects, etc.) and their identities and try to involve these actors in their programmes of action (e.g. a certain research project). The actors do not limit themselves to identifying other actors. They also try to show that it is in the interest of the latter to participate in their programme of action. They construct a story showing that they themselves and the other actors must come together (at an obligatory passage point) in order to solve a specific problem at hand, reach a specific goal, etc.

The second moment in the process of translation, *interessement*, has to do with the virtual and hypothetic nature of every problematisation. The "other actors" called upon in the problematisation of a set of actors can accept or refuse to join the programme of action (also non-human actors can accept or refuse: In Callon's example of scientists and their study objects, the latter refuse, for instance, when their integration into a laboratory setting for experiments fails). However, there are strategies at hand for the group of actors to convince the other group. *Interessement* is, thus, the group of activities through which one entity of actors tries to define and stabilise the identity of another group of actors.

Interessement can lead to *enrolment* but does not have to. If it does, then enrolment does not imply a set of pre-defined roles the actors called upon can occupy. Rather it denotes the negotiation process within which related roles are defined and assigned to actors who accept them (or not). Along the process, the actors whose programme of action engages other actors, are continually transformed as is their programme of action.

The last phase in the process of translation is *mobilisation*, where the question who is a representative speaker for whom is negotiated and settled. It is the collective of an actor's translation efforts which defines his or hers (or its) programme of action (cf. Belliger and Krieger 2006).

What we want to show with this short presentation of main concepts of the Sociology of Translation is that the concepts can be applied empirically and offer an analytical benefit. In looking at innovation processes, they can help to identify moments along the way where a certain group of human or non-human actors calls upon another group of human or non-human actors to join the process. The latter group can accept or refuse, become enrolled or not, act as a speaker or representative for other actors or not.

A differentiation Latour (2007) proposes to explain the dynamics of actor-networks is that between *mediators and intermediaries*. Intermediaries transport meaning or force without transformation. Defining an input is enough to anticipate the output. Mediators, by contrast, transform, translate, distort and modify the meaning or the elements they are supposed to carry. Input is not a good predictor for output, in the case of mediators (ibid., 39). We have stated that in innovation processes mediators become associated. During this association, both ends of the association experience a transformation. They are translated, not simply connected or transported. Chains of associations get complex not only from an observer's perspective but also from the actors, forming part of them. There is a need to stabilise parts of the chain of associations so that actors can rely on getting a stable output when providing the same input. Mediators or groups of mediators are transformed into intermediaries or groups of intermediaries. This process is called *black-boxing* (cf. Latour 1994). Parts of the chain get black-boxed and, for a while, the other actors involved do not have to bother about them. However, a black-box can always be opened; the process of black-boxing is reversible.

The construction of machines, the training of lab assistants and the definition of experimental setups are examples of processes of black-boxing. Someone has developed laptop and beamer technology in complex actor-networks over considerable amounts of time. Nevertheless, I can engage with an audience, a laptop, a beamer and a subject in the setting of an academic presentation. As long as the laptop and the beamer do not break down, the process of transforming codified knowledge input (the presentation) into visually available information (the image on the wall) is black-boxed and I as a speaker do not have to bother about it (neither does the conference programme, whose time schedule might be distorted).

These steps of black-boxing and opened or broken black-boxes are crucial and of relevance for empirical studies of innovation. For instance, in developing a local currency, at some point, the currency might be available as physical paper money which a certain number of people in my village, region, etc. accept as a medium of exchange. The task of negotiating and explaining the meaning of the regional currency, explaining how it becomes and holds its value, etc. is black-boxed and I only have to bother if someone questions the validity of the regional currency.

This relates to yet another ANT concept, which we consider useful for the analysis of innovations: *inscription* (Akrich 1992). ANT theorists understand as inscription the work of assigning and inscribing specific visions of the world into objects or relations between objects, humans or humans and non-humans. Following a specific *problematisation*, their views of the world and their surrounding, actors inscribe these views into the relationships they enter and develop, the things that they produce, etc. The results are "scripts". Akrich focuses more on technical objects, here, and states that the visions of an innovator or designer are embodied in the results of the innovation and design. They are thus not completely open for interpretation and use, but can be used and interpreted in certain ways. Other actors can "subscribe" to them or "de-inscribe". Inscriptions also "prescribe" demands to other actors. Again, they can accept and subscribe or revolt and de-inscribe. By contrast to these concepts describing the action and reaction of other actors, Akrich proposes the notion of "de-scription" as the analysts' work of deciphering inscriptions. While Akrich focuses very much on the relationship between designers and innovators on the one hand and technical objects on the other, we believe that inscription work is also relevant for the action of human actors towards other human actors: the type of relationships an actor or group of actors aspires to is guided by visions of the world just as this group's design of an artefact would be.

For us, empirically, it is a concept which sensitizes to acts of transfer of meaning from one actor to the other and, more broadly speaking, to the negotiations of the meaning of certain innovations. The concept is related to the first phases of the process of translation. When actors aim to inscribe meaning into other actors and relationships, the latter can accept or defy these meanings and attributions, they can become "interested" and "enrol" or not.

With this conceptual toolbox at hand, we will now re-visit an empirical case of a, so to speak, traditional technology and market-oriented innovation to see what we can gain out of ANT for the understanding of the social process of innovation.

5 Re-analysing an Empirical Case: The Van de Ven et al. Study of 3M

In their empirical and theoretical innovation research, Van de Ven et al. (2008) contradict the conventional image of innovation and come to the conclusion that innovation processes are characterised by non-linear, chaotic dynamics. The research of Van de Ven et al. was based on comprehensive, decades-long case studies accompanying potential innovation processes from their beginning in the late 1970s to their final success or failure in the 1980s and 1990s. After this field research, Van de Ven et al. tried to systematise their findings on innovation processes in a series of books with "The innovation journey" being their latest major publication (ibid.).

One of the most impressive accounts given by Van de Ven et al. of a commercial innovation initiative is the case of the 3M company and its attempt to introduce the first cochlear implant (a device enabling deaf persons to hear partially) into the market (ibid.: 223ff.). The 3M case shows how a completely rationally framed endeavour (large industrial infrastructures and resources, professional management, strategies, time plans, milestones, research units etc.) develops more and more complexity in often unintended ways: doors of opportunities open and close again, networks build up and fragment, people are hired and fired, technological trajectories develop in unanticipated ways, cooperation partners turn into competitors, new players appear and "change the game", institutional contexts impose restrictions or become themselves the object of competitive strategies etc.

The studies by Van de Ven et al. predominantly portray innovation processes as "social processes" in the conventional sense of human-to-human interaction respectively organisation-to-organisation interaction. Although they are not primarily interested in re-constructing the relations between non-human and humans, their accounts are detailed enough to comprise plenty of information on technological artefacts and their "role" in the innovation process. Van de Ven et al. used "events" as their unit of analysis when studying these cases, which were coded to be used for quantitative statistical analysis showing the co-occurrence of different types of events or more complex, multidimensional event-landscapes. We decided to use the 3M case primarily because of the detailed chronology of events that Van de Ven provide and because of the dominance of "social processes" in Van de Ven's account to re-analyse selected parts with the instruments of ANT.

The moment where Van de Ven et al. "enter" their empirical case[2] is a phase they call initiation and which is characterised by interactions between 3M and a number of other organisations like the University of Melbourne, Audiotronics California Corporation, the House Ear Institute etc. In ANT terms, what is happening here is best described with the concept of *translation* and its various phases.

3M follows a specific programme of action (which is not something they simply adopted at some point but has its own history[3] and interdependencies) where the fact that the company considers cochlear implant technology as a promising project plays a key role. From that point on, 3M initiates a search for ongoing activities in the United States in this sector and identifies a number of actors (the mentioned organisations but also existing technologies, etc.) with which it enters into negotiations. 3M, in ANT terms, develops a *problematisation*, writes a story where other actors play different roles, defines these roles (e.g. as a partner, as a to be acquired part of 3M, etc.) and establishes an obligatory passage point or, actually, a series of passage points all of which, in the view of 3M, have to be passed by a certain assembly of actors at a certain point in time. One of these passage points, for instance, is recorded as 3M engineering arguing that the company "is losing a golden opportunity in single-channel systems by not finalizing an agreement with [i.e. selling implants to] HEI [the House Ear Institute]" (Van de Ven et al. 2008, 278). In this view, HEI is considered as an actor, is assigned a role, and it is stated that 3M and HEI have to pass through the point of a formal sales agreement in order to meet their respective needs (the need of 3M to sell the implants and make money; the need of acquiring implants of HEI). The strategies of *interessement* employed by 3M are not documented. However, what we can see from the empirical material is that some of the actors who 3M approached with the story and the proposed role distribution *enrolled* and others didn't. For instance, 3M and the University of Melbourne could not reach an agreement over cooperation. The University of Melbourne instead enrolled in another programme of action by the Australian Department of Productivity, which extended funds under the condition that the cochlear device would be developed indigenously by the University in Australia.

---

[2] It also becomes clear from analyses like Van de Ven et al. (2008) that innovation processes have no clear beginning nor end.

[3] Again: no clear beginning.

Along the complex innovation processes around the cochlear implants, with different generation devices and different groups of associated mediators, 3M has to deal repetitively with the US' Food and Drug Administration (FDA). The FDA has to approve the respective versions of the device and the negotiations with FDA figure prominently in the accounts of Van de Ven et al. The dealings of 3M with FDA are recorded as such that the company on several occasions "provides inputs" (e.g. to shape FDA guidelines), "informs FDA" (e.g. about the "remarkable results achieved"), "organises" (e.g. a seminar for FDA staff), etc. (Van de Ven et al. 2008, 281). While Akrich's (1992) concept of *inscription* is proposed for innovators and designers inscribing their views of the world into the artefacts they develop, we believe that it is pertinent to apply the notion here and that this application even offers feedback to the conceptual underpinnings of ANT: In Akrich's usage, the term inscription introduces or presupposes a clear separation between the inscribing actor and the rather passive object something is inscribed into. In the case of the FDA guidelines, it is not so clear who the inventor or innovator is. FDA has some responsibility, but at the same time 3M tries to inscribe its own visions of the world into the guidelines. What is invented is no artefact in the narrow sense, but a regulation codified in an artefact, which is relevant for 3M's dealings, i.e. an actor incorporating other actors' visions and, in turn, shaping these actors' views.

The example of the FDA guidelines suggests to look at another term of ANT's conceptual space, this time linked to Latour: form. "A form is simply something which allows something else to be transported from one site to another. Form then becomes one of the most important types of translation. [...] It can be a paper slip, a document, a report, an account, a map" (Latour 2007, 223). The FDA guidelines as a form can be seen as transporting a decision (to accept or not accept certain devices) from a concrete physical site to potentially unlimited sites of other actors developing similar devices. Only if they want to contest the guidelines do they need to approach the original site of the negotiations of the form. The specification of a form as a type of translation is interesting: The FDA guidelines incorporate a problematisation, define actors and their roles. Its strategy of interessement is to be out there and approach all other actors that want to engage in cochlear implant development. These actors can choose to enrol to the guidelines' programme of action or contest it.

In a way, in its acting as a type of translation, the guidelines define a new group of actors: those potentially developing cochlear implants. This group has not existed as such before the form of the guidelines was in place. We find other examples of new groups of actors shaping in the course of the fragmented process of innovation when looking at Van de Ven et al.'s documented data: There is a moment where 3M is suggested by FDA to look at a device for children. With this problematisation, a new actor or actor group appears on stage: children with hearing difficulties. At this point in time, it is not clear yet whether the new group of actors will enrol into the programme of action (would they accept wearing a specific type of cochlear implant? etc.), nor is clear who speaks for them. However, they started to exist as an actor "making a difference" for 3M's development of cochlear implants. The extension of the target group for cochlear implants from deaf people to the residual hearing population is a similar case.[4]

In the end, 3M's innovation initiative dissolved – the establishment of a new and stable actor-network failed, because too many intermediaries turned to mediators that behaved in unexpected ways rendering the rational planning of 3M ineffective. Finally, 3M had no other option than to sell their cochlear implant technology to their direct competitor, a company called Nucleus.

6 Conclusions

We have analysed three exemplary phases in the innovation process around cochlear implants: 3M's approaching of other actors and creation of research, production and sales networks; the contested development of FDA guidelines and the appearance of novel groups of actors.

All these processes are predominantly "social" in the conventional sense, although they are inextricably linked to the process of innovation in cochlear implants. If we would substitute a case that considered a social innovation (e.g. a local currency system) for the cochlear implant story, we would not be able to find any formal or qualitative difference in the process, only content-related differences, i.e. the actors would naturally be different, but the mechanics of the innovation process would not. If an actor pursues a social innovation, it is crucial for her/him/it to define and approach actors, target groups, etc. There will also be guidelines, forms, documents, reports which appear as relevant actors (e.g. a document defining the local currencies relationship to the mainstream currency or an approval of the local currency from the national bank) and which are inscribed views of the world. New actors will appear along the way, for instance when one target group splits into those enrolling in the programme of action and in those who won't. Actors would try to black-box parts of the chain of associations, for instance by defining and communicating the rules of the game for the local currency. Once all actors in a given region know what this local currency is and know how to deal with it, a part of the process chain is black-boxed (negotiating with currency users and convincing people will not be that important and resource consuming any more). However, if a group of actors contests the local currency system, not accepting the bills anymore, then the black-box is opened, intermediaries turn into mediators and negotiations have to start again.

Interestingly enough, it is Latour with his emphasis on bringing the material realm to the fore who offers us a perspective on innovation that does not discriminate between technological and non-technological innovation (with the former usually considered more important). For sociological studies of innovation

---

[4] "Program manager states intention to extend reach with cochlear implants into the residual hearing population to expand market potential" (Van de Ven et al. 2008, 283).

(and STS research), this non-discrimination has an impact on a theoretical as well as an empirical level: Forms of innovation that are currently labelled differently in mainstream discourse have to be analysed using the same vocabulary. It is this aspect that we have focused upon most prominently in this text.

However, the theoretical insights also suggest to maintain a normative and programmatic notion of social innovation: When so called technological and non-technological innovation processes are not different in their nature, then they also have to follow the same normative standards and have to be evaluated correspondingly. Furthermore, this conceptualisation allows for the possibility of (societal and theoretical) learning and generating insights how to design innovation processes in a sustainable, inclusive form.

Based on this understanding, we propose to conceptualise social innovation as a new paradigm for innovation management, research and assessment rather than being considered a distinct form of innovation in itself. "Social" is not a criterion that would allow to differentiate social innovation from economic or technological innovation. All innovations are social processes of interaction and communication and we currently also see a development where business innovation in the mainstream economy becomes more participative in using focus groups, crowd sourcing, or open innovation models. Furthermore, all innovation outputs – from the washing machine to the mobile phone – potentially have social outcomes and impacts, for instance by changing the organisation of household work or by changing communication patterns, and sometimes they meet social needs quite directly. Of course, all this happens within the constrained economic logic of competitive advantage, means efficiency, market entry, consumer decisions and profits (the exact logic that led the 3M cochlear implant to failure). This logic, in not being "holistic" and in partly excluding other logics as for instance ecologic sustainability or social inclusion, currently causes un-intended (but well known) negative side-effects and generally externalises many "costs". The *gradual* difference between *conventional* economic/technological innovation and social innovation might thus be the extent to which different societal logics are combined and integrated in the design, management, research and assessment of innovations. This is where the "social innovation paradigm" comes in.[5]

We can refer to Latour in formulating some elements of the social innovation paradigm. He draws our attention to the hybrid actor-networks that we produce in innovation and to the fact that we cannot isolate these actor-networks from our "human society". We therefore need instruments that allow us to monitor innovation and diffusion processes much more extensively ("social impact assessment" would probably be such an instrument) to see how innovation changes our society. ANT shows us that the innovation process never really stops, innovation is never just a product; it rather establishes a new actor-network of humans and non-humans that lives on in the collective. It has to be maintained, monitored and re-assessed. Following ANT we may furthermore suggest that we need more "speakers"

---

[5] As a side note: Akrich et al. (2002a, b) themselves ventured into generating inputs from their theoretical edifice to professional (commercial, market-oriented) innovation management.

(cf. Akrich et al. 2002b) and a better articulation of different logics and action programmes in the management of innovation but also in the assessment of innovation outcomes on multiple dimensions: social, cultural, individual, ecologic, political and economic. Practically, this means that we will have to explore new modes of how stakeholders can articulate themselves and can actively participate in innovation processes. Since we cannot determine once and for all what "the good society" is, we will rely on meta-values such as pluralism, participation, consensus building and responsiveness to perceived social problems (cf. Etzioni 1968 to name but one possible reference). These meta-values should be used to assess the aims and outcomes of innovation as well as to guide the innovation process. The aims of innovation will have to take diverse advantages and disadvantages articulated from different stakeholders in society into account. Social innovation will also have different criteria for the "efficiency" of innovation processes – where the additional time needed for discussion, negotiation and decision making will be counterbalanced by direct positive side-effects of the process itself and more sustainable and accepted results.

The social innovation paradigm would thus encompass all forms of innovation without being restricted to "purely social" activities which only include direct human-to-human interaction being isolated from technological and economic innovation per se. This new paradigm is already at work changing the innovation landscape, it becomes visible as civil-society driven innovation, as social entrepreneurship driven innovation, or as innovation driven by cross-sector cooperation. And it already has many instruments at hand that transform innovation processes and outcomes – from participation models to new forms of impact assessment. And maybe most importantly – a broader understanding of social innovation can help us to identify, support and assess the gradual transformation from conventional innovation processes to social innovation processes that will hopefully be more responsive to social needs and problems, will be more accepted, will have less negative side-effects and will make society as a whole more flexible in dealing with societal challenges.

References

Akrich, M. (1992). The de-scription of technical objects. In W. E. Bijker & J. Law (Eds.), *Shaping technology, building society. Studies in sociotechnical change* (pp. 205–224). Cambridge: MIT Press.

Akrich, M., Callon, M., & Latour, B. (2002a). The key to success in innovation part I: The art of interessement. *International Journal of Innovation Management, 6*(2), 187–206.

Akrich, M., Callon, M., & Latour, B. (2002b). The key to success in innovation part II: The art of choosing good spokespersons. *International Journal of Innovation Management, 6*(2), 207–225.

Belliger, A., & Krieger, D. (2006). Einführung in die Akteur-Netzwerk-Theorie. In A. Belliger & D. Krieger (Eds.), *ANThology. Ein einführendes Handbuch zur Akteur-Netzwerk-Theorie* (pp. 13–50). Bielefeld: Transcript.

Bloor, D. (1991/1976). *Knowledge and social imagery* (2nd ed.). Chicago: University of Chicago Press.

Callon, M. (1986). Some elements of a sociology of translation: Domestication of the scallops and the fishermen of St Brieuc Bay. In J. Law (Ed.), *Power, action and belief: A new sociology of knowledge?* (pp. 196–233). London: Routledge.

Callon, M., & Latour, B. (1981). Unscrewing the big Leviathan: How actors macrostructure reality and how sociologists help them to do so. In K. Knorr-Cetina & A. V. Cicourel (Eds.), *Advances in social theory and methodology. Toward an integration of micro and macro sociologies* (pp. 277–304). Boston: Routledge & Kegan Paul.

Etzioni, A. (1968). *The active society. A theory of societal and political processes.* London: Collier-Macmillan.

Latour, B. (1987). *Science in action. How to follow scientists and engineers through society.* Cambridge: Harvard University Press.

Latour, B. (1992). Technology is society made durable. In J. Law (Ed.), *A sociology of monsters: Essays on power, technology and domination* (pp. 103–131). London: Routledge.

Latour, B. (1994). On technical mediation – philosophy, sociology, genealogy. *Common Knowledge, 3*(2), 29–64.

Latour, B. (1999a). On recalling ANT. In J. Law & J. Hassard (Eds.), *Actor network theory and after* (pp. 15–25). Oxford: Blackwell.

Latour, B. (1999b). *Pandora's hope: Essays on the reality of science studies.* Cambridge: Harvard University Press.

Latour, B. (2007). *Reassembling the social.* Oxford: Oxford University Press.

Latour, B. (2008). *Wir sind nie modern gewesen. Versuch einer symmetrischen Anthropologie.* Frankfurt am Main: Suhrkamp.

Phills, J. A. J., Deiglmeier, K., & Miller, D. T. (2008). Rediscovering social innovation. In *Social innovation review (Fall).* Stanford: Stanford Graduate School of Business.

Rammert, W., & Schulz-Schaeffer, I. (2002). *Können Maschinen handeln? Soziologische Beiträge zum Verhältnis von Mensch und Technik.* Frankfurt am Main/New York: Campus.

Van de Ven, A. H., Polley, D., & Garud, R. (2008). *The innovation journey.* Oxford: Oxford University Press.

Zapf, W. (1994). *Modernisierung, Wohlfahrtsentwicklung und Transformation.* Berlin: Wissenschaftszentrum Berlin für Sozialforschung WZB.

Social Innovation: What Is Coming Apart and What Is Being Rebuilt?

Denis Harrisson

Abstract The paper examines the conditions under which the concept of social innovation is being cast. Three features of modern society were first identified as the hallmarks of a changing world: the dominance of large multinational firms, the decline of the welfare state and the individualisation of citizens. From this, we see how the society is being rebuilt through the constituency of social innovation in three key facets: the public interest and common good, a new approach to the concept of service and the networks strengthening the bonds of trust between citizens.

1 Introduction

Social innovation may be associated with two ways of regarding social reality and anticipating motivations for action. The first one is rational, based on an instrumental vision of reality with human beings motivated mainly by efficiency and effectiveness (Boudon 2004). The second one is based on moral and idealistic motivations with human beings searching for harmony and freedom (Etzioni 2004). With both of these conceptions, the theory consists of discovering patterns of social innovation. These positions are also affected by the tensions between individualist and collectivist representations of action. Do individuals always act to expand their interest before thinking of relationships with others, or is this, in contrast, a search for the social arrangement that initially justifies the individual actions concerned? Individualist theories regard collective structures as being external to individuals and standing as constraints. Actors respond rationally to the situation this imposes. On the other hand, collectivist theories admit that actors have motivations other than interest-based rationality. Ideals and emotions, along with selflessness and solidarity, are also motivations for collective action.

D. Harrisson (✉)
University of Quebec in Montreal, Montreal, Quebec, Canada
e-mail: harrisson.denis@uqam.ca

Interactions form a basis for giving meaning to action. Actors have creative strategies (Mumford 2003); they are capable of initiatives, even though the problems to tackle are huge, they are involved in the solution as long as the solution falls within the general interest.

In this paper, I shall attempt to deal with the issue of social innovation from a theoretical standpoint. To this end, the text is divided into two parts. I will begin first with a brief explanation of what has changed in present-day society that leads us to regard social innovation as a major process of social transformation. Social innovation is linked to social change, it is not the only way to rebuild the community bonds but it is one of the main and most promising ones. In order to comprehend that, we must know what has been altered in the former society so that some space is made for social initiative coming from the citizens involved in their community. Next, I will approach social innovation by examining what we have understood about it up to now. I believe the best way to understand it involves actual experience in social innovation. This is undoubtedly why the knowledge we possess on social innovation comes as much from the area of practice as from university research, at least up to now. Social innovation is then presented as an initiative taken by a social entrepreneur connected to the community and able to link people to grow up services. People are ready to join this new social activity taking into account the inability of institutional resources to support emerging needs. Social innovation is then treated as a service and a process based on networking and trust.

Theorising about social innovation means first of all formulating a conception of social creativity to resolve human and social problems, secondly, dealing with the flow of knowledge, ideas and resources, and thirdly, developing a conception of the connection with social relationship, civil society and democracy. Social innovation is a term that is used prolifically and, increasingly, with no particular meaning attached to it. There is, however, one constant: citizen participation in the conception of solutions to problems in a spirit of co-construction with other social actors who hold power. This is a novel way of conceiving social action. Within this more general conception, there lie scales of social innovation, with many looks being cast at problems of varied scope. Social innovation is now possible because society has changed under the combined effect of the transformation of capitalism, the changing role of the State and increasing individualisation of the citizen. This is the context that we now turn briefly.

2 What Is Coming Apart?

The most influential sociologists early in the twenty-first century have coined an expression for identifying our post-industrial society: advanced modernity (Giddens 1990), the second modernity (Beck 2003), liquid modernity (Bauman 2001), or the social world of fields (Bourdieu 1994). This second modernity is characterised by a weakening of the welfare state, growing individualisation of responsibility for "life cycles", and domination by large multinational firms in a context of economic globalisation. Bauman (2001) sees two elements as turning the new modernity into a new context that differs from the previous situation. Firstly, this society is marked by an end to illusions of a just society, free of conflicts, aspiring to a state of equilibrium between the major social actors, a benevolent society seeking only to satisfy its citizens in perfect control of its destiny, if such a society ever existed. Secondly, the deregulation and privatisation of public services is having the effect of splitting the bases of collective responsibility to the benefit of individual involvement in which only the most determined, those possessing resources in the form of human capital, material capital and social capital, manage to carve a place for themselves. Bauman sees this society as being characterised by an absence of ideals, a feeling of powerlessness in coping with the hazards of life, and difficulty in acting rationally. The mentality that takes shape is a short-term one. On the labour scene, "flexibility" is the driving concept, engendering insecurity and uncertainty with the vagaries of life. Government no longer provides protection, at least much less so than in the past. Moreover, it no longer promises to protect, nor does it claim any longer to pledge universal guarantees. This creates conditions for strengthening a sense of being left on one's own and for developing individualistic reflexes and strategies rather than tending toward strengthening social ties and defending the common interest. Fears and anxiety-causing tensions are experienced in a lonely setting. The citizens do not join forces nor bring about common causes likely to form strategies of solidarity found in social movements and activist organisations. In the following section, we will see what has changed and in what sense this is leading us to a renewed conception of social innovation in the three components identified here: the economy, the state and individualisation.

2.1 Large Multinational Firms

The new world economic order, the development of communication technologies and the sway of multinational corporations over economic development are among the shifts transforming society by creating, among other factors, new winners and new losers, with the rise of inequalities between social classes, and originating new conditions imposed by the market. It is now the private sector that dominates the public sector. The new economy is producing a widening gap between the richest and poorest in society. The latter, in addition to facing a scarcity of material goods essential to survival on a daily basis, are also being positioned as "socially excluded people" from the networks to which it has become essential to belong to establish a place in society. As for the others, who form a majority that is integrated and connected to various networks, the threat of social fragmentation lies in the conversion of citizens into consumers, who become dissociated from the conduct of civic life. The dominant value is economic, and it resides in large multinational firms (Sennett 2007).

We cannot ignore the transformations of capitalism, with a general trend resulting in the creation of contradictions. While capitalism may be prospering (shareholder strength, short-term yields, new information and communication technologies, and wealth creation), other trends are waning, as shown by the collateral damage, the socially excluded people and other social groups that are suffering losses. Employment is not expanding at the same pace, and jobs are of uneven quality, with a higher percentage of unstable jobs, fixed-term contracts and lower wages. Government social protection and union defence are dwindling. There are all conditions for social innovation.

2.2 The State

The Welfare State as built up since the Second World War is under attack through a budgetary crisis questioning its legitimacy. The Keynesian state is having difficulty regulating the socio-economic problems for which it was created, such as unemployment, education, health care and aging, and it is not managing to curb the unforeseen effects arising from the new risks caused by technological change, the dwindling qualifications of those who are out of work for too long, youth unemployment, the aging of the population, single-parent families, separations and divorces, and immigration problems (Esping-Andersen 2002). No over-all solution can address these difficulties. The problem of the welfare state lies less in restrictions on its actions than in the structuring of its priorities, marked by the ideological preferences of social actors fighting for hegemony in setting the orientation to be given to the state.

The Welfare State is a passive institution that responds to demands without being able to prevent or anticipate them. In addition, its preferred form of intervention, in particular through professionalization and rationalisation of the services it provides, hardly encourages citizens to be accountable. On the other hand, the welfare state is not characterised solely by its effectiveness in dispensing services but also by its capacity for inclusion and for bringing citizens together and by its ability to create social cohesion between social classes and socio-economic categories. Richard Sennett sees this as its primary source of legitimacy: an effective state is one that provides stability and solid foundations for society (Sennett 2007). However, this last aspect is losing force in an intense search for efficiency that is leading (misguidedly, in my view) to the option of privatising public services under the pretext that private enterprise works better and at lower cost. This transfer of responsibilities is highly questionable, even without considering that is hardly motivated by the aim of ensuring a greater cohesion of society. As such, education, old-age pensions and the universal right to health care are subjected to the rule of efficiency, which resonates only to the sound of budgetary gains in government reserves.

On the other hand, citizens also seek a reduction in the size of government and a personalisation of services, doing away with red tape in the processing of requests.

The new state that redefines its role is called upon to do so with citizens who advocate participation in social life. This capacity for participation cannot be assumed. It is created in particular through projects constituting social innovation and involving, first and foremost, redistribution of wealth and opposition to poverty.

Social innovation is created above all by actors coming from civil society, they are defending their autonomy in relation to the other two sectors. It achieves this only inasmuch as it promotes democracy, relying on commitments between the various participating actors and creating spaces for solidarity. On the other hand, civil society cannot achieve its responsibility without a democratic state. Only the state can confront the major inequalities that subsist in society. The state can provide conditions that favour the proliferation of ideas and their anchoring in communities, thereby facilitating their dissemination. This involves promoting the forms of mutual cooperation made possible by the system of public political financing (tax credits, taxation, subsidies, preferential lending rates), by policies that guarantee rights and by government efforts that take a voluntary approach. The state is also the guarantor of institutional protection of the rights that allow for civil society initiatives, but this also poses a dilemma, to the extent that civil society is in a situation of competition with the state for the representation of civil participation and solidarity. On certain projects, civil society and government must be partners (Lévesque 2003).

2.3 Individualisation

Two positions are possible: either individuals are the object of government intervention and its benevolent attention in assuming the risks they face in life cycles, or individuals maintain their personal decision-making freedom in the face of a government that restricts their will of initiative, keeping them in a passive state. The notion of accountability holds that someone who is ill is accountable for his condition because he neglected advice on healthy eating and living conditions. Unemployment shows a failure of those who did not to gain the qualifications needed on the labour market or to be competitive on this market (Martucelli 2009).

No social innovation can fail to note that the collective project must encompass individual dimensions. Taking individuals into account is the mark of a deep transformation of our "social sensitivity" (Martucelli 2009, p. 15). Each individual holds a position that is a unique and typical example of the various social categories. This is what the second modernity aims for, marked by uncertainty, ambivalence and a greater distance between the objective and the subjective. It must include individuals by clearly giving importance to social positions, systems and social relationships. In analysing this, we no longer have a model's theoretical tools, with previous theories being marked by the conception of a model of stable analysis, whereas the second modernity is marked by instability and continuous change. Individual experiences must be reframed, no longer being understandable on the basis of a single grid that enables an individual to be thought of as the marker of a harmonious society. Martucelli will say that, with the diversity of identity models, individuals face various ambivalences, because they are the ones flowing between these models and individually bearing the tension of these ambivalences. Social phenomena are also understood through these models. They bear the contradictions of social systems, as Ulrich Beck says so well: "How our lives become a biographical solution to systematic contradiction" (cited by Bauman 2001, p. 47).

Society produces individuals who must be accountable for their living conditions as they affect their health and well-being. They must be responsible for their education and their employability, which means being able to get by without institutionalised employment systems for finding a job and escaping dependence on unemployment insurance and social security. This is a specific second modernity process, resulting in various institutional transformations, including the work and employment situation (the end of industrialisation, job development in the tertiary sector) and the transformation of social protection. Individuals are the ones who must think about their future and become reflexive and responsible beings.

Setbacks in life (job loss, divorce, illness) have no definitive solutions. There are tensions between various institutional judgments. Individuals are the ones who confront failure, and it is they who must find the strength, energy and resources to escape from it. These setbacks can be seen as personal faults. However, the way to correct an individual's course in life cannot come solely from collective bodies or social networks. There is a need to be able to rely on others, as much as on oneself. What differences exist between individuals? Faced with similar obstacles, why do some emerge and others not? In what way can work in itself be connected with social understanding? How can individuals act, faced with their problems and with an absence of recourse in society? "Self-respect" is a basic principle of social justice in the rational conception of cooperation: openness to others is needed for freedom though friendship, family, work, education and volunteer activities. In this context, participation is important, bringing with it the notion of "individual responsibility" with regard to others in a rush of solidarity toward vulnerable fellow citizens, victims of circumstances beyond their control (Blais 2007).

Individuality frees up a huge space for initiative and the spirit of this second modernity. (Sociologists of this second modernity are prone to describe society as it has become but pay less attention to finding the way out or to re-engaging in dialogue and seeing how cohesions can be reconstituted.) We can link the issue of individuation to a capacity for creativity found only among entrepreneurs. This social innovation project must be associated with individual growth, which can be achieved only by associating with others. Individuals alone cannot resolve their problems. On the contrary, if they exert their capacity for reflection and action with others through friendship, sympathy and selflessness, they can then resist the dominant power and act so as to transform the restraining forces.

Nonetheless, nobody has great power: "Social life is the end result of micropower" (Enriquez 2009, p. 169) This is the product of many local acts that do not always have a general sense when they are undertaken but that can transform the social environment. These forms of action and interaction may prove to the outmoded after a certain time and give rise to new problems generating new areas of social conflict that require new social innovations.

In modern societies, there is a need to be able to associate individual interests and the collective good. This association is evident in day-to-day actions, outside the major institutions, for leading a "moral life" selflessly and obliging oneself to "give, receive and return," Mauss would say. In social life, it is only through others that individuality can assert itself by indicating that it belongs to its community. The freest individual is the one who cooperates most and who does so without constraint in a social environment formed by associations. This moral life must be incarnated in action and cooperation.

Collectivists advocate the primacy of the community, whereas for liberals it is the contrary. Society is divided on this matter, and social innovation is affected by this debate, especially when it is taken up by voices of capitalism, which make individuality the vector of any possible transformation of society that must in no instance be justified by a return to communitarianism and the dominant state. We will see now how social innovation takes part in this reconstruction of social links that is necessary for a cohesive society.

3 What Is Being Rebuilt

The new order is being built against a backdrop of discussion on the setting of priorities and creation of hierarchies in social and economic values, on universality in wealth redistribution measures, and on equality and equity, solidarity, social cleavage and job creation. The rebuilding of society relies on the strength of community links, the capacity of civil society initiatives, and the existence of diversified networks allowing for the flow of social actors from various socio-economic circles, resources and information. The links between government, market and civil society must be rethought (Lévesque 2003). Though we may have a sound knowledge of the welfare state and what it can bring, we know much less about future results of the new social order now being created. Social innovation is connected to the possibility of re-introducing a new sense for the common good and general interest, a new way of expanding the notion of public service and its singular process, and finally with the citizen's capacities of networking as a main tool of planning out social innovation.

3.1 General Interest

Social innovation lies within the scope of the general interest to create greater social cohesion between the various groups and socio-economic categories that are attempting a rapprochement to narrow gaps. This means rejecting a world of socially excluded people that make society resemble "islands of excellence in a sea of ignorance" (Esping-Andersen 2002, p. 3). To manage this, a number of routes are possible. The first is maintaining and strengthening the welfare state, which seems the least likely scenario, with states and their governments up against pressure to cut spending and to face the challenge of reducing deficits and debts. The second scenario forms a counterweight to this with the intervention of liberal thinkers advocating the privatisation and commodification of public services, a reduction in social protection and a more marked inclination toward individualism by making citizens more accountable for their life path and the setbacks that may affect it. The "third way", theorised by sociologist Anthony Giddens, is intended as an amalgam of the first two, relying on individual and public responsibility in which citizens are the object of "empowerment" so that they can face market vagaries and develop skills through rigorous training, enabling them to adjust to rapid and frequent change while being capable of meeting these needs.

The general interest and its state connection is cast in a new light. It no longer stems from favoured state intervention. The general interest is not exclusive to the state, and a new sharing of jurisdictions is required, both with civil society and with certain private interests. Social innovation is not the prerogative of any of these scenarios. It belongs to none of these approaches and is not claimed by any thinkers or ideologues as an essential component of their approach. Social innovation is truly an initiative of civil society, filling gaps left by market, government and family regardless of the type of society in which it is rooted. We need to ask what type of society will be most favourable to social innovation – a liberal society that provides a broad space for individual freedom and leaves the field open to social movements and associations, or a society in which the state is more interventionist through wealth redistribution mechanisms that favour a guaranteed minimum income and that reduce poverty and its consequences? If we accept the precepts of the theoreticians of innovation and of the place of institutional constraints in the process of innovation, would innovation proliferate more widely in liberal societies? Is this truly the case? Always and in every circumstance? Individual freedom, advocated by the ideologues of liberalism, is based on the premise that cooperation is primarily the result of a calculation, and solidarity between social categories is always rooted in interest. A theory of social innovation must rely on a conception other than interest (Festré and Garrouste 2008). This is why highly institutionalised societies can offer ideal conditions for social innovation if the institutional arrangements provide areas of deliberation and gatherings at the junction of networks that are essential to social innovation. In the former case, social innovation is possible, linked to the initiative of interested individuals. In the latter case, social innovation is possible by relying on the existence of vast social ramifications linked to institutions.

3.2 A Service and a Process

Because rival strategies exist, we do not know the destination, and the orientations are not predictable. This requires examining social innovation from two connected and interdependent dimensions: result and process. As several authors have noted, social innovation is not related solely to whatever is new or to any other element that finds its way into organisations or communities (Harrisson et al. 2009; Moulaert et al. 2005; Phills et al. 2008; Westley 2010). It highlights new services or answers, sometimes novel ones, to needs expressed by social actors, and a novel process leading to this service. For this to happen, ways of understanding these links do not necessarily follow from the same sets of theories. A service, the first term, may be assessed from the standpoint of performance, efficiency and effectiveness and in terms of cost, accessibility and ability to deal with a problem, removing this problem or at least diminishing it. In short, this also involves responding adequately to the problems posed initially, in a manner that satisfies users. If it is a financial service, the money has to flow; if it is a service to prevent school dropout, the effectiveness of the measures must be gauged in light of the graduation rate in a given cycle. A service must be effective for the social links to be solid, to get a better idea of the sense of social innovation. No purpose is served by debating continuously if there are no conclusive results at the end. This process is not individualised but is organised and determined by its requirements and financial performance. When social innovation is associated with production of a service, it proceeds by instilling a new dynamic among the actors. The type of service then stands out from public services because it is set among local services and the actors' mobilisation. This is not passive. Co-construction involves a process of participation applied upstream from cooperation, allowing for conceptualisation and definition of public policies. The state sets out the policies with the actors but remains the central player in regulation, while agreeing to discuss the general interest (Vaillancourt 2009).

The second term, the process, may be assessed from the standpoint of legitimacy, namely an ability to handle the problem adequately, taking account of the measures for participation, the institutional forms of these measures and the possible compromises among a range of expressed interests, considering the values to be defended and maintained, keeping them intact and authentic (Battilana and Boxenbaum 2009).

These two dimensions, however, can be separated for analytical reasons. It is possible to take an interest in social innovation for practical reasons without being concerned about the sequence of possible actions in attaining the result. Social innovation can then be harnessed, in the sense that the democratic process emphasised by civil society focuses above all on citizens' responsibility in resolving a set of social problems through common processes. These democratic processes have little resonance among actors who are looking for a result above all, without being concerned about participation and civic commitment. Here, empowerment counts for little. It should be noted that this tendency is far from negligible. The ambient neo-conservatism that characterises western societies in the twenty-first century has the effect of engendering trends that run counter to the main orientation. A social innovation approach is more unidirectional, in the selection of problems as well as in the values defended by their initiators and in the directive and centralising process that specifies it (Pol and Ville 2009). To provide a better description of these two concurrent processes, we can say that it involves a struggle between commodification and "de-commodification" (Karl Polanyi) of services. Social life is what should determine the demand and supply of services rather than the market which, contrary to what is being sought, destroys primary solidarity.

Social innovations are important for the vitality of democracy, as a way of avoiding a democracy that is merely procedural and the opposite of a democracy that is substantial and based on content. One particularity of social innovation is that it proposes activities and services for users, introducing solidarity into the community, and it rejects a conception based solely on rationality or utilitarianism. What place is provided for social justice, sharing, moral sense, social cohesion, inequalities decrease, solidarity, and democracy?

The process provides for relationships to be established between the variables involved in a split-sequence action that commit a range of social actors, each arriving with their needs, identity, knowledge, resources and strategy. Analysing a process of innovation thus consists of taking account of all these elements for each of these actors and placing it in a dynamic. This means that, upon contact with the others, each term will be modulated and possibly transformed under the action of the others in a time sequence. It is also necessary to take account of the initial density of the elements and of the impossibility or inability of some of these components to be transformed. After all, innovating consists of altering certain rules, structures, norms and interactions. But what is being changed? What is being maintained? Why do some terms change while others remain intact? What are the rules that govern acceptance of certain modifications in relationships and not others? What are the possible explanations that hold up for the duration?

The weakness of the theory of institution is change, i.e. this theory presents few explanations of the mechanisms of change (Lawrence and Suddaby 2006; Battilana and Boxenbaum 2009). This is the gap that a good theory of social innovation must fill and enrich in terms of new knowledge with a universal scope. Ideas are important in the change being undertaken as an evolutionary process or as a breach. In the latter case, this is what breaks with the present when a number of dimensions are involved.

The constraints borne by past arrangements leading to a certain social order are persistent. The nature of institutions is comprised in the formula "Path dependency" coined by Christopher Freeman (1995). It means that actors of a specific society cannot transform completely the rules, the norms and the interactions. There is always something from the former way of social action that still stands. Social innovation is a combination of the old way mixed with new way. It is this social order and the path that can be used to transform it that is defended. This is creating as great an obstacle to innovation and upsetting the fragile, hard-won balance. In addition, it is within these past institutional arrangements that "repertoires of action" may be identified. Institutions provide these "repertoires" based on knowledge of a particular society (Duymedjian and Rüling 2010).

This is why "bricolage" is an unusual process that will make us more aware of the action sequences of social actors (Duymedjian and Rüling 2010). It consists of recombining the elements of the repertory of institutional rules at the local level with actions that bring about the new practices that are desired, leading to the transformation of relationships between the social actors as well as the way collective services are provided. This process is coordinated by a "social entrepreneur" who becomes the leading figure personifying the innovation process.

The social entrepreneur is a creative person, someone endowed with cognitive complexity and greater tolerance toward ambiguity. Social entrepreneurs are comfortable with contradictory knowledge, and they understand that the future is full of uncertainty. Their thinking is intuitive and spontaneous. But they also know how to deal with an institutional and organisational environment. They can internalise several cultures, in other words the norms, habits and conventions of more than one culture. They are more creative than those who are exposed to less diversity. A social entrepreneur's challenge is to convert knowledge into its own language and to convey it to the broader community. Each problem can be analysed in numerous ways, and the social entrepreneur is at ease with the many possible interpretations of any social phenomenon (Bréchet and Prouteau 2010).

To ensure the dissemination of social innovation, it is also necessary to be familiar with its principles and practices and to codify knowledge dealing with this translated bricolage. This knowledge also deals with the chains used in successive decisions by the actors, the most active of whom are those positioned at the junction of various networks and institutions. Through dissemination, there exists harmonisation of the principles on which innovation rests.

The more social capital they have (i.e., links with associations, organisations and institutions), the more influential they are (Emirbayer and Mische 1998). These links have the effect of broadening the repertory and the possible field for the flow of the necessary ideas, knowledge and resources. With social actors operating in the social innovation process, it is these micro-processes that we must pay attention to.

The social actors represented by various associations form the basis of the new demands for redistribution mechanisms that do not rely solely on the government-market duo but that incorporate civil society in a context of a mixed economy. Accordingly, these actors seek new powers and greater autonomy with the aim of implementing projects serving the community, relying on creativity and on taking initiatives. They are intermediary institutions made of unions, pressure groups and associations.

3.3 A Network that Relies on Trust

It is impossible to achieve social and economic advances without citizens having a minimum of self-confidence as well as of trust in others and in long-lasting institutions. Trust is what allows for dreaming, for creating promising long-term projects, anticipating the future. Trust is also what allows for action. It becomes increasingly clear that, in western states, citizens have lost confidence in the ability of government to resolve structural socio-economic problems, and they have also lost confidence in private enterprise, with its enthusiasm for short-term results, the abdication of its "social responsibility" role and its weak predisposition to creating stable and satisfying jobs. The role of the public authorities in the context of new social risks appearing must be considered in a different way. This does not mean ending government intervention but rather thinking about it in another way, in particular by making it a primary actor in alliance with the actors in the two other sectors, namely businesses in the private market and civil society associations in the third sector.

Social cohesion relies on trust between members of a society. To instil confidence in a community, there is a need for constancy and regularity. People gain confidence in one another only if they find cues in the behaviour of others. The erosion of cohesion affects everyone, especially the most vulnerable. Since there are various identities that lead to different and sometimes conflicting expectations, the contract no longer suffices. Cooperation between agents works better with loyalty, confidence and mutual respect. This is the opposite of the rigidity characterising the state bureaucracy, which shows itself to be a set of codified constraints and which affects the behaviour of agents and institutionalises their relationships through rules, norms and routines that strengthen each other mutually by means of strategies, social actors and their representations.

A society's quality is measured by the quality of life of its weakest members. In today's society, solidarity towards the vulnerable citizens is replaced by utilitarianism and rational procedures that lack a capacity for judgment. The institutions forming the basis for these procedural rules weaken the sense of responsibility that requires situations to be interpreted and judged in an "ethical world" in which ambivalence and uncertainty reign. There is a need to re-conceive chances for meetings between actors, to debate and to renegotiate what comes under the general interest and the common good. Weak links bring to light the chance of developing connections with people belonging to networks we know little about. Abilities to develop initiatives and innovations would then be enhanced.

Individuals undoubtedly reject large and fit-for-all institutions but nonetheless seek the social links necessary for survival. We are in a connectionist world in which personal initiative and a will of enterprise are needed more than ever. In Sennett's eyes, to work in networks, one must be capable of ambiguity and ambivalence, able to create interpersonal links and to possess relational skills. Self-reliance is also required to compensate for failures in systems and to be able to play a proactive role in seeking solutions to problems. Moreover, inequality and poverty are not just elements denoting an absence of material goods but also indicate the weakness of links in the networks. Being excluded means being outside networks and not being able to get in – and thus not being able to benefit from the resources that are essential to life in society. Inequalities are defined increasingly in terms of social distance, in addition to the classic property of being deprived of material goods. However, being isolated and being in a social network deficit lead to phenomena of anxiety regarding the future and the problems experienced in an isolated manner – alcoholism, psychological distress, single-parent families. There is a weakening of social capital that is in keeping with the reduction in confidence between individuals and a deficit in civic and voluntary commitment.

These networks that produce a flow of people, ideas and resources are effective if they are oriented to the local and community dimension, for face-to-face relationships are essential to social innovation. A community enables social links to be established where people know one another as people. The ideas that hold sway are those that favour the ephemeral and the short-term. This leads to an ideal situation for social innovation, which can easily be adjusted since it offers great flexibility, emanating as it does from highly diversified situations.

4 Conclusion

The concept of social innovation and its characteristics can be identified as a process of change and social transformation. Social innovation is transported and distributed widely where it is believed that this is a way to improve the life of communities. Innovation is a process involved in building new social bonds deconstructed in favour of the new capitalism, the changing role of the state and increasing individualisation of citizens. The broad definition given to social innovation consists of social creativity in response to certain social needs in areas such as child protection, education, health, sustainable transportation, housing, new consumption patterns and many more. Social innovation is based on a number of achievements in the projects developed by civil society. In this paper, we have emphasized two dimensions: first social innovation as a service to citizens; second the process that led to the creation of new relational traits between innovators and other stakeholders of social innovation. Of course the role of the entrepreneur developed by Joseph Schumpeter has diverted attention from the analytical categories to a holistic interest in the role of individuals. We should not ignore all the other influential factors, the context, the community mobilization, the resource availability, the ability to create links and networks through which ideas and resources move. Social innovation is definitely a collective process.

References

Battilana, J. B., & Boxenbaum, E. (2009). How actors change institutions: Towards a theory of institutional entrepreneurship. *The Academy of Management Annals, 31*(1), 65–107.
Bauman, Z. (2001). *The individualized society*. Cambridge: Polity Press.
Beck, U. (2003). *La Société du risque – Sur la voie d'une autre modernité*. Paris: Flammarion–Champs.
Blais, M. C. (2007). *La solidarité. Histoire d'une idée*. Paris: Gallimard.
Boudon, R. (2004). Théorie du choix rationnel, théorie de la rationalité limitée ou individualisme méthodologique: quel choisir? *Journal des économistes et des études humaines, 14*(11), 1–18.
Bourdieu, P. (1994). *Raisons pratiques. Sur la théorie de l'action*. Paris: Seuil.
Bréchet, J. P., & Prouteau, L. (2010). À la recherche de l'entrepreneur. Au-delà du modèle du choix rationnel: Une figure de l'agir projectif. *Revue française de Socio-économie, 6*(2), 109–130.

Duymedjian, R., & Rüling, C. (2010). Towards a foundation of bricolage in organization and management theory. *Organization Studies, 31*(2), 133–151.

Emirbayer, M., & Mische, A. (1998). What is agency? *The American Journal of Sociology, 103*, 281–317.

Enriquez, E. (2009). Le pouvoir, l'État et le sujet dans le monde actuel. *Sociologie et Societes, XLI* (1), 159–176.

Esping-Andersen, G. (Ed.). (2002). *Why we need a new welfare state*. Oxford: Oxford University Press.

Etzioni, A. (2004). *The common good*. Cambridge: Polity Press.

Festré, A., & Garrouste, P. (2008). Rationality, behavior, institutional and economic change in Schumpeter. *Journal of Economic Methodology, 15*(4), 365–390.

Freeman, C. (1995). The national system of innovation. In historical perspective. *Cambridge Journal of Economics, 19*(1), 5–24.

Giddens, A. (1990). *The consequences of modernity*. Cambridge: Polity Press.

Harrisson, D., Bourque, R., & Széll, G. (2009). Social innovation, economic development, employment and democracy. In D. Harrisson, G. Szell, & R. Bourque (Eds.), *Social innovation and labour* (pp. 7–16). Bern: Peter Lang.

Lawrence, T. B., & Suddaby, R. (2006). Institutions and institutions work. In S. R. Clegg, C. Hardy, T. B. Lawrence, & W. R. Nord (Eds.), *Handbook of organization studies* (2nd ed., pp. 215–254). London: Sage.

Lévesque, B. (2003). Fonction de base et nouveau rôle des pouvoirs publics: vers un nouveau paradigme de l'État. *Annals of Public and Cooperative Economics, 74*(4), 489–513.

Martucelli, D. (2009). Qu 'est-ce qu'une sociologie de l'individu moderne? Pourquoi, pour qui, comment? *Sociologie et Societes, XLI*(1), 15–33.

Moulaert, F., Martinelli, F., Swyngedouw, E., & Gonzalez, S. (2005). Toward alternative model(s) of local innovation. *Urban Studies, 42*(11), 1969–1990.

Mumford, M. D. (2003). Cases of social innovation: Lessons from two innovations in the 20th century. *Creativity Research Journal, 15*(2/3), 261–266.

Phills, J. A., jr, Deiglmeier, K., & Miller, D. T. (2008). Rediscovering social innovation. *Stanford Social Innovation Review, 6*(4), 34–43.

Pol, E., & Ville, S. (2009). 'Social innovation': Buzz word or enduring term? *The Journal of Socio-Economics, 38*, 878–885.

Sennett, R. (2007). *La culture du nouveau capitalisme*. Paris: Hachette, coll. Pluriel.

Vaillancourt, Y. (2009). Social economy in the co-construction of public policy. *Annals of Public and Cooperative Economics, 80*(2), 275–313.

Westley, F. (2010). Making a difference: Strategies for scaling social innovation for greater impact. *The Innovation Journal: The Public Sector Innovation Journal, 15*(2), 2–19.

New Combinations of Social Practices in the Knowledge Society

Josef Hochgerner

Abstract Paraphrasing the famous quote from Schumpeter, who initially explained innovation as a 'new combination of production factors', social innovation can be defined as a new combination of social practices. In order to qualify as social innovations, such combinations or the creation and implementation of absolutely new practices must be intentional, aiming at solving a social issue, and produce effects in terms of novel social facts. Implementation and impact distinguish social innovations from social ideas. Social objectives and rationales, rather than economic ones, make them differentiable from business-driven innovations. However, social innovations take place in business as well as in the public sector and civil society. From a particular sociological point of view, social innovations are becoming of increasing relevance not only because of the frequently mentioned so-called 'Grand Challenges' the knowledge society faces in the twenty-first century. On the one hand, re-integration of the most effective economy ever is on the agenda in society, aiming at the 'management of abundance'. On the other, even the nexus between man-made social systems and human nature may need re-configuration.

1 The Issue: Why Social Innovation?

The potential of human society to create wealth and well-being is as formidable as that to produce threatening impacts on a global scale, together shaping a specific man-made cultural and material environment affecting social and individual life. Such capacities have expanded rapidly since the age of industrialization and are progressing at even accelerated pace under the present conditions of the globalized economy in contemporary knowledge societies. Humankind can draw on complex

J. Hochgerner (✉)
Zentrum für Soziale Innovation, Linke Wienzeile 246, Vienna 1150, Austria
e-mail: hochgerner@zsi.at

statehood, international organizations, daily improving technologies including infrastructures, efficient transport systems and worldwide communication networks, affluent food production and medical aid unthinkable just one or two generations ago. Whilst average life expectancy in Europe was at about 50 around 1900, it is about 80 for a new-born around 2000.[1] Yet potential is there as well for nuclear overkill and other disasters like climate change. Financial capital is 'making money' beyond the real economy and out of control (*financialization*, cf. Krippner 2005; Palley 2007; Radermacher 2010), producing hunger and the extreme poverty of hundreds of millions next to obscene wealth.

Increasing wealth, measured in global GDP as well as expressed in the rising numbers (and their personal wealth) of 'high net worth individuals (HNWIs), those with US$ 1 million or more at their disposal'[2] is based in fact on innovations and industrial progress achieved mainly during the second half of the twentieth century. It is neither territorially fixed, nor any more in the range of measures determined by nation states or national societies. To distribute wealth more equitably and sustainably, i.e. to secure livelihood and quality of life now and in the future, the knowledge society desperately needs knowledge and social innovations capable of turning knowledge (i.e. facts, cognition, even attitudes) into action, instigating appropriate social practices and behaviour.

The term *Knowledge Society* indicates a state in the development of humankind, in which 'knowledge' plays specific roles in everyday life, in social relations and economic dynamics from local to global scales. To an unprecedented extent, new and improved knowledge is nowadays being produced and accelerated by scientific research and effectuated by innovation. Based on this assumption, the opening paragraph of the EC Communication on the Europe 2020 Flagship Initiative 'Innovation Union' lists a number of severe problems, mentions *the crisis*, and states no less than that the future standard of living will depend on pushing innovation:

> At a time of public budget constraints, major demographic changes and increasing global competition, Europe's competitiveness, our capacity to create millions of new jobs to replace those lost in the crisis and, overall, our future standard of living depend on our ability to drive innovation in products, services, business and social processes and models. This is why innovation has been placed at the heart of the Europe 2020 strategy. Innovation is also our best means of successfully tackling major societal challenges, such as climate change, energy and resource scarcity, health and ageing, which are becoming more urgent by the day. (European Commission 2010, p. 2)

Current and future generations appear to be becoming dependants of the knowledge society. In this perspective, knowledge, represented primarily in science, technology and innovation, takes the place of industry and agriculture as the key attribute for denoting the main characteristic of the society in question. Research

---

[1] Cf. e.g. EUROSTAT 'Mortality and life expectancy statistics': http://epp.eurostat.ec.europa.eu/statistics_explained/index.php/Mortality_and_life_expectancy_statistics.

[2] Capgemini 'The World Wealth Report 2012': http://www.capgemini.com/services-and-solutions/by-industry/financial-services/solutions/wealth/worldwealthreport/.

and innovation are required to meet today's challenges, in particular the 'Grand Challenges' of the future. However, a number of critical issues seem to be disguised behind this general and in principle very optimistic assessment of what is termed the knowledge society.

Society in the twenty-first century may be labelled the 'information society', the 'knowledge-based information society', or the 'knowledge society'. Whatever phrase is used or will be used in the future when looking back with the benefit of hindsight, the present state of affairs results from the daunting success of industry, modernization, research and development in technology, transforming social structures from those of an industrial society towards what we now call the information or the knowledge society (cf. Beniger 1986; Stehr 1994; Castells 1998; Heidenreich 2003).

The concept of the knowledge society emphasizes immaterial and specific intangible features of products and services in economic processes, and of innovations in particular. Thereby the boundaries between the economic and social spheres are becoming blurred. At the same time, the traditionally predominant view of innovation as an exclusively economic concept needs adaptation and expansion. Beyond knowledge, realizing innovation requires investment, technologies and techniques, research and, frequently neglected, but indispensible, social resources such as commitment, creativity, enduring labour and co-operation. Social innovations enable new uses of knowledge, involving tacit knowledge as well as scientifically generated facts and cognition. However, the decisive criterion of the knowledge society in its fuzzy distinction from the industrial society is not sheer quantities of more or novel knowledge. For sure, the world society (cf. Stichweh 2004; Meyer 2010), emerging yet lagging behind the globalized economy, certainly requires new knowledge, but this is nothing basically new. Knowledge was and is crucial to mankind at any stage in its development to survive and generate what later generations may call progress, sometimes fundamental enough to speak of a new era. In the case of the knowledge society, it consists of new conditions of knowledge generation, new channels of knowledge diffusion and hitherto unknown methods of knowledge utilization that make the difference. Nonetheless, it should be kept in mind that the basic function of knowledge is to provide the 'capability to act' (Stehr 1994, p. 208).

New forms of knowledge generation by extended functions and roles of science have been termed by Gibbons et al. (1994) as 'Mode 2 knowledge production'. Science and scientific methods, the evaluation of facts and the verification of results have become increasingly relevant ever since Galileo Galilei attempted to communicate the findings of science to a wider public in the seventeenth century (*Dialogus*). The Industrial Age was based on exploiting new resources (extending from raw materials, energy, human resources to the scientific comprehension of *laws of nature*), breeding, by virtue of its huge turnover of matter, energy, output and labour, urgent needs for the management of such processes by new and more efficient ways of information processing and knowledge production.

During the development of the *industrial society*, scientific research, technological progress and innovation amplified the production of wealth, yet consequently led to the unbearable depletion of natural resources and many unexpected as well as undesired effects. It became a prerequisite of continuous development to acquire, store and process previously inconceivable amounts and forms of information and knowledge: 'The information society ... is not so much the result of any recent social change as of increases begun more than a century ago in the speed of material processing'. (Beniger 1986, vii) In the post-industrial era (cf. Bell 1974) of the now so-called knowledge society, scientific knowledge production, using multiple sources of data, information and knowledge, equals the importance of the traditionally accounted factors of production, i.e. soil, labour and capital.

The knowledge society not only requires more knowledge and science. It also produces the 'knowledge paradox'. Science, scientific methods and science-based knowledge are usually seen as providing appreciably more and superior knowledge. Yet they also entail more scrutiny to often controversial issues, on the one hand, and an awesome abundance of 'news', bemusing large sections of even, sometimes in particular, well educated societies, on the other. Thus, the new production of knowledge at the same time produces a cognition of nescience, i.e. the awareness of *not* knowing (Heidenreich 2003).

Gibbons et al. (1994, p. 167) summarized the inherited *Mode 1* of science as 'the complex of ideas, methods, values and norms that has grown up to control the diffusion of the Newtonian model of science to more and more fields of enquiry and ensure its compliance with what is considered sound scientific practice'. Nowadays, the generation and utilization of new knowledge requires *more* science and scientific methods, but is *less* under the control of scientists; sound scientific practice becomes mingled with other practices from a variety of professions as well as from laypersons. Knowledge is increasingly *produced* 'on demand', involving stakeholders beyond science and research organizations or funding agencies. Knowledge production relies more and more on collaboration between scientists and users of knowledge. In *Mode 2*, the modified function of science is 'knowledge production carried out in the context of application and marked by trans-disciplinarity, heterogeneity, organizational heterarchy and transience, social accountability and reflexivity, and quality control which emphasizes context- and use-dependence, results from the parallel expansion of knowledge producers and users in society'. (ibid.)

The social factor, alongside the technical one, was already emphasized as fundamentally relevant in the European Commission's 'Green Paper on Innovation' (European Commission 1995, p. 11). 'Innovation is not just an economic mechanism or a technical process. It is above all a social phenomenon. Through it, individuals and societies express their creativity, needs and desires. By its purpose, its effects or its methods, innovation is thus intimately involved in the social conditions in which it is produced.'

This statement addressed the fact that innovation has social aspects. But there was no reference to anything like social innovation. The present concept found its way into the politics, economics and science of many different countries only a few years ago, particularly achieving some significance after 2009. Now there are public debates on the topic, and many institutions are devoting themselves to social innovation. Explanations of the importance of social innovation can be found in the official documents of a number of EU Member States, as well as in the EU Flagship Initiative 'Innovation Union'.[3] The intensive examination of the topic on a European level began in the context of the 'Renewed Social Agenda' of 2008,[4] and through the preview of the future EU Innovation Policy (Business Panel 2009) initiated by the Directorate General for Enterprise and Industry of the European Commission. The so-called BEPA Report (Hubert et al. 2010) was published, and in 2011 the European-wide campaign 'Social Innovation Europe'[5] commenced. The same year, social innovation was first announced as a topic of research in the European Seventh Framework Programme for Research, Technology Development and Innovation.

Despite the growing popularity of the topic, there is still widespread uncertainty regarding what social innovations are, how they come into being, and what can be expected of them. In addition, as the 'Grand Challenges' are becoming ever more urgent (challenges ranging from climate change to ageing societies, financialization, poverty, social exclusion, migration and social conflicts), research, teaching and support of social innovations are also gaining in importance. The social, economic, and cultural changes of the twenty-first century are creating requirements for the analysis and implementation of innovation in general, and of social innovation in particular. These requirements are clearly appearing to reach out beyond the scope of economics.

With regard to the Grand Challenges, the Europe 2020 strategy[6] sets quantitatively measurable goals: to raise employment to 75 % of the work force; to increase investment in research, technology, and innovation to 3 % of the GDP of the EU; to reduce greenhouse gas emissions by 20 %, to increase energy efficiency by 20 %, and to have 20 % of the energy produced in Europe come from renewable resources; in the field of education, to decrease the rate of school drop-outs to under 10 %, to increase the proportion of university (or other higher-education) graduates to 40 % of the respective age cohort; in the fight against poverty, to achieve an absolute, fixed goal of 'less than 20 million' under the subsistence minimum. In order to reach these goals, new technologies and economic measures will be needed on an unprecedented scale and social innovations will be absolutely indispensible. The need for innovative changes to social practices exists in both the public and private sectors, as well as in civil society organizations (the 'Third Sector').

Against this background, social innovation may be considered any activity that expands the capability to act (of parts or the whole of society), *and* enables or leads to concrete action. Social innovations are components of today's general cultural and social transformation. Under the conditions of progressive mechanization and

---

[3] http://ec.europa.eu/research/innovation-union/index_en.cfm.

[4] http://ec.europa.eu/social/main.jsp?catId=547.

[5] http://www.socialinnovationeurope.eu.

[6] http://ec.europa.eu/europe2020/index_en.htm.

globalization, the significance of social innovations is increasing in many areas of society. Individuals' behaviour in informal networks can be just as socially innovative as organizational development and conflict resolution in organizations; as diversity management; as new teaching and learning models in the education system; or as systemic changes in labour, social, or tax laws. Social innovation can emerge as new rules for participation and decision-making in social processes, as services that influence the social situation of specific segments of the population, and as changed patterns of behaviour or improved concepts of social protection.

Ideas for social developments become social innovations when they result in practices which are either totally new or more effective than alternative concepts, and are thus accepted by society and put to use. Only when a social idea is implemented and disseminated does it become a social innovation, making a contribution towards the overcoming of a concrete problem and meeting one of existing social needs, a need that may be either new or long-standing. Just as technical discoveries are only counted as innovations once they have become marketable as products and processes and are disseminated, so must social innovations produce sustainable benefits to target groups.

2 Social Innovation Theory

The classical innovation paradigm comprises *new combinations of production factors*,[7] enabling the development of novelties in technology, services and business management. Such focus and confinement to the business sector does not cover the full range of innovations required to advance sustainable socio-economic and environmental development in the transition from the industrial to the knowledge society. Innovation must be considered a term much wider than is conventionally conceived. There is less necessity to justify social innovation *in addition to* innovation than to change the general concept of innovation to become more inclusive and comprehensive.

Fundamental societal changes require the inclusion of social innovations in a paradigm shift of the innovation system (Howaldt and Jacobsen 2010). The new innovation paradigm is essentially characterized by the opening up of the concept of innovation processes to societal characteristics, e.g. the new relevance of knowledge and Mode 2 Science. Besides companies and industrial corporations, now and in the future universities and research institutions, even individual citizens and customers, will become players in innovation processes. Terms and concepts such as open innovation, user-led innovation, customer integration and innovation networks[8] reflect aspects of this development. Innovation is actually a general

---

[7] The first phrase used by Schumpeter (2006) before adopting the term *innovation*.

[8] Examples from the vast literature on these developments: Franke et al. (2006), Chesbrough et al. (2006), Reichwald and Piller (2009).

social phenomenon; changes in innovation processes affect innovative products and services and their impacts on almost all walks of life (cf. Rosted et al. 2009).

Innovations in technology and business remain imperative, yet social innovations are essential in order to reap their full potential, at the same time creating beneficial social developments as inclusive as they are diverse. They not only have a share in social affairs as such, but in preserving and expanding the innovative capacity of companies and society as a whole: 'The most urgent and important innovation advance in the twenty-first century will take place in the social field. Technical innovations will continue, of course, and bring about a materially and immaterially utterly changed environment and new living conditions in comparison with previous possibilities; but the social innovations will be those that the inhabitants of this world must first produce or ensure' (translated from Hochgerner 1999, p. 37).

Innovations in economic as well as societal processes are undeniably relevant and even increasing in significance. No matter what kind of innovation we consider, any innovation constitutes empirical facts. It is the outcome of an applied idea, tested and approved by operation, success and acceptance. Therefore, the assessment and measurement of the scope and quality of innovation must be based on facts. In the case of commercialized innovations, e.g. a new technology, these are economic facts, whereas in the case of social innovations we need to watch out for social facts,[9] affected or created by *new combinations of social practices*. As regards business innovations, appropriate measures and methodologies have been developed over the past decades in very rich scientific literature, establishing statistical indicators and benchmarks to take account of innovations with primarily economic, but also social impacts (cf. OECD, EUROSTAT 2005).

Innovation without a prefix mainly refers to new products or processes based on advanced technology and new combinations or designs of technical components successfully employed in existing or new markets. In discussions and programmatic declarations on national, European and international levels, the greatest significance is attached to the acceleration and reinforcement, and also the continuous amendment, of innovation processes. Frequently, innovation is regarded as the final product of the scientific generation of new knowledge and its economic application. Indeed, by deliberately promoting research, technology and innovation, today's society has considerably expanded its potential to improve current and future living conditions. These developments are continuing and leading to overwhelming quantities of new products and consumer goods, novel infrastructures for transport and communication, longer life spans, yet also to individual and social stress in cases of unexpected and controversial impacts.

---

[9] A social fact is 'any more or less laid down form of action with the capacity to exert an external compulsion on the individual; or also generally appearing in the field of a given society and possessing a life of its own, independent of its individual expressions' (translated from Durkheim 1984, p. 5).

While the concept of social innovation is not new, it has only recently been recognized as a key component of innovation in scientific and policy circles in Europe and other world regions. Yet, despite the fact of its recognition, there is still a long way ahead to move from the already relatively high awareness to the systematic promotion and implementation of social innovations in the private and public spheres. To date social innovation is neither on a par with nor integrated in the classical notion of innovation, and in real life (in all societal sectors, including business, public and civil society) social innovations still remain a kind of second choice, largely unobtrusive and underrated in terms of impact and effectiveness. Indeed, social innovations appear petty compared with the Grand Challenges for which new and promising levers to provide solutions are being sought. In order better to meet rising expectations as regards the functions and efficacy of social innovations, a clarification of the concept is first required, followed by the establishment of reliable indicators and methods for measuring the resources used in the process of social innovation generation and the accountable effects.

Innovations are elements of the *modus vivendi* through which the economy and society ensure their existence *in flux*. Schumpeter saw economic development processes not as being driven by the commonly assumed quest for equilibrium, but by inequality and instability. The same applies to society as a whole, as social change goes on all the time (and may become modified to a certain extent by intentional social innovations). How much innovations themselves ever cause and perpetuate change, innovations must be viewed as necessities of modern economic and social systems, a means enabling the economy (and society, too) again and again to face ongoing problems and new challenges. 'The opening of new foreign or domestic markets and the organizational development of handicraft enterprises and factories into such concerns as U.S. Steel illustrate the same process of an industrial mutation – if I may use this biological expression – that constantly revolutionizes the economic structure from within, constantly destroys the old structure, 'creative destruction' is the significant fact for capitalism. Capitalism consists of it, and in it every capitalist structure must live' (translated from Schumpeter 2005, p. 137).

For more than 60 years following the Second World War, the capitalist system was marked by constant expansion and growing global power, largely unchecked after the collapse of the Soviet Union in 1991 and the disappearance of competition between the two ideological systems. Thus, it is not surprising that economic categories and expectations have dominated the innovation discourse. But development towards a post-industrial innovation paradigm is beginning to emerge in conjunction with the rapidly increasing interest in social innovations in recent years. In such a paradigm, social innovations as well as technological and economic innovations could be comprehended as integrated components of social change in a 'holistic' interpretation of innovation (Hochgerner 2009, p. 35).

The relevance of an innovation should not be gauged exclusively by the respective reference system or the rationale of the economy, society, or technology. Although economic and social innovations differ according to their objectives and logics of action, all innovations are socially relevant in that they emerge under social conditions in different contexts and have social effects. However, social innovations that do not aim primarily at economic objectives may also produce economic effects. The contexts and interactions of different innovation processes are currently gaining in importance and will continue to do so in the future. The expanding sphere of 'social innovation' is finding its way internationally into policy-making, the economy, and science, as seen in the growing number of institutions researching and/or practically supporting social innovations and in political declarations of intent, conferences, and documents addressing the topic.

As indicated previously, in short terms, social innovations are new combinations of social practices. Yet a more detailed definition involving determinable properties is required to facilitate empirical analysis. Conceptualized for such analytical purposes, *social innovations are new practices for resolving societal challenges which are adopted and utilized by the individuals, social groups and organizations concerned*. This definition can be used in empirical research, whereby social innovation should be considered as a *process*, consisting of stages from the generation of an *idea*, on to *intervention*, *implementation* and *impact* (a '4-*i*-process'). Ideas (inventiveness and creativity) underlie the concepts and measures proposed, which, after targeted intervention (as a response to social challenges) and successful implementation, become innovations (producing social facts) only when utilized. Social innovations are not determined solely by the potential of an idea, but also by whether and to what extent the potential of an idea is realized. It depends on whether the 'invention' offers benefit to target groups, and thus a social idea mutates into a social innovation in the process of the implementation of new social practices, usage and dissemination.

Just as technology is socially constructed (shaped) to a certain extent, innovations, whether technological or social in nature, also develop under concrete cultural conditions. In the present with its global and defining 'Western industrialized' world economy, the economy dominates the foreground of society. More than 200 years of industrial development and the global assertion of the capitalist value system have led to an economic model with global interdependencies, but lacking adequate institutions and structures of a world society with shared interests, objectives, and standards which might be able to end poverty and dependence by steering and utilizing in targeted ways the enormous economic productivity. Schumpeter's Austro-Hungarian compatriot and contemporary, Karl Polanyi, perceived that the modern changes in 'Economy and Society' (also the title of Max Weber's main work of 1922) had led to a separation and independence of economic processes and structures from society. In the course of this 'great transformation', different logics of development and action emerged, making society dependent on a specific type of economy, seen increasingly as something 'external' to society and socially uncontrollable (Polanyi 1978).

Accordingly, unlike earlier market forms,[10] industrially and financially developed capitalism (the 'system of the market economy') became a specific institution of

---

[10] 'Whereas History and Anthropology know of different economic forms, most of which contain the setting up of markets, they do not know of any economy before ours that was even remotely so dominated and controlled by markets' (translated from Polanyi 1978, p. 72).

enormous significance for the overall structure of society. It means no more and no less than the treatment of *society as an appendix to the market*. The economy is no longer embedded in social relations, but social relations are embedded in the economic system. Such a predominance of modern economic conditions and criteria in or *against* society implies that societal structures appear determined by the economy. In this context, it is hardly surprising that there seems to be a value difference between 'social' and 'economic' innovations. Innovations in and through the economy, whose success can be defined and measured in sales and revenue figures, stand in the limelight and are heeded, financed, and applauded. Innovations outside the world of the economy, i.e., in state and civil society domains, not only seem different, but receive less attention, funding and acceptance.

However, this dichotomy is artificial and logically untenable. Generally, innovations are considered business innovations, but innovations in public and civil society sectors may also have economic causes and consequences. At the same time, social innovations can also be found in large corporations and small businesses (Kesselring et al. 2008; Kesselring 2009). What is important here are the objectives and outcomes: *social innovations create social facts, whereas economic innovations create economic value added.* In neither case does it mean that social facts must be positively assessed and desired (by all the people affected by them) or that economic value added should be sustainable in the broader sense of the word. Moreover, the social facts resulting from new practices (e.g. maintained by groups of people or organizations when acting in new roles or adhering to different sets of values) may also have economic effects. At the same time, economic innovations and innovative technologies can lead to new social facts (e.g., Web 2.0 technologies resulting in new communication patterns).

The intention, testing, implementation and dissemination of a new social practice that is enforceable against others will lead, as an innovation, to deviations from the routine current of reproducing stereotyped practices. The features of innovations in general, and of social innovations as defined here, can be observed in the actions and behaviour of individuals and groups, and in social relations or institutionalized procedures. Hence, they are accessible to empirical research. Max Weber's concept of social action offers theoretical approaches. At the centre of Weber's theory of social action there is the subjective *meaning* of action, i.e., the intention and purpose of an intervention, and the reference of this action to 'others' (persons, groups, institutions, the social environment): "'Social action'... intends to refer to such actions that in terms of the actor or actors relate to the behaviour of *others* and take their bearings from it" (translated from Weber 2005, p. 3).

Whenever social innovations are manifested in social practices, in the diction of action theory, it follows that they either lead to new forms of social action or presuppose social action. In either case, social innovations are expressed in a new definition (dimension or direction) of what constitutes the meaning of action and its relation to the social environment. Social action in families, school classes, working groups, and also in large social systems (administrative entities, states, major concerns etc.), is determined by given roles and functions. However, a recasting of these very roles and functions can modify the social systems themselves, or even affect the processes of social change at large. The latter depends on the form and 'range' of concrete innovations, i.e. in the case of *systemic* social innovations (cf. Hubert et al. 2010) at the macro level of society.

Here, it seems necessary to refer to the difference between incremental innovations (improving innovations), in particular the frequent 'unobtrusiveness of social innovations' (Aderhold 2010), on the one hand, and 'basic innovations'[11] relevant to many people and stakeholders affected, on the other. To make the entire spectrum of social innovations accessible to scientific analysis, both small-scale (affecting individuals) and large-scale (affecting social structures) changes must be defined in categories that may be applied in any functional system or sector of society. This represents a slightly adapted recourse to some elements of Parsons' structural function theory (Parsons 1976). In this theory of social systems, *function* is understood as 'the effect of a social component making a contribution towards realizing a specific system status and *maintaining and integrating a social system*' (translated from Hurrelmann 1990, p. 41; author's emphasis).

Though innovations are elements of systems dynamics, they also support the integration of social systems, since specific ways of change (innovation) add to continuance. Innovations certainly imply change, yet they contribute to *stabilizing* systems. 'Stability' may be achieved by safeguarding the status quo or by adapting to new requirements and challenges. Nevertheless, change may create instability, of course, leading to complete system collapse, the demolition of old systems, and the building up of new ones. In these processes, which often occur in parallel in society, innovations have a special significance. As already explained in Schumpeter's innovation theory, they guarantee the survival of enterprises (maintenance of stability), but keep in motion the more comprehensive process of 'creative destruction' (dynamics of change). In comparison, social innovations sustain the success of social action in spite of imperilling challenges, whilst they are, at the same time, part of social change.

All innovations are socially relevant: those with objectives and rationality criteria to change economic parameters as well as those with social intentions affecting social practices. This also implies that, irrespective of the kind of innovation to be developed, realized or examined, the meanings and effects of innovations do not remain restricted to the respective functional system.

---

[11] [The evolution of] 'human beings ... repeatedly shows forks and sprouting branches. A fork stands for the opening of a new path, a new work method .... I term such a change in direction from the previously customary practice a basic innovation. Technological basic innovations create new trades or branches of industry, non-technological basic innovations open up new fields of activity in the sphere of culture, in public administration and in social services etc. Basic innovations create new terrain for human activity' (translated from Mensch 1975, p. 56f).

Technological and economic innovations affect or change not only the functional system of the *economy*, but also the other major functional systems dealt with by Parsons, i.e., *politics*, *law*, and *culture*. It is equally evident that social innovations not only exert an influence on *culture* or *politics*, but also on the functional systems of *law* and the *economy*. Within these systems, the functional area of *integration* has major importance for maintaining the system as well as for change.

According to Parsons, four *structural categories* come together facilitating the integration in all social systems, i.e. 'roles', 'collective', 'norms', and 'values'. *Roles* refer to the personal assignment or assumption of assignments; the *collective* stands for social relations abstracting from personal attributes; *norms* are rules of the most varied kinds (from house rules to laws and international agreements); *values* express general patterns of desirable modes of behaviour and attitudes which usually have the character of orientation, but may to a certain extent even assert normative significance. These structural categories embodied in social systems, from the roles of individuals to fundamental societal values, can be used to identify or designate different *types of social innovations*. The amended typology of innovations, usually restricted to *products, processes, marketing*, and *organization*, identified and assessed exclusively in the business sector, then includes *roles, relations*,[12] *norms*, and *values* as categories of social innovations in all functional systems of society as a whole.

Such an enlarged typology of innovations goes beyond the sector of the economy. It can also make innovations in the State (in public administration, regional bodies, etc.) and in Civil Society (the so-called 'Third Sector') into the objects of empirical research. Of course, technical and non-technical economic innovations are and remain of salient significance for the functional area of the economy, just as innovations in values must primarily be situated in the functional area of culture.

The proposed categories of innovations are intended to help analyze the influences of and interactions between new elements of social practices, the objectives of novelties, their functions, and effects in empirical research. Theoretical considerations and definitions are necessary to prepare the ground scientifically for future innovation research in order to attain a position from which to record, comprehend and evaluate the social innovations required to meet the so-called 'Grand Challenges'. A summary of the theoretical proposal here is intended to align the categories of social innovations with those established in business innovation research, which is based on four main types of innovation. These are in fact almost identical with the denotations introduced by Schumpeter a 100 years ago, when he produced his first typology of 'new combinations of production factors' (Table 1).

---

[12] Instead of Parsons' structural category 'collective', I choose the concept of 'relations', for Parsons (1976, p. 181) is also primarily concerned with interactions (based on expectations, achievements, rights and duties) that become effective in a collective.

Table 1 Amendments to common types of innovation by categories denoting social innovation

Comparison of the 'new combinations' according to Schumpeter with the 'main types of innovations' according to the Oslo Manual and the main types of social innovations

New combinations of production factors (Schumpeter 2006)	Innovations in the corporate sector (OECD, EUROSTAT 2005, 'Oslo Manual')	New combinations of social practices: social innovations, established in the form of ...
New or better products	Product innovations	Roles
New production methods	Process innovation	Relations
Opening up new markets	Marketing	Norms
New sources of raw materials	Organizational innovations	Values
Reorganization of the market position		

3 Proceeding from Theory to the Measurement and Assessment of Social Innovations

In the case of the 'main types of innovation', the Oslo Manual lays down numerous specifications and detailed sets of indicators to identify innovations and to allow the input factors and outcomes to be gauged. The main types of social innovation need to be specified and equipped with measurable indicators all the same. Approaches are, e.g. to draw on statistics supporting methodological instrumentality like the Human Development Indicators (HDI – http://hdr.undp.org), as proposed by Blasy and Gruber (2011), and the Better-Life-Index of the OECD (http://www.oecdbetterlifeindex.org/). Significant contributions have already been made by the Commission on the Measurement of Economic Performance and Social Progress, headed by Joseph Stiglitz, Amartya Sen, and Jean-Paul Fitoussi.[13] See also the contributions by Bassi and Wobbe in this book.

Hubert et al. (2010, p. 26) propose clearly distinguishing between the *process dimension* and the *output dimension* of social innovations: 'The process dimension ... implies that new forms of interaction are established' [whereas] ... 'the output dimension ... refers to the kind of value or output that innovation is expected to deliver: a value that is less concerned with mere profit, and including multiple dimensions of output measurement'. Another valuable distinction is presented in the same report by qualifying the particular social dimension of social innovations deriving from their characteristic objectives and intended impact, i.e.

---

[13] 'While many of our measures are directed at ascertaining short-run movements in the level of market activity, the Commission considers that the time has come to make a clear move from measuring production to measuring welfare, to try to close the gap between our measures of economic performance and widespread perceptions of well-being.' Stiglitz/Sen/Fitoussi, The Measurement of Economic Performance and Social Progress Revisited. Reflections and Overview, 63. www.stiglitz-sen-fitoussi.fr (accessed on October 26, 2011).

- '*The social demand perspective* ... innovations that respond to social demands that are traditionally not addressed by the market or existing institutions and are directed towards vulnerable groups in society.'
- '*The societal challenge perspective* ... innovations that respond to those societal challenges in which the boundary between social and economic becomes blurred and that are directed towards society as a whole.'
- '*The systemic changes perspective* ... innovations that contribute to the reform of society in the direction of a more participative arena where empowerment and learning are both sources and outcomes of well-being' (ibid. 2011 edition, p. 36ff).

When analyzing the outcome of social innovations, it is of the utmost importance not to get caught in the trap of normative prejudice. In the BEPA-Report, for instance, the definition used appears to be normative: 'Social innovations are innovations that are social in both their ends and their means. Specifically, we define social innovations as new ideas (products, services and models) that simultaneously meet social needs (more effectively than alternatives) and create new social relationships or collaborations. They are innovations that are not only good for society, but also enhance society's capacity to act' (Hubert et al. 2010, p. 7).

To be good for society and to enhance society's capacity to act are perfect *objectives* that should be supported by social innovations. However, generally to expect that all innovations which are 'social in their ends and means' contribute to such aims means ignoring the sociological fact that people are different and have often quite contradictory intentions based on diverse interests and needs. What may appear 'social' (beneficial) to one group, at a given time, in a certain social strata or region, may prove irrelevant or even detrimental to others.

Analysts as well as promoters of social innovations must not assume social innovations ought to be 'social' in the simplistic sense of 'good'. Anyone may hope so, but social innovations, just like any innovation, are neither invariably socially good to all social groupings or numbers of people affected, nor will they always and generally meet equal acceptance in the public. The attribute *social* is to be used in the meaning of *purposeful relation to other* individuals, social groups or institutions and organizations, as defined in action theory. It is not to be confused with caring, though, of course, social innovations are needed and possible in the socially extremely relevant domain of care (e.g. to establish institutionalized help for family carers).

Globalization accelerates ongoing social change. Under the conditions of globalization, innovations of all kinds affect increasing sections of society. They shape not only processes and trends in civil society, but also in public administration, in political institutions, in the economy, and in the professional associations of the social partners. At present and in the future, in addition to technical and economic innovations, a multiplicity of minor and major social innovations will become indispensible. Without them, peace and human development in keeping with the standards of industrial potentials will be at risk in a world society of eight to ten billion people, especially in the light of problems such as climate change and the growing gulf between the rich and the poor.

With reference to these challenges and to the assertion of society as an appendix to the economy (Polanyi 1978, p. 82), the most urgent basic innovation of the twenty-first century can be formulated as the *re-integration of the economy in society*. Apart from eliminating shortages, in terms of satisfying real needs, it is imperative to establish strategies and measures allowing for the *management of abundance* as a particularly urgent task in innovation. The ongoing financial crisis demonstrates the need for a variety of types of social innovation: New roles for the state, the banks, finance managers; changes in relations between the stakeholders; the undeniable necessity of norms and regulations and, last but not least, the enforcement of values, making societal values reliable or even the creation of new value systems. It appears irresponsible and untenable continuously to promote unlimited growth in *any sort of* market, whilst expecting the state and the world at large to balance deficits, social disparities and cope with resulting conflicts.

If social innovations are to play a (beneficial) role in the search for remedy, huge efforts will be required to generate and implement a wide variety of social innovations focusing on the *systemic changes* perspective. Among other preconditions, this would require a 'state that is in the position effectively to supervise and sustainably to tax the profits skimmed off on money markets' (translated from Bourdieu 1998, p. 119), preferential treatment of the production and services sectors over critical parts of the financial sector, special funds for a Global Marshall Plan,[14] and a ban on speculation on food. In the EU, these and additional measures should be clustered in a *New Deal for Europe* (Schulmeister 2010).

Taking into account the incredible speed of vast and sensational innovations brought into being by science, technology and industry in the short period of time since about 1960 (after overall recovery from the Second World War), the next 50 years will see no smaller changes with dramatic impacts on individual and everyday life. Before long, synthetic biology will arrive on the stage, designing and constructing new biological parts, devices, and 're-designing existing, natural biological systems for useful purposes'. (http://syntheticbiology.org/) 'Useful purposes' may perhaps be assumed *good for society*, because (many, yet maybe only privileged) people will benefit from new medical treatment in the case of illness, yet also in case they wish to enhance the body and brain. Technologies and biological interventions may improve physiological capacities (health, strength, endurance, avoidance of genetic defects by prenatal diagnosis and treatment) and cognitive competences (brain enhancement by pharmacology, nexus to computers, implanted memory . . .). Such developments will produce chimerical possibilities to create social change and have effects beyond comprehension, extending the human impact on biological processes to potentially crossing the borderline between man-made conditions of living and manipulating human nature itself.

Genetic modification and, in an even wider perspective, synthetic biology can improve the individual's capacity to act, thus enabling the adoption of new roles and engaging in additional relations in order better to cope with challenges.

---

[14] www.globalmarshallplan.org.

Moreover, technologically enhanced, super-intelligent, healthy stakeholders will be capable of implementing new norms and values. Novel norms and values may perhaps benefit the majority of people or social groups concerned. However, the reverse may also turn out to be true. All constituent elements of social innovations mentioned in this article seem to be in place. But still: Can social impact accruing from progress in biological science and innovative technologies based on genetic engineering and synthetic biology be considered *social* innovation? The answer to this question is no, even in case society adopts synthetic biology in the presumably near future, assessed by the majority as having a positive (good) impact. Here, the decisive fact is the vital necessity of society to enable the very existence of human beings. It is not only a fundamental pre-condition that humans need other persons to relate to in order to make a living, based on empathy, division of labour and many other requirements to maintain the vital functions of 'body and soul'. Beyond that, *homo sapiens* has established and advanced his own and indispensible environment of social systems, which is the key to survival as well as to social and cultural development, including features such as science, technology and innovation.

Even enhanced *individual* human properties, physical and cognitive ones alike, would not be sufficient to permit merely the least marginal way of living we know, unless our ancestors had not initiated collective learning as cultural property, including individual potentials to acquire knowledge and to become and remain creative. The human brain of us contemporaries in the twenty-first century is the result of *millions* of years of biological history. In spite of its extremely slow and long-lasting development, the brains of people now living in the *Knowledge Society* do not differ substantially from those of humans living in the *Stone Age* (Linden 2007). What makes a difference is the culture of collective learning in extremely diverse social systems and adaptive modes. On the one hand, brain enhancement cannot compensate this social advantage in an individual's seclusion, yet, on the other, biological upgrading of this sort separates learning, maybe even consciousness and personal self-concepts, from the vital primary societal base (Habermas 2005).

References

Aderhold, J. (2010). Probleme mit der Unscheinbarkeit sozialer Innovationen in Wissenschaft und Gesellschaft. In J. Howaldt & H. Jacobsen (Eds.), *Soziale Innovation. Auf dem Weg zu einem postindustriellen Innovationsparadigma* (pp. 109–126). Wiesbaden: VS Verlag.
Bell, D. (1974). *The coming of post-industrial society*. New York: Harper.
Beniger, J. (1986). *The control revolution. Technological and economic origins of the information society*. Cambridge, MA: Harvard University Press.
Blasy, C., & Gruber, F. (2011). Zur Messbarkeit sozialer Innovationen. In Zentrum für Soziale Innovation (ed.), Pendeln zwischen Wissenschaft und Praxis. *ZSI-Beiträge zu sozialen Innovationen* (pp. 165–172). Vienna-Berlin: LIT.
Bourdieu, P. (1998). *Praktische Vernunft. Zur Theorie des Handelns*. Frankfurt/M: Suhrkamp.
Business Panel on Future EU Innovation Policy. (2009). *Reinvent Europe through innovation. From a knowledge society to an innovation society*. Brussels: DG Enterprise.

Castells, M. (1998). *End of millennium. The information age. Economy, society and culture* (Vol. 3). Malden/Oxford: Blackwell.
Chesbrough, H., Vanhaverbeke, W., & West, J. (Eds.). (2006). *Open innovation. Researching a new paradigm.* Oxford: Oxford University Press.
Durkheim, E. (1984). *Regeln der soziologischen Methode* [1895]. Neuwied/Berlin: Luchterhand.
European Commission. (1995). Green Paper on Innovation. http://europa.eu/documents/comm/green_papers/pdf/com95_688_de.pdf
European Commission. (2010). Europe 2020 Flagship Initiative: Innovation Union. http://ec.europa.eu/research/innovation-union/pdf/innovation-union-communication_en.pdf
Franke, N., von Hippel, E., & Schreier, M. (2006). Finding commercially attractive user innovations. A test of lead user theory. *Journal of Product Innovation Management, 23*, 301–315.
Gibbons, M., et al. (1994). *The new production of knowledge. The dynamics of science and research in contemporary societies.* London: Sage.
Habermas, J. (2005). *Die Zukunft der menschlichen Natur. Auf dem Weg zu einer liberalen Eugenik?* Frankfurt/M: Suhrkamp.
Heidenreich, M. (2003). Die Debatte um die Wissensgesellschaft. In Stefan Böschen und Ingo Schulz-Schaeffer (eds.), Wissenschaft in der Wissensgesellschaft. Opladen: Westdeutscher Verlag.
Hochgerner, J. (1999). *Jenseits der großen Transformation. Arbeit, Technik und Wissen in der Informationsgesellschaft.* Vienna: Löcker.
Hochgerner, J. (2009). Innovation processes in the dynamics of social change. In J. Loudin & K. Schuch (Eds.), *Innovation cultures. Challenge and learning strategy* (pp. 17–45). Prague: Filosofia.
Howaldt, J., & Jacobsen, H. (Eds.). (2010). *'Soziale Innovation. Auf dem Weg zu einem postindustriellen Innovationsparadigma'. Dortmunder Beiträge zur Sozialforschung.* Wiesbaden: VS Verlag.
Hubert, A. et al. (2010). Empowering people, driving change: Social innovation in the European Union. BEPA (Bureau of European Policy Advisers) (Ed.), Brussels. Download (1.9.2011) http://ec.europa.eu/bepa/pdf/publications_pdf/social_innovation.pdf.
Hurrelmann, K. (1990). *Einführung in die Sozialisationstheorien.* Weinheim/Basel: Beltz.
Kesselring, A. (2009). Social innovation in private companies. An exploratory empirical study. In S. Roth (Ed.), *Non-technological and non-economic innovations. Contributions to a theory of robust innovation.* Bern: P. Lang.
Kesselring, A., & Leitner, M. (2008). Soziale Innovation in Unternehmen. Study commissioned by Unruhe Privatstiftung. Vienna: ZSI. https://www.zsi.at/object/publication/1444.
Krippner, G. (2005). The financialization of the American economy. *Socio-Economic Review, 3*(2), 173–208.
Linden, H. (2007). *The accidental mind. How brain evolution has given us love, memory, dreams and god.* Cambridge, MA: Harvard University Press.
Mensch, G. (1975). *Das technologische Patt. Innovationen überwinden die Depression.* Frankfurt/M: Fischer.
Meyer, J. (2010). World society, institutional theories, and the actor. *Annual Review of Sociology, 36*, 1–20.
OECD, EUROSTAT. (2005). *Oslo manual: Guidelines for collecting and interpreting innovation data* (3rd ed.). Paris: OECD.
Palley, T. (2007). Financialisation. What it is and why it matters. http://www.levyinstitute.org/pubs/wp_525.pdf. Accessed 10 May 2012.
Parsons, T. (1976). *Zur Theorie des Sozialsystems [1951].* Opladen: Westdeutscher Verlag.
Polanyi, K. (1978). *The Great Transformation. Politische und ökonomische Ursprünge von Gesellschaften und Wirtschaftssystemen [1st edition: 1944].* Frankfurt/M: Suhrkamp.
Radermacher, F. (2010). *Die Zukunft unserer Welt. Navigieren in schwierigem Gelände.* Essen: Edition Stifterverband.

Reichwald, R., & Piller, F. (2009). *Interaktive Wertschöpfung. Open Innovation, Individualisierung und neue Formen der Arbeitsteilung*. Wiesbaden: Gabler Verlag.

Rosted, J., Kjeldsen, C., & Napier. G. (2009). *New nature of innovation. Study report to the OECD Committee for Industry, Innovation, and Entrepreneurship (CIIE), jointly funded by the Danish and Finnish governments*. Copenhagen: FORA.

Schulmeister, S. (2010). *Mitten in der großen Krise. Ein "New Deal" für Europa*. Vienna: Picus.

Schumpeter, J. (2005). *Kapitalismus, Sozialismus und Demokratie [1st edition: 1942]*. Tübingen: UTB.

Schumpeter, J. (2006). *Theorie der Wirtschaftlichen Entwicklung. Eine Untersuchung über Unternehmergewinn, Kapital, Kredit, Zins und den Konjunkturzyklus [reprint of the 1st edition of 1912]*. Berlin: Duncker & Humblot.

Stehr, N. (1994). *Knowledge societies*. London: Sage.

Stichweh, R. (2004). On the Genesis of World Society: Innovations and Mechanisms, Luzern: http://www.unilu.ch/files/26stwworldsoc.pdf. Accessed 10 May 2012.

Weber, M. (2005). *Wirtschaft und Gesellschaft [1st edition: 1922]*. Frankfurt/M: Zweitausendeins.

Part II
Social Innovation in the Service Sector

What Is Social About Service Innovation? Contributions of Research on Social Innovation to Understanding Service Innovation

Heike Jacobsen and Milena Jostmeier

Abstract The emergent domain of Service Science is dominated by business management and technical views of services and their innovation potential. A sociological theory of services can supply a conceptual framework for services as processes of mediation, of mutual reference, or of interaction or communication between a production situation and a usage situation. On the users' side, participation in service processes may be understood as productive activity (J. Gershuny) in the sense of purposeful proactive engagement with persons or artefacts (objects or symbols). This change in the mode of realising a particular desired "function" can be defined as social innovation. Current discussions on socially desirable forms of service innovation and their chances of gaining widespread acceptance could well profit from this concept. Investigation of each of the elements of productive activity (time, place, resources, objectives, hurdles) and the way they are changed by the diffusion of new services is the task of current studies in the sociology of service innovation.

1 Introduction

As services become more important for the economy and for employment, academic and political interest is necessarily and increasingly drawn to service innovations. How are new services created, how do they become accepted, how do they become established in the long term? What organisational, institutional and political conditions increase service enterprises' capacity for innovation? These

H. Jacobsen (✉)
Brandenburg University of Technology, Cottbus, Germany
e-mail: jacobsen@tu-cottbus.de

M. Jostmeier
Social Research Centre, Dortmund University of Technology, Dortmund, Germany
e-mail: Jostmeier@sfs-dortmund.de

questions have formed the subject of lively debate for a number of years. The emergent domain of *Service Science* is dominated by business management and technical views of services and their innovation potential. Yet by speaking of a "service dominant logic" (Vargo and Lusch 2004) and by defining services as the "application of competencies to the benefit of another entity", a certain importance is also accorded to social factors. The assumption here is that the viewpoint of the user is gaining increasing relevance for all production processes, including the manufacture of material goods. And that this goes hand in hand with a fundamental transformation of all economic processes.

What part can sociology play in contributing to the development or critique of these ideas? Given the long tradition of research and reflection on services by sociologists and by scholars from socio-economics as well, it can be expected that sociological concepts could be very useful for understanding service innovation. In general, sociology is interested in the societal aspects of the tertiarisation process: What changes occur in the labour market, in the families and in everyday life when services sprawl all over the economy and in several realms of our private and public lives? Besides this, particular aspects of work in service functions and sectors as well as of organising services are being investigated by applying sociological concepts (e.g. Korczynski 2002; Jacobsen 2001, 2010; Jacobsen and Voswinkel 2005).

For social sciences-based innovation research the question arises of whether the tertiarisation of innovation generates new problems that fundamentally cannot be dealt with using the categories of analysing the creation, establishment and stabilisation of innovations which up to now have been developed primarily on the basis of technical and material innovations.

In this article an initial answer to this question from the perspective of social sciences-based research on services is being outlined. As a starting point, we first need a definition of services *sui generis*, in other words, not in contrast to production. Services are characterised by a form of mediation between the context of the service offering and the context of the service usage; services only exist when they are realised in practice in the usage context (cf. Jacobsen 2009) (Sect. 2). From this model some assumptions of what this implies for service innovation can be derived (Sect. 3). This leads to a reflection on how existing approaches to social innovation contribute to a better understanding of service innovation under the main question: What is *social* about service innovation? (Sect. 4) We will see that a certain view of social innovation in particular is useful to conceptualise service innovation as social innovation (Sect. 5). Finally, conclusions from this for further investigation will be drawn (Sect. 6).

2 Service Model

Very often the question about the "nature" of services is answered by pseudo-definitions stating what services are *not:* non-material, non-technical, non-storable and so forth. Another approach to defining services is merely classifying them referring back to sectors, industries or functions. Both solutions to obtain a clearer view of what is characteristic for services remain unsatisfying.

Overcoming the long tradition of defining services *ex negativo* by differentiating them from the production of material goods (on the "endless struggle over the definition" cf. Häußermann and Siebel 1995: 148ff) is an important step that needs to be taken before the question raised above whether the tertiarisation of the economy calls for fundamentally new instruments for analysing the associated innovations, can even be asked.

An important step to a substantial definition of services sui generis can be seen in developing a comprehensive service model that covers the main dimensions of services. We suggest this as follows:

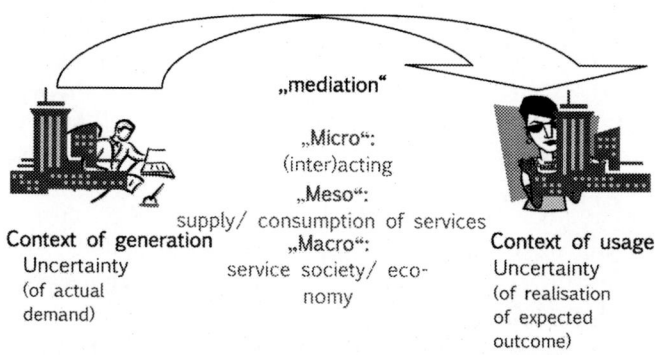

In this model, services are mediation activities between offering and using contexts. We see the two sides of a service: the context of generating or producing services and the context of using or consuming them. Both sides are fraught with uncertainty: In the context of generation it is uncertain whether the service will actually be taken up, while in the context of usage doubts arise as to whether the service is fit for purpose. Between them, the service takes place as a process of mediation, of mutual reference, of interaction or communication between a production situation and a usage situation. As we know this from the service science literature, the "application of competencies" or, more abstract, any process of maintenance in favour of the usage context can be seen as such a process of mediating.

The act of mediation can be investigated and analyzed on three levels:

- The micro-level of action in terms of social interaction;
- The meso-level of product offering by organisations and product consumption by potential users/consumers;
- And the macro-level of service societies characterised by their degree of functional integration whereby the various societal spheres are interlocked and interdependent.

In any service, these levels can be differentiated analytically. Changes on one level have an impact on the other levels. This can serve as a framework for analysing existing as well as new services, including their preconditions and outcomes.

3 Service Innovation

Service innovations represent new possibilities for mediation between the contexts of production and usage. Whether this happens with or without technology is not the crucial issue – the crucial factor for a service innovation is that there must be innovation not only in the production context but also in the usage context; the innovations offered from the production context must be actively accepted in the usage context in order for a new service to be created as mediation between the two contexts. Innovation therefore involves a change in behaviour in the course of using a new service.

Hence we are changing perspective away from the organisation that develops a new service and wants to 'penetrate the market', towards individual or social systems which have to incorporate a new service into their behaviour in order for it to be realised as an innovation. Thus, from the perspective of the user and of the using social system, a new service is a new option for action. When looking at the usage context, we are interested in the relative autonomy of the usage context compared to the production context.

From the perspective of the organisation offering the service, this is mainly just stating the limits of what is possible. A service innovation cannot be manufactured and pushed on the market; it arises in the mediation between the production and usage contexts. The analysis of service innovations requires a closer consideration of the perspective of users and of the using social system. The fact that businesses create new offerings is not a sufficient condition for a service innovation. Users have to act differently – innovatively – in order to allow such new possibilities to become part of practice. This is not an absolute difference compared to innovations of material goods but a relative one. As structural change continues in favour of services, the necessity for innovative behaviour by users becomes central to innovation processes. Innovation research therefore needs a concept for analysing the behaviour of actual or possible users revealing their original contribution to the innovation of services. We suggest that this is all the more urgent given that businesses' innovation strategies are aimed at activating the usage context a great deal more than was previously the case (see for this for example Prahalad and Ramaswamy 2004).

Jeremy Howells (2010) has recently produced a provisional summary of research on service innovation in business economics to date. He identifies three lines of tradition. Originally, new services were understood as being initiated exogenously, that is, through the development of new technologies; they were technology-driven. Countering that, the attempt was made to focus on the special features of services and to trace their innovation back to endogenous – service-driven – factors, to the greater importance of the integration of customers for the service process, for example. Finally, at the present time, a mixed – integrative – interpretation combining both approaches has become established. Integrative means that unlike the endogenous approach, fundamental differences between product innovation and service innovation are not sought, nor is service innovation seen as being initiated from outside, as in the exogenous approach. Instead, Howells states, it is assumed that innovations both of goods and of services are no longer or have not yet been captured in a sufficiently precise definition. In both cases, a change "in the fundamental operation of the economy" (Howells 2010: 4) is starting to have greater effects. According to Howells, this change has shifted the focus from products and services as such to "solutions". In the course of this transformation, networks and value chains have become more important relative to the individual enterprise. "Solutions", one could say, tend to require skills and services of multiple actors. Howells notes that so far there are not any adequate concepts that can provide a framework for distinguishing and understanding "components" and "flows" in the innovation process, and the organisational routines that link them: "[...] gaining a complete understanding of these processes, flows and interactions over time, producing an accepted definition of the elements and stages in each and then enabling this to be applied generically to all or at least parts of the service sector remain elusive" (Howells 2010: 7).

It should be noted that in these research desiderata of economics, the perspective of the "innovating" enterprise as an assertive, agenda-setting actor is largely relativized. Service innovation here is viewed as a process between suppliers or supplier networks and consumers. At the same time, the consumer perspective is being taken increasingly seriously. A more recent approach to the conceptual design of new services takes this particularly far, where the hope is to win over consumers for the "co-creation" of new service experiences (Prahalad and Krishnan 2009). According to this, the new and future basis of value creation would consist in suppliers and consumers together creating "experience environments". This would go far beyond customer support and the inclusion of the customer at the point of sale.

Unlike the "solutions based innovation" approach, which does also depart from the purely organisation-centred view and emphasises an integrated perspective on products and services, in the "co-creation" approach the consumer's life-world and "communities of consumers" are the focus of the innovation strategy. "Although products, services and solutions are, of course, all embedded in an experiences based approach, managerial attention must shift dramatically to focus on the experience space (not products and services) as the locus of innovation and on the experience network (not just the company and its suppliers) as the locus of competence" (Prahalad and Ramaswamy 2003: 16).

The concept of co-creation focuses on the designing of individual experience contexts as a goal in itself. However, action is still guided by the economic interest of the supplier, even if there is a call to move from "managing efficiency" to "managing experiences" (Prahalad and Ramaswamy 2002). The authors assume that, not least, consumers themselves are interested in influencing "value creating processes"; "armed with new tools and dissatisfied with available choices, consumers want to interact with firms and thereby 'co-create' value" (Prahalad and Ramaswamy 2004: 2).

To what extent the concept of co-creation is relevant in practice is a question which cannot be answered here. It should be noted, however, that in these at times extremely euphoric visions of service worlds jointly created by businesses and consumers, critical importance is attached to users' actions. Hence it is no longer only businesses that make offers to consumers through their own agency, for the latter become active themselves in order to create offerings that suit them. Without their active involvement, the specific service is not created. The current strategies that find reflection in these concepts are aimed at a further activation of the usage context.

4 Meanings of Social Innovation and their Relevance for the Understanding of Service Innovation

Our approach from the perspective of social sciences-based service research suggests we should first examine whether the current reassessment of the relevance of social innovation is connected to the further increase in the economic and social importance of services. Can service innovations be meaningfully understood as social innovations? Based on the definition of services as mediation between the creation and usage contexts, and following from the increasing importance of the activation of the usage context outlined above, in this section possible links between social innovation and service innovation are being summarised.

Three periods of thought on social innovation can be differentiated thus far – a classical, a modern and a contemporary one: For the classical period Joseph A. Schumpeter defined innovation as the "establishment of new combinations" of things and forces necessary for production by an entrepreneur (1912: 100). Central to this definition, therefore, is the process of inventing a new kind of combination ("invention") and the self-interested, predominantly economically oriented agency of an identifiable actor. William F. Ogburn identified non-technical inventions as well as technical ones, but for him the former were dependent on the latter: "we understand [...] invention to mean the combination or modification of existing and known material and/or immaterial cultural elements to create a new element" (Ogburn 1969: 56). In this period social innovation was mainly understood as being derived from or subordinated to technological innovation.

In a more modern period Harvey Brooks classified "almost purely technical innovations (e.g. new materials) – socio-technical innovations (e.g. the infrastructure for private motorisation) – social innovations, with the subtypes of market innovations (e.g. leasing), management innovations (e.g. new working time arrangements), political innovations (e.g. summit meetings) and institutional innovations (e.g. self-help groups)" (Brooks 1982 quoted in Zapf 1989: 177). Wolfgang Zapf (1989) freed social innovation from technological determinism by seeing it not – as Ogburn did – as following on from technological innovation, but by seeing it equally as a conditioning factor: social innovations "can be preconditions, attendant circumstances or consequences of technical innovations" (Zapf 1989: 177). On the other hand, he can evidently also imagine social innovation without a direct technological reference when he proposes the following definition: "social innovations are new ways of achieving goals [...] which change the direction of social transformation, are better at solving problems than earlier practices, and which are therefore worth imitating and institutionalising" (Zapf 1989: 177). Social innovation here is understood as a process of problem-solving. If a direction is attributed to social transformation, it is natural that this direction can also be changed, if problems occur in the course of the transformation. The rational society which is implied here, or at least a large number of insightful individuals, can then decide to protect this change of direction institutionally. Understood in this way, a social innovation always means an improvement on a previous state. This ameliorative assumption is based on the idea of an evolutionary process of social development. In this process, conflicts and polarisations are ultimately overcome through insight. Just as, for Schumpeter, the individual entrepreneur has an interest in the establishment of a (technological) innovation, for Zapf society as a whole has an interest in the establishment of a social innovation. However, the parallel ends when it comes to the source of Schumpeter's creative destruction – namely the competition between the various self-interested actors. What drives social innovation, if the competition motive is lacking? Zapf leaves unanswered the questions of what drives social innovations, whether there are driving actors, and who these might be. Following directly on from Zapf, Katrin Gillwald (2000) seeks an answer to this. She also argues from a modernisation theory perspective and emphasises the factors of action, of novelty and of enduringness. However, her definition primarily focuses on the social benefit of a social innovation. Her more differentiated treatment of the level of action makes it possible to distinguish various dimensions of benefit and forms of rationality. Accordingly, the benefit may be ecological, cultural, economic, social or political. Rationalities may be along the lines of protecting the environment, satisfying "higher" needs, efficiency, integration or maintaining the ability to act politically. This portrayal nudges empirical studies of social innovation into the realm of the feasible. However, it is based on the amelioration assumption that Zapf also made, and supposes a holistic idea of social development and social progress.

Over the past few years research on social innovation has been renewed: Geoff Mulgan et al. *(2007)* defined social innovation as "new ideas that work in meeting social goals" and explicitly are not motivated by profit interests. Alexander Kesselring and Michaela Leitner (2008) also share this understanding but focus on a concept of social innovation which can be used for empirical work. They argue for a "parallelisation" of technological and social innovation; they wish to keep them "to a certain extent on the same level" (2008: 19f) Firstly they separate social innovation from social transformation, by attributing to social innovation a "specific practical context, [...] intendedness and hence also the presence of a certain infrastructure (organisations, institutions, organised groups) and responsible actors" (2008: 28). However they include an important limitation in their definition: "Social innovations are elements of social transformation which create new social facts, i.e. they discernibly influence the behaviour of individual people or particular social groups and direct it towards recognised goals which do not primarily follow economic rationality" (Kesselring and Leitner 2008: 28). They state that social innovations have to "generate social benefit" (Kesselring and Leitner 2008: 29), as a result of which they may also come into conflict with other forms of rationality – they explicitly mention economic rationality. The most recent definition has been developed by Howaldt and Schwarz (2010): They focus on "changes in social practices" and in "usage regimes". In doing so, they aim at dissolving some of the constraints implied by former definitions. However, implicitly also they often refer to the common good as being the objective of social innovation when they use examples for their definition.

This overview of the discussion about the definition of social innovation raises some fundamental issues. First, social innovation usually is being *related to technological innovation* either as being subordinated or opposed to technological innovation or as being paralleled with it. It seems to be still difficult to think about innovation without at least clarifying which role new technologies play in them. Social innovation *sui generis*, without reference to technological innovation, mostly seems to remain unusual and sometimes even unthinkable. Second, social innovation usually is seen in connection with *value rationality*, either explicitly or implicitly. Social innovation, so most authors agree upon, should be seen in connection with socially desirable outcomes, they should contribute to the benefit of a society.

Both of these issues raise the question of what is meant by "social" in concepts of social innovation. Three meanings of "social" are to be distinguished:

Discipline	Typical use	Meaning
Psychology	A *social* person or type	s.o. is interested in the wellbeing of others, s.o. likes being together with others
Political Science	A *social* problem	Individualised problems become generalised and addressed as *issues of common interest* (social politics)
Sociology	*Social* action, process, structure	Mutual dependency, humans as fundamentally social beings (socialised)

- A psychological meaning that refers to a personal attitude or character: someone is a social type, is interested in the wellbeing of others or likes being together with others
- A political meaning in the sense of addressing a social problem, that means in talking about generalised individual problems that should be addressed as issues of common interest and for that social politics should find a solution
- A sociological meaning in the sense of social action, social processes and/or social structures. In this meaning the mutual dependency of human acting and the fundamentally social existence of individuals come into the forehand.

The political meaning is overwhelmingly present in existing concepts of social innovation. This is a hindrance to understanding the relevance of social innovation for service innovation. Instead, a more sociological understanding of social innovation is much more useful for this. Innovation that relies on changes in practices of users and consumers can be addressed as social innovation.

5 Users Productive Activity as Key to Understanding Service Innovation

An interesting approach to such a sociological understanding of service innovation as social innovation was already developed nearly three decades ago: Jonathan Gershuny defined social innovation as follows: "(...) over time, the relative desirabilities of two alternative modes of provision for a particular function may change (...) with the consequence that the household changes from one mode of provision to the other. This change in the mode of provision for particular functions (...) will be referred to as 'social innovation'" (Gershuny 1983: 2).

Classical examples for such changes in the mode of provision are transitions from public transport to private automobility forth and backwards or from commercial cleaning services to private washing machines also forth and backwards.

This definition of social innovation therefore focuses on the action and the decisions of users. It is based on the idea that, from the perspective of households, there are functional necessities which can be fulfilled in different ways. How households choose between the alternatives may vary over time. Changing from one option for fulfilling the function to another is called social innovation.

Gershuny reflects that the respective function is not fulfilled as it were automatically once households/users have decided on a particular form. Rather, having made the decision, they still have to act accordingly. He calls this action for the purpose of fulfilling the function "productive activity" (1983: 32ff) Productive activity generates a direct benefit by fulfilling a household-related function – for example, going food shopping serves to bring food into the house. Gershuny separates productive activity from work which generates not only a direct but also an indirect benefit, in particular an income that is available to the household as an exchange value.

Gershuny places his approach in the context of the socioeconomic analysis of tertiarisation and finds that with increasing use of technology, the functions necessary for social reproduction are performed in changing forms of the division of labour. When households decide to buy goods with which they themselves fulfil a specific function "productively actively" instead of consuming the relatively expensive final service, they thereby contribute not to the formation of a society characterised by services but to a self-service society (Gershuny 1981; cf. also Jacobsen 2005).

Compared to the uses of the term "social innovation" that are outlined above, Gershuny's interpretation is fundamentally different in two respects: firstly, social innovation here is conceived not in opposition to technological or organisational innovation, but *sui generis*. Accordingly, social innovation takes place in the action of individuals indicating changes in their routine behaviours – namely the change from one form of function realisation to another.

Secondly, Gershuny's definition of social innovation breaks with the *value rationality* mentioned above, in the sense of goals which are considered socially desirable. Households decide according to the respective benefits to them. At the same time, benefit should not be understood in a narrow sense as economic benefit, such as cost savings, for example. Benefit gains are equally conceivable in other dimensions, such as gains in autonomy in the self-service arrangement. As a result, decisions orientated to the benefit can also be made according to value-rational considerations, but these values do not necessarily refer back to social desirability. Instead, they are primarily orientated to what the individual desires.

This definition of social innovation is helpful for the sociological understanding of service innovations because it explicitly focuses on the action of users. The change of form in which a function is realised starts with the action of the individual and with the decisions taken in the household. In contrast to the definitions mentioned earlier, rather than social innovation "taking place" independently of individuals, individuals now set social innovation in motion through their action and allow it to become part of practice.

Above all, however, this approach also means that social innovation in Gershuny's sense is not something that can be "done" directly by interested enterprises. Efforts to influence users' experience through service innovations, to create new experience environments with them and then exploit these for economic gain, have their origin in businesses' utilisation interests. A definition of social innovation which like Gershuny's can also be related to commercial services but does not view the establishment of these kinds of service innovations as a largely unidirectional way of enterprises impacting on users' life worlds, opens up new possibilities for a better understanding of the process of tertiarisation and the processes of service innovation.

However, important arguments against this concept are its functionalist restriction and its political-economic bias. These critical points make it difficult to apply this understanding of social innovation to service innovation in general. It does not cover sufficiently so many services that are made for fun in a broader sense, and that do not contribute directly to elementary aspects of social and material reproduction, as for example today using social media. We could very well live without them; but today they have become an important part of service sector activities, just to name one example. In addition it does not refer to the fact that individuals get socialised by using or substituting services. This is to say that a more applicable concept of service innovation as social innovation would need to integrate the repercussions of service use and consumption on the individual's life.

6 Résumé

For a first conclusion some general assumptions shall be made:

First, it is useful to analyse the social aspects of service innovation but we have to develop that further carefully avoiding the traps of value rationality and hierarchical orders of technical/non-technical innovation.

Second, service innovation takes place when actors in the usage context are ready to change their expectations and their behaviour – in this sense it is a social innovation. This process is influenced by both sides of the service process, the production as well as the usage context. Service innovation cannot be applied unidirectionally by innovative service providers but must consider the necessary integration of users.

Third, users do not only take part in service production as co-producers but for them services are an integral part of life. Users get socialised when and by using services. Questions in this regard include those of how users access the options for action which open up with new service offerings, what problems they encounter, what opportunities and risks arise for the individual, and what the social consequences are.

Finally, service innovation takes place on all of the three levels of micro, meso and macro interaction more or less at a time and this is not only very interesting for sociology but also useful to be taken into account when politics embark on setting the market objectives (e.g. sustainability or social integration).

References

Brooks, H. (1982). Social and technical innovation. In S. B. Lundstedt & E. W. Colglazier (Eds.), *Managing innovation. The social dimension of creativity, invention, and technology*. New York: Pergamon Press.
Gershuny, J. (1981). *Die Ökonomie der nachindustriellen Gesellschaft. Produktion und Verbrauch von Dienstleistunge*. Frankfurt am Main/New York: Campus.
Gershuny, J. (1983). *Social innovation and the division of labour*. Oxford: Oxford University Press.
Gillwald, K. (2000). *Konzepte sozialer Innovation (Paper der Querschnittsgruppe Arbeit und Ökologie P00-519)*. Berlin: Wissenschaftszentrum Berlin für Sozialforschung.
Häußermann, H., & Siebel, W. (1995). *Dienstleistungsgesellschaften*. Frankfurt am Main: Suhrkamp.
Howaldt, J., & Schwarz, M. (2010). *Soziale Innovation im Fokus. Skizze eines gesellschaftstheoretisch inspirierten Forschungskonzepts*. Bielefeld: Transcript Verlag.
Howells, J. (2010). Services and innovation: New theoretical directions. In F. Gallouj & F. Djellal (Eds.), *Handbook of innovation and services: A multi-disciplinary perspective (Part I, Chapter 3)*. Cheltenham: Edward Elgar.
Jacobsen, H. (2001). Produktionskonzepte im europäischen Einzelhandel: Deutschland, Italien und Schweden. In H. Rudolph (Ed.), *Aldi oder Arkaden* (pp. 23–57). Berlin: Unternehmen und Arbeit im europäischen Einzelhandel.
Jacobsen, H. (2005). Produktion und Konsum von Dienstleistungen: Konsumenten zwischen Innovation und Rationalisierung. In H. Jacobsen, S. Voswinkel (Eds.) Der Kunde in der Dienstleistungsbeziehung – Beiträge zur Soziologie der Dienstleistung (pp. 15–36). Wiesbaden: VS Verlag für Sozialwissenschaften.
Jacobsen, H. (2009). Soziologie der Dienstleistung, Unpublished Habilitation Thesis, Dortmund.
Jacobsen, H. (2010). Strukturwandel der Arbeit im Tertiarisierungsprozess. In B. Fritz, G. Günther Voß, & W. Günther (Eds.), *Handbuch Arbeitssoziologie* (pp. 203–228). Wiesbaden: VS Verlag.
Jacobsen, H., & Voswinkel, S. (2005). *Der Kunde in der Dienstleistungsbeziehung – Beiträge zur Soziologie der Dienstleistung*. Wiesbaden: VS Verlag.
Kesselring, A., & Leitner, M. (2008). *Soziale Innovation in Unternehmen*. Vienna: Zentrum für Soziale Innovation.

Korczynski, M. (2002). *Human resource management in service work.* Houndmills: Palgrave.
Mulgan, G., Rushanara, A., Halket, R., & Sanders, B. (2007). In and out of sync. The challenge of growing social innovations. Research report. London, Download von: youngfoundation (http//www.youngfoundation.org/files/images/In_and_Out_of_sync_Final.pdf, Abruf: 27.10.2010).
Ogburn, W. F. (1969). *Kultur und sozialer Wandel. Soziologische Texte* (Band, Vol. 56). Neuwied/Berlin: Luchterhand.
Prahalad, C. K., & Krishnan, M. S. (2009). *Die Revolution der Innovation. Wertschöpfung durch neue Formen in der globalen Zusammenarbeit.* München: Redline Verlag.
Prahalad, C. K., & Ramaswamy, V. (2002). The co-creation connection. *Strategy and Business, 27,* 1–12.
Prahalad, C. K., & Ramaswamy, V. (2003). The new frontier of experience innovation. *MIT Sloan Management Review, 44*(4), 12–18.
Prahalad, C. K., & Ramaswamy, V. (2004). Co-creation experiences: The next practice in value creation. *Journal of Interactive Marketing, 18*(3), 5–14.
Schumpeter, J. A. (1912). *Theorie der wirtschaftlichen Entwicklung.* Leipzig: Duncker & Humblot.
Vargo, S. L., & Lusch, R. F. (2004). Evolving to a new dominant logic for marketing. *Journal of Marketing, 68*(1), 1–17.
Zapf, W. (1989). Über soziale Innovationen. *Soziale Welt, 40*(1–2), 170–183.

Social Innovation and Service Innovation

Faridah Djellal and Faïz Gallouj

Abstract Social innovation and service innovation issues have developed separately over the last two decades, with too rare intersections between them. Both issues share many points in common, however, and sometimes even describe the same socio-economic reality. This contribution aims to help establish dialogue between these two still marginal but promising fields of economic theory and the social sciences in general. It briefly describes each of these two fields, puts them into perspective, and examines the links between them in a number of different ways.

1 Introduction

The issues of social innovation, on the one hand, and service innovation, on the other, still play a very marginal role in economic theory. The main reason for this neglect is probably the relationship to the market, in the first case, and the relationship to materiality in the second case. In fact, social innovation is often considered as a response to market (and also state) failures and services are primarily defined by their lack of materiality.

However, although these issues are not central to economic theory, they have been the subject of a growing body of literature over the last two decades, and this trend shows no signs of slowing. This success can be explained in particular by the chronic socio-economic crisis experienced by developed economies since the 1970s, demographic change (ageing populations in rich countries, in particular), the failure of development policies, the rise of environmental concerns, and the return to favour of the service society in economic thought and institutional and political debate. What we are witnessing is the challenging of the myths of unproductive services, of low capital intensity, low levels of innovation, poorly

---

F. Djellal (✉) · F. Gallouj
Lille University, Lille, France
e-mail: faridah.djellal@univ-lille1.fr

suited to exchange, on the one hand, and, on the other, the myth of the service society as a "society of servants" (Gallouj 2002a).

As we highlight in this chapter, these two issues have many points in common. Firstly, social innovation is very often a service innovation (a new intangible solution), whether it emerges in a service sector organisation (innovation in services), the industrial or agricultural sectors (service innovation), civil society, social movements or heterogeneous collective entities in which stakeholders from these different fields are involved. However, more generally, beyond this potential identity, efforts to define social innovation and service innovation come up against the same obstacles: a degree of invisibility (to traditional indicators for measuring innovation, such as R&D and the registering of patents), the key role played by informal processes and interaction (co-production), appropriation regime issues, and the failure or inadequacy of public support policies.

Despite these commonalities and this identity (in certain cases), these two research trajectories have rarely intersected, with few exceptions (Gershuny 1983; Crozier et al. 1982; Harrisson et al. 2010, for example). This does not mean, of course, that the economics and socio-economics of services never address the issue of social innovation or that social innovation specialists never touch on the subject of services. It does mean, however, that the substantive dialogue, to the extent that it can be given a tangible form, for example through the exchange of references (mutual citations) between these two scientific communities, is particularly limited. Therefore, in their efforts to define social innovation, social innovation specialists often take the established and solid field of technological innovation as their benchmark and ignore the debates, though close to their own, but less well-established, in the field of innovation in services.

There are several explanations for this strange mutual ignorance. The first explanation, as far as services are concerned, would appear to be the initial focus in the literature on technologist approaches, based on the principle of assimilation, which assumes that innovation in industry and innovation in services have a similar identity, whereas social innovation tends more immediately towards the intangible, non-technological aspects of innovation. A second explanation may be the initial focus of these studies on knowledge intensive business services (KIBS) to the detriment of "proximity" personal services, or public services, which are more sensitive to social innovation. Another explanation is the disciplinary division of labour apparent in these studies. In fact, social innovation is more likely to be a subject addressed by sociologists, whereas the service innovation or innovation in services fields are (mainly) dominated by economics and management sciences.

In the field of innovation in services, the weakening of the "assimilationist" or technologist approach and the rise of "service-based" (demarcative) and "integrative" approaches, alongside the shift from empirical studies of knowledge intensive business services (KIBS) towards less complex services (personal services, local services, "care" services and public services), and the rise of multi-disciplinary approaches, provide a strong argument for a closer relationship between the two issues.

The very aim of this article is to help establish this dialogue between these two issues. The next two sections are devoted to a brief account of the two notions of social innovation and service innovation, from the point of view of their nature, and the way in which they have emerged and are organised. For each notion, they highlight the different analytical perspectives that make them scalable in scope. The fourth section puts the established results into perspective and examines, in different ways, the links between social innovation and services and service innovation.

2 Social Innovation: The Desperate Quest for a Definition

Social innovation remains a particularly fuzzy notion, despite numerous efforts to clarify its meaning. It is heterogeneous, eclectic and flexible in scope (Cloutier 2003; Moulaert et al. 2005; Harrisson et al. 2010; Harrisson and Vezina 2006; Harrisson and Klein 2007; Pole and Ville 2009; Howaldt and Schwarz 2010; Phills et al. 2008; Hamalainen and Heiskala 2007).

Both the noun "innovation" and the qualifier "social" in the expression "social innovation" are problematic. The term *innovation* raises the traditional question of where to draw the line between change and actual innovation. This question is especially relevant to social innovation. A relatively more flexible and looser definition of newness seems to be used in the socio-economics of social innovation, compared with the traditional innovation economics. The qualifier *social* raises even tougher problems to the extent that it can be interpreted in many different ways. It can, in principle, be used to describe any human activity, a particular sector, a particular type of problem, a particular way (method) of approaching a problem (involvement and empowerment), a particular motivation or intention on the part of the innovator, a particular impact of the innovation, the non-economic aspect of economic interventions, etc. (Harrisson et al. 2010; Phills et al. 2008). We therefore need to define the limits of social innovation if we want this concept to have a certain usefulness and relevance. The most common solution consists of defining social innovation with reference and in opposition to business innovation.

2.1 Social Innovation in Opposition to Business Innovation

In their search for an operational definition for and a theory of social innovation, the specialists concerned have naturally turned towards the well-established field of innovation economics, particularly the founding works of Schumpeter and the Neo-Schumpeterian school. Social innovation is therefore considered in opposition to what, for the sake of convenience, we might call business innovation to essentially describe technological innovation, but also organisational innovation.

This general perspective is aptly illustrated by the typology in Table 1 (adapted from Hochgerner 2009). Business innovation includes the categories found in the Oslo Manual (OECD). It covers, as a result, technological product and process innovation and non-technological organisational and marketing innovation. Social innovation, on the other hand, relates to civil society, social movements, the state,

Table 1 Typology of innovation (after Hochgerner 2009)

Technological innovations in economic production		Non-technological innovation on company levels		Social innovations in business, civil society, state		
Product[a]	Process[a]	Organisation[a]	Marketing[a]	Participation	Procedures	Behaviours

[a]Innovation as defined by the Oslo Manual (OECD 2005)

but also business. Hochgerner subdivides social innovation into three sub-categories which are indicative examples: stakeholder involvement, procedures in decision making and behaviours.

This typology raises a number of comments.

1. While it includes technological product and process innovations and several forms of non-technological innovations (organisation, marketing, participation, procedures and behaviours), it omits non-technological product innovation (service innovation). Although excluded from the Oslo Manual for the moment, it is a frequent form of innovation in the services sector. Examples of such forms of innovation include new financial products, new insurance contracts, new fields of consultancy expertise, etc. It is important to include this type of non-technological product innovation within both business innovations and social innovations (cf. Table 2).

2. To better account for social innovation in businesses, we suggest separating it from other fields of social innovation (those implemented by civil society and the state), by introducing a separate type of innovation (Table 2). Social innovation in business may therefore include participation, procedures and behaviours, as well as a product, process, service, organisation and marketing. According to Hillier et al. (2004), "orthodox social science studies in the 1990s used the term 'social innovation' primarily in reference to the transformation of organisations to optimise their efficiency". In other words, social innovations are organisational innovations, such as total quality (see Franz 2010), re-engineering, just-in-time production and self-service. Cloutier (2003) confirms the finding that social innovation in business refers essentially to new forms of work organisation. According to her it is possible, however, to distinguish between two different perspectives in social innovation studies. In the first perspective, social innovation is "a new social arrangement that promotes knowledge creation and technical innovation" without any particular reference to quality of life at work. The second perspective describes new forms of work organisation as social innovations because their primary purpose is to improve quality of life at work.

These discussions highlight a number of problems that arise when we try to draw a line between different types of innovation, starting with the difference between "pure" ("non-social") organisational innovations and social organisational innovations. It is also difficult to draw a line between different types of social innovation, that is, between social innovations relating to participation, procedures and behaviours, on the one hand, and organisational or process innovations, on the other hand. These two groups appear, in certain cases, to be identical and redundant.

Table 2 A new typology of innovation

Business innovation							Social innovation					
Innovation in firms									Innovation in civil society, state			
Technological innovations in economic production		Non-technological innovation on company levels			Social innovations in business				Social innovations in civil society, state			
Product	Process	Organisation	Marketing	Participation	Procedures	Behaviours	Participation	Procedures	Behaviours			
		Nt product (Service)	*Nt process*	*Product* *Marketing*	*Process* *Nt product (Service)*	*Organisation*	*Product*	*Process*	*Organisation*	*Nt product (service)*		

3. Social innovation in civil society, social movements and the state is likely to involve not only procedures, participation and behaviours, as suggested by Hochgerner's typology, but also organisations, processes (unless these two categories are identical to the previous three) and "products", as well as services.
4. This typology should not lead to a static interpretation of, or blind us to, the dynamic relationships between different types of innovation. It is important to note that, as stated by numerous economists (Schumpeter 1942; Freeman 1991), "business" innovations are not independent of social innovations. Technological innovation needs to rely on social innovations to develop effectively. The success of the automobile as a technical artefact is closely linked to social or service innovations, such as garages, petrol stations, driving schools, road signs, insurance and rescue services, car loans, and traffic management systems. Conversely, social innovation can give rise to technological innovations.
5. Neither should this typology restrict innovation, either technological or social, to institutional limits (an organisation or business, civil society, or the state). On the contrary, like technological innovation, and probably to a greater extent, social innovation can develop in heterogeneous networks of variable sizes and involving multiple agents. The open nature of social innovation does not, it should be stressed, make the process of identification and measurement any easier.

2.2 General Characteristics of Social Innovation

Various attempts to define social innovation have highlighted a number of characteristics which help reveal the (fluctuating) outline of this innovation without providing us with a satisfactory definition. Social innovation is therefore often defined in the following terms, which describe its form or nature, its process and stakeholders, its target, and its purposes: it is supposed to be intangible, non-technological, organisational, non-market, informal, local, designed to solve social problems, etc. However valuable in helping us define social innovation these different characteristics do not provide us with indisputable technical criteria.

2.2.1 The Target of Social Innovation

As Cloutier notes (2003) in her excellent review of the literature on the subject, social innovation can aim at three interlinked targets: the individuals whose well-being it seeks to ensure, the environment or territory (considered at a local, regional, national and supranational level) of which it needs to ensure the economic development and moderate any adverse effects (urban growth, pollution, inequality, etc.), and finally the firm or organisation, of which it seeks to increase the performance. In the latter case, social innovation refers mainly to new forms of work organisation and changing power structures.

2.2.2 Form and Nature

Socio-economic studies often refer to social innovation as an intangible or immaterial entity (a new service, organisation, procedure, behaviour, institution, law, etc.). As Cloutier (2003) stresses, "[social innovation] refers mainly to 'ways of doing', actions and practices. It is the opposite of the idea of product." This intangibility assumes that social innovation is the opposite of technological innovation and very closely related to organisational innovation. However, the relationship between social innovation and intangibility is debatable. Without going so far as to consider all technological innovation as a social innovation since it resolves a social problem, there are many examples of technological (and therefore material) innovations with a social purpose (even in the limited sense of inclusion or social cohesion). These could include, for example, clean technologies, generic drugs and telephone help lines. These examples also challenge the strictly organisational nature of social innovation.

2.2.3 Process and Stakeholders

Social innovation differs from traditional innovation not simply in its "nature" but also in its modes of production and its stakeholders. Another key characteristic of social innovation is its local or grass-root nature and the essential participation of users in its emergence and implementation. User participation includes the notion of co-production, which is central to service economics and management. However, its scope may be even wider, since it may also mean the capacity of the user to take charge of or take back control over their life, environment (and territory) and future. Some authors go so far as to define social innovation mainly or even exclusively in relation to this active participation element alone (Lallemand 2001). The production processes in question are often local or grass-root processes in which informality and a variety of stakeholders play a major role. It is not difficult to imagine how a social innovation that is technological in nature could be developed in laboratory conditions without the participation of the user. In the same way, we can find exceptions to the "informal" and "local" ("grass-root") dimensions of social innovation. For example, within a historical perspective, it is possible to list the major changes in the social economy and national political governance within a formalized "top-down" perspective.

2.2.4 Purposes

The purpose of social innovation is not (directly) economic. Promoters of this form of innovation are generally not motivated by the prospect of maximising their profits. Generally, their activity is not-for-profit or generates little profit. The purpose of social innovation is to resolve social problems that cannot be resolved by "traditional" innovation due to market or state failures or disinterest.

More generally, in the search for solutions to different types of problems, the purpose of social innovation is to increase the quality and quantity of life of an individual or group of individuals (Pole and Ville 2009) or enhance their "better-being" (Bouchard et al. 1999). However, the purpose of certain social innovations is also business development. This covers, for example, inclusion schemes for people in difficult social situations, microfinance (the granting of microloans and saving or insurance schemes for poor people excluded from the traditional banking system).

3 Service Innovation: Making "Invisible Innovation" Visible

Although much remains to be done across a range of fields to do justice to and make the most of the business activities driving today's economies to a large extent, the literature on innovation in services has undeniably taken off in recent years (Gallouj and Weinstein 1997; Sundbo 1998; Miles 2002; Gallouj 2002b; Rubalcaba 2006; Windrum and Garcia-Goñi 2008; Tether 2005; Hipp and Grupp 2005). A number of literature reviews have been produced recently (Howells 2007; Gallouj and Djellal 2010). Rather than going into detail about the content of these different works, we will provide an overview of certain results, which are important in our eyes, as a basis for debate with the social innovation field.

3.1 The Specific Nature of Services and Their Impact on Innovation

Extending Adam Smith's observation that "services perish in the very instant of their production", economic studies in this field have sought to define the intrinsic characteristics of these activities. Services are therefore considered as immaterial or intangible and interactive (co-produced).

The fuzziness (immateriality and intangibility) of output has a number of implications for innovation analyses. It can deflect analyses towards the most tangible components of the service, particularly processes (whether they are innovative or not). It makes it difficult to distinguish between product innovation and process innovation, to estimate the degree of newness, and to enumerate the innovation or assess its economic impact (in terms of jobs or impact on sales, for example). The intangible and volatile nature of the "product" compromises efforts to protect the innovation and facilitates its imitation. On the other hand, intangibility makes it possible to envisage the existence of intangible product and process innovations, as well as forms of innovation that aim to make the service less fuzzy (formalization innovation).

Interactivity, the second characteristic of services, refers to a certain form of customer participation in the production of the service. It has different theoretical consequences for innovation, both in terms of its nature and the way in which it is organised. It reveals the importance of certain specific forms of innovation – custom-made innovation and ad hoc innovation – which escape both theoretical apparatus and traditional measurement tools. It does not appear to be compatible with the traditional linear conception of innovation which assumes the existence of specialist R&D structures independent of production and marketing structures. On the other hand it is particularly consistent with the interactive innovation model (Kline and Rosenberg 1986), which focuses in particular on project groups of varying sizes, involving different company professionals as well as customers. Therefore, the customer is not only the co-producer, he may also be the co-innovator, which raises innovation appropriation problems.

3.2 Taking into Account "Invisible" Innovation

As far as the overall concept of innovation in services is concerned, there has been a shift in perspective (according to the framework developed by Gallouj 1994) from assimilation to demarcation followed by integration. The initial reduction of innovation in services to production and, more generally, to the simple adoption of technical systems, was followed by attempts to identify specific forms of innovation invisible to traditional apparatus; innovation in services and in goods were then considered in terms of integration, in a context of convergence between goods and services. *Integration* assumes that innovation in goods and in services, technological innovation (visible innovation) and non-technological innovation (invisible innovation) must be analysed using the same tools.

Visible innovation is innovation measured by traditional indicators, such as R&D and patents. It reflects a technological and assimilationist vision of innovation in which innovation is, in the main, rooted in the production of science-based technical systems. Limiting innovation to such a conception leads to a result in which services are relatively less innovative than industry, despite the advances associated with the inclusion of ICTs. This technological and scientific conception of innovation only reveals the tip of the innovation iceberg.

Invisible or hidden innovation represents a major and still largely neglected field of research that requires further exploration. Invisible innovation is not a homogeneous category. Its diverse expressions are often grouped under the heading of non-technological innovation. This convenient expression hides the sheer diversity of innovation forms, including social innovations, organisational innovations, methodological innovations, marketing innovations, and intangible product and process innovation.

3.3 From a Linear Model to an Open Model

The dynamics of innovation can either be spontaneous (unpredictable) or planned (predictable). Innovation is planned and predictable when it takes place within clearly identified structures (for example, R&D departments and project groups) and in accordance with pre-established processes. Planned innovation activities of this type are, of course, implemented by service organisations. There is a strong theoretical tradition within the management sciences that recommends applying New Product Development (NPD) methodologies to services, that is, considering the creation of new services as part of planned and systematic processes within the framework of a theoretical perspective termed New Service Development (NSD) (Scheuing and Johnson 1989).

However, the literature on innovation in services has focused on the role of interactive structures and processes, forming part of a general open innovation perspective and covering a range of more or less sophisticated and formalised cooperative models.

The general open innovation perspective includes Kline and Rosenberg's chain-linked interaction model or interactive model mentioned earlier. However, it also covers a certain number of unplanned or emergent models such as the rapid application model, the practice-based model, bricolage innovation and ad hoc innovation. The rapid application model is a model in which planning does not precede production, as in the traditional linear model. Once the idea has emerged, it is immediately developed as the service in question is being provided. As such, the service provision process and the innovation process are one and the same (Toivonen 2010). The practice-based model consists of identifying changes in service practices, developing them and institutionalising them. The bricolage innovation model describes change and innovation as the consequence of unplanned activities performed in response to random events, characterised by trial and error and "learning on the job" (Fuglsang 2010; Styhre 2009). Ad hoc innovation (Gallouj and Weinstein 1997) can be defined as the (original) solution development process for a corporate customer problem. This interactive process, which requires the participation of the customer, is described as ad hoc because it is "unplanned" or "emergent", which means that it is consubstantial with the service provision process from which it can be separated only in retrospect. Ad hoc innovation is only recognised as such after the event.

Open innovation also covers specific innovation networks – Public-private innovation networks in services (servPPINs) – that are still relatively unknown[1] but which develop in a dominant service economy. These servPPINs describe the collaboration (co-operation) between public, private and third-sector service organisations in the field of innovation (Gallouj et al. 2013).

---

[1] These innovation networks were the subject of a European project called ServPPIN (The Contribution of Public and Private Services to European Growth and Welfare, and the Role of Public-Private Innovation Networks, FP7).

4 First Elements of a Dialogue Between Social Innovation Studies and Service Innovation Studies

This fourth section puts social innovation, on the one hand, and services and service innovation, on the other, into perspective in order to outline potential areas for debate between the two fields. We will start with a brief overview of what services studies tell us about social innovation and what social innovation studies tell us about service innovation.

4.1 What Services Studies Tell Us About Social Innovation and What Social Innovation Studies Tell Us About Services

As we pointed out in the introduction, social innovation and service innovation issues have, in the main, developed separately with very little interaction between them. In theoretical terms, mutual references between the two fields are therefore rare. Below are some exceptions to the rule.

4.1.1 Gershuny's Vision of Social Innovation: A Restrictive, Technological and Economic Conception

Among the service economics specialists, the author who has taken a close interest in the field of social innovation is Gershuny (1983), the promoter of the self-service theory. According to Gershuny, the advent of the self-service society (or the relative decline of services) can be explained by social innovation, defined as a change in the way a need (function) is satisfied by the consumer. Consumer needs can, in fact, be satisfied in two different ways, either by calling on the *formal* sector (acquiring services from an external service provider) or the *informal* sector (the combination of two factors: a purchased good (equipment) and the work necessary to implement it). There are many examples of this choice including the leisure function, which can be satisfied by going to the theatre, cinema or a concert, or by buying audio-visual equipment. Social innovation is the transition from formal to informal satisfaction. It consists of a dual technological and social component. The implementation of this conceptual apparatus at the analytical and statistical levels leads Gershuny to conclude that social innovation has given rise to a shift from a service society to a self-service society (that is, a preference for the "informal" satisfaction of a need).

4.1.2 Beyond Technological Conceptions of Social Innovation

The social content of social innovation makes it possible to consider an element neglected up to now in purely technological approaches: the participation of the users and their intervention as consumers who have to choose between different solutions. However, Gershuny's contribution from this viewpoint remains limited because he considers social innovation as only consubstantial with material technology.

Normann (1984: 84) gives a much broader meaning to the social content of social innovation. According to him, one of the reasons why service innovation is less spectacular than industrial innovation is that it is founded on social innovations, that is, "innovations that create new types of social behaviour, use social or human energy more efficiently, and link social contexts in a new way". As such, social innovation is not limited to the way in which the customer participates or makes a choice, but also includes:

- Using technical or human production capacities which are unused and which are there to be used. Some IT service firms have therefore been set up to use the overcapacity of the IT departments of large firms (Crozier et al. 1982).
- The introduction, in an organisation, of new functions leading to new roles or sets of roles. An established and well-known example of this type of social innovation is Club Med's "nice organisers" (or G.O.s).
- Linking up contexts and stakeholders with potentially complementary needs. J.C. Decaux is an example of this type of social innovation. The service provided by this company is based on linking up four groups of stakeholders: local authorities to whom bus shelters are provided free of charge and which they are not responsible for maintaining; the advertisers who rent quality, well-maintained advertising media (bus shelters); passengers of buses and the general public who benefit from the advantages offered by this "urban furniture".

4.1.3 Integrating Social Innovation into Representations of Services and Innovation in Services: Characteristics-Based Approaches

The characteristics-based approach to services is a theoretical construction (inspired by the work of Lancaster), which claims to provide an integrated theoretical representation of innovation in goods and services. Gallouj and Weinstein (1997) (see also Gallouj 2002a) define the product as the interlinking of vectors of characteristics and competences: service characteristics [Y], internal [T] and external [T'] technical characteristics, internal [C] and external [C'] competences. Innovation then emerges through the dynamics of these characteristics, which can be added, subtracted, associated, dissociated, etc. Gallouj (2002b, see also Djellal and Gallouj 2010) considers that such a representation is able to take into account certain "social" aspects and certain dimensions of social innovation. It can include sustainable service characteristics, on both a socio-economic and an environmental level (for example, socio-civic service characteristics), and any corresponding technical competences and characteristics.

4.1.4 What Social Innovation Studies Tell Us About Service Innovation

The bridges established by the social innovation school with the innovation in services school seem to be more fragile. Social innovation is much more concerned with forging links with the theory of (industrial) innovation and constructing an identity in relation to it.

Although from a theoretical point of view social innovation tells us nothing or not so much about service innovation, that does not prevent services from often being mentioned in definitions of social innovation (cf. Mulgan et al. 2007; European Commission 2011).

In the same way, many works are devoted to social innovation in particular service activities, without any real link being made with the field of the socio-economics of innovation in services. These service activities include home help services (Degrave and Nyssens 2008), public services in general (Barreau 2002), etc.

A few rare (and recent) works, lastly, confine themselves to briefly highlighting (without going into detail) the need to add innovation in services issues to the research agenda on social innovation. This is the case for Howaldt and Schwarz (2010) and Mulgan et al. (2007).

4.2 Putting Social Innovation and Service Innovation into Perspective

We will address a number of points (similarities, differences, etc.) in this section that merit debate or should form the subject of a more in-depth debate between social innovation and service innovation.

4.2.1 Social Innovation: Innovation in Services and Service Innovation

The links between social innovation and services can be considered from two different angles: one sectoral (social innovation as innovation *in* services) and the other functional (social innovation as service innovation).

A specific characteristic of social innovation is that it can develop in any socio-economic field and any sector: inside and outside firms, in the public, semi-public and private sectors, in services, in the industrial and agricultural sectors, in civil society, etc. It is often a service innovation, even when it does not emerge in the services sector. In fact, whatever the sector in question (including industry and agriculture), social innovation often consists of supplying "services" to address socio-economic problems.

However, although it transcends economic sectors, tertiary and service activities are a particularly fertile environment for social innovation. While it concerns all services, it has enjoyed particularly strong growth in the following sectors: the public sector, personal services and in particular the sector of social and solidarity economy or "third sector". This key relationship between social innovation and service sectors can be explained in a number of ways. It can be explained primarily by the particular nature of service activities, which are based on intensive social interactions between consumers, users and producers. It can also be explained by the nature of the values (fairness and solidarity) prevailing in the public and third sectors.

4.2.2 Theoretical Perspectives

The field of innovation in services, like that of social innovation, seeks for theoretical frameworks capable of taking into account their nature and dynamics. The obvious point of reference for both fields is industrial innovation and it is therefore not surprising that they have attempted to develop and define themselves in relation to the solid academic field of industrial innovation. However, despite this common anchoring point, these theoretical perspectives have followed different paths to arrive at the same result: taking into account both the technological and non-technological dimensions.

In fact, as we mentioned in the first section, in the services field, the issue of innovation has moved through a number of stages, from a lack of recognition to an assimilation to technological (or more generally industrial) innovation, then to demarcation and finally integration or synthesis. The assimilationist perspective (according to which innovation in services is similar to innovation in industry) has long been the dominant approach and it continues to be influential today.

It is the demarcation perspective, on the other hand, which immediately dominated the social innovation field, defined as it is in opposition to industrial innovation (technological innovation). The assimilationist (or at least partially assimilationist) perspective which takes into account certain forms of technological innovation in social innovation (such as green technologies) is a fairly late development.

4.2.3 The Nature and Measurement of Innovation

Intangibility is an obvious point in common long debated by both the social innovation and service innovation literature. This commonality underlines how certain service innovations are social innovations. However, it is not, of course, sufficient to systematically establish an identity between service innovation and social innovation. In fact, as seen in section two, certain "intangible" results of social innovation are not products/services but rules, behaviours, laws and institutions. In addition, innovation in services, just like social innovation, is not necessarily intangible, since it can in both cases be embodied in a technical artefact.

Like service innovation, social innovation is difficult to grasp in a survey. Since they exist in a wide variety of forms, including products, services, processes, organisations, principles, laws and institutions, and especially a combination of all or part of these elements, they are difficult to measure. A sustainable tourism package or fair trade, for example, is difficult to fit into the official categories of questionnaires. They are combinatorial by nature and newness is often the result of a combination of already existing elements. Sustainable tourism combines elements such as hotels, restaurants, transport, booking arrangements, natural landscapes, etc. The problem, in the case of social innovations, also relates to the institutional unit that takes responsibility for them. It no longer concerns just the firm. It also involves analytical categories - citizens or heterogeneous groups containing a large number and variety of stakeholders - which are difficult to adapt to surveys. However, although international institutions have made considerable efforts to develop indicators to facilitate the measurement of innovation in services (Oslo Manual, OECD), this is not the case for social innovation.

4.2.4 The Issue of Appropriation

Within the framework of service innovation, the issue of appropriation regimes focuses not on the legitimacy of protection but on the technical methods of appropriating innovations which do not fall within the scope of conventional technical methods, such as patents (Blind et al. 2010). Within the social innovation framework, the issue of protection is rarely raised or is not considered as a legitimate issue. A social innovation is a success when it goes beyond its promoters, in other words, when it is imitated by others. This applies to microcredit, for example, and the famous Grameen Bank created by Muhammad Yunus and which won the Nobel Peace Prize, or the Restos du cœur food service for the homeless. This conclusion should be put into context, of course, because it is more difficult to apply when considering material artefacts. In addition, appropriation can be a source of conflict when social innovation is delivered by hybrid networks containing stakeholders from varying backgrounds (public, private and civil society). In fact, appropriation regime approaches differ between public and non-profit organisations and private organisations. The first are working in the public interest and distribute knowledge to a wide audience. The second are concerned with private appropriation of value added sources.

4.2.5 Organisational Modes for Innovation

The participation of the customer and the user (co-production) plays a central role in both service innovation and social innovation. In the case of social innovation, certain authors do not hesitate to define the essential nature of social innovation in relation to co-production, in other words, to identify the nature of innovation with its mode of organisation. The linear innovation model is conceivable in both fields of research. In both cases, material artefacts can be developed in a laboratory system according to a linear procedure. In the same way, the implementation of certain new services (particularly financial or insurance services) can fall within the scope of the linear and "stage-gate" approach of the "New Service Development" (NSD) models. However, in social innovation, as in service innovation, what dominates is openness and interaction, along with informal and unplanned activities. The partnerships, which we have called public-private innovation networks in services (servPPINs) (Gallouj et al. 2013), are new institutional arrangements that take into account the way in which different stakeholders interact to produce not only technological innovations but also social and service innovations.

4.2.6 Performance Measurement Issues

To assess the performance of service organisations, the services economics has developed a multi-criteria assessment tradition that can be applied to social innovation, whether it relates to services or otherwise (Gadrey 1996; Djellal and Gallouj 2008). Drawing freely on the work of the School of Conventions (Boltanski and Thévenot 1991), it is assumed that the effects of social innovation can be defined and evaluated according to different justificatory criteria corresponding to the five following types of performance: industrial and technical performance (focusing on volume and traffic evaluations), market and financial performance (focusing on monetary and financial operations), relational performance (relating to interpersonal links), civic performance (relating to equality, fairness and justice), and reputational performance (relating to brand image).

5 Conclusion

Social innovation and service innovation are two still marginal but particularly dynamic fields of research that are in what Kuhn describes as a pre-paradigmatic phase, that is, a period in which a multitude of definitions and more or less contradictory theories compete with each other without one imposing itself on the others. These fields have both been developed (in positive and negative ways) based on the well-established academic fortress of industrial and technological innovation. Despite numerous analytical affinities (and even sometimes the same identity), and similar theoretical and methodological problems, these two fields have developed in parallel, only intersecting on rare occasions.

This chapter has endeavoured to establish a certain dialogue between these two fields of research, with mutually rewarding results for both. The fact that social innovation is often a service innovation but also just as often (and increasingly) an innovation *in* services makes this dialogue all the more desirable. In fact, the services sector is a particularly fertile ground for social innovation. This is true of market services, taking into account the density of social interactions (particularly with customers) that characterise them. It is even more true of public administrations, in which the density of these social interactions is formed in a "public service spirit" based on the principles of fairness, equality of treatment and continuity. This is also true to an even greater degree for the rapidly expanding conglomeration of tertiary activities in developed economies, which are grouped under the term "third sector".

The areas for dialogue raised in this exploratory contribution are the theoretical perspectives favoured, the nature of innovation and the question of its identification and measurement, its modes of organisation, its appropriation regimes and the evaluation of its impacts. However, other areas would also merit attention, in particular public policies to support social innovation and service innovation. A better understanding of social innovation in the light of service innovation and vice versa is likely to help reduce even further the hidden or invisible innovation gap in our economies and enable us to advance towards a new comprehensive innovation paradigm.

References

Barreau, J. (2002). In F. Djellal & F. Gallouj (Eds.), *Les services publics français et l'innovation sociale* (pp. 165–185).
Blind, K., Evangelista, R., & Howells, J. (2010). Knowledge regimes and intellectual property protection in services: A conceptual model and empirical testing. In F. Gallouj & F. Djellal (Eds.), *The handbook of innovation and services*. Cheltenham: Edward Elgar.
Boltanski, L., & Thévenot, L. (1991). *De la justification. Les économies de la grandeur*. Paris: Gallimard.
Bouchard, C. (1999), Recherche en Sciences Humaines et Sociales et Innovations Sociales. Contribution à une Politique de l'Immatériel. Conseil Québécois de la Recherche Sociale, Groupe de Travail sur l'Innovation Sociale.
Cloutier, J. (2003). *Qu'est-ce que l'innovation sociale?*, Cahier de recherche du CRISES, no ET0314, UQAM, novembre.
Crozier, M., Normann, R., & Tardy, G. (1982). *L'innovation dans les services*, Mission à l'innovation, rapport no. 8, mars.
Degrave, F., & Nyssens, M. (2008). L'innovation sociale dans les services d'aide à domicile. Les apports d'une lecture polanyienne et féministe, *Revue française de socio-économie*, 2008/2, 79–98.
Djellal, F., & Gallouj, F. (2008). *Measuring an improving productivity in services: Issues, strategies and challenges*. Cheltenham: Edward Elgar.
Djellal, F., & Gallouj, F. (2010). Innovation in services and sustainable development. In C. A. Kieliszewski, P. P. Maglio, & J. C. Spohrer (Eds.), *The handbook of service science* (pp. 533–557). New York: Springer.
European Commission. (2011). FP7 Cooperation Work programme 2011, theme 8, Socio-economic sciences and humanities.
Franz, H.-W. (2010). Quality management is ongoing social innovation. In K. Müller, S. Roth, & M. Zak (Eds.), *Social dimension of innovation* (pp. 115–130). Prague: Linde.
Freeman, C. (1991). Innovation, change of technoeconomic paradigm and biologico analogies in economics. *Revue économique*, no. 2, mars, 211–232.
Fuglsang, L. (2010). Bricolage and invisible innovation in public service innovation. *Journal of Innovation Economics*, 1(5), 67–87.
Gadrey, J. (1996). *Services: la productivité en question*. Paris: Desclée de Brouwer.

Gallouj, F. (1994). *Economie de l'innovation dans les services, Logiques économiques*. Paris: Editions L'Harmattan.

Gallouj, F. (2002a). Innovation in services and the attendant old and new myths. *Journal of Socio-Economics, 31*, 137–154.

Gallouj, F. (2002b). *Innovation in the service economy: The new wealth of nations*. Cheltenham: Edward Elgar.

Gallouj, F., & Djellal, F. (Eds.). (2010). *The Handbook of Innovation and Services: A multidisciplinary perspective*. Cheltenham: Edward Elgar.

Gallouj, F., & Weinstein, O. (1997). Innovation in services. *Research Policy, 26*(4–5), 537–556.

Gallouj, F., Rubalcaba, L., & Windrum, P. (2013). *Public private innovation networks in services*. Cheltenham: Edward Elgar (forthcoming).

Gershuny, J. (1983). *Social innovation and the division of labour*. Oxford: Oxford University Press.

Hamalainen, T. J., & Heiskala, R. (Eds.). (2007). *Social innovations, institutional change and economic performance* (pp. 52–79). Cheltenham: Edward Elgar.

Harrisson, D., & Klein, J. L. (2007). Introduction: Placer la société au centre de l'analyse des innovations. In J.-L. Klein & D. Harrisson (Eds.), *L'innovation sociale: Émergence et effets sur la transformation des sociétés* (pp. 1–14). Québec: PUQ.

Harrisson, D., & Vézina, M. (2006). L'innovation sociale: une introduction. *Annals of Public and Cooperative Economics, 77*(2), 129–138.

Harrisson, D., Klein, J.-L., & Leduc Browne, P. (2010). Social innovation, social enterprise and services. In F. Gallouj & F. Djellal (Eds.), *The handbook of innovation and services: A multidisciplinary perspective* (pp. 197–218). Cheltenham: Edward Elgar.

Hillier, J., Moulaert, F., & Nussbaumer, J. (2004). Trois essais sur le role de l'innovation sociale dans le développement territorial. *Géographie Economie et Société, 6*, 129–152. 2004/2.

Hipp, C., & Grupp, H. (2005). Innovation in the service sector: The demand for service-specific innovation measurement concepts and typologies. *Research Policy, 34*(4), 517–535.

Hochgerner, J. (2009). Innovation process in the dynamics of social change. In J. Loudin & K. Schuch (Eds.), *Innovation cultures. Challenge and learning strategy* (pp. 17–45). Prague: Filosofia.

Howaldt, J., & Schwarz, M. (2010). Social Innovation: Concepts, research fields and international trends, Sozialforschungsstelle Dortmund ZWE der TU-Dortmund.

Howells, J. (2007). Services and innovation: Conceptual and theoretical perspectives. In J. R. Bryson & P. W. Daniels (Eds.), *The handbook of service industries* (pp. 34–44). Cheltenham: Edward Elgar.

Kline, S., & Rosenberg, N. (1986). An overview of innovation. In R. Landau & N. Rosenberg (Eds.), *The positive sum strategy: Harnessing technology for economic growth*. Washington, DC: National Academy Press.

Lallemand, D. (2001). *Les défis de l'innovation sociale*, Issy-les-Moulineaux, ESF Editeur.

Miles, I. (2002). Services innovation: Towards a tertiarization of innovation studies. In J. Gadrey & F. Gallouj (Eds.), *Productivity, innovation and knowledge in services* (pp. 164–196). Cheltenham/Northampton: Edward Elgar.

Moulaert, F., Martinelli, F., Swyngedouw, E., & Gonzalez, S. (2005). Toward alternative model(s) of local innovation. *Urban Studies, 42*(11), 1969–1990.

Mulgan, G., Tucker, S., Rushanara, A., & Sanders, B. (2007). Social innovation: What it is, why it matters and how it can be accelerated, Skoll centre for social entrepreneurship, Oxford Said Business School, Working paper, The Young Foundation.

Normann, R. (1984). *Service management: Strategy and leadership in service business*. New York: Wiley.

OECD. (2005). *"Proposed guidelines for collecting and interpreting technological innovation data", Oslo manual*. Paris: OECD.

Phills, J. A., Deiglmeier, K., & Miller, D. T. (2008). Rediscovering social innovation, *Stanford Social Innovation Review, 6*(4), 34–43.

Pole, E., & Ville, S. (2009). Social innovation: Buzz word or enduring term? *The Journal of Socio-Economics, 38*, 878–885.
Rubalcaba, L. (2006). Which policy for innovation in services? *Science and Public Policy, 33*(10), 745–756.
Scheuing, E. E., & Johnson, E. M. (1989). A proposed model for new service development. *Journal of Service Marketing, 3*(2), 25–35.
Schumpeter, J. (1975[1942]). *Capitalism, socialism and democracy*. New York: Harper.
Styhre, A. (2009). Tinkering with material resources: Operating under ambiguous conditions in rock construction work. *The Learning Organization, 16*(5), 386–397.
Sundbo, J. (1998). *The organisation of innovation in services*. Copenhagen: Roskilde University Press.
Tether, B. (2005). Do services innovate (differently)?: Insights from the European innobarometer survey. *Industry and Innovation, 12*, 153–184.
Toivonen, M. (2010). Different types of innovation processes in services and their organisational implications. In F. Gallouj, & F. Djellal (Eds.), *The handbook of innovation and services* (pp. 221–249). Cheltenham: Edward Elgar.
Windrum, P., & Garcia-Goñi, M. (2008). A neo-Schumpeterian model of health services innovation. *Research Policy, 37*(4), 649–672.

Innovators at Risk in the Public Service

Stuart Conger

Abstract Innovation is a threat to the status quo in the public service and therefore there are many barriers for the innovator. Several of the barriers will be illustrated including: (1) top management desires innovation but is stymied by special interests deeper in the organization; (2) management thinks its innovative by instituting only incremental change; (3) management initiates an innovation without adequate support; (4) the apparent buy-in by various levels of management masks their opposition; and (5) the arrival of new management with a new agenda. Innovators have a short life expectancy in government.

1 Introduction

For some 35 years I worked on innovative projects in the Canadian public service and had to acknowledge that innovation in government is virtually a violation of the rules of a well-organized bureaucracy. Joyce (2007) identified risk of failure and rewards, incentives and disincentives as key problems in the Government of Canada.

In this paper I will examine four risk areas, then I will present some personal observations and experiences I had trying to move innovations forward. I could find no literature describing the perils that innovators face and, as a result, I have had to rely on 50 years of personal observation during which time I personally promoted certain innovations and witnessed other people doing the same.

1. *Risk of Failure*: "Media and opposition parties are always eager to expose public sector failures and pillory public servants involved, with potentially disastrous effects on their careers" (Borins 2006). These and similar factors that result in significantly lower risk tolerance in the public sector are inherent to most

S. Conger (✉)
Retired from Canadian Ministry for Human Resources and Skills Development, Ottawa, Canada
e-mail: stuconger@gmail.com

government and public sector structures. They can be moderated but it is unrealistic to expect risk tolerance for public sector innovation to be brought into line with that in the private sector.
2. *Rewards and Incentives; Resistance and Disincentives*: In Canada, opinions expressed by Deputy Ministers "that the reports of the Office of the Auditor General had an inhibiting influence on innovation and risk-taking among public servants" prompted the Auditor General and the Public Policy Forum to collaborate in a round table discussion to inquire more generally into constraints on innovation. A useful discussion paper prepared for that discussion identifies six areas of constraint including the following (Public Policy Forum 1998). All quotes are from the report.

   2.1 *Accountability – or blame?*: "The reality is that over the last decade or more, politicians have demanded more and more that public servants be held accountable for departmental actions" and that "there is a perception that public servants who make mistakes, even if under the orders of their superiors, will pay a heavy price" (pp. 5–6).
   2.2 *Empowerment and changing infrastructure*: It is suggested that the lack of success of the government's 'Public Service 2000' initiative in reducing barriers to empowerment "would seem to indicate that the current environment in the public service is not conducive to creating the dynamic, fluid context needed to foster innovation and risk-taking among managers and staff in government" (p. 6).
   2.3 *Capacity*: "Managers are still being asked to 'do new with less' without being given the required support" (p. 7).
   2.4 *Values and ethics*: The paper rather depressingly concluded, "It may be that in the current government culture, heroic efforts will be required to counteract the effects of the disbelief system on the attitudes of executives and staff towards risk-taking" (p. 8).

3. *Leadership*: David Albury (2005) notes that a "senior level champion for each innovation is vital, especially for support and determination through the hard times which nearly all innovations encounter during their development" (p. 51). He goes on to note that the culture of creativity and diversity that is necessary to generate innovation needs "leadership which provides clear direction and goals but without detailed control" (p. 53).
4. *Funding*: Although small-scale innovation may be able to proceed without funding, or by squeezing necessary funds out of an individual manager's budget, any significant innovation project will need adequate funding if it is to succeed. This factor is particularly important given that innovation projects have an inherently high risk of failure. Although inadequate resources were not the most frequently reported obstacle cited in Borins' study, it was the one that innovators overcame the least frequently (Borins 2006). Albury similarly noted short term budgets and planning horizons as a barrier to innovation (2005).

As has already been suggested there are many barriers lurking in the shadows to frustrate the innovator. I'd like to address several of the classic cases, illustrated by some real life examples that I have witnessed and experienced. The innovators worked conscientiously to improve the effectiveness of the departments, and they were given ample funds for their projects, but they were on their own when difficulties arose.

2 Classic Situation Number One: Management Desires Innovation but Is Stymied by Special Interests Deeper in the Organization

From time to time senior executives recognize that new ideas and new methods are required to deal more effectively with the needs of the organization or of its clients. They have heard of a variety of problems in their organization including: bureaucratic slowness; poor communications between departments; lack of coordination; inefficiencies; and, failures by their clients to benefit from the programs intended to help them. These executives look at the key people reporting to them and wonder if any is capable of making or even accepting an innovation because generally they have grown up in the organization, have a commitment to traditional ways of working, and have an empire based on current practices which they want to protect. The staff are also aware that some employees who have attempted to introduce innovations have run afoul of strong interests in the organization that are not keen on the innovations and who seek opportunities to restrict the new efforts, to humiliate the champions of change and even engineer their removal or redeployment. This symptom is sometimes given inadequate attention by authors enamoured of innovation, as in the following examples:

Example 1. Advocates of innovations enthuse over the role of the innovator and fail to recognize that the champion of an innovation may become a sacrificial lamb on the altar of doing.

Example 2. Kay (2010) argued that a social innovator must be entrepreneurial. Someone who is an entrepreneur-innovator starts by dreaming up, thinking over, and becoming excited about putting together specific ideas for an innovative proposal. He or she wages a relentless and enthusiastic campaign with no opposition (except possibly apathy). He or she is a happy warrior Kay has seriously underestimated the power and influence of those opposed to innovations and innovators.

3 Classic Situation Number Two: Management Thinks It's Responding to the Need for Innovation by Instituting Incremental Change

Much as a few government departments and social agencies may claim that they want to see innovation, they leave it up to individuals to take the initiative rather than establishing an adequately resourced branch charged with innovation that will create or find new methods and then demonstrate their merits within the organization. The organizations may have an office to ferret out waste but not one to introduce changes other than mere procedural efficiencies.

4 Classic Situation Number Three: Management Initiates from Top Down Without Adequate Support or Follow-Through

Sometimes senior executives or even boards of directors are persuaded to adopt an innovation that they are convinced will enhance the organization's operations but they may not have ascertained if the organization actually wants it and has the resources to implement it. Because it is something new, the practitioners may well resist implementing it in favour of current practices.

Example 1. There are many school boards in Canada who invested in excellent computer-assisted career guidance systems because Board members thought that career guidance was very important and that computer-assisted career guidance was superior to what was being offered students in the schools. These new systems were seldom used because the school counsellors were burdened with administrative tasks and saw an urgent need to provide personal, rather than career, counselling. The Boards failed to recognize that additional staff would be required to implement the computer-assisted career guidance system. The original advocate was happy that he made the sales of the computer systems but dismayed that they were not used to the extent that he had expected.

5 Classic Situation Number Four: Hostility to an Innovator Is Displaced

Employees with the talent for the creation of innovative services often have difficulty rising in the organization structure unless they hide their innovative ideas. This is a frustration for senior executives who want innovation to come up through the ranks. One approach that is often used by executives in the hope of innovations is to spot these people and give them a special project to create something new and have them report directly to the executive. The fact that the individual has worked in the lower ranks gives some assurance that the resulting innovation will be practicable.

Innovations are likely to cause changes in the status of some individuals and groups within the organization and thereby prompt opposition to the changes. Sometimes the opponents of an innovation are afraid to criticize the innovator directly and engage in creating collateral damage. For example, I was assigned to prepare recommendations for the Canadian "War on Poverty" and I came up with several proposals. One was quickly approved by my boss's boss but equally disliked by my immediate superior. He was angry with me but did not want to confront me directly because of his boss's enthusiasm for the project and his resentment was directed at my secretary by refusing to speak to her! Management desiring progress on approved innovations must remain alert to roadblocks and work to keep everyone involved onside.

6 Classic Situation Number Five: Apparent Buy-in by Key Highly Placed Management, Masking their Unstated Opposition, or Even Hostility

Example 1. There can be passive opposition even at senior levels.
I had suggested to the deputy minister of a government department that there was a need for a certain new policy and he readily agreed. After a draft of the policy was prepared he put it on the agenda for a senior executive committee meeting comprising the senior executives at headquarters and the 10 regional offices. Most of the regional executives were opposed to the proposed policy because it would result in forcing them to reorganize their district and local offices and give a certain priority to one activity that was low on their priority lists. At the beginning of the meeting the deputy minister praised the proposed policy and then asked for comments. The first executive to speak praised the policy in specific terms and the deputy said: "I see you have some notes there and I would ask you to give them to the secretary to put in the minutes." In handing his notes to the secretary he said: "My notes are in two columns: one in favour of the policy and one opposed. Ignore the latter for the minutes, I just came prepared to support the boss and am glad he made his opinions known at the first." His lack of commitment later showed up in his indifferent efforts to implement the approved policy. The executive committee that was reluctant to voice objections approved the new policy unanimously. Like some other senior executives who are pleased with an innovation, the deputy minister failed to see the opposition in the immediate rank below him. The policy was implemented but with a greater struggle than would have occurred if the deputy minister had seen the opposition and addressed the issues.

7 Classic Situation Number Six: Opposing Forces Within the Organization Can Lead to Disaster or Success Depending on How Potential Allies Are Mobilized

Example 1. Success through making useful tactical concessions: National union offices can have different priorities from local offices.
It is natural to think of unions as likely to oppose innovations on the grounds that they might have a negative impact on their members. Yet some unions have been known to advocate and even negotiate for changes that might not be popular among all the

union membership. The counsellor training program in the Canadian employment service is a case in point. The national union had argued for some time that all employment counsellors should be trained to a much higher level. This demand was the starting point for a plan for the competency-based employment counsellor training program. An important element of the plan was examinations of competence.

At first the national union resisted the idea of its members being tested but finally agreed providing there would be very good training and that the counsellors could take the exams more than once if they failed. There was, however, considerable opposition by the regional union leadership and they insisted that they should be heard before the national union committed itself further. As a result, the national union asked headquarters staff responsible for the proposed program to meet with representatives of the regional branches for one day per region (there were 10). The meetings were tense and the visitors dealt with the union's concerns at length, focussing on the safeguards to their members. The locals were still not keen but the national union, having argued for a training program, would not back down and the project was formally approved by the union and implemented by the department. Some counsellors took early retirement or re-assignment rather than take the training. Unions, like other organizations, have different priorities at different levels, and the innovator needs to know where support will come from.

Example 2. Success through cultivating the potential beneficiaries: National associations also have different priorities between head office and local branches. At one time I was working for the Canadian Department of Industry where I was responsible for creating and implementing a national small business management training program. Following examples that I had seen in Denmark and Switzerland I had decided that the courses should be organized in local communities by the local chambers of commerce or similar organizations and taught by local subject matter specialists using prepared teaching guides. Because I wanted to involve the local chambers of commerce I thought it would be helpful to get the support of the national office of the Chamber. When I went to their headquarters I got a cold and unsympathetic audience who demanded to know how much money the government was spending on this project. Dismayed but not discouraged, we approached many local chambers who quickly became enthusiastic and organized many courses. In time, the head office of the Chamber heard of the success that its branches had with the program and complained to the government that they had not been consulted! I was delighted to report the name of the person I had met and the date.

Shortly after I had got the training program implemented across the country there was an election and the government changed. The new minister of Industry said that he wanted the department to focus on policy and discontinue programs such as mine. As it so happened, another federal department was providing funding to the provinces to implement my program and when it learned that my program was to be cancelled it arranged to have the program and me transferred to it. It was then that I learned the advantage of being sponsored by two different departments or agencies. I likened it to the first principle of child psychology: what you can't get from mom you can get from dad. It is a great protection for an innovation, and the innovator.

Example 3. Success through osmosis from allies. Innovation doesn't necessarily end with the new idea or invention, but often requires creative thinking along the entire path from invention to widespread implementation. An interesting example arose in the Canada Revenue Agency that collects Canadian federal government taxes. CRA was always in the forefront of the application of information technology, but when they came to the point of actually putting the computer in the hands of the front line staff, they had to learn and apply a few lessons that took them beyond mere technology. Case Management, a breakthrough innovation back in the eighties, is an interactive technique for enabling a case worker such as an auditor or a collector to conduct all his or her work without reference to hard copy documentation or reference material, including even the original tax returns. To the IT organization's dismay, the older collectors viewed this approach with great suspicion and refused to accept it on the stated basis that it would reduce their productivity, while the younger ones, possibly more computer literate, were apprehensive but curious and willing to give it a try.

After exhaustive education, information sessions, reassurance and promotion, all to no avail, the organization decided to allow those who were willing, to try the new technology, while those opposed were permitted to stay with the traditional method. The only stipulation was that both groups had to be intermingled and were to compare errors, objections and case closing results on an ongoing basis. It wasn't very long before the traditionalists could observe the enthusiasm and greatly improved outcomes of the automated group, and gradually they asked to be converted over. Today, no one would consider going back, and on the contrary, the older more experienced collectors became the richest source of suggestions and ideas for system enhancement. The lesson here is that sometimes for the innovator, it works well to go with the resistance, bend with the wind, and learn how to develop allies.

8 Classic Situation Number Seven: The Forces of Darkness Sometimes Win

Innovators have a short life expectancy in government. Innovation does not strengthen the status quo and threatens the established practices and organization. Innovators are born not trained. They have an unusual combination of scientific interest and entrepreneurial drive. The entrepreneurial orientation makes them frustrated with bureaucratic procedures and they often find innovative ways of getting things done. For example, many workers at all levels tend to interpret their jurisdiction quite narrowly whereas enterprising innovators consider the official definition of their jurisdiction as a starting point.

I knew a man at a senior level in a government department who was quite possibly the greatest innovator in all of the Canadian government. He conceived and implemented a number of renowned innovations that included federal and provincial departments, companies, colleges and schools. He was very persuasive, had a contagious enthusiasm and was very successful and well regarded by all who knew him outside his department. But many in the department were jealous of the resources that he was able to get for his projects and they decided that he was doing so many things so fast that perhaps he was cutting corners. They successfully urged the financial management people to conduct an audit of his management practices. They found that he was awarding contracts to consultants without always going through the standard competitive bidding process. They were successful in branding him a renegade and having him transferred to an obscure office with little or no authority.

As director general of worker client services in the Canadian employment service I was responsible for the professional development of employment counsellors and for the invention of career guidance methods and materials. We made the latter freely available to the schools although they fell under provincial jurisdiction. In meeting individually with the provincial government officials responsible for student services I found that, with but a few exceptions, they did not know each other and did not share ideas. I invited them to Ottawa so they could meet each other, learn of the projects that each was doing, and perhaps engage in some joint planning. After I called the meeting another branch of the department officially responsible for youth complained that I had invaded their territory and it would have taken steps to stop me except that we both had the same boss and he had approved my initiative.

Over the years I encountered many objections that my people and I were usurping the domains of others. As the enemies of change increased they speculated that, because I was ignoring the traditions of the department, I was probably ignoring the rules governing the commitment and expenditure of funds. Finance and accounting people (the most conservative and suspicious group in government) were happy to oblige the enemies of innovation by searching for any "irregularities" in my office. I had observed over the years that the enemies of innovation always asked the financial officers to investigate the innovators handling of expenses. To taunt them I often used the phrase "it's only money" but at the same time I would not make any commitments of funds without my administrative officer initialling the documents indicating her approval. That way I protected myself from that particular source of defeat.

9 Classic Situation Number Eight: Policy of Appointing Deputy Ministers and Assistant Deputy Ministers from Other Departments

The government adopted a policy of promoting across departments rather than appointing the most senior executives from within. This policy has resulted in deputy ministers (DMs) and assistant deputy ministers (ADMs) who have no insight into the issues surrounding the delivery of departmental programs and services, and have no professional understanding of their clients or even provincial counterparts who may deliver their services through cost-sharing arrangements.

Furthermore some of these transient executives have a very negative view of the ultimate clientele such as convicts, the unemployed, sick and homeless. Given their ignorance of the strengths and shortcomings of departmental policies, structure, programs and services they see no need for innovation and do not encourage it.

10 Classic Situation Number Nine: Arrival of New Management with New Agendas

A dangerous time in the life of an innovation is when the boss of the champion is changed and the new boss is either unsympathetic or caters to the opponents in the hope of ingratiating her/himself with the opponents who usually vastly outnumber the innovators. It is surprising how many new bosses do not realize that they have a responsibility to defend their staff. I have seen this happen when a newly appointed ADM advised the champion that there might not be a place for him in a forthcoming reorganization. After he left she tried to ingratiate herself with the deputy minister, who had no conception of the need for innovation, by accepting as a replacement a redundant executive who was notably incompetent in several previous assignments. The DM attended the man's retirement party and was astounded to hear the high praise for the unusual and excellent initiatives that the retiring executive brought to the department and began to question his opinion of the ADM. Eventually the ADM regretted her docility but the damage was done and in due course she, herself, was transferred out. In the meantime all creativity in the branch disappeared and practice returned to normal.

Besides the appointment of an incompetent manager there are other problems that a new manager can present. For example, when I was appointed chair and executive director of Saskatchewan NewStart I found that they had started a community development project in a nearby rural community, but my interpretation of NewStart's mission was that it was a curriculum development project and I cancelled the community development function. The staff were excellent but could not accept my decision and left.

11 Classic Situation Number Ten: Proposals for Innovations Are Approved or Rejected on the Whim of the Most Senior Executive

It is the thesis of this paper that governments are not interested in innovations unless they promise to result in major cost savings and that deputy heads approve innovative projects only if they personally see the need and also have confidence in the proponent as very competent in directing the development of the innovation and in promoting its eventual adoption. In some cases their approval is based on purely personal motives.

Example 1. Success through strategic timing of the proposal. I was the psychologist with the after-care department of a large provincial mental hospital and thought that the re-entry of patients to their homes, jobs and neighbourhoods would be greatly facilitated if they were involved in group therapy sessions dealing with handling critical incidents in each of these areas. The director of the department agreed with me but opined that the hospital superintendent would be negative unless, he said, we get an appointment for 4:30 pm and keep arguing the advantages of the project until the superintendent got restless and agreed to our proposal just to get us out of his office so he could get home for his usual early dinner. That is exactly what happened.

Example 2. Success through persuading the executive's family of the merits of the project. We were developing a sophisticated computer-assisted career and educational guidance system and like many computer-based programs we exhausted our budget and needed more money. The most difficult person to persuade was going to be the executive director of finance. We had a very good prototype ready for pilot testing in the schools and we learned that the finance chief had a daughter in a certain school and decided to offer that school an opportunity to pilot the system. The school principal agreed and also concurred with using the class of the girl in question. The pilot test was successful and the students were encouraged to take their printouts of their personal results home to show their parents. Subsequently we asked for and got the additional funds.

Example 3. Failure with an indecisive executive. We were asked to make a proposal to prepare a training program to help front line immigration officers recognize their ethnic and racial biases and to understand certain cultural features of would-be immigrants' societies. Our assistant deputy minister liked our proposal but asked us to make it to the DM who suggested that we do further research and get back to him. We recognized this as a typical stalling tactic and through some discreet enquiry found out that he felt we were too confident in our presentation. We should have been more hesitant to correspond with his own nature.

Example 4. Funding of innovative projects does not include resources for dissemination of successful projects. There is a certain ethic that is widespread among public servants to the effect that advertising, promotion and marketing are wasteful practices and should not be supported. This was extremely evident in a very large national program of financing innovative projects to encourage students to stay in school and complete their studies. As part of their contract all projects were required to file one copy of the final report of their results. Absolutely no money was provided for even the outstanding projects to disseminate the methods that they had found to be effective in retaining students in school.

12 Conclusion

Innovation in government is not for the faint of heart or the risk-adverse person but rather for the dedicated professional who has a passion for making the system work in new ways and has the sense of personal security to take the arrows of opponents in stride and the ability to win and keep the confidence of his or her superiors, and finally to secure the resources necessary for innovations.

References

Albury, D. (2005). Fostering innovation in public services. *Public Money and Management,* 25(1), 51–56.
Borins, S. (2006). The challenge of innovating in government (second edition): IBM Center for the Business of Government. Retrieved 10 Jan 2010 http://www.businessofgovernment.org/report/challenge-innovating-government.
Joyce, M. (2007). *Performance information and innovation in the Canadian government.* Kingston: School of Policy Studies, Queen's University.
Kay, A. (2011) The Life of a Social Innovator. Retrieved from http://www.alanfkay.com/status/life_of_social_innovator.shtml on Jan. 10, 2011.
Public Policy Forum. (1998). Innovation in the Federal Government: The risk not taken. Retrieved 10 Jan 2011 http://www.oag-bvg.gc.ca/internet/English/meth_gde_e_10193.html. Published at: http://www.innovation.cc/discussion-papers/risk2.htm.

Part III
Social Innovation and Welfare

Social Innovations in Ageing Societies

Rolf G. Heinze and Gerhard Naegele

Abstract To meet the challenges of population ageing, currently is one of the most striking political and societal tasks in nearly all European countries. Population ageing can be regarded as both drivers for social change as well as point of departure for social innovations which are seen as one of the adequate answers to tackle with its challenges. This paper starts with our own understanding of social innovation. Secondly we describe population ageing in its different challenges for both the ageing population as well as for the society as a whole. It will be shown that population ageing affects more or less all sectors of society and in consequence asks for cross-sector policy approaches. The special focus of this paper is to look at social innovations answering to population ageing in the context of the "productivity discourse". In doing this we are presenting the integrated use of technology and social services in order to support independent housing/living at home even in the case of being needy of care as an example of age-related social innovation. In the wake of population ageing new potentials for social innovation are generated which are insofar of essential importance as there are many new products and services developed especially for the elderly, which support 'independent living' in old age. Moreover, at the same time they generate positive effects on economic growth and employment (market innovation) which will be discussed under the heading of 'Silver Economy'. In this context networked living (or: Ambient Assisted Living – AAL) will be presented as a special type of social innovation being at the interface between technology and social services. Networked living is not only understood as integration of information and communication technologies but also as social cross-linking of different industries, technologies, services and other key players.

R.G. Heinze (✉)
Ruhr University Bochum, Bochum, Germany
e-mail: Rolf.Heinze@rub.de

G. Naegele
Dortmund University of Technology, Dortmund, Germany
e-mail: Gerhard.Naegele@fk12.tu-dortmund.de

1 Preface

With our following remarks we take an approach towards the term ,innovation', which goes beyond scientific-technological product and process innovation or market innovation and which stresses social respectively socio-political dimensions. We speak of social innovation if there is an intentional, purposeful *new configuration of social practices* realised by a certain group of stakeholders respectively constellations of stakeholders. The objective here is to solve or satisfy socio-political problems or needs better than it would be possible on the basis of established practices. This means that it is about the founded and explicitly intended integration of various constellations of stakeholders and practices into new socio-political methods of operation and organisation. Social innovations can thereby be market-oriented or 'non-respectively without profit' (see diverse contributions in Howaldt and Jacobsen 2010).

What is inherent to social innovations is their 'focus on values', since they are explicitly oriented towards 'societal goals' which are understood to be worthy. This means that social innovations are useful to tackle 'societal challenges' such as the collective ageing as a part of the demographic change which can be observed in almost all industrial countries. Thus social innovations aim at producing 'societal benefits'. We think it is the reference to societal usefulness that makes social innovations *real* innovations. Social innovations should not only be focused on typical (and mostly commonly known) social challenges and problems but should be strong when they are about socio-political challenges of overarching importance. In this context social innovations should be – but do not immediately have to be – socially accepted, contextually introduced into a relevant societal sphere of activity and finally institutionalised as *new social practices* and become the norm.

2 Criteria and Preconditions for Social Innovations

In Europe the term *social innovation* is a relatively new one, although social innovation is not new as such. Moreover, it is often confounded with social enterprise or is limited to the social field. We follow the following definition being used by the European Commission:

> Social innovation is about new ideas that work to address pressing unmet needs. We simply describe it as innovations that are both social in their ends and in their means. Social innovations are new ideas (products, services and models) that simultaneously meet social needs (more effectively than alternatives) and create new social relationships or collaborations (European Commission 2010).

This definition is explained in detail as follows:

> Many organisations – charities, foundations, government agencies, businesses – are developing new ways to solve social problems, inside and outside the EU. Social innovation could take place in hospitals, social housing, education, in cities and in rural areas. Many

initiatives result in new types of public services and sometimes also new business models. So, many social innovations lead to new forms of organization in the public, not-for-profit and in the private sectors. They can create novel interactions between the public sector, third sector, social enterprises, the social economy, economic operators and civil society, to respond to social issues. Social innovation activities are often started at local level, meeting specific unmet needs, for example eldercare. They thereby help addressing a societal challenge (ageing society) and, through its process dimension (e.g. the active engagement of the elder, new services) it contributes to transform society in the direction of participation, empowerment and learning (European Commission Enterprise and Industry 201).

To summarise: in our own conceptualization we are speaking of social innovations, if the following preconditions are fulfilled:

- Orientation towards outstanding societal challenges/social issues
- New solutions in the sense of a real understanding of newness
- Specific new configurations of social practices/arrangements
- Overcoming the traditional dichotomisation of technological and social innovations
- Integration/collaboration of heterogeneous stakeholders that usually do not (have not) co-operate (co-operated)
- Integrated patterns of action
- Reflexivity and interdisciplinary approaches
- Orientation towards the key goal of societal usefulness
- Sustainability of measures (in the sense of social practice/facts)
- New growth potentials in terms of regular employment
- Integration of the end-users ("user co-production")

3 Population Ageing as a Driver of Social Change and Starting Point for Social Innovations

To meet the challenges of population ageing, currently is one of the most striking political and societal tasks in nearly all European countries. Population ageing can be regarded as both drivers for social change as well as point of departure for social innovations which aim at tackling with its challenges. In other words: Age is increasingly becoming a determinant/'driver' of social change and societal development instead of a 'result'. In doing this we regard population ageing as integral part of overarching demographic mega-trends which can be outlined as follows (see diverse contributions in Heinze and Naegele 2010a; Walker and Naegele 2009):

- Shrinking of the population as a whole
- Declining resp. stagnating birth-rates
- Increase of the so-called 'further life expectancy'
- Increase of the average age of the population
- Shrinking and "greying" of the workforce
- Increase of the very old ('double' and 'threefold' population ageing)

- Considerable growth of the proportion of the older in relation to the younger generation
- Further rise in the proportion of (in many countries also ageing) foreigners within the overall population
- Apart from the Eastern European countries, Germany and Italy belong to those countries in the EU with the most prominent demographic challenges.

The point of departure for our paper is the assumption that population ageing can be regarded as an outstanding societal challenge referring to the key dimensions of social innovations mentioned earlier. This can be proven by the following dimensions of ageing societies for which on the EU level plenty of empirical evidence is available. Although the following socio-political challenges of population ageing are typical for Germany, they are also true for many industrialized European countries:

- There are fundamental changes in both the living- and family structures as well as in social networks of the ageing population. This goes in line with a structural change in the household composition of older people. Whereas multi-generational households are diminishing, older single households, mainly female, have increased substantially ('singularisation of old age'). One of the consequences is a decline in the informal and/or family-bound helper potential.
- The demographic change does not stop in at the doors of enterprises and public administrations. Additionally, the 'baby-boomer' generation is retiring. In many countries, a substantial lack of younger workers moving up is expected. This particularly refers to skilled workers. Older and/or female workers are regarded as substitutes to fill the various bottlenecks. Consequently, in the future companies will run their businesses with shrinking and at the same time on average older staff members. However, at least in Germany older workers show a far-spread positive early retirement-consciousness and elderly women are increasingly faced by the new burden of reconciling work and (family) long-term care. Many women are at the same time still engaged in looking after their elderly children ("sandwich generation"). At the same time EU governments have raised (or at least are planning to do so) retirement ages. The question how to manage to keep an ageing workforce longer active is at the top of the policy agenda in many European countries.
- Population ageing goes along with an increase of age-specific morbidity and long-term care. Multi-morbidity, poly-pharmacy, an increasing numbers of older people suffering from dementia and long-term care – the two latter particularly among the very old – are typical for the morbidity structure of an ageing population. In consequence, there is a need of both adapting the health treatment systems as well as the provision of long-term care according to the special needs of an ageing population. The optimistic assumptions concerning the thesis of compression of morbidity so far seem to be only true for middle and upper class seniors.
- Not only in Germany, among the older generation a strong wish for maintaining independent living in their own 'four walls' as long as possible can be stated. Moving into a home for the elderly or to other forms of institutionalized/sheltered

housing is regarded only as a "worst case scenario" option. In consequence, new answers are necessary to meet the challenges linked to autonomous housing and living in old age even in the cases of being needy for help and/or long-term care.
- Population ageing is leading to an increased need for lifelong learning in all stages of life. This does not only refer to older workers maintaining and promoting their workability and employability. Life-long learning is also a necessity for those already being retired. E.g., self-supporting and/or self-managing independent living by a better use of IC-technologies requires the according knowledge and qualifications. This also refers to the demands of the slogan of 'active ageing' which puts life-long-learning also in old age at the top of the agenda.
- In many European countries like Austria, Belgium, France, Germany, Italy, the Netherlands and the UK, one can observe an ethnic-cultural differentiation of old age. The so-called 'guest workers' are growing old. The traditional answers which are in practice for the resident older population cannot simply be transferred to 'older migrants'. There is a need for new and innovative 'culture-sensible' answers.

Parallel to this, the phase of age as such is changing fundamentally. In line with the dimensions of ageing societies mentioned earlier it can be argued that not only population ageing as such can serve as a point of departure for social innovation but also internal differentiations in the phase of old age as such. In their wake a new *social heterogenisation* among the ageing population has developed. In this context – among others – gerontological research points out:

- The phase of old age is becoming longer and internally more differentiated. The needs of the 'young old', as a rule, are completely different from those of the very old. At the same time age is increasingly becoming female to the double effect of both gender differences in the age when getting married as well as gender differences in the further life expectancy. At the same time, age is becoming more and more 'singularised', which mainly affects women.
- At the same time age is becoming 'younger'. This dimension refers to the increasing discrepancy between self-perception and real chronological age. For Germany there is empirical evidence for a discrepancy of more than 10 years at least among the "young olds". In consequence, when asking for self-responsibility and/or society-oriented (and labour world oriented) activities in old age, one has to take into account that chronological age is of little explanatory power.
- At the end of the phase of age, life is becoming increasingly vulnerable. Long-term care and/or dementia treatment are core challenges in ageing societies. E.g. in Germany currently more than 2.3 million mainly very old persons are in need of long-term care according to the German Long-Term-Care Insurance, and around 1.3 million also mainly very old persons are suffering from dementia. These figures are expected to rise to around 3 and 1.6 million people in 2030.
- The mega-trends so far reported are overlapped by an increase of social inequality in life situations in old age. More or less all spheres of life of older people are characterised by social differences regarding their chances of getting old satisfactorily. Evidence for social inequality in old age can be found e.g. in the

income situation, comfort of housing/living, social integration, access to social and health services and in the further life expectancy. The pessimistic thesis of medicalisation seems to be true for older persons from the lower social strata.

When evaluating German (and EU) policies trying to meet the challenges of population ageing – among others – the following key types of approaches and/or measures can be distinguished (Bäcker et al. 2010; Heinze et al. 2011). We regard them – following our own conceptualisation – as point of departures for social innovations:

4 Population Ageing as a Cross-Sector Task of Shaping

Population ageing is more than just demographic change. It affects more or less all sectors of society and in consequence asks for cross-sector policy approaches. This however stands in a sharp contrast with the hitherto (not only in Germany) prevailing fragmentation of policy sectors. To understand the cross-sector dimension of population ageing and to transfer this view into comprehensive policy concepts can be understood as a social innovation in its own right.

4.1 Demographic-Sensitive Adjustment of Working Conditions

Ageing of the workforce and the staff is a severe challenge for economy, employment policies, social partners, companies and the ageing workforce/older workers itself/themselves. 'Simple' and one-sided solutions are not needed, on the contrary, comprehensive approaches are called for to meet the diverse challenges, including integrated activities vis-à-vis all relevant key stakeholders. These have to be developed mainly on the corporate level. Respective corporate age-management strategies should at least include health protection, ergonomic measures, life-long learning and skills promotion, job and task reorganization, innovative working time schedules, career planning, measures to reconcile work and care and flexible retirement schemes – embedded in an overarching demographic-sensitive organizational culture. It goes without saying that such comprehensive approaches can be interpreted as social innovations.

4.2 To Promote Workability and Employability of an Ageing Workforce

The concepts of workability and employability (Ilmarinen 2005) refer to a multi-disciplinary approach to stabilizing and promoting the individual working potential. Usually they include measures to promote the health status as well as skills and the work-motivation of an ageing workforce. To take account of the private life situation of older workers also plays a key role and demands particularly for measures aiming at an age-related work-life-balance. Core aim is to promote the quality of working life in its multidimensional conceptualisation. Respective measures call for integrated (socially innovative) approaches.

4.3 To Adapt/Reconstruct the Health Treatment and Long-Term Care Systems

Traditionally, particularly in Germany, public health treatment systems are not focussing on chronic but on acute diseases. Aiming at the health-related requirements of an ageing population a change of paradigm is necessary. Integrated solutions are regarded as best answers to the new challenges of multi-morbidity, chronic diseases, long-term care and dementia. This requires sector-overarching collaboration of (1) different professions (e.g. general practitioners, nurses, carers, social workers), (2) different institutions (e.g. medical practices, hospitals, care services, homes for the elderly), (3) different organizational systems (e.g. for Germany Statutory Health Insurance, Statutory Long Term Care insurance, health prevention and rehabilitation, palliative care) and (4) different statutory responsibilities (for Germany the Federal, Länder- and local level). The more networking is aimed at the more socially innovative solutions are in sight (Naegele 2009).

4.4 To Adapt Housing Conditions to Allow Longer Independently Living

The older a person gets, the more time he/she spends at home. Thus the private household increasingly becomes the centre of life for an ageing person. Currently, in Germany the wish to live independently in his/her own house/flat is ranking on top of the scale of necessaries among the ageing population. Housing/living in old age is a multidimensional concept including different aspects like controlling, mobility, security, affordability, sociability, health-protection and others. (Socially innovative) Integrated answers are the logical consequence (Naegele 2010b).

4.5 Adapting the 'Front-Oriented' Education to Lifelong Learning Systems

In Germany educational systems are traditionally 'front oriented', that means, aiming at the first phases of learning life. Further and/or adult education is hardly developed, nor is learning in old age institutionalised. Traditional learning places like primary schools, popular high schools or universities have to open themselves to adult/aged learners; however, this requires not only a change in paradigm within the strategic educational concepts but also a supportive legislation and financing which both – at least in Germany – so far are missing.

4.6 Stakeholder and Policy Mix

Most of the examples of social innovation dealing with meeting the challenges of population ageing better stand for the requirement of collaboration of both different fields of action and policies as well as responsible stakeholders, administrations and political levels. Taking into account that population ageing has to be understood as a cross-sector task, cross-sector collaboration of both different fields of action/ policy as well as different stakeholders is crucial when it comes to look for and establish comprehensive solutions.

4.7 New Types of Involvement of the Ageing Population

User involvement and user engagement usually are seen as valuable instruments to secure sustainability and effectiveness of measures. Concerning population ageing this is a comparatively new understanding keeping in mind that in the past older persons used to be object of mainly welfare measures and not subject. The recently established change of paradigm treating them as "customers" on welfare markets and no longer as "clients" of social services need to be accompanied by new forms of user involvement. Three different approaches are visible: (1) to involve older customers in the process of developing, designing and quality assuring of age-related products and services, (2) to use their potential for civic engagement, and (3) to use their potential for social volunteering. All approaches call for new ways of involving older persons in societal tasks, either self-oriented or oriented to third parties, following the well-known concept of *active ageing* (Walker 2010).

5 Social Innovations Answering to Population Ageing in the Context of the "Productivity Discourse"

Population ageing belongs to the main societal challenges for all welfare states. In Germany, the perception of ageing has changed towards an emphasis of competences and potentials in recent years. Economists regard population ageing also as an economic resource of rising importance both on the supply side of work ("older workers as a resource to fill future gaps in skilled labour") as well as on the demand side as consumers on 'silver markets' (Heinze et al. 2011). Against the background of an increasingly positive valuation of the "grey" economic power, the societal comprehension of old age is beginning to change from worst-case scenarios towards a more optimistic emphasis of competences and potentials ('productivity approach'). In many cases, however, the special resources of an ageing population need to be both identified as well as further developed. If the economic potentials are better used and promoted, population ageing can even serve as a driving force for innovation, particularly with respect to the "silver economy" and to the employment sector.

However, gerontologists argue that the productivity of an aging population should not only be judged in terms of the traditional criteria of profitability ('"formal" economy'). Not only referring to the rising amount of civic engagement and social volunteering in old age (Ehlers et al. 2010) one can state: "Intergenerational relations and social commitment can hardly be measured in terms of 'cash flows.' The productivity contribution of the elderly strengthens the cohesion of society" (Amann et al. 2010). Consequently, when speaking about the productivity of an ageing population one has to take into account two dimensions: a socially integrative one as well as an economic one.

German experience shows that the potentials of an ageing society do not develop on their own. Political and societal action is needed in order to identify, promote and to use them. In this context the following message of the 5th Federal report on ageing in Germany can be cited (BMFSFJ 2006):

> If the potentials of population ageing are both identified as well as being utilised and promoted, collective population ageing can serve as a driving force for general social, technological and economic innovation.

Among others the Fifth Federal report on ageing in Germany points out the following points of departure:

- Better use of the potentials of older employees
- Age management in companies, workplace design and ergonomics for an ageing workforce
- To promote the 'silver market' for a better use of the economic power of old age
- To fight socio-economic inequalities across the entire life-course
- To promote social and civic participation in old age
- To transfer the concept of active ageing into practice
- To promote lifelong learning in order to support healthy ageing by self-determined health promotion and prevention
- To let technology become part of older people's lives.

6 Interim Conclusions

Social innovations are regarded as suitable instruments to put the productive potentials of an ageing society into practice. These potentials should aim at interactive learning processes and the networking of heterogeneous stakeholders and patterns of action. Undoubtedly, simple technological product- and market innovations are not enough to meet the challenges of population ageing best. Particularly when it comes to meet the challenges of population ageing adequately, new types of *configuration of social practices* realised by a certain group of stakeholders which typically did/do not collaborate so far are needed. In consequence, social innovations are dependent on the socio-spatial environment and stakeholders, the willingness to co-operate and in consequence on new types of institutionalized collaboration. However, when it comes to look for adequate social innovations, there is no ‚one best way'. In all, efficient interface management is one of the prime prerequisites for success.

To establish successful types of social innovations both existing social configurations as well as the 'blockades' of the stakeholders involved have to be overcome. However, this is hard to realise, above all in a highly fragmented and regulated policy system (like the German one). This is particularly true for the health treatment and long-term care sector (Heinze 2009; Bäcker and Naegele 2011, vol. II). Therefore, good practice, benchmarking and the exchange of experiences are additional, necessary preconditions for sustainable social innovations aiming at the diverse challenges of population ageing. In this context we also regard social innovations being of growing importance for both stimulating economic growth as well as creating new employment chances.

7 Ageing of Society as a Driver for Social Innovations in Germany: The Example of Housing/Living in Old Age and It's Support by Modern ICT

Primarily, our own conceptualisation of social innovation explicitly aims at integrating social, organisational and institutional innovations. A second interpretation of social innovations aims at the sustainable collaboration of action and/or policy fields. Particularly in the sector of housing/living in old age both approaches form ground for diverse new strategic alliances. Starting from the socio-political goal of promoting independently living in old age as long as possible even in the cases of being in need of external help or even being in need of care the following fields can be addressed: housing as such, ICT, architectural and infrastructural and environmental adaptation, social services, social volunteering and health treatment.

The latter refers to the fact that private households are increasingly developing into the direction of a 'third location' of public health treatment (apart from medical treatment by general practitioners and hospital treatment) (Heinze et al. 2011a). Health@home can improve the quality of health treatment as well as it can save public (social security) money. In recent German literature about health economy aiming at older persons besides the traditional sectors, nutrition, wellness and communication are included. Private households as health locations in their own right are evaluated by many experts as a sector full of social and economic developmental potential; keeping in mind that in Germany only 5 % of the ageing population is living in special living places for the elderly like homes for the elderly or new types of sheltered housing. Particularly new types of collaboration in the action and policy fields of health treatment and long term care can be regarded as a social innovation with a strong future in ageing societies.

'Living and housing in old age' include social and household-oriented services as well as environmental support, design and construction or new high-tech products (like ICT). It also addresses the traditional sectors such as the retail trade or the professional small trade social and care services sector. In German literature this multi-complexity of housing in old age is very often addressed as 'networked housing/living' (Heinze 2010). The specific dimensions of independent living at home are embedded in the overall wish of older persons concerning quality of living/housing, especially regarding the dimensions of comfort, mobility, security and affordability. Housing/living in old age has developed to a central segment of the so-called 'silver market' and population ageing is one of the mega trends when looking at driving forces. Although high-tech infrastructure for promoting independent living in old age even in the case of dependency and vulnerability (e.g. tele-medical treatment and tele-care) already exists, in most cases successful models for both networking sectors and developing business concepts are still missing (Heinze and Ley 2009; Heinze 2010).

In general, modern ICT progressively transforms the environment of people into an interconnected system. These systems often consist of barely perceptible intelligent sensors that can be integrated into a comprehensive network. The technological base for "smart" homes has been available for more than 10 years. A 'smart' environment is one that can react to the presence of people and, depending on their needs, provides different services. The reactions and services are usually made available by computers that are almost invisible to their users. These computers are interlinked and have sensors gathering and analysing information about their environment. In addition, they are also fitted with actuators with which they can influence their environment. AAL (or smart living) can be deployed in all areas of life; from monitoring to emergency alarms. In the past few years, many homes have been technically upgraded and increasingly have universal information technology infrastructures at their disposal. Meanwhile, the setting up of an internet access is possible in (almost) every existing home and even the number of older users is increasing, at least among the younger older persons.

This stands in line with empirical findings showing that older persons in general do not principally refuse new IC-technologies, rather they are able to handle and use new technologies productively when being introduced accordingly. Currently particularly the very old in many cases still need help in accepting, learning to use ICT and supporting to integrate it in their everyday life. In These cases human support either by professionals or by volunteers is needed but new 'man–machine-systems' can also be regarded as social innovations. However, it can be expected that still existing mental barriers to new technologies will be successively overcome in the coming years, as the future old will differ from the current generation in that they are significantly more open to technological innovations, e-health or even for tele-care.

Meanwhile, various building companies are offering modules of smart living. Without the increasing use of modern 'welfare technologies', the care for the chronically ill and persons in need of nursing will be virtually impossible. In the field of prevention too, home automation appears to be a growing market. But if e-health and telemedicine applications can both raise the quality of treatment and lower the costs, the question arises why the available findings have not yet been taken up across the board and been put to practice in standard care. Meanwhile, the pilot phase has been more than completed and the housing industry and the tenants are ready for practical implementations. First isolated projects have already demonstrated the positive aspects of home networking. There are, however, various barriers that have to be overcome. Empirical experience shows that the new technical solutions are often perceived as impersonal and technocratic. Therefore technology-supported, value-added services should not be too technology-centred but also have to take into account social innovations. Technical solutions will only be successful and establish themselves in the market if a distinct added value is generated for the user, which can only consist in an improvement of the quality of life and a facilitation of daily activities. Moreover, the technical solutions have to be coordinated with the offers and services of the traditional providers of the health industry.

Furthermore, housing/living in old age should not be restricted to the adaptation and modification of 'four walls' as the immediate living space. It is also important to develop comprehensive concepts that include adequate modifications of both infrastructure and living environment, on the one hand, as well as supply with shops and services in a living-quarter, on the other hand. The latter refers to the overarching idea of linking housing and quarter-managing ("Quartiersmanagement") which is seen by experts as necessity particularly for ageing cities (Naegele 2010a, 2010b).

There is plenty of evidence for links of housing/living in old age with the 'silver economy'; but the 'silver economy' is not an independent economic sector that is easily definable, rather a mixed market. Adapting housing and living according to changed necessities of older people and, at the same time, to raise their level of satisfaction and quality of life can develop to an economically attractive field of action for local builders, craftsmen, IT-producers and salesmen, financing institutions, and other sectors working on the local level. To stimulate their collaboration new 'strategic alliances' need to be set up, which include more . This is of particular importance for the local level where 'new strategic alliances' as (local) social innovations are needed which include more and other stakeholders than those representing the traditional old age-related welfare practices, long-term care etc. For Germany this can be seen as a new task for local authorities according to their responsibility for the requirements of the local community (Naegele 2010a). To attract also the target group 'seniors', it is important to expand and adequately qualify those advisory services that are centred around the distribution of age-related products and services concerning housing and independent living. It is not only professional work that is needed in this context; there is also an attractive field for establishing informal support and social volunteering structures.

In order to put social innovations like the mentioned into practice there needs to be a proof of an increased effectiveness and fiscal saving. There are some qualitative empirical studies ('surplus-analyses') focusing on networked-housing/living. However, an assessment focusing explicitly on fiscal effects is difficult, since it refers to welfare-mix-analyses in a sector where so far no benchmarking has been practiced and no experiences and 'best ways' are available. Furthermore, so far sustainable financing models at national level are missing. The success-model 'outpatient before in-patient care' also needs financial promotion. However, it can be assumed that both the older residents and the social security systems benefit from new types of networked-housing/living. The surplus value of these social innovations can be assumed in several dimensions:

- The integration into a network has preventive effects.
- In co-operative forms of living and in active living quarters the quality of life is increasing.
- Older persons can stay longer independent. Moving to in-patient forms of housing takes place later. Consequently welfare-state support is less in demand.
- An increase of efficiency in the care systems is likely.

8 Conclusions and Summary

With increasing age more time is spent at home. Thus the own flat/house increasingly becomes the centre of life. This is combined with increased demands regarding the quality of life, especially in terms of independency, comfort, security and affordability. Networked housing/living will definitely increase in the wake of population ageing. The technological infrastructure already exists, although in many cases suitable networking and business models are still missing. Social innovations can only be successful if there is a change of institutional arrangements and if e.g. the infrastructural preconditions and structures of cooperation for networked – 'housing/living' are created. Older people should not only be seen as consumers but as co-producers of social innovations. There is innovative power of the 'economic factor age' regarding the combination of civic engagement (or 'social capital'), innovative micro-system technology and new social services linked with economic concepts for process optimisation. Co-operation is therefore the keyword.

Our society needs the potentials of the older generation due to both social and economic reasons (taking into account the costs for residential home care compared to outpatient care). 'Living independently' has become a key issue in the process of population ageing. It refers to both social and household-oriented services as well as to many products supporting independent living in old age. Especially the linkage of both aims independent living and promotion of health is considered to be a significant future growth market. Here the active participation of the central health care providers in the German health sector plays a major role for the successful implementation of new, in the broadest sense, welfare technologies in the health sector in particular. Now that the technical infrastructure is available, the next step after the model project phase should be the concrete implementation and the setting up of socially innovative alliances.

Older people need both individuality and community. Intelligent living facilities and housing-related services can offer both. Care for those in need will probably not be possible without an increased use of an integrated supply network combined with civic engagement and the use of modern IC-technologies. The option that a country like Germany with one of the 'oldest' populations worldwide could develop a 'lead market' for social innovations regarding 'age' has not been discussed at great length.

References

Amann, A., Ehrgartner, G., & Felder, D. (2010). *Sozialprodukt des Alters: Über Produktivitätswahn, Alter und Lebensqualität.* Wien: Böhlau-Verlag.

Bäcker, G., Naegele, G., Bispinck, R., Neugebauer, J., & Hofemann, K. (2010). Sozialpolitik und soziale Lage, 5. Auflage, 2 Bände. Wiesbaden: VS-Verlag für Sozialwissenschaften.

BMFSFJ. (ed.) (2006). Fünfter Bericht zur Lage der älteren Generation in der Bundesrepublik. Potenziale des Alters in Wirtschaft und Gesellschaft. Der Beitrag älterer Menschen zum Zusammenhalt der Generationen. Bericht der Sachverständigenkommission an das Bundesministerium für Familie, Senioren, Frauen und Jugend. Berlin.

Ehlers, A., Naegele, G., & Reichert, M. (2010). Volunteering by older people in the EU. Published by the European Foundation for the Improvement of Living and Working Conditions, Dublin 2011.

Heinze, R. G. (2009). *Rückkehr des Staates? Politische Handlungsmöglichkeiten in unsicheren Zeiten.* Wiesbaden: VS-Verlag für Sozialwissenschaften.

Heinze, R. G. (2010). Smart living in old age. Options and implementation. in Gerobilim H. 1/2010, 2ff

Heinze, R. G., & Ley, C. (2009). Vernetztes Wohnen. Ausbreitung, Akzeptanz und nachhaltige Geschäftsmodelle, Forschungsbericht Bochum/Berlin.

Heinze, R. G., & Naegele, G. (Eds.). (2010a). *Einblick in die Zukunft. Gesellschaftlicher Wandel und Zukunft des Alterns. Dortmunder Beiträge zur Sozial- und Gesellschaftspolitik, 61.* Berlin: LIT-Verlag.

Heinze, R. G., & Naegele, G. (2010). Intelligente Technik und "personal health" als Wachstumsfaktor für die Seniorenwirtschaft. In Fachinger, U. & Henke, K.-D. (Hrsg.): Der private Haushalt als Gesundheitsstandort. Theoretische und empirische Analysen. Baden-Baden: Nomos: 109ff.

Heinze, R. G., Hilbert, J., & Paulus, W. (2011a). Care is coming home: Towards a new architecture of health service in Europe. In K. Krüger, & e. de Gier (Eds.), Long-term care services in 4 European countries: Labour markets and other aspects. Barcelona u. a., 147ff.

Heinze, R. G., Naegele, G., & Schneiders, K. (2011b). *Wirtschaftliche Potenziale des Alters* (Grundriss Gerontologie, Vol. 11). Stuttgart: Kohlhammer-Urban Taschenbücher.

Howaldt, J., & Jacobsen, H. (Eds.). (2010). *Soziale Innovation: Auf dem Weg zu einem postindustriellen Innovationsparadigma.* Wiesbaden: VS-Verlag.

Ilmarinen, J. (2005). Towards a longer working life. Ageing and the quality of worklife in the European Union.Helsinki. Institute for Occupational Health

Naegele, G. (2009). Sozial- und Gesundheitspolitik für ältere Menschen. In A. Kuhlmey & D. Schaeffer (Eds.), *Alter, Gesundheit und Krankheit* (p. 46). Bern: Verlag Hans Huber.

Naegele, G. (2010a). Kommunen im demographischen Wandel – Thesen zu neuen An- und Herausforderungen für die lokale Alten- und Seniorenpolitik. *Zeitschrift für Gerontologie und Geriatrie, 43*, 2.

Naegele, G. (2010b). Selbstbestimmt leben und wohnen im Alter. In Theorie und Praxis der sozialen Arbeit, 62. Jg., H. 5. Oktober 2011: 339ff.

Walker, A. (2010). The emergence and application of active ageing in Europe. In G. Naegele (Ed.), *Soziale Lebenslaufpolitik* (p. 585). Wiesbaden: VS-Verlag für Sozialwissenschaften.

Walker, A., & Maltby, T. (1997). *Ageing Europe* (Rethinking Ageing). Buckingham/Philadelphia: Open University Press.

Walker, A., & Naegele, G. (2009). Major policy challenges of ageing societies: Britain and Germany compared. In A. Walker & G. Naegele (Eds.), *Social policy in ageing societies. Britain and Germany compared* (p. 1). Basingstoke: Palgrave Macmillan.

Social Innovation or Social Exclusion? Innovating Social Services in the Context of a Retrenching Welfare State

Flavia Martinelli

Abstract In the last 20 years, publicly provided social services – a pillar of the Post-WW2 welfare states – have experienced significant restructuring throughout Europe. An important stream of research emphasizes the socially innovative impact of many restructuring experiences in specific social services and territorial contexts. In particular, great expectations are placed on the devolution of authority from the central state to local governments, the growing role of the third sector, and the increasing involvement of users, for their positive consequences in terms of response to needs, empowerment and democratic governance. However, these expectations are not fully supported by empirical evidence, some of which highlights how the growing stratification of supply is bringing about inequalities in access and quality, undermining the principle of social citizenship. Innovation in social services may thus involve new forms of social and territorial exclusion. While questioning the mainstream notion of social innovation, the paper argues that a new research agenda should address the challenge of conjugating social innovation with universal social rights and citizenship, through a renewed role for the state.

1 Introduction

This contribution lies at the crossroads of three partially overlapping streams of research: social services and social policy, social innovation, and social sustainability, addressed from a planner's perspective. The title provocatively challenges the broadly shared view of social innovation as inherently conducive to social inclusion. The main argument put forward here is that the current mainstreaming of the notion of social innovation is weakening its very 'social' dimension. Social innovation cannot be considered a 'panacea' for the retrenching

---

F. Martinelli (✉)
Mediterranean University, Reggio Calabria, Italy
e-mail: fmartinelli@unirc.it

welfare state, as is increasingly assumed. A key topic for any new research agenda on social innovation is thus how social innovation can be conjugated with social inclusion, within and with the support of an active – albeit 'reinvented' – welfare state.

In the following pages the implications of – and relationships between – social services, social innovation and social sustainability will first be unravelled. I will then provide a definition of social innovation in the context of social services, stressing the importance of universal access to social services and the sustainability of innovations, and testing recent restructuring trends in the domain of social services against these requirements. Finally, the need to bring the state back into the picture in order to ensure the sustainability of social innovation in social services will be stressed, as a key topic for any new European research agenda on social innovation.

2 Social Services

Together with social security provisions, 'in-kind' publicly provided social services – education, health and care services – were a pillar of the European Fordist-Keynesian welfare state. Significant differences existed among countries, as stressed by Esping-Andersen (1990) and others, who analysed and classified national welfare 'traditions' or 'models' (Arts and Gelissen 2002; Jensen 2008; Kazepov 2008). But beyond differences, this major component of the post-WW2 welfare state – best implemented in the 'socialdemocratic' or 'Scandinavian' model – was strongly anchored in a basic egalitarian principle: equal access to equal – good quality – services, regardless of place, income or origin (Blomqvist 2004). In other words, social services were major carriers of universal social rights and citizenship. It should also be noted that the public provision of social services did not only have a redistributive and universalistic aim, as it also contributed to sustain accumulation, by lowering – socialising – the costs of the reproduction of labour (Swyngedouw and Jessop 2006).

Since the 1990s – with the end of Fordism and the beginning of the neo-liberal restructuring of the state – major changes have occurred in the regulation and organisation of social services. Three major trends have been observed across countries, although with different intensities. First, there has been a generalised *reduction* in the direct public provision and/or funding of such services. Secondly, a *diversification* of suppliers – what Kazepov (2008) has called 'horizontal' subsidiarity – has occurred, involving liberalisation (i.e. allowing/encouraging the entry of, and competition among, non-public suppliers) and out-sourcing of production (i.e. funding private suppliers, whether for profit or non-profit). Thirdly, there has been *devolution* of authority – or 'vertical' subsidiarity – from national to local governments.

These changes were brought about by several transformative pressures. On the supply side, the increasing budgetary difficulties – fiscal crisis – of the nation states, the alleged cost/quality inefficiencies of the public sector, the rigid and bureaucratic character of supply; on the demand side, the claims for greater consumer choice, better customisation of services (i.e. adaptation to user needs), and more democratic governance. An odd convergence thus occurred between top-down neo-liberal restructuring strategies, on the one hand, and bottom-up mobilisation of users and civil society for better or effective services, on the other. The former introduced deregulation, liberalisation, and privatisation, with the ostensible aim of increasing efficiency and competitiveness in social services, in line with New Public Management principles and the belief in the superiority of the market as an allocative mechanism. The latter succeeded, in many places, to improve the supply–demand nexus or to trigger the supply of needed services, through the mobilisation of the local civil society.

A large body of research has been accumulated on the above restructuring trends, highlighting some common trends and outcomes, despite the great variety of national and regional trajectories. A first generalised outcome is the increased role of the *third sector* in the supply of social services, whether regulated and funded by the state or substituting for a retrenching public supply (see next section). A second generalised outcome is the increased diversification of supply – which in many cases has also involved a straightforward *stratification* of services, i.e. an increase in access selectivism and exclusion.

3 Social Innovation

3.1 Defining Social Innovation in Social Services

Although it has risen to prominence in the last 15 years and is now ubiquitous, the notion of social innovation is not new (see e.g. Chambon et al. 1982; also Moulaert 2009 for a survey). It is a rather enticing notion, mobilised in a variety of disciplines and across different domains, which has become a keyword in contemporary policy discourses. The European Union has made it a central item in its research and policy agenda (Hubert 2010; EC 2011) and the *Challenge Social Innovation* Conference in Vienna has, indeed, taken up the 'challenge'. However, the very transversal nature of social innovation also makes it a 'loose' notion, with ambiguous analytical rigour (Moulaert 2009). There is no single, exhaustive, or accepted definition of social innovation. Moreover, the recent success of the notion and its mainstreaming in policy discourse has paradoxically 'emptied' it of its innovative dimension, exposing it to the concrete danger of becoming hollow – or, worse, instrumental – rhetoric.

Borrowing from the works developed by Moulaert and others in the course of several European projects, as well as by Harrisson, Klein and others at the CRISES (SINGOCOM 2001–2004; KATARSIS 2006–2009; SOCIAL POLIS 2007–2010; MacCallum et al. 2009; Moulaert et al. 2010, 2013; Klein and Harrisson 2006), 'social' innovation, as opposed to other narrower notions of innovation, is characterised by the following features:

- It contributes to *satisfy human needs* that would otherwise be ignored;
- It contributes to *empower individuals and groups*;
- It contributes to *change social relations*.

Thus, and differently from the 'economic' reading of Schumpeterian innovation, i.e. as geared to gain competitiveness, the distinctive aim of social innovation as defined in the above literature is *social justice* or *social cohesion*, through innovation in *processes* as much as in content.

In the specific *context of social services*, social innovation, then, can be defined as any changes, whether top-down or bottom-up engineered, output or process related, organisational, legislative, or cultural, that contribute to:

- Reveal and/or (better) respond to social needs – whether material or existential – either by improving the quality of existing social services (e.g. adapting them to specific needs, making them more user-friendly or improving their cost/effectiveness) or by creating new services and/or delivery systems for ignored needs.
- Empower users and/or specific social groups, i.e. enhancing their capabilities to act, by providing greater information, knowledge, recognition, voice, or power.
- Modify social – and power – relations among providers and users, thereby improving governance processes, by e.g. making planning procedures more transparent and decision-making more participatory.

To the above three forms of 'canonical' social innovation, however, two further requirements, specific to social services, must be added. Social innovation in social services must also contribute to:

- Ensure, preserve and/or increase *equality of access*, the main characteristic of 'old' social services and warranty of *social citizenship*.
- Upscale and 'institutionalise' innovation, i.e. acquire a relatively *durable* character and become an *embedded societal acquisition* that can last beyond the initial mobilisation/innovation moment and until the next round of innovation. This may sound contradictory with the notion of innovation, which is a highly dynamic process, but in fact, the very essence of Schumpeterian innovation works by waves and any innovation is bound to be adopted, to be adapted and to diffuse into the system, until it is superseded by another.

3.2 Social Innovation and the Restructuring of Social Services

In what follows I will test the above working definition of social innovation against three main features of the recent restructuring of social services, i.e. those allegedly most related to social innovation: (a) the devolution of authority to local governments; (b) the growing role of the third sector; (c) the growing mobilisation of users.

The *devolution of authority* concerning the funding, planning and delivery of social services from the national government to local authorities has been a major and much studied feature of the recent restructuring of social services. In some countries, such as Sweden, this decentralisation started in the 1970s, in others, such as Italy, only much later. In the literature there is widespread agreement among scholars that the establishment of what have been called 'Local Welfare Systems' (Andreotti et al. 2012) can significantly contribute to improve the interface between the demand and the supply of social services, and therefore the identification of needs, the adaptation and customisation of services to local specificities, and the involvement of users and the local civil society in the planning and delivery of services (see also Allen 2006). As such, devolution would definitely be conducive to social innovation in the forms outlined earlier. However, evidence from empirical research is mixed. The above positive improvements generally occur in places already endowed with a developed social capital and/or adequate financial resources – whether transferred from the central state or locally levied (Thorgaard and Vinter 2007). In other contexts, where the civil society and the local governments are less innovative and/or financial resources limited, devolution often ends up worsening the local supply of social services (Bifulco and Vitale 2006). What devolution is bringing about, thus, is greater territorial differentiation in the level and quality of social service delivery, across and within countries, depending on previous welfare traditions, levels of national regulation and funding, and local endowment of social and financial resources (Evers et al. 2005; Allen 2006).

The increased involvement of the *third sector* – and non-profit organisations in general – is also ubiquitously saluted as a positive 'social' innovation per se. This type of supplier is considered a viable alternative to the traditional direct public provision of social services from several points of views. First, third sector organisations are generally less bureaucratic and more user-sensitive than public service administrations, thereby more capable to tailor services on users needs. Secondly, they have a strong – built in – solidarity and reciprocity content, in contrast to both the 'assistance' and the profit drivers of the traditional welfare state and the market, respectively. In fact, the third sector is often equated with the 'social economy' (Laville and Nyssens 2000; Hulgard and Spear 2006; Nyssens 2006). Finally, this type of supply organisation is supposed to enhance the transparency of the process and the participation of users and the civil society, not only in the planning and delivery of social services, but also in their production. Not surprisingly, third sector organisations were considered a central actor in the New Labour 'Third Way' strategy in the United Kingdom during the 1990s, which had the ambition to conjugate social rights with social duties (Allen 2006). However, on this aspect too, empirical evidence is mixed and a great variety of situations is observed. A key element is the relationship between the third sector and the state, in terms of both funding and regulation. In some instances, such as in Denmark (Thorgaard and Vinter 2007; Hulgard 2006) the state has out-sourced production to third sector organisations, in order to better respond to needs, while maintaining the funding and monitoring functions (over the quality of output, the work environment, access, etc.). In other cases, such as adult care in the United Kingdom (Newman et al. 2008) or Italy (De Leonardis and Vitale 2002), out-sourcing to third sector organisations has obeyed merely to cost-cutting imperatives, with a visible worsening of social workers contractual conditions and professional qualifications, which inevitably reverberated on the quality and coverage of output. In other cases yet, such as for integrative education for immigrant children in Greece (Baharopoulou and Siatitsa 2007), third sector organisations simply substitute for an absent or retrenching public sector and are, thus, completely dependent on the availability – and vagaries – of social and financial resources.

Last, but not least, the growing *mobilisation and involvement of users* in any phase of the social services production-delivery process is by definition considered a major component of social innovation, strongly related to both the above features. It is widely acknowledged that encouraging this participation cannot only contribute to more democratic governance and to the empowerment of users but also to better – user-friendly – and even cheaper services, all key components of the definition of social innovation. Participation in the planning, as well as in the production of social services – through co-production (Pestoff 2006) – not only increases the awareness and voice of social services recipients, it also changes their attitudes, reducing their sense of dependence and enhancing their agency capabilities, while actively contributing to the customisation of services to specific needs. Empirical evidence on this form of innovation in social services can be grouped in two categories. The first includes *bottom-up* initiatives, generally community or neighbourhood actions that evolved *outside* established delivery systems, often precisely to fill in for inadequate or absent responses to pressing needs or to challenge existing delivery systems and practices (Moulaert et al. 2010, 2013; KATARSIS 2006–2009). The other includes *top-down* restructuring of existing (public) social service delivery systems oriented to give greater voice and power to users. Among the latter we can mention the Italian reform of social services enacted with the Law 328/2000, which both devolved the responsibility of planning social services to regional and local governments and introduced significant participatory procedures (Bifulco and Centemeri 2008), or the UK 'modernisation' of care services towards greater user empowerment carried out in the 2000s (Newman et al. 2008). The impact of both types of experiences is generally very positive but is contingent upon a number of conditions. For the former type a major issue is funding, the availability of which has clearly proved to severely condition the survival of whatever mobilisation. For the latter, the unequal availability of financial resources has also proved a central issue, together with the conservative culture of some public administrations, leading to greater unevenness in service coverage and quality (Bifulco and Vitale 2006).

4 The Sustainability of Social Innovation

The very diverse empirical evidence on the actual results of the above three restructuring processes in different contexts underscores that innovation in social services does not automatically mean social innovation. In my definition of social innovation in the case of social services, key criteria to fully assess the constitutive three dimensions of social innovation (satisfaction of human needs, empowerment, and changes in social relations) are whether they also ensure: (a) the maintenance or enhancement of universal access and (b) the social sustainability of innovation.

4.1 From Universalism to Stratification: The Growing Social and Territorial Exclusion

As stressed earlier, social services are key carriers of citizenship. Access to education, health assistance and care services, independently of origin, income, age, gender, religion or place is a universal right (Williams 1992; Thompson and Hogget 1996), the basis of social citizenship as conceived in the 1948 Universal declaration of human rights (articles 21, 22, 25 and 26). In other words, social services are a major vehicle of social sustainability. The universal right to these services has been recently reaffirmed by the European Commission, in the context of the debate on services 'of general interest' (CEC 2007). Their special contribution to social cohesion and the dangers of liberalisation have been recognised, setting them apart from other such services. However, *how*, universal access to social services is to be ensured in the context of a retrenching welfare state and reduced public spending capacity remains fuzzy.

In fact, while the welfare state of old had attempted to, and imperfectly succeeded in, ensuring a quasi-universal system of social services, even if at the cost of some rigidity, standardisation and inefficiency, the new delivery system that has been taking shape in the last 20 years is characterised by a strong diversification of supply, which has inevitably created stratification and, in many instances, sheer exclusion (Martinelli 2013). And while the early discussion about the restructuring of the welfare state had been rather critical about liberalisation and privatisation – what Crouch and others have called the 'marketisation of citizenship' (Crouch et al. 2001) – the recent stress on social innovation has somewhat obscured the exclusionary processes at work. The debate has been caught in the 'subsidiarity trap', i.e. the belief that diversification and devolution – horizontal and vertical subsidiarity – are socially innovative *by default* and, hence, inherently better.

Empirical evidence shows that this is not the case. On the whole, liberalisation, privatisation and devolution have increased inequalities in social services quality and access, among countries and places, as well as among social groups. The poorest localities and the poorest people – among these, especially immigrants – do not benefit from the diversification of supply and are increasingly excluded from access to social services or have access to inadequate ones. And social innovation, where it has occurred, has often remained episodic in both time and space, a feature that leads to the next issue, i.e. how to sustain social innovation.

4.2 Sustaining Social Innovation in Time and Space

There are two dimensions in the sustainability of social innovation in services. The first is sustaining innovations over time; the second is the up-scaling of innovation from the micro and the local to a broader societal level. Although the mobilisation of local communities, users and civil societies, often through third sector organisations, has in many instances successfully compensated for inadequate or absent social services, thereby effectively accomplishing social innovation, empirical evidence also shows that 'sustaining' and 'up-scaling' such initiatives is rather difficult (Moulaert et al. 2010; Murray et al. 2010).

First of all, not all places and groups are capable of rallying the necessary social and financial resources to launch socially innovative initiatives; and the poorest groups and places are generally also those less endowed with these resources. Secondly, when social resources are mobilised and socially innovative initiatives do develop, huge amounts of energies and time are devoted to raising financial resources and/or meeting requirements for obtaining funds (Moulaert et al. 2010). Many such initiatives do not last beyond the mobilising and pioneering phase. Most importantly, very often the social innovation accomplished at the local level does not 'trickle-up' to the broader scales, i.e. does not upgrade into a durable – institutionalised – societal acquisition, available to other places and groups. The issue then becomes how to translate bottom-up and local socially innovative experiences into universally available and durable service delivery institutions.

5 A New Research Agenda: Reinventing the State

5.1 Social Innovation and Social Exclusion

The current use of the notion of social innovation in research and policy arenas has become somewhat too obsequious to neo-liberal discourses which see the state as a hindrance and the liberalisation, privatisation and devolution processes as carriers of social innovation per se. This mainstreaming of the notion of social innovation is particularly deceptive in the domain of social services, where social innovation is often perceived as a way to substitute and/or compensate for the retrenchment of an inefficient or bankrupt welfare state. I contend that social innovation should not be considered the magic wand that can redress the growing social and territorial inequality in access to social services, which to a large extent is a consequence precisely of the recent restructuring of social services.

This ambiguity is reproduced in many research and policy circles. In the 2012 call of the FP7 Cooperation Work Programme in Socio-economic Sciences and Humanities, for example, the 'Social innovation against inequalities' topic (SSH 2012 2.1.1) urged proponents to 'investigate what the role of social innovation could be in tackling inequalities', because 'despite achievements in economic development and welfare, inequalities in Europe are persistent or even rising', candidly assuming that 'as social innovation often flourishes bottom up between state and market, particularly through being embedded in the activities of the third sector, (...) social innovation against inequalities [should] be spotted, encouraged and harnessed in policymaking processes at local, national or European level' (EC 2011:22). The BEPA report also argues that 'at a time of major budgetary constraints, social innovation is an effective way of responding to societal challenges, by mobilising people's creativity to develop solutions and make better use of scarce resources' (Hubert 2010:6). Similarly, the Young Foundation report deploys an unwavering faith in the wonderworking virtues of social innovation, through which 'the most pressing issues of our time' can be solved, particularly 'where government policy on the one hand, and market solutions on the other, have proved grossly inadequate' (Murray et al. 2010:3).

On the basis of the literature and empirical evidence, I believe that social innovation in social services *cannot* be sustained *outside* or *in alternative to* the state, as is frequently implicitly or explicitly assumed, but must be promoted *within* and *with* the state. Even if socially innovative experiences often develop outside the state, they need to be sustained and up-scaled and this can only be ensured by the state.

5.2 Reinventing the State

A major item on any new research agenda on social innovation should, indeed, be *the role of the state*. This is particularly pressing in the case of social services, which, as vehicles of social citizenship, cannot be entrusted to the market, neither to the third sector or users alone.

Towards this objective, two strongly related key topics should be explored. The first concerns what new – innovative – *division of labour* could be envisaged between the state, the market, the third sector and users, in the different phases of the social services production system (planning, financing, producing and delivering), that could maintain/restore universal access to social services, while taking into account the reduced financial resources available to governments and the need for improved output. The second concerns the *specific role of the state*. We certainly cannot go back to the welfare state of old and a new role must be envisaged, but a major role nonetheless. 'Reinventing the state' was, indeed, one of the most voted research topics at the 'Challenge Social Innovation' Vienna conference (see 'Vienna declaration' in CSI 2011). The role of this reinvented state should be to foster, steer, and institutionalise social innovation in general, as well as in the specific area of social services. Here, it should especially ensure that social innovation is conjugated with social inclusion, diversity with universalism, empowerment with redistribution.

In particular, research should focus on the following state elective tasks, which are crucial for ensuring universal access: (a) funding; (b) regulation; (c) (co-) production.

Access to *financial resources* is a basic requirement for both social innovation in and universal access to social services. Empirical evidence shows that the most successful innovative experiences in this area were those that could rely on some level of stable and reliable public financial flows, either local, national or EU. Conversely, many innovative experiments, both top-down and bottom-up, did not work or survive for lack of funding. A case in point is the devolution implemented in Italy, which did not accompany the transfer of responsibility with a mechanism to ensure reliable and equitable funding to municipalities. The scarcity of financial resources is particularly penalising for the poorest places. In the absence of adequate funding neither local authorities, nor third sector organisations can ensure social services to the people most in need, thereby perpetuating or even increasing inequality in access. Innovative financial mechanisms will have to be identified and implemented to ensure: (1) the promotion and support of *virtuous innovations* in social services; (2) a basic level of financial *redistribution* in favour of the weakest social groups and places.

Regulation, the ultimate prerogative of the state, can significantly contribute to both social innovation and social inclusion in at least three ways: (1) close *coordination and monitoring* of responsibilities and tasks among the different levels of government and the different actors in the social services system; (2) *minimum quality standards and requirements*, not only in output, but also, e.g. in the area of employment (training and contractual relations of social workers); (3) *up-scaling and/or mainstreaming* of innovative practices.

In many social services, those that represent a historic conquest and established pillar of the modern state, such as education or selected health services, a decentralised but highly regulated *direct public provision* should be maintained and forms of *co-production* involving the civil society and users should be envisaged, with the explicit aim to ensure high quality services to all. Here social innovation should be encouraged to improve both the efficiency and the efficacy of public supply, without giving up the role of the state as universal provider. A virtuous example in this area is the Danish case, where both vertical and horizontal subsidiarity have been accompanied by strong central monitoring of processes and standards (Hulgard 2006; Thorgaard and Vinter 2007; Rauch 2008).

In conclusion, social innovation *and* social inclusion can and should be conjugated, *within* and *with* the state at its different scales, i.e. bringing back in the state as the ultimate guarantor of social justice and the common good.

References

Allen, P. (2006). New localism in the English National Health Service: What is it for? *Health Policy, 79,* 244–252.
Andreotti, A. Mingione, E., & Polizzi, E. (2012). Local welfare systems: A challenge for cohesion. *Urban Studies 49*(9) 1925–40

Arts, W., & Gelissen, J. (2002). Three worlds of welfare or more? A state-of-the-art report. *Journal of European Social Policy, 12*(2), 137–158.

Baharopoulou, A., & Siatitsa, D. (2007). Education and training in Greece, WP1.2 Annex E, KATARSIS-FP6 Coordinated Action. http://katarsis.ncl.ac.uk/wp/wp1/papers.html.

Bifulco, L., & Vitale, T. (2006). Contracting for welfare services in Italy. *Journal of Social Policy, 35*(3), 495–513.

Bifulco, L., & Centemeri, L. (2008). Governance and participation in local welfare: The case of the Italian Piani di Zona. *Social Policy & Administration, 42*(3), 211–227.

Blomqvist, P. (2004). The choice revolution: Privatization of Swedish welfare services in the 1990s. *Social Policy and Administration, 38*(2), 139–155.

CEC-Commission of the European Communities. (2007). Services of general interest, including social services of general interest: A new European commitment, Document accompanying the Communication on a single market for 21st century Europe. http://ec.europa.eu/services_general_interest/interest_en.htm.

Chambon, J.-L., David, A., & Devevey, J.-M. (1982). *Les innovations sociales*. Paris: Presses Universitaires de France.

Crouch, C., Eder, K., & Tambini, D. (Eds.). (2001). *Citizenship, markets and the state*. Oxford: Oxford University Press.

CSI-Challenge Social Innovation (2011). Vienna declaration. http://www.socialinnovation2011.eu/vienna-declaration-2011

De Leonardis, O., & Vitale, T. (2002). Les coopératives sociales et la construction du tiers secteur en Italie. *Mouvements, 19*, 75–80.

EC-European Commission. (2011). FP7 Cooperation Work Programme: Socio-economic Sciences and Humanities, Brussels: EC. http://ec.europa.eu/research/participants/portal/page/cooperation?callIdentifier=FP7-SSH-2012-1.

Esping-Andersen, G. (1990). *The three worlds of welfare capitalism*. Princeton: Princeton University Press.

Evers, A., Lewis, J., & Riedel, B. (2005). Developing child-care provision in England and Germany: Problems of governance. *Journal of European Social Policy, 15*(3), 195–209.

Hubert, A. (2010). *Empowering people, driving change: social innovation in the European Union*. Brussels: BEPA – Bureau of European Policy Advisers.

Hulgard, L. (2006). Danish social enterprises: A public-third sector partnership. In M. Nyssens (Ed.), *Social enterprise at the crossroads of market, public policies and civil society* (pp. 50–58). London/New York: Routledge.

Hulgard, L., & Spear, R. (2006). Social entrepreneurship and the mobilisation of social capital in European social enterprises. In M. Nyssens (Ed.), *Social enterprise at the crossroads of market, public policies and civil society* (pp. 85–107). London/New York: Routledge.

Jensen, C. (2008). Worlds of welfare services and transfers. *Journal of European Social Policy, 18*(2), 151–162.

KATARSIS – Growing Inequality and Social Innovation: Alternative Knowledge and Practice in Overcoming Social Exclusion in Europe, FP6 Coordination Action 2006–2009. www.katarsis.ncl.ac.uk/.

Kazepov, Y. (2008). The subsidiarization of social policies: Actors, processes and impacts. *European Societies, 10*(2), 247–273.

Klein, J.-L., & Harrisson, D. (Eds.). (2006). *L'innovation sociale. Émergence et effets sur la transformation des sociétés*. Québec: Presses de l'Université du Québec.

Laville, J.-L., & Nyssens, M. (2000). Solidarity-based third sector organizations in the 'proximity services' field: A European Francophone perspective. *Voluntas: International Journal of Voluntary and Nonprofit Organizations, 11*(1), 67–84.

MacCallum, D., Moulaert, F., Hillier, J., & Vicari Haddock, S. (Eds.). (2009). *Social innovation and territorial development*. Farnham/Burlington: Ashgate.

Martinelli, F. (2013). Learning from case studies of social innovation in the field of social services: balancing top-down universalism with bottom-up democracy. In F. Moulaert, D. MacCallum,

A. Mehmood, & A. Hamdouch (Eds.), *A handbook of social innovation: Social innovation, collective action, social learning and transdisciplinary research*. Cheltenham: Edward Elgar (forthcoming).

Moulaert, F. (2009). Social innovation: Institutionally embedded, territorially (re)produced. In D. MacCallum, F. Moulaert, J. Hillier, & S. Vicari Haddock (Eds.), *Social innovation and territorial development* (pp. 11–23). Ashgate: Farnham and Burlington.

Moulaert, F., Martinelli, F., Swyngedouw, E., & Gonzalez, S. (Eds.). (2010). *Can neighbourhoods save the city? Community development and social innovation*. Oxford/New York: Routledge.

Moulaert, F., MacCallum, D., Mehmood, A., & Hamdouch, A. (2013). *A handbook of social innovation: Social innovation, collective action, social learning and transdisciplinary research*. Cheltenham: Edward Elgar (forthcoming).

Murray, R., Caulier-Grice, J., & Mulgan, G. (2010). *The open book of social innovation*. London: The Young Foundation and Nesta.

Newman, J., Glendinning, C., & Hughes, M. (2008). Beyond modernisation? Social care and the transformation of welfare governance. *Journal of Social Policy, 37*(4), 531–557.

Nyssens, M. (2006). *Social enterprise at the crossroads of market, public policies and civil society*. London/New York: Routledge.

Pestoff, V. (2006). Citizens and co-production of welfare services. Childcare in eight European countries. *Public Management Review, 8*(4), 503–519.

Rauch, D. (2008). Central versus local service regulation: Accounting for diverging old-age care developments in Sweden and Denmark, 1980–2000. *Social Policy & Administration, 42*(3), 267–287.

SINGOCOM – Social Innovation, Governance and Community Building, FP5 2001–2004. cordis.europa.eu/documents/documentlibrary/100123951EN6.pdf.

SOCIAL POLIS – Social Platform on Cities and Social Cohesion, FP7 Coordination Action 2007–2010. www.socialpolis.eu/.

Swyngedouw, E., & Jessop, B. (2006). Regulation, reproduction and governance, WP2 Discussion Papers, DEMOLOGOS – Development Models and Logics of Socio-economic Organisation in Space, FP6 – Specific Targeted Project, Contract CIT2-CT-2004-505462, Newcastle, GURU. http://demologos.ncl.ac.uk/wp/wp2/disc.php.

Thompson, S., & Hogget, P. (1996). Universalism, selectivism and particularism. Towards a post-modern social policy. *Critical Social Policy, 16*(1), 21–43.

Thorgaard, C., & Vinter, H. (2007). Rescaling social welfare policies in Denmark. National report, Social Policy and Welfare Services Working Papers 10, Copenhagen: The Danish National Institute of Social Research.

Williams, F. (1992). Somewhere over the rainbow: universality and diversity in social policy. In N. Manning, & R. Page (Eds.), *Social Policy Review 4* (pp. 200–19).

Part IV
Social Innovation and Social Entrepreneurship

Social Innovation, Social Entrepreneurship and Development

György Széll

Abstract Social innovation and development have to be placed in the perspective of sustainability. Overcoming poverty and pauperisation is not only an issue for the Third World; however, the so-called developed nations, i.e. mainly the OECD countries, are facing increasing social inequality and pauperisation after their short dream of ever-lasting prosperity (Lutz 1984). Mini-credits have been regarded as a means of overcoming pauperisation first in Third World countries, later in developed countries as well, and the idea has been compensated by the Nobel Prize for peace in 2006. But not only since the recent conflict about its initiator, Muhammad Yunus, there has been rising critique, especially in India. Strategies for sustainability include Corporate Social Responsibility, the development of a strong civil society, the quality of democratic participation, and by it strengthening the trade unions as the largest democratic institutions in our societies.

Civil society is not only in the core of democratisation but also for social innovation. Since the Age of Enlightenment science and its institutions are the centre for innovation and social innovation. The reference here is not only in regard to Schumpeter but for Karl Polanyi too.

Since the 1970s there is a debate about zero growth and alternative measurements for the quality of life and working life, beyond GDP (Széll, G., & Széll, U. (Eds.) (2009). Quality of Life & Working Life in Comparison. Frankfurt/M: Peter Lang).

Parts of this article are published in 'The social economy: its role, importance, and prospects', in Veli Matti Autio (ed.), *Contemporary Corporate Culture under Globalization*, Vol. III, A Memorial Book for Professor Erkki Asp, Helsinki, FEMDI/Finnish Employers' Management Development Institute, 2012: 265–278.

G. Széll (✉)
University of Osnabrück, Osnabrück, Germany
e-mail: gszell@uos.de

1 Introduction

After the terrible twentieth century the world is facing again the most fundamental transformations. The hegemony, which the West could realize during the past centuries, is questioned. We are speaking of the Pacific era, which shall replace the Atlantic one. After the implosion of the Soviet Empire in Europe, the Japanese-American author Francis Fukuyama was announcing the end of history in 1992. However, regimes of really existing socialism still continue like the ones in North Korea, Laos, Myanmar, Vietnam, Cuba and not to forget China.[1] But it is evident that these regimes are confronted with serious economic or/and social problems, and they have to transform their economic and social policies, and at last probably their regimes themselves; otherwise the survival of the political class in power and eventually the whole nation is in danger.

Capitalism needed 1,000 years, since its first beginnings in the eleventh century, to arrive at its peak today. There is no question that capitalism has developed the productive forces more than any other system of relations of production. Even today we witness at any moment technological revolutions, namely in the domain of information technologies and the media. For one part of humanity this has brought an unimaginable well-being. This well-being has certainly been distributed in a very unequal manner, not only between whole nations, but also within the rich nations as well.

With the development of the productive forces the social relations were revolutionized themselves. Namely the English, American and French revolutions have ended feudal regimes. Modern civilisation, civil society, parliamentary democracy, universal rights, the Nation-state have been invented and exported into the whole world. Certainly not out of altruism – although quite often missionaries propagated them – and not right away. The notion of progress – technological progress, economic progress, social progress – endorses this vision of the world. Education and sciences – i.e. social innovations – play in this context a primordial role (Sünker et al. 2003).

2 Social Innovation and Social Entrepreneurship

The ICICI Conference 2011 in Vienna, of which this book is a prominent outcome, gave a large space to the *Open Book of Social Innovation* by Robin Murray, Julie Caulier-Grice and Geoff Mulgan, financed and published by the Young Foundation in 2010.[2] There we can read:

---

[1] Although there are quite a few other states, which still have a reference to socialism in their constitution: Bangladesh, Guyana, India, Portugal, Sri Lanka, Syria and Tanzania.

[2] The list of 527 examples in the book is quite impressive, however, it lacks a proper assessment in regard to the impact and importance of each of them.

> The field we cover is broad. Social innovation doesn't have fixed boundaries: it happens in all sectors, public, non-profit and private. Indeed, much of the most creative action is happening at the boundaries between sectors, in fields as diverse as fair trade, distance learning, hospices, urban farming, waste reduction and restorative justice.
> The term 'social innovation' is a relatively new one, but social innovation itself is not new. There are many examples of social innovation throughout history, from kindergartens to hospices, and from the co-operative movement to microfinance. A 'field' of social innovation is, however, a new idea. ... Social innovation is about new ideas that work to address pressing unmet needs. We simply describe it as innovations that are both social in their ends and in their means. Social innovations are new ideas (products, services and models) that simultaneously meet social needs (more effectively than alternatives) and create new social relationships or collaborations. (Murray et al. 2010)[3]

The European Commission, DG Enterprise and Industry, used this citation on its homepage on Social Innovation Europe (2012). Apparently there is a risk in this context – as the main title reads 'Industrial innovation' – that social innovation might be subdued to it. The European Foundation for the Improvement of Living and Working Conditions is anxious about this danger. In so far the commitment by the European Commission has to be followed very closely by the social actors and academia.

Joseph Schumpeter gave capitalism a human face: the entrepreneur (1943, 1951, 1967), not any more the ugly capitalist. Nowadays – with the domination of stock exchange companies – managers are the main entrepreneurs (Mills 1956), although their personal responsibility is quite limited, as the recent scandals demonstrate. Due to these and other scandals in the past we have a debate and strategies about Corporate Social Responsibility (CSR), which includes environmental responsibility as well (Széll 2006). Social entrepreneurship can therefore not only be found within the social economy itself, but within capitalist business sometimes, too. CSR has been a trend and social innovation for about 30 years; however, it has developed a strong drive since the 1990s.

In 2001, the European Commission published the Green Paper 'Promoting a European framework for corporate social responsibility', which was followed by a large number of initiatives, also at the national level. The responsibility for this programme lies with the Directorate General Social Affairs, Employment and Inclusion (2002). Therefore the issue is stakeholder democracy vs. shareholder value dictatorship.

Actually already in the past, foundations like Rockefeller, Ford, Thyssen, Bosch or Bertelsmann, the biggest German one, practiced social entrepreneurship in managing the company. Quite a number of foundations are the owners of the companies with management responsibilities. That was quite a social innovation in their time. Ashoka, a foundation, which has been promoting social entrepreneurship for 30 years, defines a social entrepreneur as follows:

---

[3] The citation is not to be found in a book, however, in a dispersed way, on the internet page of Social Innovator http://www.socialinnovator.info/about/why-social-innovation (retrieved 9 January 2012).

Social entrepreneurs are individuals with innovative solutions to society's most pressing social problems. They are ambitious and persistent, tackling major social issues and offering new ideas for wide-scale change. Rather than leaving societal needs to the government or business sectors, social entrepreneurs find what is not working and solve the problem by changing the system, spreading the solution, and persuading entire societies to take new leaps. Social entrepreneurs often seem to be possessed by their ideas, committing their lives to changing the direction of their field. They are both visionaries and ultimate realists, concerned with the practical implementation of their vision above all else. Each social entrepreneur presents ideas that are user-friendly, understandable, ethical, and engage widespread support in order to maximize the number of local people that will stand up, seize their idea, and implement with it. In other words, every leading social entrepreneur is a mass recruiter of local change-makers—a role model proving that citizens who channel their passion into action can do almost anything. Over the past two decades, the citizen sector has discovered what the business sector learned long ago: There is nothing as powerful as a new idea in the hands of a first-class entrepreneur. (Ashoka homepage 2012)

One of the most interesting experiments in social entrepreneurship is by the Brazilian Ricardo Semler, who gave his very successful company Semco to his workers for self-management (1993). There were a few similar experiences in the past (Lip, Photo Porst), which quite often unfortunately failed, because of the lack of competence on the side of the employees.

One of the biggest social innovations in this field was the introduction of micro-credits on a large scale some 20 years ago by Muhammad Yunus from Bangladesh, for which he received the Peace Nobel-Prize in 2006 (Yunus 2008), although there were some earlier experiences already since the 1970s in Latin America (Sebstad and Cohen 2001). In recent years, however, problems – linked to micro-credits – spread, because usury has usurped this kind of finance and ruined many farmers, especially in India (Dash 2011).

Another important social innovation in the Third World was the invention of the participatory budget in Porto Alegre and the State of Rio Grande do Sul in Brazil (cf. Murray et al. 2010: 153). This shows that important social innovations are not limited to the developed world, quite to the contrary.

The social entrepreneur seems to be in contrast to purely philanthropic foundations like the Melinda and Bill Gates Foundation e.g., the biggest in the world, which just redistribute their wealth. But even there – due to the enormous fortunes – entrepreneurship is absolutely necessary.

A large understanding of the social economy would include also the public sector, as it should produce first of all public goods and therefore not be profit driven. But the past has shown that the state on its different levels had and has quite successful companies producing goods and services, mainly as 'public goods', but also partly for the market (Wikipedia 2012a).

Within the social administration the main purpose is the redistribution of surplus or wealth produced in society. In so far entrepreneurship is not necessarily needed; but on the other hand, there is a growing trend to regard public administration as a kind of business, following its rules. The appropriate training is more and more required and accordingly offered in the meantime. Anyway, social innovation in the

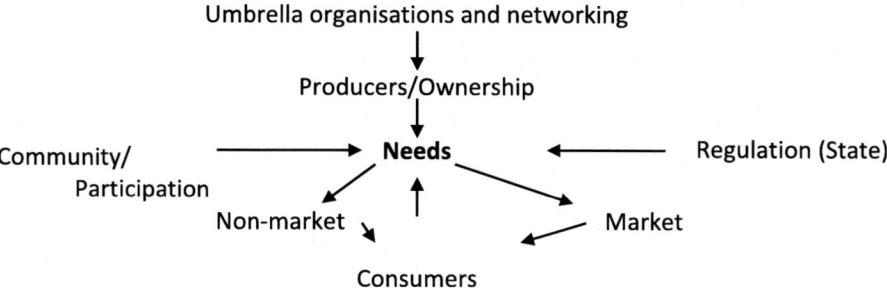

Fig. 1 The social economy model

public sector is quite necessary as new demands emerge and new social structures have to be respected.

Non-Governmental or Non-Profit Organisations (NGOs/NPOs) have been playing a prominent role in social, political and economic life for many years. One of their main activities concerns the environment. They have become observers or even members of many local, regional, national and international bodies. They have created hundred thousands of jobs. Some of them – e.g. Greenpeace – have become big companies and have to be run like that. Out of this turn, the notion and praxis of Sustainable Entrepreneurship or Sustainability Entrepreneurship, short Sustainopreneurship, emerged (Wikipedia 2012c). All these organisations – and many foundations, too – survive only thanks to fundraising, which has become really professionalized. One of the main activities in promoting social entrepreneurship is therefore through training. In the meantime there exist quite a number of institutions, which offer this kind of qualification.

The social economy by its alternative approach to the economy (cf. Fig. 1) is a fundamental social innovation by itself. It settles itself as an alternative between so-called free market capitalism and state socialism or in other words state capitalism.

A substantial element of the social economy is to overcome alienation of human beings, as has been defined by Karl Marx and Friedrich Engels (2009):

1. The alienation from him/herself,
2. The alienation from the other,
3. The alienation from the production process and finally the
4. The alienation from the means of production.

This alienation of man by the forms of scientific management and of Fordism led to the destruction of competencies and to that most employees practice an attitude and behaviour of irresponsibility, not only in the capitalist countries but in those of really existing socialism as well. Was it not called 'organised irresponsibility' (Kornai 1992)?

The Kibbutz experience in Israel should not be neglected in this context as a very radical social innovation, trying to realise communism in praxis – although it has been in heavy waters for a number of years. (Ben-Rafael 1988; Rosner 1992)

Another form of social economy are the self-help groups (Dash 2005), which exist also in the form of neighbourhood initiatives where neighbours construct together their homes without any money compensation. Money-free exchange of labour in form of social/citizen co-operatives is a new form of social economy. Here the members of the co-operative take care of elder members as long as they are themselves fit and accumulate by this activity a credit, which will be used in the future so that the next generation will take care of them. In this sense the term of generation solidarity gets a completely new and very concrete meaning. A rather new form within the social economy are the public-citizen partnerships (PCP).

Volunteer and charity organisations are other historic and widespread forms within social economy. Social networks developed also historically and recently with the help of internet adopted new and global forms (Freeman 2006). So, e.g. *facebook* has now nearly one billion 'friends'. However, social networks like *YouTube* and thousands of others, initially started just for communication, have become companies, worth billions of US dollars.

The social economy created second labour markets, where the production is not targeted in producing surplus and profits but socially useful services and goods. The so-called alternative production instead of arms in the 1980s is still a very important example (Cooley 1987/1980). The alternative Nobel-prize winner and former technical director of the Greater London Enterprise Board, Mike Cooley, elaborated his philosophy of socially useful goods, first presented in the Lucas Aerospace Combine plan (cf. Wainwright and Elliott 1982).

Since the end of the nineteenth century, trade unions started to establish their own companies and banks, often in the form of co-operatives. The idea was also to create a third sector besides capitalism and the state, which was not submitted to the rules of the market and profit. In Germany this sector is named *Gemeinwirtschaft*, which might be translated into English as 'co-operative economy'. It was rather successful at the beginning. In the 1970s the trade unions controlled the fourth biggest bank in Germany, the biggest construction company in Europe etc. Unfortunately this model failed due to corruption and incompetence as well (Széll et al. 1989).

On an even larger scale workers' self-management was developed in Yugoslavia since the 1950s – again as an alternative to capitalism and state socialism, integrating social economy and social life. The basic units of production are autonomous organisations (Széll 1988). Unfortunately, this experience of the most democratic form of the economy ended with the break-down of the Yugoslav nation and system.

Similar experiences of workers' self-management were practiced within the soviets after the First World War in Russia and within the Chinese communes in the 1950s. However, much earlier these kinds of social-economic utopias were already experimented, so e.g. the New Lanark co-operative by Robert Owen (1813). The two Swiss authors Holenweger and Mäder spoke, for the case of Switzerland, of 'islands for the future', which will incrementally grow together (1979).

3 Co-operatives

In the field of the social economy the co-operatives are vanguard institutions, although with different success and ideologies (European Commission 2012). They developed as a third way between private and state ownership, based on solidarity and equality of all its members (Wikipedia 2012b). (http://en.wikipedia.org/wiki/Co-operative) The International Labour Organisation (ILO), the oldest UN-organisation and a tripartite body of state, employers and trade union representatives has since its very beginning in 1919 very much focused on the development of co-operatives to improve the quality of life and working life (Széll and Széll 2009). Thus they state:

> A co-operative is defined as an 'autonomous association of persons united voluntarily to meet their common economic, social and cultural needs and aspirations through a jointly owned and democratically controlled enterprise'. ... The ILO views co-operatives as important in improving the living and working conditions of women and men globally as well as making essential infrastructure and services available even in areas neglected by the state and investor-driven enterprises. Co-operatives have a proven record of creating and sustaining employment – they provide over 100 million jobs today; they advance the ILO's Global Employment Agenda and contribute to promoting decent work. Based on the only international governmental instrument on co-operatives, the ILO Promotion of Co-operatives .... (ILO 2002)

In the same vein, the United Nations have proclaimed 2012 the International Year of Co-operatives. The resolution A/RES/64/136 passed on 18 December 2009 by consensus, was proposed by 55 UN Member States.

Since their very beginnings in nineteenth century, a big debate started about the political nature and strategies of co-operatives. Friedrich Engels in a letter to Bebel stated in 1886 that Karl Marx and he himself were fully convinced that co-operatives were a necessary phase on the way to a communist economy (1970: 426). But on the other hand, the German co-operative movements, led by Friedrich Wilhelm Raiffeisen and Hermann Schulze-Delitzsch (Trappe 2001), were rather conservative, and are still so today. One may argue that they even should have served the function to prevent farmers and workers to join socialist, communist or anarchist movements. Nevertheless even the most successful co-operatives have quite often suffered corruption and careerism. They had (?) to adapt to the rules of the market, although they are not driven by the profit motive.

3.1 The Role of Umbrella Organisations

In today's world no institution, no co-operative can be created nor survive without the support of umbrella organisations. However, as can be learnt from the failure of really existing socialism, we have to be careful in regard to a too strong state. That is why own structures need to be created, independent from the state, which are based on democratic principles (Széll 1988). A federal and decentralised system is much more appropriate for the needs of local structures, and it impedes at the same time the drift towards an authoritarian system. A federal system with support structures for management, training, and finances is the best tool. But one has always to watch out that the bureaucracy does not become too independent and powerful. These support institutions therefore have to play more the role of a midwife than the one of almighty experts. The historical experiences of the largest cooperative complex in the world, Mondragón in the Spanish Basque region (cf. Széll 1992) tells this story as well as the other great cooperative system, Desjardins in Québec, Canada. For all of them the central role of an own bank was the key for the success. This is not surprising, as we know from really existing capitalism that the financial sector is the driving and dominant force (Polanyi 1944). To cope with it, you have to develop your own strength in this domain as well.

4 The Role of Education

Education is the central system of social reproduction of each society (Bourdieu and Passeron 1990), but also for social innovation. Herein the fundamental norms and values are created and transmitted as well as the know-how and technological, social, economic and cultural knowledge. Therefore for the functioning of society education is central – for its continuity as well as for change and adaptation to new challenges. The development of capacities for a new culture of management for co-operatives asks for an appropriate educational system.

Our educational system through its heritage of authoritarian systems, even feudal ones, is still centred on the production of the capacity to subordinate, to execute more than of responsibility and innovation. Vocational training to work in teams is lacking on all levels enormously. But co-operation, co-operatives demand to take responsibility on all levels.

Education in the modern world cannot be restricted to basic training. Management of modern companies and namely of co-operatives necessitates a permanent apprenticeship for original solutions to new problems – always more complex because global. Life-long learning is therefore an absolute must.

To arrive at an efficient educational system the link with research is absolutely indispensable. The universities and schools have a special responsibility in this regard. Not only because they have to detect the technological, economic, cultural and social changes, and they have to open new ways, in forecasting the impacts and risks of action, but also because they are the centres of innovation for the solutions of these new problems. And also they have to train permanently the persons in charge of the institutions in all sectors and domains.

5 The Perspectives

What are then now the perspectives for the social economy, co-operatives and social entrepreneurship at the beginning of the third millennium? (European Union 2012) It may seem hypocrite to dare to make some forecasts in these difficult periods. Co-operation is the most basic form of human life. No individual can survive without co-operating with others, even biological reproduction necessitates social co-operation within the family, a clan, a tribe, in neighbourhood – without even mentioning economic co-operation. All technological, cultural, social progress results from co-operation. The first co-operatives date back thousands of years, because they stem from the birth of humankind.

Modern capitalism has replaced and even destroyed traditional forms of economic, social and cultural production and reproduction, which allowed living together in harmony with nature too, therefore in a sustainable way. The return to these forms of production and reproduction is not possible, nor is it reasonable, because they included also slavery, oppression of women, permanent warfare, no laws etc. The totalitarian regimes of traditional villages are not acceptable anymore in a world of reason and enlightenment. We have always to defend the universal rights against all forms of authoritarian regimes; insofar progress has been made over the last centuries.[4]

Certainly modern co-operatives, as they developed since the nineteenth century, have other qualities than the traditional structures of co-operation. And they have differentiated themselves into different forms like the co-operatives for production, for consumption, for building, for management, for services etc. Above all the legal frameworks of bourgeois societies have influenced their structures and management.

The modern co-operatives have to be able to co-exist together with the capitalist sector, definitely still for a long time dominant on the global level. That is why new structures have to be developed, i.e. social innovation is asked for. These new structures have to incorporate the advantages of all the systems. In this sense a new co-operative entrepreneurship is asked for.

Those societies and regions, which have been marginalized and exploited by modern capitalism, do not have any other chance of survival than to base their future on the development of their own forces. Only a self-centred development gives this chance. A certain de-globalisation – as it has started with the World Social Forum (2012) and attac – is therefore necessary, but neither in a naïve nor ideological manner, as in the 1960s and 1970s. The slogan of this movement – with many local, regional, national and continental initiatives – is socially very innovative and inspires innovation: Another world is possible!

In the capitalist countries we witness a slow renewal of co-operatives during the last couple of years. Namely in the industrial districts of the Emilia Romagna in Italy the co-operatives have demonstrated that their structures were often more flexible and even more capable to defy global competition than the big bureaucratised companies. Piore and Sabel (1984) called these forms 'industrial regions or clusters', where innovation developed best. This holds also true for the

---

[4] Although with the rise of nationalism, Fascism and Stalinism in the nineteenth and twentieth centuries, or religious fundamentalism today progress is questioned.

large co-operative sectors in Japan, France, and Greece – Spain and Québec have already been mentioned. For several years, the *Crédit Agricole* bank from France has been even the biggest bank in the world. Today there are more than 800 million people organised in co-operatives. "Small is beautiful" (Schumacher 1991) seems therefore to be realised on a large scale. To succeed even more, it is worthwhile to concentrate on the necessary preconditions, enumerated above.

Two conditions have still to be fulfilled for the success of a culture of co-operative entrepreneurship. There is first the principle of responsibility, described by the German philosopher Hans Jonas in 1979, and also the Principle of hope by another German philosopher, Ernst Bloch, in 1954. It is true that the philosophers have so far only interpreted the world differently, but we have to change it, if we regard the miseries of the world! (Karl Marx' 11th Feuerbach thesis.) So, the task of today is to re-launch the culture of co-operative entrepreneurship! Scientists, educators and practitioners from all over the world, in a global solidarity, should cooperate in this endeavour (Zoll 2000).

In this same vein of ideas and experiences, it is worthwhile to remember briefly the short, however, famous Prague spring in 1968. There the Czech formulated the Third Way. Authors like Ota Sik (1992) have elaborated this idea, which should today be enlarged by the ecological dimension (Széll 1992). Some prominent political leaders, who have been saying to pursue Third Way policies include Tony Blair from the United Kingdom, Romano Prodi from Italy, Bill Clinton from the United States, Gerhard Schröder from Germany, José Luis Rodríguez Zapatero from Spain, Kevin Rudd of Australia, Jean Chrétien from Canada, Helen Clark from New Zealand, Wim Kok from the Netherlands, and Ferenc Gyurcsány from Hungary (Giddens 1998, 2000, 2001). Although, this initiative seems to have vanished in the last years, and none of the initiators is anymore in power, there is no necessity to resign too early, because the on-going ecological and social crises put us under even more pressure than a decade ago (Harrisson et al. 2009; Kim and Széll 2011).

So, what is the conclusion? Innovation has always taken place through the clash of cultures: practical, scientific, technological, economic, business etc. Often it is just the new combination of old ideas and practices. Today social innovation, social entrepreneurship and development with the aim to improve the quality of life and working life and to allow a sustainable development, have to build on the past, combining old and new in an innovative way. The conclusion of session 10 'Social Innovation and Development' of this conference, which was taken up as one of the 14 prioritised research topics of the Vienna Declaration (see Annex), was phrased: conditions of participation and self-management in social innovations aimed at overcoming poverty and pauperization (cf. also Széll 2012). So, to end alienation and exploitation, the ultimate goal should be self-management (Széll 1988). Hopefully, Europe may take the lead in social innovation again, as it has done three centuries ago in the Age of Enlightenment (Postman 1999). A real utopia (Bloch 1995).

References

Ashoka. (2012). http://www.ashoka.org/. Retrieved 7 Jan 2012.
Ben-Rafael, E. (1988). *Status, power and conflict in the Kibbutz*. Avebury: Gower.
Bloch, E. (1995). *The principle of hope* (Vol. 3). Cambridge, MA: MIT Press.
Bourdieu, P., & Passeron, J.-C. (1990). *Reproduction in education, society and culture*. London: Sage.
Cooley, M. (1987/1980). *Architect or bee? The human price of technology*. London: Hogarth.
Dash, A. (2005). The social economy of self-help groups. In G. Széll & C.-H. Bösling (Eds.), *Hartkemeyer, labour, globalisation and the new economy* (pp. 301–318). Frankfurt/M. et al.: Peter Lang.
Dash, A. (2011). Social innovations and institutional challenges in microfinance. Contribution for challenge social innovation. Session 10 'Social Innovation and Development', Vienna.
Engels, F. (1970). Engels an Bebel'(20. Januar 1886). In K. Marx, & F. Engels (Eds.), *Marx-Engels Werke/MEW* (424–428). Berlin: Dietz.
European Commission, DG Employment & Social Affairs. (2001). Promoting a European framework for corporate social responsibility. Green Paper, Brussels.
European Commission, DG Employment and Social Affairs. (2002). Corporate social responsibility: A business contribution to Sustainable Development. Brussels, COM(2002) 347 final http://www.Europa.eu.int/comm/employment_social/soc-dial/csr/csr_index.htm.
European Commission/DG Enterprise and Industry. (2011). Social innovation Europe http://ec.europa.eu/enterprise/policies/innovation/policy/social-innovation/index_en.htm. Retrieved 7 Jan 2012.
European Union. (2012). http://www.socialeconomy.eu.org/spip.php?article1113. Retrieved 7 Jan 2012.
Freeman, L. (2006). *The development of social network analysis*. Vancouver: Empirical Press.
Fukuyama, F. (1992). *The end of history and the last man*. New York/Montréal: The Free Press/ l'Université de Montréal.
Giddens, A. (1998). *The third way. The renewal of social democracy*. Cambridge: Polity.
Giddens, A. (2000). *The third way and its critics*. Cambridge: Polity.
Giddens, A. (Ed.). (2001). *The global third way debate*. Cambridge: Polity.
Harrisson, D., Széll, G., & Bourque, R. (Eds.). (2009). *Social innovation, the social economy and world economic development. Democracy and labour rights in an era of globalization*. Frankfurt/M. et al.: Peter Lang.
Holenweger, T., & Mäder, W. (Eds.). (1979). *Inseln der Zukunft? Selbstverwaltung in der Schweiz*. Zürich: Limmat Verlags-Genossenschaft.
International Labour Organisation/ILO. (2002). ILO Promotion of co-operatives recommendation (R. 193). Geneva.
Kornai, J. (1992). The Socialist System. The Political Economy of Communism. Princeton: Princeton University Press.
Kim, Y., & Széll, G. (Eds.). (2011). *Economic crisis and social integration*. Frankfurt/M. et al.: Peter Lang.
Lutz, B. (1984). Der Kurze Traum immorwähronder Prosperität. Eine Neuinterpretation der industriell-Kapitalistischen Entwicklung im Europa des 20. Jahrhunderts. Farnkfurt a.M. & New York, Campus.
Marx, K., & Engels, F. (2009). *Die deutsche Ideologie*. Berlin: Akademie-Verlag.
Mills, C.W. (1956). The Power Elite. New York, Oxford University Press.
Murray, R., Calulier-Grice, J., & Mulgan, G. (2010). Open book of social innovation. London: Young Foundation.
Owen, R. (1813). *A new view of society. Essays on the formation of human character*. London: Cadell & Davies.
Piore, M., & Sabel, C. (1984). *The second industrial divide. Possibilities for prosperity*. New York: Basic Books.

Polanyi, K. (1944). *The great transformation. The political and economic origins of our time*. Boston: Beacon.
Postman, N. (1999). *A bridge to the eighteenth century*. New York: Alfred Knopf.
Rosner, M. (1992). Kibbutz. In G. Széll (Ed.), *Concise encyclopaedia of participation and co-management* (pp. 461–468). Berlin/New York: de Gruyter.
Schumacher, E. F. (1991/1973). *Small is beautiful: Economics as if people mattered*. Berkeley Heights: Wildside Press.
Schumpeter, J. A. (1943). *Capitalism, socialism and democracy*. London: G. Allen & Unwin.
Schumpeter, J. A. (1951). In R. V. Clemens (Ed.), *Essays on entrepreneurs, innovations, business cycles, and the evolution of capitalism*. New Brunswick/London: Transaction Publishers.
Schumpeter, J. A. (1967). *The theory of economic development*. Oxford: Oxford University Press [original edition in 1931].
Sebstad, J., & Cohen, M. (2001). Microfinance, risk management and poverty. Washington, DC: CGAP & World Bank http://www.microfinancegateway.org/gm/document-1.9.27070/2468_file_02468.pdf.
Semler, R. (1993). *Maverick: The success story behind the world's most unusual workplace*. New York: Warner Books.
Sik, O. (1992). Self-management. In G. Széll (Ed.), *Concise encyclopaedia of participation and co-management* (pp. 729–742). Berlin/New York: de Gruyter.
Social Innovator. (2012). http://www.socialinnovator.info/about/why-social-innovation. Retrieved 9 Jan 2012.
Social Innovation Europe. (2012). http://www.socialinnovationeurope.eu/. Retrieved 7 Jan 2012.
Sünker, H., Farnen, R., & Széll, G. (Eds.). (2003). *Political socialisation, participation and education: Change of epoch – processes of democratization*. Frankfurt/M. et al.: Peter Lang.
Széll, G. (1988). Participation, workers' control and self-management. Trend report and bibliography (vol. 36, # 3). London: Sage, Current Sociology.
Széll, G. (Ed.). (2006). *Corporate social responsibility in the EU & Japan*. Frankfurt/M. et al.: Peter Lang.
Széll, GY (Ed.) (1992). Concise Encylopaedia of Participation and Co-Management. Berlin & New York, de Gruyter.
Széll, G. (2012). Some historical perspectives on participation. In E. Ben-Rafael, O. Yaakov, & M. Topel (Eds.), *The communal idea in the 21st century*. Leiden/Boston: Brill Academic Publishers.
Széll, G., & Széll, U. (Eds.). (2009). *Quality of life & working life in comparison*. Frankfurt/M. et al.: Peter Lang.
Széll, G., Blyton, P., & Cornforth, C. (Eds.). (1989). *The State, trade unions and self-management. Issues of competence and control*. Berlin/New York: de Gruyter.
Széll, G., Bösling, C.-H., & Hartkemeyer, J. (Eds.). (2005). *Labour, globalisation and the new economy*. Frankfurt/M. et al.: Peter Lang.
Trappe, P. (2001). Co-operatives. In G. Széll (Ed.), *European labour relations* (Vol. 1, pp. 221–238). Aldershot: Gower.
United Nations/General Assembly. (2009). Resolution 64/136 'Co-operatives in social development' http://daccess-dds-ny.un.org/doc/UNDOC/GEN/N09/469/99/PDF/N0946999.pdf?OpenElement. Retrieved 7 Jan 2012.
Wainwright, H., & Elliott, D. (1982). *The Lucas plan. A new trade unionism in the making?* London/New York: Allison & Busby.
Wikipedia. (2012a). Social economy. http://en.wikipedia.org/wiki/Social_economy. Retrieved 7 Jan 2012.
Wikipedia. (2012b). Co-operatives. http://en.wikipedia.org/wiki/Co-operative. Retrieved 7 Jan 2012.
Wikipedia. (2012c). Social entrepreneurship. http://de.wikipedia.org/wiki/Social_Entrepreneurship. Retrieved 7 Jan 2012.

World Social Forum. (2012). http://www.forumsocialmundial.org.br/main.php?id_menu=4&cd_language=2. Retrieved 8 Jan 2012.
Yunus, M. (2008). *Creating a world without poverty*. New York: Public Affairs & Dhaka: Suberna.
Zoll, R. (2000). *Was ist Solidarität heute?* Frankfurt/M: Edition Suhrkamp.

Social Innovations and Institutional Challenges in Microfinance

Anup Dash

Abstract As a tool of development, microfinance represents an extremely complex landscape. As distinct from commercial finance, microfinance is "development finance" – finance for the creation of longer-term social and developmental value (i.e., social profit). Thus, its focus is to blend values, to re-cycle money to multiply social impact. The international policy debate, influencing the development of the sector, has been dominated by two schools – the development school and the finance school. The field has grown through innovations flowing into the sector from both traditions. The first wave, with the most original fundamental social innovation in the form of a new social design for solidarity lending through groups, did create new economic and emancipatory space for the poor women. With the entry of commercial capital, microfinance grew with a new momentum driven by a new logic, but with a "change of heart" changing its focus from the clients to the institution and its sustainability, giving rise to a second wave of innovations in institutional development, market development, product development, and technology development. However, commercialization and its focus on institutional sustainability led to a mission drift. Driven by distorted market logic and a uni-dimensional narrow economism, it has run into a deep crisis today with a "reputation risk", as hard questions are raised about the credibility, ability and intention of the MFIs to serve the poor. Microfinance is now disintegrating as a compelling tool for poverty alleviation. The present crisis creates an opportunity for a third wave of innovations for MFIs to grow to maturity as "blended value" organizations, moving from efficiency to effectiveness, and to produce credible results in terms of social impact, to achieve ever higher social returns on investment. Future innovations should be driven by the need to create institutions which cost less, perform well, and produce impact.

A. Dash (✉)
Utkal University, Bhubaneswar, Orissa, India
e-mail: dashanup@hotmail.com

1 Introduction

Microfinance was invented locally as a small innovative project which was experimented in a Bangladesh village in the 1970s as an answer to the problem of poverty. It began with a great *transformative* potential for building better lives through poverty alleviation and empowerment. It was the beginning of a *new movement*, which was not just about money or credit for the poor, but about unleashing human potential and unlocking human dream for a "life with freedom and dignity". In the context of the failures of the subsidy-based, delivery-oriented, publicly-funded anti-poverty programmes, which treated the poor as *passive* recipients of welfare benefits, it is based on a new entrepreneurial approach to poverty alleviation, making the poor (women) *active* participants in the economy as "makers and shapers" of their own life. Fundamentally, a distinct approach to poverty alleviation, and a new approach to capitalism (to make profit and the market work for the poor), it assumes even greater relevance today in the aftermath of the global financial crisis of 2008 in repairing the damaged lives of innocent victims at the margins of the society (Dash 2010). With the failures in the world of the "big money", the importance of microfinance has increased, necessitating further innovations to strengthen "the power of the small money" to rebuild damaged lives at the bottom of the pyramid.

With its promise as a tool for poverty alleviation, microfinance has been in the centre of the global development policy agenda, especially in the context of the Millennium Development Goals. A very fast-growing, dynamic and vibrant sector, it has been a wonderful meeting ground of the (otherwise ideologically hostile) left and the right of the political spectrum. Politically it appeals to the left as being redistributive and as a programme for direct poverty alleviation and empowerment of the poor women through "solidarity" building, fostering collective action towards social transformation; and to the right as facilitating a process to engage the bottom half in growth and give the poor effective purchasing power through the emergence of a "penny capitalism". For the liberals, microfinance has introduced a remarkable financial innovation in rural credit delivery, while for the radicals, it makes strong claims to empower poor women economically and socially and transform structures of subordination and social relations through "solidarity" group building (Rankin 2002; Mosley and Hume 1998).

2 The First Wave of Innovations

The field of microfinance has been a breeding ground of innovations. Originally developed as "microcredit", it was based on a *new social design* – the *fundamental social innovation* – that marked the birth of the modern architecture of microfinance. Due to weak institutional infrastructure in rural areas, both private and government institutions have faced serious problems in meeting the credit needs of the rural poor. Poor and imperfect information resulted in problems of adverse selection and moral hazard, leading to both high transaction costs and high default rates in rural credit. Screening potential borrowers, monitoring loan use, and enforcing credit agreements obviously become extremely difficult and costly affairs, especially where loans are very small, with no documented credit histories of clients and a complex as well as expensive legal system. There is also the further problem of collaterals, which the poor are not able to provide (asset less, as they are) for the banks to cover their risks. In such difficult situations, banks have followed the policy of "credit rationing", leaving large numbers of the poor without access to institutional credit. Local money lenders have traditionally filled this gap created by credit market failure for the rural poor, but with extremely usurious rates of interests and under exploitative terms forcing the poor into servile social relations and personalized dependence, suppressing their capacity for individual self-initiative and risk taking, with the resultant erosion of their self-esteem and confidence limiting the possibilities of emancipatory collective action.

The innovation of this *new social design* – formation of groups of poor (women) to serve as *social* collateral substituting for the financial collateral – for the delivery of small credits through *solidarity lending* made the group jointly liable for the loan. This proved to be extremely efficient and successful, as the group members (with their comparative information advantage) not only guaranteed each other's loans, but also reduced transaction costs in the whole process of credit management through peer screening of members and borrowers, peer monitoring of loans, and peer pressure against default. The repayment of loans became very high reaching near 100%. Building on this original social innovation, there have been many different *variants* in the design of the group lending methodology (e.g., the Self-Help Groups in India, The Grameen Bank model of Joint Liability Groups, the Solidarity Groups in Latin America, the Village Banks etc.) which have come up through further institutional innovations, but essentially based on this original invention, where the groups of poor (women) pledge their social capital in lieu of the material assets that commercial banks require as collateral. These models differ in terms of the complexity of roles the groups are designed to play, the level of autonomy (in decision making and group management) of the groups, and the amount and types of resources the groups internally generate and control. Based on these criteria, the model is either credit-led or savings-led. The Indian Self-Help Group (SHG) model, for example, is designed to make the groups autonomous community-based organizations of poor (women) for more complex social-developmental roles, with mechanisms to create and manage their own funds (as a precondition to access external loans), and thus, is savings-led.

At a theoretical level, the major strengths of this approach are that: (1) it is rooted in the concept of poverty, not as a social condition, but as a social construction; (2) poverty and wellbeing are multi-dimensional (in contrast to the money-metric reductionism); (3) it is based on an empowerment strategy that builds on "the power within" – power which cannot be given, but has to be generated through collective self-confidence to resist and challenge "the power over"; (4) it builds on a social mobilisational strategy to build up the community and the peoples' sector as an answer to the failures of the state and the market, but outside conventional philanthropy; (5) The process *blends values* (economic with social) by moving on a strong complementarity and mutual reinforcement between access to tangible financial resources (credit) and access to intangible resources of social networks, organizational strength, solidarity and social capital, leadership, new skills and consciousness etc.; (6) it stimulates societal self-(re)organization at the bottom and starts with the realities of the poor women, based on the premise that the real life world of the poor does not change as fast as the logic of economics assumes.

The success of these programmes entirely depends on the *quality of the groups*, because, it is the group's cohesiveness and its self-management capacity that enables them to lower the costs of financial intermediation by creating an "information asset" as a guard against adverse selection, loan misuse and default. Therefore, financial intermediation, in order to be successful and sustainable, does need to build on effective and intensive *social intermediation* – the process through which investment is made in the building up the human capital, social capital as well as the institutional capital of the poor preparing them to engage in formal financial intermediation, and increasing their capacity for entrepreneurship and leadership roles, group management, collective action, and self-reliance. Group formation is an extremely complex and difficult process. Once formed, the groups need to be nurtured with great care, skill, and above all, patience and the fragile groups need to be strengthened against the various internal as well as external threats inherent in the empirical realities of the poor women (Dash 2003). Members require a whole range of training and capacity support (beginning from social skills like leadership, conflict resolution, negotiation and participation to techno-managerial skills, financial literacy, accountancy, records keeping, business management skills etc.) to function as active members of a matured group. Strong and sustaining groups are the *social infrastructure* on which the entire edifice of microfinance operates. Thus doing good microfinance necessitates heavy investment in the groups (the infrastructure) for developmental returns (Dash 2005a).

The groups (especially in the Indian SHG model) are founded on a much more critical approach to participation, and the SHG is designed to provide an emancipatory space for the poor and disenfranchised women. It is a *locus* for i. building new solidarities around common goals based on "civic" as against the "primordial" sentiments and universalistic principles, ii. expanding circles of support for poor and excluded women, iii. a new social learning, as well as a personal transformation, and iv. new leadership building among women in the community. Thus the SHG is not only a vehicle for the delivery of microfinance services, but more importantly, it is a *social design* for stimulating change in the lives of the poor women through emancipatory collective action. The SHG is: i. a *public sphere*, characterized by symmetry, reciprocity, non-hierarchy, and "unmediated" for women; ii. a *free sphere*, separate from the apparati of the state and the market; and iii. a *democratic sphere*, for promoting the cultural competencies of participation (Dash 2003, 2005b).

The members view the groups, not in the same way as an employee views the farm or a client looks upon a bank, but as an entity that is very much *central to their lives* – offering the members an institutional space as well as a social environment that provides not only cohesion, support, and security, but also gives them identity, confidence and hope. The group has very significant intrinsic value for the member, and is not limited only to an instrumental purpose. It is based on the republican value of active citizenship. These groups are a first step to change poor women's life experience from one woven around "protection networks" to one around "innovation networks" and change their life world from one structured around "vertical ties" to one based on "horizontal ties". This process of a *creative destruction* in poor women's lives expands into wider levels, as the groups (themselves developed on poor women's "bonding" social capital) begin to build up "bridging" social capital through their federations and other networks, then further creating "linking" social capital as they begin to relate with banks, government bureaucracies, and the wider market. Women increase their status in terms of their bargaining power within the home, awareness of social and political issues, mobility and transactions with the outside world (unmediated by men), recognition of their contribution and role as central to the family and community, their self-esteem and confidence.

But for this to happen, the poor women as much as their groups need capacity more than capital, and without capacity, capital could have damaging effect. The danger of producing backlash in hierarchically structured traditional patriarchal societies, in the form of domestic violence or alcohol abuse, or male appropriation of female loans is not uncommon. While formation of microfinance groups creates opportunities for poverty alleviation and empowerment, they are not *automatically* lifting the poor above poverty or empowering them. Group formation is a necessary, but not sufficient condition for poverty alleviation and empowerment. Access to credit does not automatically translate into positive impact. To realize its positive impact, the process has to be socially engineered through constant social intermediation. In the absence of adequate and rigorous social intermediation, the groups can develop pathological behaviour (such as internal power dynamics as a constraint to implement sanctions on defaulters, leadership abuses in monopolizing loans, misappropriations, other transparency and accountability problems in group management, member drop-outs etc.), leading to the collapse of the whole programme. Therefore, social intermediation is the life blood and a concomitant process that fuels and propels financial intermediation. As Abed and Matin (2007) say, "the greatest power of microfinance lies in the *process* through which it is provided" (p. 4, emphasis added). The promotional role of the microfinance institutions (MFIs) is an extremely critical input to their role as microfinance providers. Doing real microfinance well, i.e., living up to its poverty alleviation and empowerment claims, is therefore an extremely complex and difficult process, much like riding a bicycle which requires constantly balancing its two wheels (social intermediation and financial intermediation) and very creatively blending values(economic with social) to build better lives and wellbeing for poor people.

With its *bi-dimensional* (economic and social) goal, it pursues an arranged marriage between capitalism (income growth) and democracy (participation and inclusion). While economic transactions are an important aspect of the group activity, the groups do have a more holistic design and a much broader developmental goal. When they grow to maturity they do play a developmental role as a force of change in the community (Dash 2003). As a social infrastructure, the well-functioning SHG in India becomes a point of service for different development initiatives and governmental inputs. This creates possibilities for creatively developing credit-plus (as against the minimalist credit-only) strategies and linking microfinance to other development programmes. Where microfinance is joined up with other developmental inputs, it creates groups which go beyond a *narrow economism*.

3 The Commercial Revolution and the Second Wave of Innovations

In the early years, philanthropic capital investing for social returns supported NGOs, who successfully validated the wisdom that "the poor are bankable". But, behind this success, there was a strong commitment to their social mission, a very high level of social motivation, and a rigorous social mobilization strategy focused around the formation of groups geared to create a new economic and socio-political space for innovation and collective action. The *social rigor in the process* was the secret of the "magic bullet". But, soon it was realized that the philanthropic capital market is very uncertain and extremely limited by the amount of social surplus it generates. Further, it cannot recycle the capital, hence is not sustainable. It is too small to match the huge capital needs for scaling up the early successes in microfinance to make any significant impact in the fight against global poverty. Therefore, the participation of the mainstream commercial capital (both public and private) was needed. Also, the early successes convincingly demonstrated that the poor are a good credit risk, and thus, microfinance appeared to be a great market opportunity for commercial finance. As a result, microfinance, which was born in the philanthropic capital market, is now growing in the commercial capital market.

With commercialization, microfinance got a new momentum driven by a new logic. Provision of sustainable financial services, not to the very poor but to low income people with active economic activity in the under-served market niches became the goal of microfinance; the emphasis shifted from the *depth* of outreach to the *cost* of outreach. The commercial revolution brought about "a change of heart" in microfinance – a paradigm shift from "poverty lending" to "institutional sustainability". As a result, the entry of the mainstream commercial capital has increasingly brought the MFIs under tremendous pressure to drift away from their social mission and gravitate towards a focus on building financially sustainable microfinance institutions (Dash 2009).

Lack of institutional capacity for *efficient* financial intermediation was perceived as a more binding constraint on the scale of outreach than availability of funds. Thus innovations were directed towards institutional capacity building of MFIs with systems and processes to improve their efficiency for accessing the mainstream financial capital market. Key innovations were made in the areas of institutional development, market development, and technology development. The major foci in the process of commercialization became business development, product development, management information system, financial management, efficiency and productivity enhancement, and profitability. The most significant innovations, as summarized by the United Nations Capital Development Fund in its May 2005 issue of *Microfinance Matters*, are: *product innovations* (e.g., micro-savings, remittances, housing, insurance, pension etc.) for the poor in response to market needs, and *technology innovations* (introduction of biometrics into the credit data system, ATMs (electronic messages) with picture and voice prompts for the illiterate rural poor, Smart Cards and wirelessly connected point of service, cell-phone based banking for remote villages etc.). The other important innovation has been the institutional transformation and a *trend towards formal financial institutions*. Yet another important area, where substantial innovation has come up is the development of *the financial market infrastructure* (e.g., excellent progress has been made on the quality of information on financial performance at the institutional level through refined systems and standards; a shared information system with client credit histories, like credit bureau; the Microfinance Information Exchange – the MIX, a centralized database for microfinance reporting – with an increasing number of microfinance institutions and funds reporting high quality data). As the State of the Microcredit Summit Campaign Report (2011) says, these innovations have been extremely critical for the development of "a vibrant microfinance ecosystem" (p. 6) to support and sustain the growing microfinance industry, which today reaches out to 190 million clients globally. The Self-Help Group movement in India alone now includes 68 million women.

4 The Current Crisis and Institutional Challenges in Microfinance

In spite of its spectacular innovations and growth, microfinance has today run into a deep crisis, which has recently rocked the sector. Hard questions are now being raised about its future. More specifically in India and Bangladesh (its own home), serious concerns are raised questioning its ability and intention to serve the poor and "lift them out of poverty". Recent reports of increasing cases of suicide by microfinance clients in India have taken the air out of the microfinance balloon, giving rise to a "legitimation crisis" of the microfinance sector. This crisis has been exacerbated by unbridled greed, abuses and tyranny of the microfinance institutions – unethical and aggressive marketing, multiple lending and high interest rates on loans leading to over indebtedness on the part of the poor clients, coercive and abusive methods followed by the MFIs for loan recovery, and the resultant increase in social and psychological pressures on the poor clients driving them even to the point of suicide. Naturally this has stirred intense public criticism as well as growing regulatory heat. The MFIs have become "loan-sharks" and, in the words of the Bangladesh Prime Minister Sheikh Hasina, are "sucking blood from the poor in the name of poverty alleviation" (quoted in the *New York Times*, dated January 5, 2011).

Clearly, the present crisis in microfinance is a *crisis of its own making*. The critical risks facing the microfinance sector globally today are: credit risk, reputation risk, unfair competition, mission drift, corporate governance, and inappropriate regulation (CSFI 2011). While the sector is faced with multiple risks, the two most important of all are the reputation risk and the credit risk. Credit risk is the result of over-supply of credit and bad credit management leading to over-indebtedness by millions of borrowers, who have accumulated larger debts beyond their capacity to repay, leading, in turn, to the threat of the breakdown of financial discipline with the potential danger of increased delinquencies and huge loan loss. Over indebtedness, as a consequence of loans from multiple sources, not only results in an impoverishment of the MFI's asset quality, but also damages clients' wellbeing. The impact of the reputation risk is extremely severe, bringing the credibility and legitimacy of the MFIs under question and serious scrutiny. The microfinance sector is not equipped to cope to these risks effectively at present. Although the present crisis is symptomatic of its collapse, it is *not* the end of microfinance. Rather, the crisis builds up the steam to learn from failures and push for a third wave of innovations in microfinance to "do good" by "doing well".

5 What Has Gone Wrong with Microfinance? Market Versus Morality

Market and morality are uneasy bed partners. Rent-seeking and free-riding, fuelled by what Keynes termed as the "animal spirit", increasingly become the drivers of market "success" for MFIs. Multiple MFIs crowd into the same local economic space, chasing the same poor clients; push-selling badly designed and highly priced loan products and dumping them on the poor borrowers in quick and successive cycles. Then they use coercive and abusive methods with the clients to recover their loans in gross violation of the minimum standards of fair practice and consumer protection norms. Not only the *costs* of loan are high, its *risks* are also great for the poor client. Instead of enabling the poor clients to slowly climb up the opportunity ladder, the MFIs create a loan ladder for the clients, which make them even more vulnerable. The stories behind the "efficient" MFIs – their rosy balance sheets, impressive growth curves, and excellent ratings – are extremely ugly. Clients have to burn the candle on both ends to make the microfinance institutions "successful" and "sustainable" – sell their furniture and utensils, cut down on their food and eat less, borrow from other loan sharks and take second jobs to pay off their loans (Brett 2006). The microfinance industry has produced "a pandemic of revenue-maximizing institutions, many of which have *forgotten* the social mission they may once have had" (Rippey 2007: p. 113, emphasis added), breeding a race of financial institutions "with no conscience at all" (p. 115). The interests of the poor women borrowers are often in conflict with the interests of the institutions, and when interests diverge, MFIs have shown more interest in their own institutional well-being at the cost of the well-being of the poor women borrowers. The father of micro lending, Muhammad Yunus has been warning that high growth and high profits (in the name of cost covering) have been corrupting the industry. The concept of microcredit, as he told the *Wall Street Journal*, "is being blatantly abused".

As a result, microfinance is increasingly disintegrating as a compelling gender-focused tool for poverty alleviation, empowerment and development as evidences are mounting to show that it can and does have serious damaging effects on the poor women clients. "Feminization of debt" (the other side of "credit") destroys a client's self-respect and sometimes even her life. A study of Indian Self Help Groups clearly shows that "even after 5 or 7 years, around half of member households are still below the poverty line" (Sinha 2007: p. 76). Rahman (2007) concludes his analysis of Bangladesh with the observation that "the poverty fighting power of microfinance is limited" (p. 202). One of the most comprehensive literatures in respect of Impact Assessment of microfinance programmes under the USAID supported AIMS programme (Assessing the Impact of Micro enterprise Services), on the basis of extensive literature review and case studies of some leading MFIs, asserts that the relationship between microfinance and poverty reduction is *not* straightforward (Barnes and Sebstad 2000: p. 1).

There is something seriously flawed in the current architecture of the microfinance industry. In operational terms, microfinance today has degenerated into a *narrow economism*, as MFIs are increasingly guided by the mantra: "Greed is good". Commercial investors want to see aggressive growth, profits and the potential for scale, luring the MFIs away from the moral adherence to their social goal. In fact, the trend of "commercialization of microfinance" has given rise to a growing sense of uneasiness internally within the microfinance community for quite some time now. A recent book (Dichter and Harper 2007), based on "a stock taking" of the microfinance industry globally, comes to the powerful conclusion that "there is quite a lot *wrong* with microfinance" (Harper, *ibid.*: 257, emphasis added). The first generation of micro finance innovations convincingly demonstrated that "the poor are bankable", they are a good credit risk. The present generation of "efficient" and "sustainable" microfinance institutions has transformed this mantra into a market intelligence that "banking with the poor is profitable", thanks to the neo-liberal revolution. The drive to be financially sustainable robs MFIs of their (social) soul. "Institution building" has replaced "client building" as the goal of MFIs. The logic driving the growth of the industry during the last decades is distorted. Financial sustainability is no more a *means* to achieve valued social *goals*; it has become an *end in itself*. Giving primacy to financial sustainability is like putting the cart before the horse.

The pressure to be financially sustainable and institutionally efficient requires MFIs to measure, monitor, and manage their financial performance – the single bottom line – very carefully to build an impressive portfolio (e.g., in terms of portfolio quality, profit and loss, delinquency, portfolio yield rates, subsidy dependence etc.) and to go to scale with aggressive business strategy. The pendulum swings in the direction of the "Right", more and more as the MFIs operate on a distorted logic with the exclusive focus on the single bottom line of their financial performance. The Rating agencies are also to share part of the blame for the misplaced emphasis on *financial performance* of the MFIs. The Rating Instruments, currently used by the donors to assess the recipient microfinance institutions suffer from the same serious weakness in terms of the uni-dimensionality of narrow economism. They are designed to only assess the MFI's financial health. Thus, for example, Lowell et al. (2005) in their study point out three major weaknesses of the rating agencies: (1) they rely too heavily on simple analysis of ratios derived from poor-quality financial data, (2) they overemphasize financial efficiency while ignoring the questions of programme effectiveness, and (3) They generally do a poor job of conducting analysis in important qualitative areas. Further they argue that "donors make important decisions using potentially misleading data and analysis, and *the agencies' potential to do harm may outweigh their ability to inform*" (p. 40, emphasis added). Such rating systems ignore questions of *social performance and impact*; and also do a poor job in assessing MFIs qualitatively in such areas as governance quality, organizational transparency, depth of poverty outreach, ethical practices, social impact etc.

In the run up for quick financial profit, the new breed of "efficient" MFIs have hardly the patience, skill, motivation and commitment to invest in microfinance groups (SHGs) and poor (women) clients which are the very foundation of their business. Group meetings are devoted to routine and boring matters of credit, repayment, and savings alone. The quality of interaction, the attendance and the duration of the meetings go down as the value of the groups is reduced for the members. Groups begin to perform poorly as the pathologies of group dynamics are manifested through abuse of power by the leaders, free riding, and erosion of transparency. The complexity of pathological group dynamics obscures the myths about the role of social capital in peer lending programmes. In the context of Bosnia and Herzegovina, Bateman (2007) argues that the present model of microfinance "very actively *destroys* social capital" (p. 218). As community development and support activities are recast as commercial and strict cost-recovery operations, there is "a degeneration of local solidarity, interpersonal communication, volunteerism, trust-based interaction and goodwill" (p. 219). Losing focus on their social goals, MFIs tend to behave as pure market players, driven by market forces and principles. Market players, as they are, they try to externalize costs (of group building and social intermediation). Everyone loves the champagne, but no one tends the vine, leading to the *tragedy of commons* syndrome in the group-based microfinance model.

6 Future Innovation Needs

The *first generation innovations* in microfinance were the most basic and fundamental *social* innovations in the form of "new social designs" through which the gaps between the poor and the financial institutions were bridged, opening up a huge world of developmental possibilities for the poor. The *second generation innovations* were driven by the institutional needs of the MFIs to go to scale and to be more "efficient", albeit in managing the single bottom line (financial). These "efficiency-driven innovations" were more market-oriented, geared to product diversification, and based on application of new technology, innovations in internal systems and tools of MFIs. These innovations made microfinance institutions more efficient, but at the expense of making them more effective in terms of their social performance; responsive to the markets rather than to their mission – separated from the very core social rationale that is the very basis of their being and legitimacy.

The present crisis – exacerbated by the goal-less and soul-less growth driven by a distorted logic and a uni-dimensional narrow economism of MFIs to create profit at the bottom of the pyramid – throws up critical challenges for the sector, but also breeds opportunities for a *third wave of innovations*. The institutional pressure on the MFIs to build public credibility, legitimacy and accountability by demonstrating that they add distinct value to the society cost effectively better than other players should drive *future innovations*. Future innovations need to focus on creating microfinance institutions which not only *cost less*, but also *perform well*, and *produce impact*. In other words, the next generation of innovations has to be directed towards institutional change in microfinance to *blend values*, to show positive results in the following core themes, as articulated by the Microcredit Summit Campaign: (1) reaching the poorest, (2) empowering women, (3) building financial self-sufficiency, and (4) ensuring social impact.

Reaching the poorest, empowering the women, and ensuring social impact are strategic social goals which can only be achieved through conscious, sustained and rigorous processes of targeting, tracking and measuring social performance, the same way as it is done for financial performance. In order to fully realize their potentials for positive social impact, MFIs have to be tightly aligned with their social mission, improve their knowledge management systems based on a sophisticated understanding of their clients and the environment in which they operate, as well as to build up their organizational capacity for social performance management with a focus on deepening outreach and designing appropriate services leading to economic and social changes in the lives and behaviour of the clients, their family, their business, and the wider community.

Microfinance, in essence, is "development finance", and clearly it is distinct from "commercial finance". It is "finance against poverty", or rather, "money with a (social) mission". In contrast to commercial finance which is exclusively driven by profit and measured in terms of the single bottom line of financial returns on investment and creation of short-term market value, microfinance is a social investment for the creation of longer-term social and developmental value (i.e., social profit). It is a different approach to investment – investment to maximize both financial and social returns, to blend values, to re-cycle money to multiply social impact and to generate long-term social developmental benefits. Yet, there are no credible mechanisms to structure the microfinance investment for social value creation. Neither do MFIs have robust internal organizational systems and management tools so as to be able to authentically translate their social mission into practice, nor are there any credible and comprehensive rating tools available to ascertain the degree to which the MFIs blend values – economic with social and ethical. In the absence of a structured mechanism built into the management strategy of the MFIs as development institutions, and more importantly, the investment decisions of the social investors, some "do-gooders" at best try to create a social face and claim to be "doing development" by some sporadic social activities as an add-on, not as a strategic tool to maximize their social return on investment (SROI).

Since appropriate tools have not been developed to capture the realities of blended value organizations like MFIs and assess them on a *social screen* alongside the financial screen, mainstream capital market resorts to the standard short-term financial measurement system as a guide to investment decisions. Financial performance tools tell us about the health of the microfinance institutions, but not about the health and wellbeing of their clients. In the absence of *social rating tools*, the rating agencies use wrong tools and distort the microfinance market and build compelling pressure on the sector as a whole to limp with one (financial) leg to the exclusion of their social leg. They do more harm in the process by providing distorted information to the social investors who want to see their capital bring long-term positive social returns. By ignoring the social bottom line, MFIs not only risk their credibility and reputation, but also miss potential opportunities. The current crisis in the microfinance sector has thrown up this challenge to evolve comprehensive *social rating* systems for the MFIs which could serve the purpose of accounting to external stakeholders, managing internal operations, and producing credible results in terms of social impact.

There are, however, serious problems inherent to this field of social impact which remains a challenge for researchers – the qualitative and the subjective nature of the social values. Indicators of social performance are more complicated than indicators of financial performance. Many different kinds of changes can be brought about by a programme (both as direct and indirect consequences), and each possible change can be measured by a number of different indicators (Imp-Act 2005). Social values are not objective facts, neither are they governed by any hard and concrete law with regularities and precision to fit to the logical construction of a log frame or social value metrics and show that financial inputs perfectly translate into social outputs and outcomes. Their qualitative and complex nature is especially challenging for social science research experts (especially the dominant section among them which comes from the logical-positivist tradition) to frame them in a reliable, and objectively measurable metrics to match with the sophistication in the financial metrics. Thus social performance metrics and social rating systems, measurement and monitoring of social and developmental values, and measuring the social return on investment are front-line areas for research innovation as well which would improve the institutional framework of social investment capital market as much as the microfinance management *praxis*.

There have been some fragmented initiatives in recent years to develop social and ethical accountability systems for the MFIs. The Imp-Act programme's Social Performance Management, the CGAP's Poverty Assessment Tool (PAT), Micro Finance Transparency, The Smart Campaign, and the microcredit Summit Campaign's initiatives to develop the "Seal of Excellence" are some of the notable developments in this direction. However, these are still some loose ideas, which need further development and innovation with regard to standardized indicators, general consensus across the diversity of MFIs, enforcement mechanisms etc. For example, the Smart Campaign takes a modular approach and treats consumer protection principles as a module, which could be integrated with the financial rating, or could form part of a social rating, or can be a stand-alone system with certification by the Smart campaign. The buy-in for the Smart Campaign is rather easy, compared to; say, the Seal of Excellence, because there already exists some amount of consensus on the general principles of client protection. The Seal of Excellence is more focused on impact, but is generally perceived as top-down, and not relevant for a large part of the sector that aims at "access" and "inclusion" as their goal. Again, there remain the questions of a credible enforcement mechanism (State of the Microcredit Summit Campaign Report 2011). Thus the field remains patchy, fractured, and lacks a robust, tight, coherent and integrated framework with rigor and relevance, and with credible mechanisms for enforcement and benchmarking standards.

Microfinance remains a sector that does not yet channel resources towards impact. For this, we need institutional innovations to be "client focused" and not "institution focused" (Datar et al. 2008), and to grow to the next level of maturity moving from efficiency to effectiveness and impact. This implies innovations to be more creatively engaged with the clients, enriched by a more refined understanding of gender, poverty and development. Today, in the twenty-first century, we are far more developed in our conceptual framework to understand poverty, the nuances of gender, and the goal of development. There are at least three areas of microfinance focus, which MFIs need to build on recent advances in knowledge – (1) expanding and deepening their understanding of *poverty as multidimensional*; (2) moving beyond the income-centric to *a wellbeing-focused approach* to development; and (3) developing *gender diagnostic* tools to guide female targeting of programmes drawing insights from advances in feminist economics.

We have learnt that there is more to development than just income and GDP. Development involves more basic objectives, and we have a sharper awareness of the means-end confusion – income and growth are the *means* to achieve more basic developmental goals. Development is about people and their *agencies* – their happiness and wellbeing, their capabilities, choices and freedom "to lead the kind of life they value" (Sen 2000). Wellbeing as a critical element of development requires closer attention to the lived experiences of the poor and the deprived, the marginalized and the excluded that have no opportunity to share the growth of the country's GDP. The GDP is a very bad indicator of a country's development performance – fatally flawed, as it privileges a narrow economism at the expense of social, environmental and ethical breakdown (Széll 2011). A very strong unifying theme and the key message which emerges from the report of the Commission on the Measurement of Economic Performance and Social Progress (CMEPSP), set up by the French President Nicholas Sarkozy, (with Joseph Stiglitz as its president and Amartya Sen as its advisor) is that "the time is ripe for our measurement system to *shift emphasis from measuring economic production to measuring people's wellbeing*. And measures of wellbeing should be put in the context of sustainability" (2008: p. 12, emphasis in original). Thus, it is very important that *wellbeing* of the clients, their families and community becomes the centre of development and the goal of microfinance services.

Both wellbeing and poverty are multidimensional in nature, and are more agency-focused in approach which capture the realities of the poor better than a reductionist economic construct and its money-metric measure. The famous *Voices of the Poor* study of the World Bank, based on interviews held with poor people in 60 countries, comes to clear conclusions which are very important and informative for the microfinance community. The lessons we get from this series are: (1) Poverty needs to be viewed in a multidimensional way. Hunger is part of our common understanding of poverty, but equally strong are the sense of powerlessness, voicelessness, and humiliation that come with being poor. Poor people want access to basic services and infrastructure, but they know that education is the escape from poverty. Bad health is a trigger that drags people deeper into poverty. Poor people do not just want an income or a subsidy. They know that they have to increase their assets, whether land, water, or knowledge, to get a better return on those assets; (2) People trust their own (community) institutions more than the state institutions and rely on their informal networks; (3) Households are under deep stress, gender relationships are crucial to understanding poverty; (4) The social fabric is often the poor people's savings grace, and it is under threat (Narayan et al. 2000).

There has been a steady dilution of the gender goals in microfinance under the influence of the neo-liberal minimalists. Feminist economics offers a much better and more relevant conceptual guide for microfinance; therefore, doing good microfinance requires a change of lens from neo-classical to feminist economics. Feminist economists have argued that capitalism is patriarchal (Vaughan 2007) and the orthodox mainstream economy suffers from an inherent *androcentric bias* (Best and Humphries 2003). In making a historical analysis of the women's relationship to the world of money making and investment in the nineteenth century America, Yohn (2006) describes the women entrepreneurs as "crippled capitalists" in the otherwise "male preserve" of financial markets, credit systems, and capitalist accumulation. Women were expected to turn their energies to the production of *social* capital and "social housekeeping". Obviously, women's business in this period remained small, under-capitalized, and limited in their reach and profit potential (p. 98), as women had to carve out an alternate and female space in which to do business by highlighting the connections between their entrepreneurial activities and domestic concerns (pp. 100–01). What has changed from the nineteenth century scenario in the twenty-first century is that women are today "encouraged", "promoted", and "organized" to do business and run enterprises as a matter of public policy – more so through microfinance programmes. But what women have still not been able to do is to challenge the "gendered nature of enterprise development". Even today, as in the nineteenth century, in spite of all the efforts and investments to promote women entrepreneurs through the microfinance programmes, women enterprises remain small, under-capitalized, and limited in their reach and profit potential, as women have to run enterprises within the "female space" harmonizing their "productive" and "reproductive" roles.

As a result, women's enterprises, supported by MFIs are mostly home-based, because of cultural constraints on women's mobility and the need to integrate their culturally structured roles in the productive and reproductive economies, restricting them to only those kinds of business which provide the needed flexibility. Home (or close to home)-based operations means that interruptions to their work are frequent (arising out of the need to simultaneously attend to their reproductive work) with the resultant loss in the efficient functioning and loss of productivity in the enterprise. They reduce the geographical scope of their business activity to cut down travel time. Women hire fewer employees than men for their enterprises, and again they hire mostly same-sex workers, from the known social circles because the relationships are easier, at the cost of efficiency. The barriers to entry into a competitive market are too many for them – all flowing from the structures of subordination in a patriarchal system. Thus, microfinance programmes promote women's enterprises within the accepted "female space" shaped by the patriarchal hegemony and do not enable them to challenge this space and overcome patriarchy. Hence, the conventional minimalist microfinance does not move beyond the androcentric capitalism, resulting in an *adverse inclusion* of poor women entrepreneurs into capitalism.

A well-functioning group-based microfinance programme demonstrates that markets and hierarchies are not the only two alternative modes of coordination as advocated by orthodox economists. It also moves beyond the ontological construct of the *homo oeconomicus* – a neo-classical concept rejected by the feminist economists as an atomistic and under-socialized individual, exclusively self-regarding, autonomous, and instrumentally "rational". The members of the self-help groups resemble more with the contrastive explanation of the "human agency" offered by the feminist economists – The "Relational" woman (in contrast to the "Rational man"), the model of non-deterministic multi-dimensionality and relatedness, in which both material and non-material motivations drive human behaviour. Interdependent and interconnected group actors (and not isolated individuals) are at the centre of economic activities, and heterogeneity of human needs (and not simply economic calculus) defines human wellbeing. With the very notion of a "separative" self, which is "androcentric" in its very core, understanding *collective action* is an endless problem in orthodox economics (Best and Humphries *op.cit.*). Feminist economics informs us better the phenomenon of these self-help groups getting things done collectively and helps us better to understand the groups and the members who are driven by multiple logics rather than a calculative logic pursuing their own private goods only. The group is a social entity that enables members to develop their "capability space" in ways that cannot be bought in the market place or through market mechanisms. The emancipatory goals of the microfinance movement ought to be anchored in the shared interests of the poor women and their "situated" *agency*.

Sen emphasizes that women's *agency* – their ability to be active agents of change, to define their own goals and act upon them – is crucial to ensuring their well-being. Women's well-being can be furthered by highlighting agency amid structures of constraint and thereby directing action to everyday practices of subordination and discrimination. Giving women the freedom to exercise their agency should be the goal of development policy, and microfinance institutions should check how much their services realize this goal. Credit alone does not enable women to challenge patriarchy, and change the complex structures of subordination, inequalities, and discrimination within the household, the market, or the wider society. Conversely, such technically structured microfinance programmes more often gets co-opted into the hegemonic patriarchal structures. In the minimalist credit programmes, women frequently exhibit, what Sen calls, "adaptive preferences" – preferences that have adjusted to their second-class status (1990).

If microfinance has to have significant and lasting positive impact on women's lives, it must also work to change the power relations that constrain their abilities to control and benefit from improvements in household income (Kantor 2005: p. 65). It is both strategic and more immediately necessary that MFIs move beyond viewing women as mere "recipients of credit", "responsible payers" or "a new market". They need to expand their role in supporting investment in social reproduction while also contributing to doing this in ways that change gender relations. There is a need to conceive of microfinance more innovatively and more creatively in terms of its social promise appropriate to the realities of the poor women in order to unleash its true emancipatory and transformative potential. We need future "market-makers" in the social investment capital market who push frontiers in defining and benchmarking standards to blend values, enhancing transparency, and innovating more efficient operations to achieve ever higher social returns on investment.

References

Abed, F. H., & Matin, I. (2007). Beyond lending: How microfinance creates new forms of capital to fight poverty. *Innovation, 2*(1–2), Winter and Spring, 3–17.

Barnes, C., & Sebstad, J. (2000) Guidelines for microfinance impact assessments. Discussion paper for the CGAP 3 virtual meeting (October 18–19, 1999). Assessing the impact of micro enterprise services (AIMS), Washington DC.

Bateman, M. (2007). De-industrialization and social disintegration in Bosnia. In D. Thomas & H. Malcolm (Eds.), *What's wrong with microfinance?* Warwickshire: ITDG/Practical Action.

Best, M. H., & Humphries, J. (2003). Edith Penrose: A feminist economist? *Feminist Economics, 9*(1), 47–73.

Brett, J. A. (2006). We sacrifice and eat less: The structural complexities of microfinance participation. *Human Organization, 65*(1), Spring, 8–19.

CSFI. (2011). Microfinance banana skins 2011: Losing its fairy dust. Centre for the Study of Financial Innovation, www.csfi.org.uk.
Dash, A. (2010). Gender, poverty and microfinance: The global economic crisis and beyond. Contribution for the annual conference of the international association for feminist economics, Buenos Aires.
Dash, A. (2009). Microfinance, poverty and the social economy of empowerment. In D. Harrisson et al. (Eds.), *Social innovation, the social economy and the world economic development*. Frankfurt am Main: Peter Lang.
Dash, A. (2005a). The social economy of self-help groups. In G. Széll et al. (Eds.), *Labour, globalisation and the new economy*. Frankfurt am Main: Peter Lang.
Dash, A. (2005b). Emancipation through micro credit. *Appropriate Technology*, 32(1) March, 12–13.
Dash, A. (2003). Strategies for poverty alleviation in India: CYSD's holistic approach to empowerment through the self-help group model. *IDS Bulletin, 34*(4), October, 133–142.
Datar, S. M., Epstein, M. J., & Yuthas, K. (2008). In Microfinance, clients must come first. *Stanford Social Innovation Review*, Winter, 38–45.
Dichter, T., & Harper, M. (Eds.). (2007). *What's wrong with microfinance?* Warwickshire: ITDG/Practical Action.
Imp-Act. (2005). Social performance management in microfinance: Guidelines. *Imp-Act* Programme, Institute of Development Studies at the University of Sussex, Brighton
Kantor, P. (2005). Determinants of women's microenterprise success in Ahmedabad, India: empowerment and economics. *Feminist Economics, 11*(3), 63–83.
Lowell, S., Trelstad, B., & Meehan, B. (2005). The ratings game. *Stanford Social Innovation Review*, Summer, 39–45.
Microcredit Summit Campaign (2011). State of the microcredit summit campaign report. www.microcreditsummitcampaign.org.
Mosley, P., & Hume, D. (1998). Microenterprise finance: Is there a conflict between growth and poverty alleviation? *World Development, 26*(5), 783–790.
Narayan, D., Patel, R., Schafft, K., Rademacher, A., & Koch-Schulte, S. (2000). *Voices of the poor*. Oxford/Washington D.C./New York: The World Bank/Oxford University Press.
Rahman, S. M. (2007). A practitioner's view of the challenges facing NGO-based microfinance in Bangladesh. In T. Dichter & M. Harper (Eds.), *What's wrong with microfinance?* Warwickshire, UK: ITDG/Practical Action.
Rankin, K. N. (2002). Social capital, microfinance, and the politics of development. *Feminist economics, 8*(1), 1–24.
Report by the Commission on the Measurement of Economic Performance and Social Progress (CMEPSP) (2008). www.Stiglitz-sen-fitoussi.fr.
Rippey, P. (2007). Princes. peasants, and pretenders: The past and future of African microfinance. In T. Dichter & M. Harper (Eds.), *What's wrong with microfinance?* Warwickshire: ITDG/Practical Action.
Sen, A. (2000). *Development as freedom*. New York: Anchor Books.
Sen, A. (1990). Gender and cooperative conflicts. In I. Tinker (Ed.), *Persistent inequalities*. New York: Oxford University Press.
Sinha, F. (2007). SHGs in India: Numbers yes, poverty outreach and empowerment, partially. In T. Dichter & M. Harper (Eds.), *What's wrong with microfinance?* Warwickshire: ITDG/Practical Action.
Széll, G. (2011) (Guest Editor). Special issue on "Beyond GDP". *The Indian Journal of Industrial Relations*, 46(4) April, 545–552.
Vaughan, G. (Ed.). (2007). *Women and the gift economy*. Toronto: Inanna.
Yohn, S. M. (2006). Crippled capitalists: The inscription of economic dependence and the challenge of female entrepreneurship in nineteenth-century America. *Feminist Economics, 12*(1/2), January/April, 85–109.

Social Innovation and Social Enterprise: Evidence from Australia

Jo Barraket and Craig Furneaux

Abstract 'Social innovation' is a construct increasingly used to explain the practices, processes and actors through which sustained positive transformation occurs in the network society (Mulgan, G., Tucker, S., Ali, R., Sander, B. (2007). Social innovation: What it is, why it matters and how can it be accelerated. Oxford: Skoll Centre for Social Entrepreneurship; Phills, J. A., Deiglmeier, K., & Miller, D. T. *Stanford Social Innovation Review,* 6(4):34–43, 2008.). Social innovation has been defined as a "novel solution to a social problem that is more effective, efficient, sustainable, or just than existing solutions, and for which the value created accrues primarily to society as a whole rather than private individuals." (Phills, J. A., Deiglmeier, K., & Miller, D. T. *Stanford Social Innovation Review,* 6 (4):34–43, 2008: 34.)

Emergent ideas of social innovation challenge some traditional understandings of the nature and role of the Third Sector, as well as shining a light on those enterprises within the social economy that configure resources in novel ways. In this context, social enterprises – which provide a social or community benefit and trade to fulfil their mission – have attracted considerable policy attention as one source of social innovation within a wider field of action (see Leadbeater, C. (2007). 'Social enterprise and social innovation: Strategies for the next 10 years', Cabinet office, Office of the third sector http://www.charlesleadbeater.net/cms/xstandard/social_enterprise_innovation.pdf. Last accessed 19/5/2011.). And yet, while social enterprise seems to have gained some symbolic traction in society, there is to date relatively limited evidence of its real world impacts. (Dart, R. *Not for Profit Management and Leadership,* 14(4):411–424, 2004.) In other words, we do not know much about the social innovation capabilities and effects of social enterprise.

In this chapter, we consider the social innovation practices of social enterprise, drawing on Mulgan, G., Tucker, S., Ali, R., Sander, B. (2007). Social innovation: What it is, why it matters and how can it be accelerated. Oxford: Skoll Centre for

J. Barraket (✉) • C. Furneaux
Queensland University of Technology, Brisbane, Australia
e-mail: jo.barraket@qut.edu.au

Social Entrepreneurship: 5) three dimensions of social innovation: new combinations or hybrids of existing elements; cutting across organisational, sectoral and disciplinary boundaries; and leaving behind compelling new relationships. Based on a detailed survey of 365 Australian social enterprises, we examine their self-reported business and mission-related innovations, the ways in which they configure and access resources and the practices through which they diffuse innovation in support of their mission. We then consider how these findings inform our understanding of the social innovation capabilities and effects of social enterprise, and their implications for public policy development.

1 Introduction

In a global risk society (Beck 1992) characterised by increasing economic and environmental interdependencies, the role of civil society actors and cross-sectoral collaborations in delivering innovative responses to 'wicked problems' (Weber and Khademian 2008) has gained increasing attention. Within this context, there has been growing interest in social enterprise in a number of world regions by governments, businesses, and the not for profit sector over the past decade. This growth in interest has played out in Australia; yet, little is known about the dimensions or impacts of the existing social enterprise sector in this country (Barraket 2004; Lyons and Passey 2006; Barraket 2008). As Mulgan (2006) has noted more broadly, surprisingly little is known about social innovation that occurs in the not for profit sector, and amongst social enterprises.

In response to this gap in knowledge, a research project was undertaken to identify the activities of social enterprises in Australia, and to report on the size, composition and the social innovations initiated by this sector of the social economy. This chapter considers the main findings of this study in relation to the social innovation found in the sector.[1] The chapter contributes to our understanding of the social enterprise sector in Australia, and the ways in which social innovation has occurred within this sector. It considers the self-reported activities of Australian social enterprise in light of Mulgan et al.'s (2007) conceptualisation of social innovation, discussed further in Sect. 2.1 below.

2 Defining Terms

The notion of social enterprise has been the subject of definitional debate amongst scholars, practice experts and policy makers for over a decade. Different policy actors tend to focus on particular forms of social enterprise with a view to achieving specific policy goals, while different socio-cultural contexts have given rise to

---
[1] For the full results, see Barraket et al. (2010).

differing organisational compositions (Kerlin 2006; Defourny and Nyssens 2010). Finding an operational definition of social enterprise for the purposes of the study was an important objective and was derived from a review of the available policy literature, preliminary responses to an initial discussion paper promoted online, and input via three project workshops with key informants about what defines social enterprise (see Barraket and Collyer 2010). For the purposes of this study, social enterprise was consequently operationalised as businesses or ventures that:

- Are led by an economic, social, cultural, or environmental mission consistent with a public benefit[2];
- Trade to fulfil their mission[3];
- Derive a substantial portion of their income from trade[4]; and
- Reinvest the majority of their profit/surplus in the fulfilment of their mission.

2.1 Social Innovation and Social Enterprise

'Social innovation' is a construct increasingly used to explain the practices, processes and actors through which sustained positive transformation occurs in the network society (Mulgan 2006; Phills et al. 2008). Social innovation has been defined as a "novel solution to a social problem that is more effective, efficient, sustainable, or just than existing solutions, and for which the value created accrues primarily to society as a whole rather than private individuals" (Phills et al. 2008: 34). Phills et al.'s definition stresses that social innovation is characterized not just by 'newness' but by improved responses to societal needs. We find Phill et al.'s (2008) definition operationally problematic, because it is normatively framed: that is, it presumes the possibility of consensus within society about what constitutes 'more efficient, efficient, sustainable, or just' solutions to complex social problems. Rather than seeking to define social innovation as such, Mulgan et al. (2007) aim analytically to identify its characteristics. These authors suggest that social innovation can be conceptualized as comprising three core dimensions: new combinations or hybrids of existing elements; cutting across organisational, sectoral and disciplinary boundaries; and leaving behind compelling new relationships. In this chapter, we draw on Mulgan et al.'s (2007) characteristics of social innovation to better understand social innovation practices amongst our sample.

---

[2] This may include member benefits where membership is open and voluntary and/or benefits that accrue to a subsection of the public that experiences structural or systemic disadvantage.

[3] Where trade is defined as the organised exchange of goods and services, including:
Monetary, non-monetary and alternative currency transactions, where these are sustained activities of an enterprise; contractual sales to governments, where there has been an open tender process; and trade within member-based organisations, where membership is open and voluntary or where membership serves a traditionally marginalised social group.

[4] Operationalised as 50 % or more for ventures that are more than five years from start-up, 25 % or more for ventures that are three to five years from start-up, and demonstrable intention to trade for ventures that are less than 3 years from start-up.

Emergent ideas of social innovation challenge some traditional understandings of the nature and role of the third sector, as well as shining a light on those enterprises within the social economy that configure resources in novel ways. Social enterprises have attracted considerable policy attention as one source of social innovation within a wider field of action (see Leadbeater 2007). And yet, while social enterprise seems to have gained some symbolic traction in society, there is to date relatively limited evidence of its real world impacts (Dart 2004). In other words, we do not know much about the social innovation capabilities and effects of social enterprise. To date, the social innovation produced by social enterprise has been largely presumed rather than empirically demonstrated. In the remainder of this chapter, we consider the composition and self-reported business and social innovations of the Australian social enterprise sector, based on our survey data.

We then consider how these findings inform our understanding of the social innovation capabilities and effects of social enterprise, and their implications for public policy development.

3 Methodology

The research was carried out in several phases. The methodology for the project is summarised in Fig. 1 below.[5]

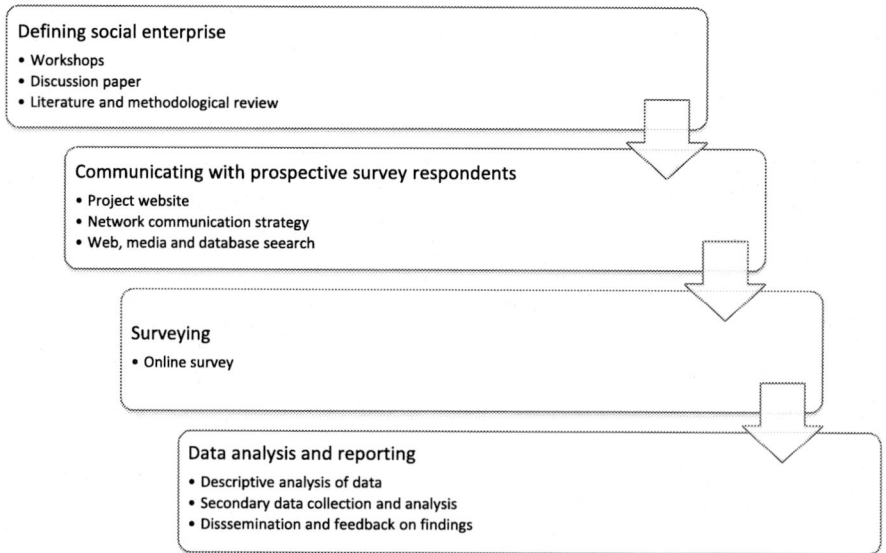

Fig. 1 Overview of methodology

---

[5] Parts of this section are reproduced from Barraket et al. (2010).

3.1 Literature and Methodological Review

A detailed review of social enterprise mapping projects conducted internationally was carried out to identify different approaches to sampling and available research instruments – such as existing surveys and interview schedules – from which previously validated survey items could be used.

3.2 Website Establishment

A project website was set up and a preliminary discussion paper on defining social enterprise was developed and promoted on the site for comment. Four responses to the definitional discussion paper were received via the project website. The website also provided opportunities for people to tell us about a social enterprise they knew and/or to register for a copy of the full project report. One hundred and fifty-seven social enterprises were recommended for inclusion in the research via individuals who contacted us through the project website.

3.3 Framing and Defining Workshops

In April–May, 2009, the research team conducted three workshops and two meetings to explore with key informants definitions of social enterprise. Informants were purposively selected based on their reputation for leadership in Australian social enterprise development, social enterprise research, and/or their affiliation with organisations and government departments with oversight of social enterprise development. Thirty-four people participated in these discussions. Participants were asked to articulate the core features of social enterprise, and to consider how best to operationalize the concept for the purposes of identifying and surveying the sector. Participants' intuitive understanding of social enterprise was also explored using specific examples that 'tested' articulated definitions.

3.4 Identification of the Population

At the time of commencing the study, there was no known population of social enterprise in Australia. Social enterprises in this country are incorporated under a variety of legal structures and, given the relative newness of terminology, many organisations that are social enterprises do not identify themselves as such. An inductive, or bottom-up, approach was taken to identify the population for surveying. A systematic search for Australian organizations consistent with our definition of social enterprise was conducted via:

- A review of publicly available information from relevant regulatory bodies (for example, the consumer affairs agencies in each state);
- A review of case study and resource sites pertaining to social enterprise in Australia;
- A comprehensive web search for not for profit trading organizations;
- A media search of local and national print media over the past 2 years;
- Requests for information, where privacy requirements permitted, through the research team and partner organisation's existing networks; and
- Promotion of the project and project website through relevant networks, seminars and newsletters, and via Twitter.

In total, 4,460 prospective organisations with available contact details were identified via these methods. Based on the organizational information available through the search process, not all of the organizations identified could be verified as social enterprises. We thus sought to be inclusive in our invitation to participate in the survey, and used filtering questions in the survey instrument to determine which organizations were valid social enterprises, according to our definition.

3.5 Survey Design and Administration

A detailed online survey instrument was designed based on our original research aims, existing survey instruments used to map social enterprise, existing survey instruments utilized as part of Australian business data collection, and issues raised by workshop participants. The survey was piloted online with three people involved with social enterprise development and subsequently refined. Most refinements related to the technological interface of the online survey, with two minor substantive amendments to survey questions. The online survey was opened for 7 weeks between October 2009 and November 2009. Direct invitations to participate were sent by email to 4,460 organisations. Taking into account email bounce backs, 4,000 valid email invitations were distributed. One follow-up reminder was issued by email. The survey was actively promoted at major relevant events, including the Social Enterprise World Forum in Melbourne, and Jobs Australia national conference in Hobart. Two half-page advertisements were placed in consecutive editions of a widely distributed social enterprise magazine, The Big Issue. The survey was also promoted in the digital newsletters and/or on the home pages of at least 12 not-for-profit and social enterprise intermediaries, as well as four government agencies. Finally, telephone follow-up reminders were made by members of the research team and partner organisation staff to 274 organizations.

3.6 Data Analysis

Once completed, survey data were cleaned, analysed, and a summary report provided to participants. A total of 539 responses to the survey were received.

Of these 365 respondents were considered valid according to our operational definition of social enterprise and retained within the sample. Survey data were subjected to descriptive and inferential analysis. Inferential analysis pertaining to social innovation practices of our sample are presented here.

3.7 Limitations of the Study

The findings of this research may not be generalizable to all settings. The absence of a known population of social enterprise prior to conducting the research, and the consequent use of inductive methods to identify the sample, limit the extent to which we can generalize from the findings. Also, the relatively low response rate to the survey constrains the validity of our results. The resulting sample was, however, internally diverse, including enterprises of all ages, sizes and operating within every industry of the Australian economy. On this basis, we discuss our findings here as findings true of our participating sample, which can yield some insights into the social enterprise sector more broadly.

4 Findings

Our purpose in this chapter is to consider the self-reported aspects of social innovation reported by our sample, in light of Mulgan et al.'s (2007) three dimensions of social innovation. Full details of the research findings and demographics are available online (see Barraket et al. 2010).

4.1 Finding 1: Variety in Social Enterprises

Mulgan et al. (2007: 5) argue that the first dimension of social innovation is new combinations or hybrids of existing elements. In other words, social innovation both stimulates, and is constituted in, variety in the combinations of existing forms of organization. Our findings highlight the considerable variety that exists in the social enterprise sector in Australia. In every dimension that the survey measured there was notable diversity: in terms of organisational form, the size of the organisations, age, ownership structure, primary mission, number of ventures, industry involvement, source of income, or types of innovation.

4.1.1 Demographics of the Population of Social Enterprises

The majority (74 %) of responding organisations were comparatively small, 22 % were medium sized and around 4 % were classified as large organisations. The Australian Bureau of Statistics classifies organisations as small if they have less than 20 staff; medium if greater than 20 but less than 200; and large if they employ 200 people or more. According to the Australian Bureau of Statistics (2004) 32.8 % Small and medium enterprises (416,000) employed one to four people, 10.9 % (139,000) employed 5–19 people, and 56.3 % (715,000) were non-employing businesses. Thus compared to small and medium business, the percentage of social enterprises classed as 'small' within our sample was considerably higher than the business sector in general.

In terms of their age, organisations were also asked how long they had been operating. The majority of social enterprises (around 62 %) were over 10 years old, 11 % were aged from 6 to 10 years old, 13 % were aged 2–5 years old, and the remainder were less than 2 years old, or not fully operational. This finding is consistent with other research, which found that older more established, not for profit organisations are more likely to operate a commercial venture compared to organisations that were established in the last 15 years (Department of Families and Community Services 2005).

4.1.2 Primary Mission of the Social Enterprise

Figure 2 sets out the main purpose identified by responding organisations

The survey found notable diversity in the missions of participating social enterprises. The primary purpose of the majority of social enterprises was to create opportunities for people to participate in their community, while the second most common was to develop new solutions to social, cultural, economic and environmental problems, the latter finding that social innovation is an explicit objective of many social enterprises in our sample.

Mulgan et al. (2007) suggest in their conceptual framing that social innovation both contributes to, and is signified by, new combinations of structures. The survey

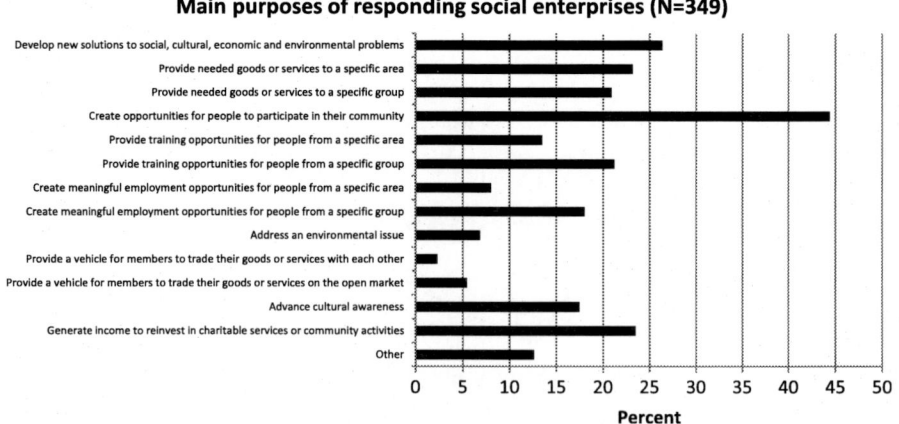

Fig. 2 Primary purpose of social enterprises

found evidence to support this, with variety in the structure and legal status of social enterprises, as well as diversity of ownership structure, industry involvement sources of income and targeted beneficiaries.

4.1.3 Organisational Structure of the Social Enterprises

As Fig. 3 shows, the majority of social enterprises were fully incorporated entities, although a range of alternative arrangements were represented in the sample.

4.1.4 Legal Status of Social Enterprises

As Fig. 4 shows, the most common legal form of social enterprise within our sample was incorporated association, followed by company limited by guarantee. While typically organisations in the third sector are not for profit entities, social enterprises that participated in the study included both profit distributing, as well as non-profit distributing forms (Table 1).

It is instructive, in terms of examining new combinations, to consider how legal status and organisational structures are correlated in the data. This is set out in Table 2 below.

As Table 1 demonstrates, there is considerable hybridity in the combinations of organisational legal status and forms from organisations completing the survey. While the majority of combinations conform to prevalent understandings of not for profit organisations in Australia (e.g. an incorporated/registered entity which was

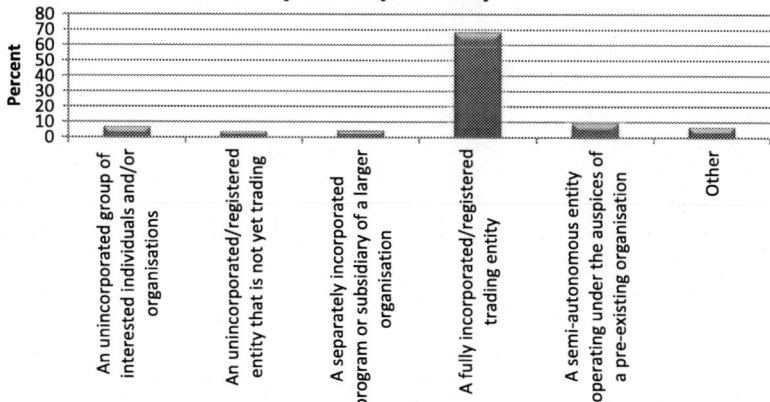

Fig. 3 Organisational structure of social enterprises

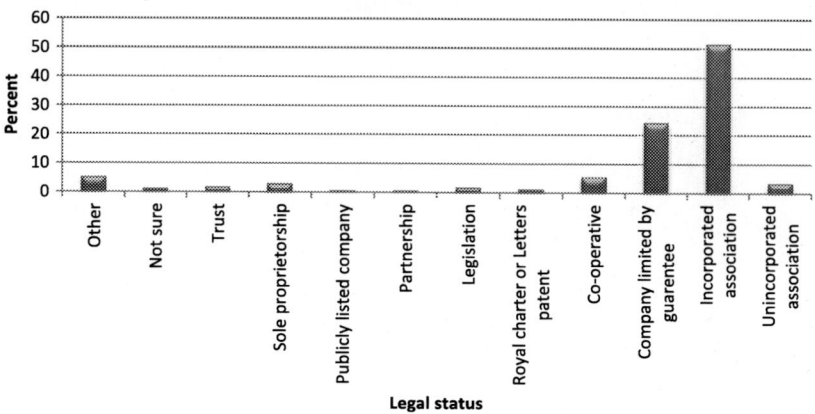

Fig. 4 Legal status of social enterprises

Table 1 Non-profit status and organisational legal status (N = 338)

		Is your organisation not for profit		
		Yes	No	Don't know
Organisation's legal status	Unincorporated association	12		
	Incorporated association	166	4	3
	Company limited by guarantee	69	15	
	Co-operative	14	4	
	Royal charter or Letters patent	4		
	Legislation	6		
	Partnership		1	1
	Publicly listed company		2	
	Sole proprietorship		10	
	Trust	5	1	
	Not sure	4		
	Other	14	3	
	Total	294	40	4

either and association or company limited by guarantee), a large number of alternative combinations of structures were also found. These differences were statistically significant [χ^2 (1,55) = 224.08, $p < 0.001$].

4.1.5 Ownership Structure of the Social Enterprise

Figure 5 demonstrates that the primary ownership structure of the social enterprises was an organisation owned by a non-profit agency (over 50 %). This coheres with

Table 2 Cross Tabulation of organisational structure with organisational legal status (N = 328)

		8. What best describes the organisational structure of your enterprise right now?				
		An unincorporated group of interested individuals and/or organisations	An unincorporated/ registered entity that is not yet trading	A separately incorporated program or subsidiary of a larger organisation	A fully incorporated/ registered trading entity	A semi-autonomous entity operating under the auspices of a pre-existing organisation	Other
9. What is your organisation's legal status?	Unincorporated association	7				5	
	Incorporated association	4	4	7	143	8	12
	Company limited by guarantee	1	4	4	65	7	4
	Co-operative		2		15	1	1
	Royal charter or Letters patent					3	1
	Legislation	1	1		1		
	Partnership	1			1	3	
	Publicly listed company		1		1		
	Sole proprietorship	5	1		1	1	2
	Trust			1	5		1
	Not sure	2		2		1	
	Other	3			6	4	3
	Total	21	13	12	232	29	21

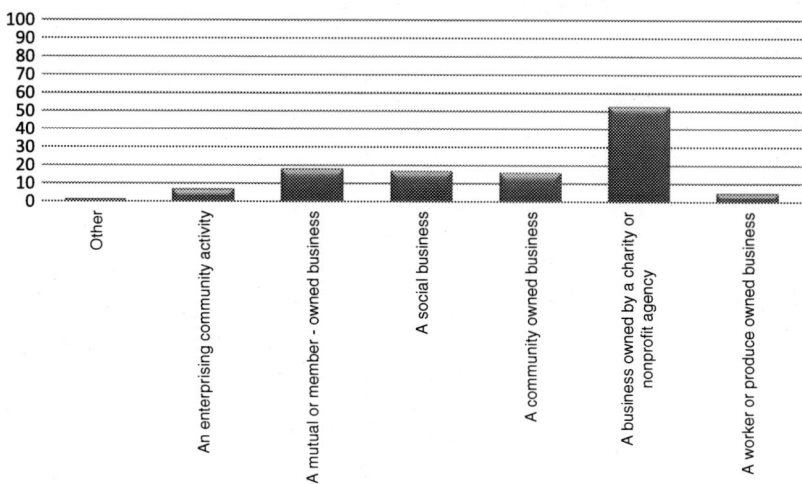

Fig. 5 Structure of social enterprises

other research, which found that, in 2003–04, over one quarter (29 %) of not-for-profit organisations operated a commercial venture or social enterprise (Department of Families and Community Services 2005).

4.1.6 Main Industry Involvement for Social Enterprises

Figure 6 demonstrates that human services, education and research, and culture and recreation are all categories that feature prominently within our sample. When asked to classify the industries within which their enterprise operated, the majority of organisations responding to the survey operated in education and training (41.28 %) and arts and recreation services (31.4 %). Findings from the BALTA Social Economy Survey in Canada show slightly different results with the majority of enterprises operating in social services (37.4 %), teaching and education (34.6 %) and arts and culture (33.2 %). While there is difficulty correlating the data given the different industry classifications, it is evident that a larger percentage of social enterprises in Australia that participated in our study were involved in the education sector compared to Canada. Perhaps more importantly, the data suggest that social enterprises are involved in a large variety of industry settings not typically associated with the not for profit sector (e.g. electricity, gas and mining). Indeed, it is notable that, across our sample, social enterprise operated in every industry of the Australian economy.

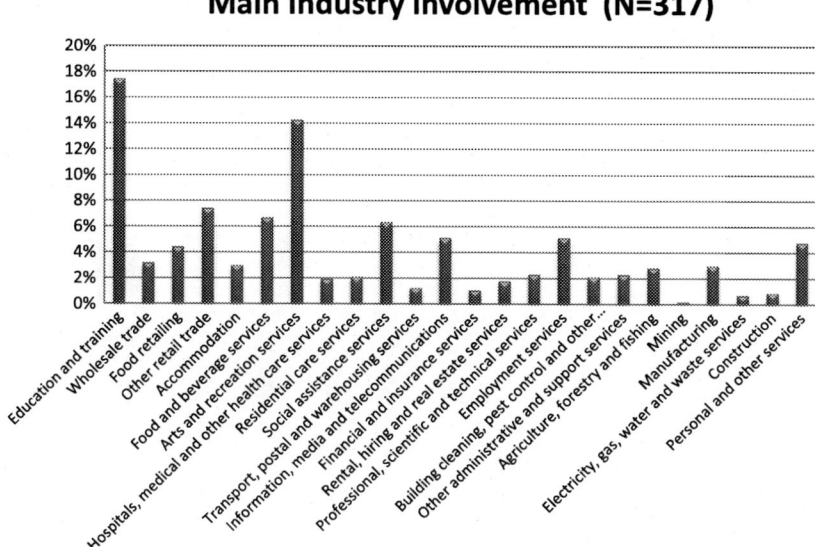

Fig. 6 Main industry involvement of social enterprises (Some organisations indicated more than one industry involvement)

4.1.7 Income of Social Enterprises

For any organization, income can be derived from a range of sources.

As can be seen from Fig. 7, the main source of income reported was through the sale of goods and services, followed by payment from government for service delivery.

4.1.8 Reinvestment of Surplus by Social Enterprises

While income and expenditure is important, a key issue for social enterprises is what they do with the profits from the enterprise. Typically a not for profit organisation in Australia, has to reinvest their surplus in the operations of the enterprise, and would never distribute surplus to shareholders or owners (as this would make the enterprise for profit). The blurring of this boundary can be seen clearly in Fig. 8 below, were the distribution of funds amongst social enterprise is more diffuse than is allowed for in the traditional understanding of a not for profit organisation.

The vast majority of surplus was spent in improving or growing the social enterprise.

The targeted beneficiaries of social enterprises participating in our study were extremely diverse (see Fig. 9), reflecting the variability of collective human

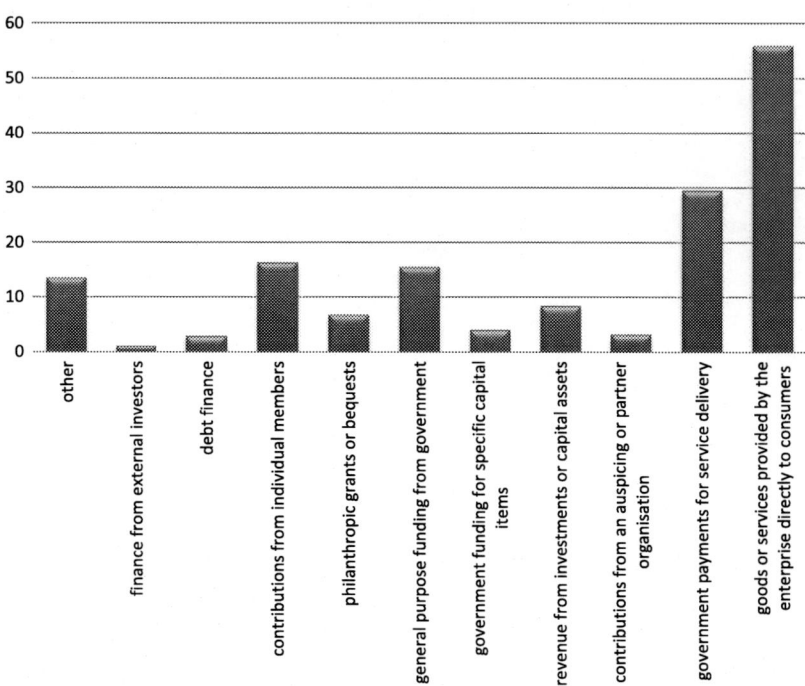

Fig. 7 Income derived from different sources

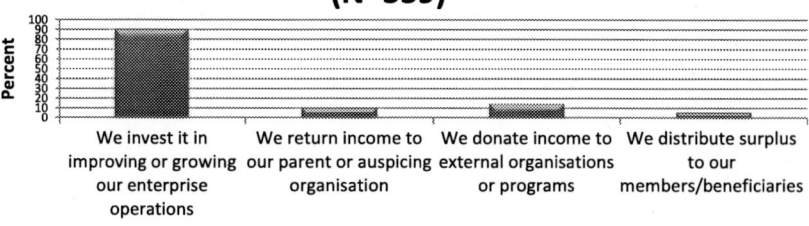

Fig. 8 Reinvestment of surplus

aspirations enacted through civil society organizations. Young people were the most frequently cited beneficiaries. However, it is notable that more than 20 % of responses to this question fell into the 'other' category, with respondents citing a wide range of highly specific target groups and/or locations.

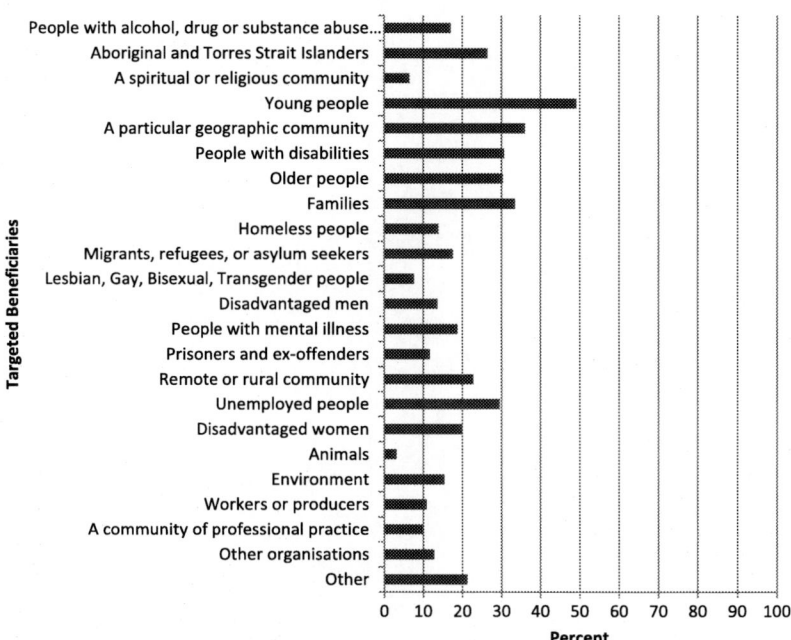

Fig. 9 Beneficiaries of social enterprise

4.2 Finding 3: New Relationships

Mulgan et al. (2007) suggest that new relationships are formed in order to facilitate social innovation. One source of evidence for these relationships is the sources of information used by social entrepreneurs and social enterprise managers. Figure 10 details these sources of information.

While some of these relationships may be instrumental in nature, the data suggest that social enterprises, as organisations that inhabit both social and economic domains, are involved in diverse relationships in support of both mission fulfilment and business success.

4.3 Innovation in Social Enterprises

While the framework provided by Mulgan et al. (2007) has proven useful in terms of establishing some of the organisational forms, relationships and combinations,

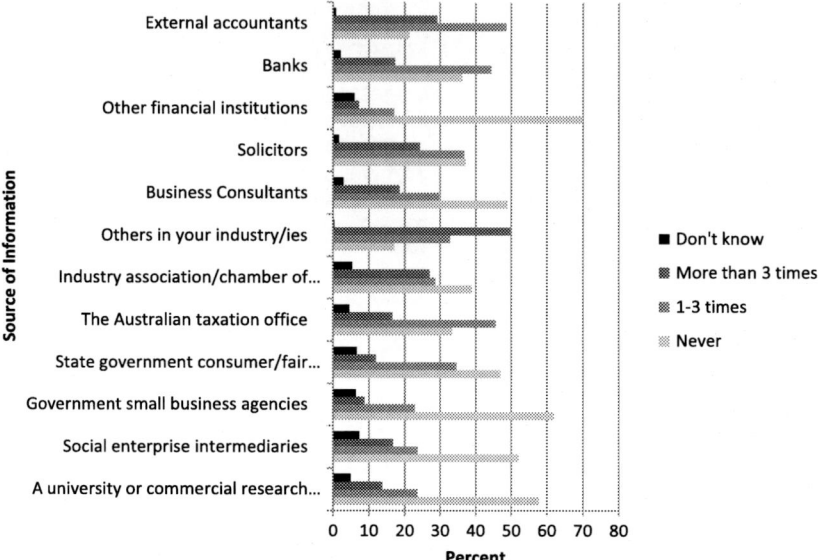

Fig. 10 Source of information used by social enterprises

such assessment stops short of detailing the nature of the innovations themselves, and their impact upon profitability of the organisation. Insofar as we have captured these in our research, they are detailed below:

4.3.1 Type of Innovation

Social enterprises are widely held to be innovative organisations. In our study, we asked respondents to indicate in what areas they innovated. Following typical OECD coding, we examined goods (product) innovation, service innovation, process innovation, and organisational innovation. Allowing for the mission-driven nature of social enterprise, we also asked for organisations to specify whether the goods, services and processes were primarily for the benefit of their beneficiaries or the benefit of the organisation itself. This information is summarised in Fig. 11 below.

Examining Fig. 11, there seemed to be a distinct difference in the responses – particularly in relation to the goods produced. There seemed to be an inverse proportion of organisations that did not undertake goods innovation of any sort, compared to the other types of innovation. Additionally, as the answer to these questions was yes/no binary answers, there was overlap between them, with some

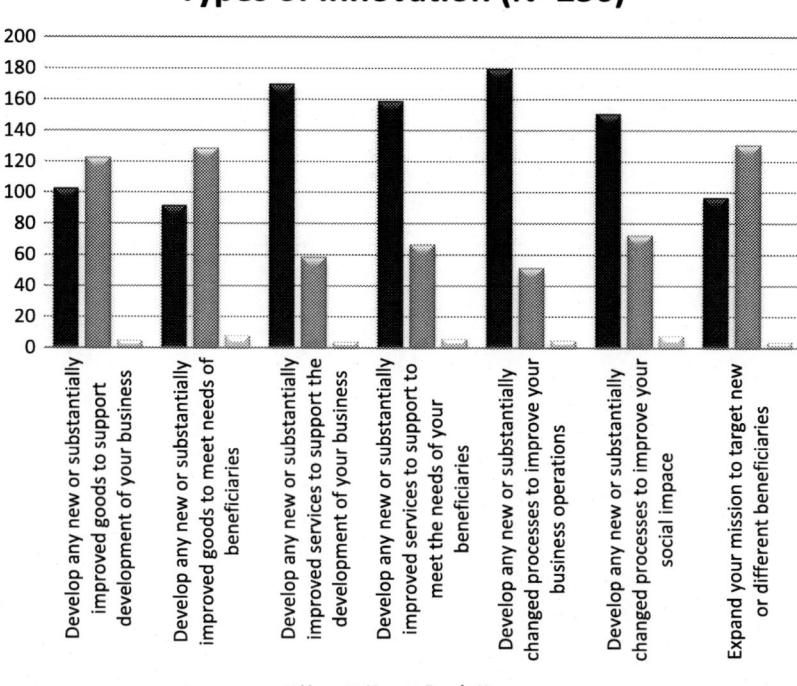

Fig. 11 Types of innovation (The total number of innovations implemented is higher than the total number of respondents, as a number of organisations undertook more than one type of innovation)

organisations undertaking multiple forms of innovation. Given this correlation and complexity in the binary data, further analysis of potential underlying components within the dataset was warranted.

4.3.2 Clusters of Innovation Activity

Given that many organisations undertook multiple forms of innovation, direct correlation analysis was a challenge. A Principal Component Analysis (PCA) was undertaken in order to look for underlying patterns in the innovation data. This showed that there was a simple structure in the data with two main components. From analysis of these data, innovation tended to take on two main types: either innovation in processes, services and organisational goals; or in goods. The full PCA can be found in Appendix A. However the graphed plot of the components can be seen in Fig. 12 below:

Further exploratory analysis was needed in order to determine how many social enterprises fitted into each component, which can be seen in Fig. 13 below.

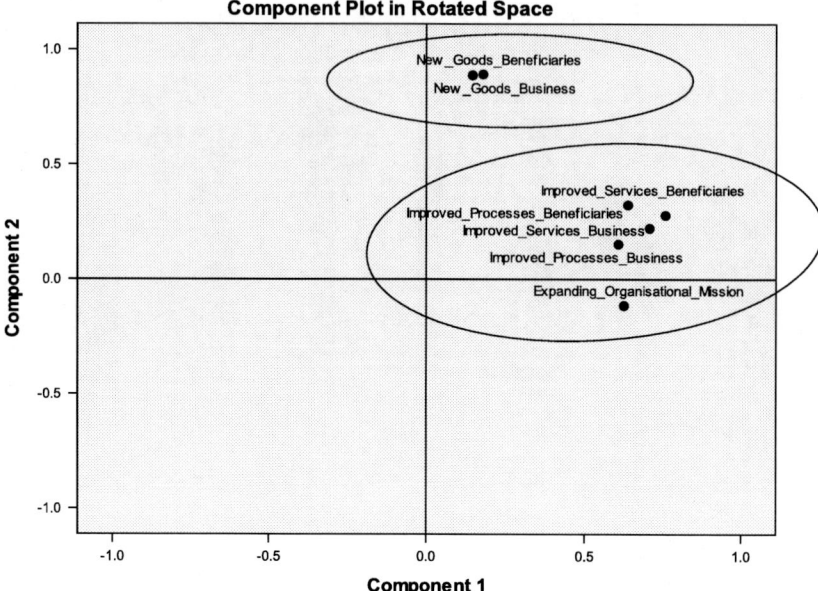

Fig. 12 PCA component plot in rotated space

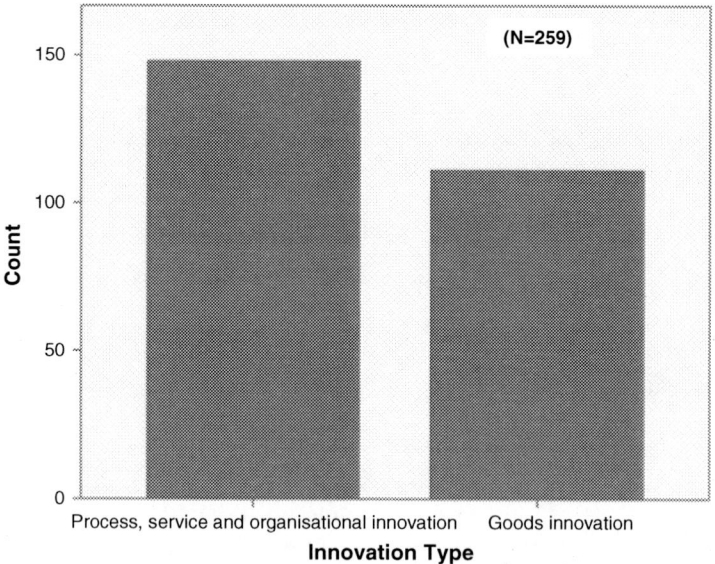

Fig. 13 Number of organisations in each component of innovation

Analysis of the raw data indicated that all organisations that undertook innovation in goods for beneficiaries were included in the second group, and none of those who didn't. In other words, the the split in the data found by the PCA makes practical sense as well. Cross tabulations showed that 111 organisations undertook goods innovation for their beneficiaries, and 148 did not, and this difference was highly significant.

Thus there is a distinct split in the data concerning innovation, with some organisations undertaking innovation of goods, while others definitely didn't. This is perhaps not surprising as the majority of social enterprises operate in the service economy. More interesting is the impact that this difference had upon cash flow.

4.3.3 Relationship Between Innovation and Profit/Loss

While plots indicated that social enterprises undertaking innovation in goods had a much higher overall income than social enterprises that undertook other forms of innovation, this was offset by higher costs. An Analysis of Variance (ANOVA) was undertaken to examine different profit between the two main groups of innovators. This found that goods and service innovators had a higher profit overall compared to process, services and organisational innovators [$F(1,107) = 5.099, p < .026$].[6]

In each case there is a distinct difference between those organisations that undertook goods innovation and those that did not. Social enterprises that reported innovating in goods, also reported earning more, spending more, and having greater surplus compared to those social enterprises that didn't. The two greatest losses also occurred in the group that undertook goods innovation. Thus goods innovation has potential for greater returns as well as greater losses, and therefore the risk profile of goods innovation for social enterprises is higher than social enterprises that undertake process, service or organisational innovation (Fig. 14).

5 Discussion and Conclusion

The Australian social enterprise sector is extremely diverse in its mission orientations, legal structures, market orientations and business models. Within this diversity, the sector self-identifies as being active in social innovation, with a large proportion of our research respondents identifying that their major purpose is to create new solutions to complex social, environmental, cultural and economic problems. Following the framework advanced by Mulgan et al. (2007), we have found evidence that social innovation amongst our participating social enterprises:

---

[6] Due to the nonparametric nature of the data, the log of these values was used.

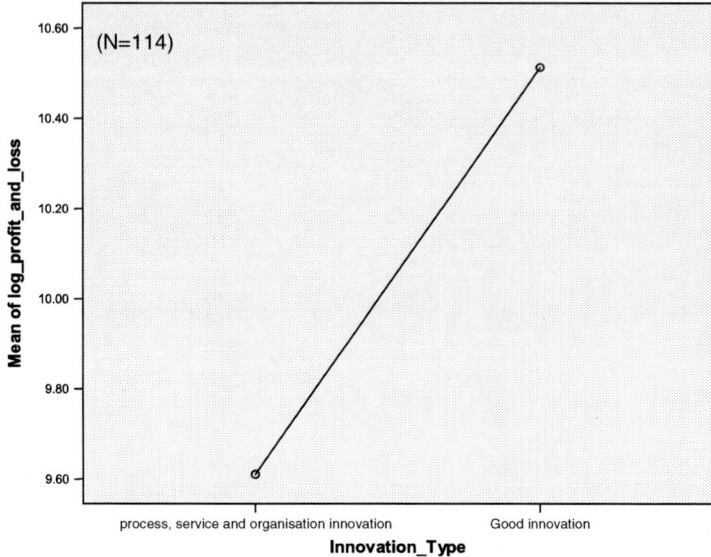

Fig. 14 Comparison of [log] Profit and Loss between SE which under took goods innovation and those that didn't

- Involves **new combinations or hybrids** of organisational structure, form and operations;
- Cuts **across boundaries** – in terms of geography, intended beneficiaries, and operations; and
- Simulates **new relationship**s to achieve both mission and business goals.

Our findings also suggest that adoption of different innovation practices produces distinct outcomes in terms of the dimensions of sectors of our society and economy, and in terms of organisational-level financial performance amongst our participating social enterprises. With regard to the latter, our findings suggest that different aspects of innovation produce different risk profiles for social enterprises and, consequently, their beneficiaries. Better understanding of these risk profiles and their effects on the mission fulfilment of social enterprises could enable policy makers and social enterprise intermediaries to develop more effective policy frameworks to support high impact social enterprise development. Social enterprises are characterised by hybridity – of mission orientation, industry location, organisational structure and the dual fulfilment of social and business functions. As a consequence, they typically sit rather uncomfortably within traditional policy frameworks. This hybridity, which is a presumed strength of social enterprises' innovative capabilities, is undermined by the limited capabilities of policy regimes to embrace hybridity. Insofar as social enterprise is active in social innovation, its full potential will only be realised where institutional levers are able to support it.

With regard to sector dimensions, our research evidence indicates that social enterprises challenge traditional organisational categories within the social economy, incorporating profit distributing forms that were entirely consistent with our operational definition of this form of activity. As Defourny and Nyssens (2006) have suggested, social enterprise combines the public orientation of traditional charities with the trading activity more typical of traditional cooperatives and mutuals, thus internally reconfiguring the social economy. The emergence of 'profit for purpose' social enterprises, that use profit distributing forms as vehicles for the fulfilment of public or community benefit further challenges the presumed boundary between civil society and the private business sector. This growing 'grey space' produces both new sites of contestation and co-optation of social change agendas, suggesting that critically informed understandings of the enabling and constraining effects of social innovation on substantive social change are required.

The research presented here tells us a little about *what* types of innovation practices are undertaken by social enterprise in the Australian context. Although consistent with other research on business innovation, the self-reported nature of these practices means that there is no independent validation of the innovation, although this is an inherent challenge for all survey data. In addition to this limitation, further research is needed to understand *how* these self-reported innovations are initiated and *to what end*, or what kinds of impacts they produce. Greater understanding of the practices and effects of social innovation amongst social enterprise would assist us to move beyond the uncritical conferral of symbolic legitimacy upon social enterprises as sources of social innovation to an understanding of the practical legitimacy – including what kinds of social and environmental equity these organisations can, and cannot, facilitate – of these and related social economy organisations.

Appendix: Principal Component Analysis

Principal Component Analysis (PCA) is a method of determining the empirical association between a number of variables (Tabachnick and Fidell 2007: 610), by generating a unique mathematical solution which analyses variance (Tabachnick and Fidell 2007: 635). Consequently Principal Component Analysis, with Oblique rotation and Kaiser Normalisation, was used to examine the relationship of the covariance matrix of the types of innovation used in social enterprises. Analysis of the screen plot indicated that there was an elbow, indicating two components in the data. This is confirmed by examining the rotated component matrix (with higher loadings shown in bold) (Table 3):

Table 3 Rotated Component Matrix[a] for the Principal Component Analysis

	Rescaled Component	
	1	2
Improved Processes – Beneficiaries	**.757**	.280
Improved Services – Business	**.714**	.219
Expanding the Mission of the Organisation	**.631**	−.120
Improved Services – Beneficiaries	**.630**	.331
Improved Processes – Business	**.603**	.154
New Goods – Beneficiaries	.175	**.893**
New Goods – Business	.146	**.884**
Extraction method: Principal Component Analysis. Rotation method: Varimax with Kaiser Normalization.		

[a]Rotation converged in three iterations.

Consequently, two components were found in the data differentiating between organisations which undertook goods innovation and those who undertook process, service and mission innovation.

References

Australian Bureau of Statistics. (2004). *Characteristics of small businesses, Australia, 2004*, Cat. No. 8127.0, Canberra.

Barraket, J., & Collyer, N. (2010). Mapping social enterprise in Australia: Conceptual debates and their operational implications. *Third Sector Review, 16*(2), 11–28.

Barraket, J., et al. (2010). Finding Australia's social enterprise sector: Final report, Brisbane: Social traders and the Australian centre for philanthropy and nonprofit studies. Available at: http://www.socialtraders.com.au/sites/www.socialtraders.com.au/files/FASES_9.7.10.pdf. Accessed October 28, 2010.

Barraket, J. (2008). Social enterprise and governance: implications for the Australian third sector. In J. Barraket (Ed.), *Strategic issues for the not for profit sector* (pp. 126–142). Sydney: UNSW Press.

Barraket, J. (2004). Social and community enterprise: What role for government? http://www.dvc.vic.gov.au/Web14/dvc/rwpgslib.nsf/GraphicFiles/CommunitySocialEnterpriseMarch2006.pdf/$file/CommunitySocialEnterpriseMarch2006.pdf.

Beck, U. (1992). *Risk society towards a new modernity*. London: Sage Publications.

Dart, R. (2004). The legitimacy of social enterprise. *Not for Profit Management and Leadership, 14*(4), 411–424.

Defourny, J., & Nyssens, M. (2006). Defining social economic organization. In M. Nyssens (Ed.), *Social economy organization. At the crossroads of market, public policies and civil society* (pp. 3–26). London: Routledge.

Defourny, J., & Nyssens, M. (2010). Conceptions of social enterprise and social entrepreneurship in Europe and the United States: Convergences and divergences. *Journal of Social Entrepreneurship, 1*(1), 32–53.

Department of Families and Community Services. (2005). Giving Australia: Research on philanthropy in Australia, Summary of findings, Canberra, http://www.cafaustralia.org.au/uploads/files/Giving_Australia_Summary_Oct05.pdf.

Kerlin, J. (2006). Social enterprise in the United States and Europe: Understanding and learning from the differences. *Voluntas, 17*(3), 247–263.

Leadbeater, C. (2007). 'Social enterprise and social innovation: Strategies for the next 10 years', Cabinet office, Office of the third sector http://www.charlesleadbeater.net/cms/xstandard/social_enterprise_innovation.pdf. Last accessed 19/5/2011.

Lyons, M., & Passey, A. (2006). Need public policy ignore the third sector? Government policy in Australia and the United Kingdom. *Australian Journal of Public Administration, 65*(3), 90–102.

Mulgan, G., Tucker, S., Ali, R., & Sander, B. (2007). Social innovation: What it is, why it matters and how can it be accelerated. Oxford: Skoll Centre for Social Entrepreneurship.

Mulgan, G. (2006) The Process of Social Innovation. *Innovations, Technology, Governance, Globalization 1*(2), 145–162.

Phills, J. A., Deiglmeier, K., & Miller, D. T. (2008). Rediscovering social innovation. *Stanford Social Innovation Review, 6*(4), 34–43.

Tabachnick, B. G., & Fidell, L. S. (2007). *Using multivariate statistics* (7th ed.). Boston: Pearson.

Weber, E. P., & Khademian, A. M. (2008). Wicked problems, knowledge challenges, and collaborative capacity builders in network settings. *Public Administration Review, 68*(2), 334–349. Business Source Elite, EBSCOhost (accessed October 17, 2011).

Part V
Social Innovation at the Workplace

Social Innovation at Work: Workplace Innovation as a Social Process

Peter Totterdill, Peter Cressey, and Rosemary Exton

Abstract What happens in the workplace has enormous social as well as economic implications. Workplace innovation is the process through which "win-win" approaches to work organisation are formulated – good for the sustainable competitiveness of the enterprise and good for the well-being of employees. Workplace innovation is also an inherently social process involving knowledge sharing and dialogue between stakeholders.

The knowledge economy that lies at the heart of the Europe 2020 Strategy is inconceivable without the active involvement of employees. There is however an unhelpful policy dualism between rights-based representative participation and discretionary task-based participation. Representative participation can drive, resource and sustain participative work practices, integrating the strategic knowledge of leaders with the tacit knowledge of employees. The paper demonstrates that, at the heart of such cases, the systemic incorporation of opportunities for "productive reflection" can be found throughout the organisation.

> The authors would like to acknowledge the support provided by *the* European Foundation for the Improvement of Living and Working Conditions *for the preparation of this paper. The case studies described in this paper were undertaken for this project except where otherwise referenced.*

P. Totterdill (✉) • R. Exton
UK Work Organisation Network, Nottingham, UK
e-mail: peter.totterdill@ukwon.net

P. Cressey
University of Bath, Bath, UK

1 Why Is Workplace Innovation a Key Dimension of Social Innovation?

According to the *Innovation Union* Flagship Initiative, social innovation concerns the creation of new solutions to social problems and new social capital; its modus operandi focuses on building new social relationships and models of collaboration with an emphasis on empowerment and engagement.

What happens in the workplace, in other words, the ways in which work is organised and people are managed, has enormous social as well as economic implications. Work organisation exerts a strong influence on performance, productivity and innovation in products and services, preconditions for a stable and equitable economic base. Economic performance is the main factor in the growth of welfare, creating the new jobs and wealth that facilitate the solution of social problems. However work organisation also shapes social outcomes which lie at the heart of the Europe 2020 Strategy such as the health, skills, employability and inclusion of employees and the consequences of demographic change.

Workplace innovation is the process through which "win-win" approaches to work organisation are formulated – approaches which are good for the sustainable competitiveness of the enterprise and good for the well-being of employees. Workplace innovation also represents the 'high road' to economic performance: it is, or should be the inherently European way, characterised by high wages and high productivity.

Most importantly, workplace innovation is an inherently social process. It is not about the application of codified knowledge by experts to the organisation of work. Rather it is about building skills and competence through creative collaboration. Workplace innovation is about open dialogue, knowledge sharing, experimentation and learning in which diverse stakeholders including employees, trade unions, managers and customers are given a voice in the creation of new models of collaboration and new social relationships.

2 Workplace Innovation: An Underused Resource

Policy responses to an increasingly volatile global environment have been largely fragmented. Predominant policy interventions have focused on the macro-system level, for example by reforming benefit systems and pensions to encourage greater labour market participation and tax incentives for R&D. With a few notable exceptions the workplace has been largely invisible.

Policymakers tend not to understand workplaces or the organisation of work. Work organisation is regarded as a private matter for employers, at best involving consultation and participation involving employees or trade unions but this is only sporadically reinforced by regulation or active policy. It is as though European politicians have failed to understand that work is where the majority of the population spend their most active hours for most of their lives, and that how work is organised is vitally important for individual human happiness and fulfillment, and has a direct impact on the health and wealth of society.

In consequence workplace innovation has become an underused resource for European public policy at both EU and Member State levels. The design of work processes and the extent to which organisational practices facilitate or inhibit employee participation actively influences the achievement of EU social and economic goals including the ability of organisations to compete, innovate in products and services or address environmental issues. Workplace factors exercise a major influence on the extent to which employees can utilise their skills and develop them further, and therefore on the return which employers and the state realise from their investment in vocational training. Work organisation is also a determinant of employees' quality of working life, shaping the extent to which they gain satisfaction and personal growth from their working lives; it therefore shapes their level of engagement, their ambition, their retention by the organisation (not least in the case of older workers able to retire or mothers considering whether to return to work after the birth of children), and not least their mental and physical health. Yet the evidence suggests that only a small proportion of workplaces, public or private, are deploying participative working methods systemically across the whole organisation.

3 Taking Stock

The current European policy model for the workplace, and much of the academic debate, is grounded in an unhelpful dualism between rights-based representative participation on the one hand and discretionary task-based direct participation on the other.

There have been significant EU legislative developments in relation to employee rights, the protection of employees' dignity, and opportunities for personal development at work. Directive 2002/14/EC passed by the European Parliament and Council established a general framework for informing and consulting employees in the EU. At Member State level, many of the "old" EU 15 have long had in place mechanisms providing for employee information and consultation at the workplace. These include statutory works councils (for example in Germany and France), encompassing collective agreements backed by legislation which provide the primary means of regulating information and consultation in countries like Denmark and Belgium, and the hybrid Italian model in which a statutory framework allows for sectoral agreements to flesh out the detailed operations of works councils.

In exploring the impact of the various forms of participation on outcomes, there has been extensive debate about whether direct or representative practices have the greater effect. (Guest and Peccei 2001, p. 207) argue that neither representative nor direct forms of participation are necessarily beneficial when applied in isolation.

Representative participation has no significant positive effect on employee attitudes and behaviour and, if implemented on its own, can have a negative impact on performance. One possible explanation for this is that representative participation in isolation will fail to overcome low levels of management trust in the workforce. Employees themselves may also become cynical about formal partnership structures and agreements that appear remote and have little visible impact on their own working lives (Pass 2008; Guest and Peccei 2001, p. 207).

Nonetheless there does appear to be evidence of a connection with organisational performance; for example the Involvement and Participation Association (IPA) study *The Partnership Company: Benchmarks for the Future* found that almost all the companies with representative structures responding to a survey felt that their approach to management-employee relations keeps them up with or ahead of their competitors (Guest and Peccei 1998). Moreover this is supported through case study evidence demonstrating that there is a positive relationship between the existence of works councils and economic performance as measured by productivity growth (Fernie and Metcalf 1995).

An important body of research has begun to show not that representative partnership has a direct impact on performance, but rather that it exerts a positive influence on the development of activities and practices that may do so. When partnership arrangements exist alongside participative workplace practices they result in mutual benefits through improved information sharing and greater levels of trust between employers, unions and employees (Oxenbridge and Brown 2004, p. 388) and to a heightened impact on performance (Batt and Applebaum 1995). Representative committees may create a culture and instigate concrete practices which inspire managers to implement and sustain direct forms of involvement. The new generation of line managers, union representatives and employees appear more at ease with a combination of inclusive (direct and indirect) rather than exclusive (direct versus indirect) voice practices. Wilkinson et al. (2004) argue that in a UK context managers are becoming more confident in organising direct exchanges of opinion with employees, while union representatives and employees increasingly expect them to do so.

This combination of representative and direct practices has been characterised in terms of "employee voice" (Boxall and Purcell 2003). For employee representatives there is evidence that formal partnership enhances the degree of influence they are able to exert over employment and workplace issues through consultation and early involvement in decision making (Ackers et al. 2005). It also strengthens the robustness of the structures, such as works councils and trade unions, within which they work (Guest and Peccei 2001, p. 207). Union representatives are adapting and carving out new roles, leading to greater involvement in establishing joint rules and procedures (Bacon and Storey 2000, p. 407). From an employee perspective the evidence suggests that representative partnership creates opportunities to exercise greater autonomy and direct participation (Batt and Applebaum 1995). Moreover employers pursuing high-performance, high-involvement practices are "likely to be impatient with traditional adversarial approaches to collective representation" (Kessler and Purcell 1995).

The importance of employee voice in this sense is that it is directly linked to greater workforce commitment to the organisation, reflected in lower levels of absence, turnover and conflict, and improved performance (Applebaum and Batt 1994; Huselid 1995, p. 635). Partnership can lead to the enhancement of employment standards, enabling the decent treatment of employees to be seen as integral to the achievement of high performance. Purcell et al. argue that employees who experience consultation and involvement are more willing to "go the extra mile" (2003). Where unions and management collaborate, employee trust is enhanced (Bryson 2001, p. 91) supporting a more positive psychological contract (Rousseau 1995; Guest 2000) thus creating higher levels of organisational commitment, motivation and job satisfaction. Likewise Teague (2005) argues that partnership can be the conduit to improve organisational competitiveness by mediating between employee wishes for decent work and managerial efforts to upgrade performance.

Describing innovation as "the successful exploitation of new ideas" Bessant et al. (2006) argue that the perceived work environment (comprising both structural and cultural elements) does make a difference to the level of innovation in organisations. Improved collaboration, upskilling and opportunities to share tacit knowledge are created through more effective communication and the direct involvement of employees in problem-solving, design and improvement of work processes (Bryson et al. 2005, p. 451; Ichniowski et al. 1996, p. 299). Similarly Kark and Carmeli (2008) suggest that employee creativity makes an important contribution to organisational innovation, effectiveness, and survival but that it is influenced by the work environment and levels of encouragement.

A US study (Kim et al. 2010, p. 371) finds that team voice improves labour productivity but only when the interaction effect with representative voice is taken into account. Involving the expertise of workers directly in the work process via teams may contribute to the plant's labour efficiency. They also found that worker representatives' voice showed a positive relationship with productivity when the interaction with direct voice is included.

Teague (2005) argues that an overarching "enterprise partnership" can harness an organisation's resources, including the tacit knowledge of employees, more effectively than the leadership models which currently dominate the change management literature. Martinez Lucio and Stuart (2002) argue that partnership is central to the modernising agenda as a means of permanently substituting cooperative relations for conflict at work. Cooperative relations in this sense are predicated on an extension of employee rights and a commitment by representatives to work with employers, rather than against them, in the interests of improving organisational performance (Danford et al. 2005, p. 593). Guest and Peccei (2001) take up this theme and argue that the balance of advantage must be mutual.

A major test of representative partnership's impact on performance therefore concerns its ability to increase the level of employee influence not just at policy level but over day to day operations (IPA 1997). Viewing partnership as systemic, deeply embedded and far-reaching is central to this perspective. In short, combining direct and representative participation together with an emphasis on job design and quality has the most positive effect on employee attitudes and behaviour relating to productivity, output quality and innovation (Guest and Peccei 2001, p. 207; Beaumont and Hunter 2005; Wers 1998). This builds a climate of trust where individual employees are confident that their contribution will be valued (CBI/TUC 2001). Recent research also highlights the importance of a set of internally consistent policies and practices in ensuring that human capital contributes to the achievement of an organisation's business objectives: these include compensation systems, team-based job designs, flexible workforces, quality improvement practices and employee empowerment (Lado and Wilson 1994, p. 699; Huselid et al. 1997, p. 171). As Teague (2005) suggests: "Organisations with mutually reinforcing employment practices achieve superior performance as their collective impact is greater than the sum of individual measures."

4 Towards a New Understanding

There are cases in which representative participation drives, resources and sustains "high road" participative work practices. The "win-win" outcome in such cases lies in integrating the strategic knowledge of leaders with the tacit knowledge of employees. According to the HI-RES study, a meta-analysis of 120 cases of workplace innovation across ten European countries, the common factor in organisations that have achieved a degree of convergence between high performance and high quality of working life is related to knowledge sharing and dialogue (Totterdill et al. 2002): ". . . a clear concentration on those factors in the work environment which determine the extent to which employees can develop and use their competencies and creative potential to the fullest extent, thereby enhancing the company's capacity for innovation and competitiveness while enhancing quality of working life."

In much literature as in practice the employee participation debate and the organisational use of competence are often seen as separate and distinct. At the heart of both these factors lies the systemic incorporation of opportunities for "productive reflection" throughout the organisation. The concept of productive reflection attempts to unify them by jointly appreciating the role that organisational structures have in articulating employee voice together with the active use of employee's formal and tacit skills and competences in the process of improvement, innovation and change.

Thus productive reflection "must not be seen as an abstract concept or a separable subjective event. Rather it is about new forms of self-management, about how competence is distributed inside companies, about the processes of monitoring and intervention that are constructed. Crucially, it is about the embedding of reflexive approaches to problem solving and change. As the table indicates this embedding of *productive reflection* draws upon the creation of contextualised workplace learning that allows and releases the capacity of the workforce, via de-centralised and flexible project groups, the use of multi-functional networks and multiple stakeholder perspectives" (Boud et al. 2006).

Productive reflection in the organisational context is a social process grounded in the ability to reflect about and anticipate the impacts of change. Good and sustainable organisations build a set of internal reflexive mechanisms. They embed them in the organisation to enable smooth transitions. Reflexivity focuses on bringing the thinking and active subject (employee/representative/union) into the centre of work practices, to underline the importance of continuing learning and the necessity to prioritise worker's tacit and explicit knowledge if the organisation is to be sustainable in the long run.

Productive reflection has both an organisational and an individual character. At organisational level it is vitally necessary for innovation and the development and production of quality goods and services. For the latter it means "making sense of one's work" not as a sociological or abstract issue but in finding meaning, a key factor for experiencing a sense of coherence, wellbeing and resilience in the workplace. This may be even more significant for a younger and less deferential generation of workers who are less tolerant of boring, repetitive or badly designed jobs that provide limited opportunities for self expression (Knell 2001).

Reflexivity is then appropriate within both individual and group settings. The first is a form of self-reflection directed inwards and separated from immediate action and reflection directed outwards at the ongoing situation in which somebody is acting. Collectively it is compatible with the literature on learning organisations and lifelong learning, which demands continuous learning to address continuous change and restructuring.

Reflexivity in this context means conscious, active decisions on measures to promote, facilitate and support reflection and learning. However, the issues of reflection and learning are often not formally allotted priority on the management agenda and the prerequisites for these activities will be steered by values, norms and practices that have simply evolved and are not the product of clear thought. Hence we need proactive measures for reflection and learning in the form of learning mechanisms. These mechanisms may be cognitive, cultural, structural or procedural. Learning mechanisms are formalised strategies, policies, guidelines, management and reward systems, methods, tools and routines, allocations of resources and even the design of the physical facility and work spaces.

There are three social dialogue forms, organisational, technical and physical, which should be considered in relation to such reflexivity:

The most common *organisational forms* are forums or arenas that provide legitimacy for reflection and provide the formal opportunity for a collective or group to meet and "discuss things". These include regular team meetings in so far as they provide structured opportunities for reflection and learning about what has gone well and what went badly, or for a routine review of existing practices. Continuous improvement groups and quality circles also fall into this category. Sometimes flexible structures such as task groups or ad hoc "time out" sessions are introduced to cope with the immediate scope, discontinuity, or variability of issues facing enterprises. They may also be coupled to a specific development project, policy revision or planning task, existing "until further notice".

Technical learning mechanisms are generally based on the use of information and communication technology. The internet has given rise to virtual communities which are essential for many people in their daily work as a basis for knowledge sharing, joint problem solving and dialogue. Virtual networks are often more important to professionals than their social networks at the workplace.

The *physical design* of the workplace can support interaction and collective reflection between members of an organisation. Apart from formal meeting rooms there may be "free areas" where coffee and meal breaks are held; some employers actively discourage staff from eating at their desks to stimulate dialogue in such communal areas at mealtimes. Other places may be provided where people can sit informally, perhaps with access to a whiteboard for "buzz sessions". In one hospital, the paediatric department was designed with wide corridors incorporating seating and play areas to promote informal interactions between different professions, parents and children. In short the emphasis here is on the creation of settings where reflective dialogues can occur as part of daily work routines.

5 Embedded Collective Productive Reflection

We have seen above how different phases of participation have moved from a rights based agenda to one that centres upon the production of knowledge and ideas, and joint problem solving. The argument can develop further to place collective reflection at the core of workplace practice. This can be represented as a series of mutually reinforcing practices in which workplace social dialogue sustains, informs and is informed by productive reflection. The concept of productive reflection attempts to unify workplace social dialogue and work organisation by understanding the interaction of organisational structures for employee voice on the one hand and the active use of employee's formal and tacit skills in work and change processes on the other.

Figure 1 demonstrates how productive reflection becomes embedded when workplace social dialogue acts as a bridge for knowledge sharing between different levels of the organisation. In this context representative participation acts as the guarantor and enabler of direct participation and voice at the frontline. Dialogue about knowledge sharing through both formal and informal channels becomes "the new collective bargaining" in which employees offer their tacit knowledge and creativity in return for knowledge of and influence in strategic decision making (see for example the Tegral case below). But here the outcomes of bargaining can be win-win rather than zero sum, offering (in the words of the HI-RES study cited above) the prospect of workplaces in which "employees can develop and use their competencies and creative potential to the fullest extent, thereby enhancing the company's capacity for innovation and competitiveness while enhancing quality of working life."

This brings into question the union role in encouraging direct participation and reflection in a way that does not contradict collectivism and representation.

Fig. 1 Workplace social dialogue and productive reflection

The issue pulls unions into considering how they can best represent their members in issues previously thought to be outside their accepted sphere of activity: issues of creativity, strategy, internal dialogue that enable active intervention in design and practice. Often the need is to confront the nature of entrenched interests and the barriers imposed in real-life situations which result from accretions of practices and expectations that have grown up over decades and cannot be eliminated overnight.

Evidence should be sought on how unions and worker representatives fulfil their potential role as competent suppliers and guarantors of reflective practices in workplaces. Participation here makes up for lack of dialogue up and down the line management hierarchy, which can act as a serious limitation on productive reflection. Productive reflection can draw on different authorial voices, for instance combining formal trade union knowledge of the rules with frontline employees' competences and know-how.

The need identified here is for a workforce input that can critically challenge systems thinking rather than celebrate it, in other words for non-formal networks of *dialogue* and *reflection* that operate outside enclosed system loops. To see the issue of employee involvement from this perspective means a re-alignment of issues around how best to use expertise, how to engage people in specific processes of reflection and dialogue and a finer appreciation of the createdness of enterprise added value. Workplace practices and processes are socially constructed in the sense that they reflect complex interactions of power relations, knowledge and history as well as external influences; the outcome of these interactions shapes the distinctive character of each workplace and the ways in which dialogue and reflection take place.

Table 1 Formal and informal workplace social dialogue in strategic and task-based decisions

Forms of social dialogue

Strategic Decisions

	1	2	
Formal	Clear rules Tangible outcomes Bounded areas	Ad hoc communication Informal routes Spontaneous forms	Informal
	3	4	
	Direct forums Improvement groups Defined areas Clear goals	Active process of involvement Difficult to measure Intangible Loosely defined	

Task-Based Decisions

Such trends also raise larger questions for future employee participatory forums, including the balance between institutionalisation and active intervention of workers as individuals. Case study evidence points to the existence of companies with no formal structures or procedures relating to information, consultation and participation but in which high levels of dialogue, reflexivity and entrepreneurial behaviour can be found at all levels (see for example the Lindum Group case described below).

The relationship between formal and informal structures at both strategic and task-based levels is summarised in Table 1 below:

Formal, strategic manifestations represented by Box 1 correspond with rights-based representative participation, but managers may also use other less structured approaches for drawing on employees' tacit knowledge and creativity in high level decision making (Box 2). Likewise formal structures for direct employee participation such as continuous improvement groups (Box 3) may not entirely substitute for more spontaneous forms of engagement in improvement and innovation (Box 4). In short, we need to identify the ways in which both formal and informal structures support knowledge sharing through productive reflection.

Looking at past research we can see how the EPOC study in the 1990s (European Foundation for the Improvement of Living and Working Conditions 1997) rendered Box 3 visible, revealing the development and scope of formally constituted direct participation across Europe. What this paper suggests is that there is a further need to make visible other emergent forms that exist in the boxes towards the right hand side of the table. Most of the evidence for these forms comes from case studies, generating what we call the "weak signals" of new corporate practice.

While the traditional debate has placed more emphasis upon the forms and empirical spread of institutionalised participation rather than the constituents of that involvement in terms of reflection, learning and creativity, we can now identify a trend in employee participation, a relatively weak signal that nonetheless begins to bridge that gap.

6 Case Study Evidence

Where are the weak signals that indicate the possible emergence of a new formulation of workplace relations in which dialogue, or bargaining, about the two way distribution of knowledge provides the bridge between representative and direct participation? We can elaborate the conceptual framework by drawing on case study evidence to identify the organisational processes and structures which integrate workplace social dialogue, participative forms of work organisation and productive reflection. In terms of Table 1 (above) we are looking for evidence of two way connections between formal strategic social dialogue in Box 1 and both the informal and task-based quadrants (Boxes 2–4).

We have discussed knowledge distribution in terms of a bargaining process in which the establishment of mutual trust can allow for the forging and negotiation of win-win outcomes. A graphic illustration of how this might work in practice is illustrated by the case of *Tegral Metal Forming Limited*, a steel cladding and roofing company based in County Kildare, Ireland (Totterdill and Sharpe 1999). Previous industrial relations had taken a traditional path in which every change in employment or working practice was subject to separate agreement, leading to inflexibility and complexity.

In 1996 management and unions entered into a partnership agreement as a result of the company's participation in the ESF-funded *New Work Organisation in Ireland* (NWO) programme. A partnership forum was established with the participation of management and unions (including full time union officials) with the aim of ensuring greater employee involvement in company decisions. This enabled the complex legacy of previous agreements to be replaced by a "gainsharing" arrangement based on "win-win" principles. The partnership climate reduced the time spent by management and unions on industrial relations issues and also enabled the introduction of annualised hours and the elimination of overtime.

Partnership also transcended the industrial relations sphere at *Tegral*. A series of partnership-based task teams were established to identify operational improvements, including one on the handling of scrap which immediately led to significant waste reduction savings. It was clear from interviews with frontline employees by the independent evaluators of the NWO programme (Totterdill and Sharpe 1999) that they had known of the potential for such savings for a considerable time. It was only the establishment of partnership culture and practices that encouraged them to bring this to the attention of management.

In a second stage of development, the partnership forum instigated self-organised teamworking throughout the company as a means of extending partnership culture to the frontline. Employees received training in team-based practice and a layer of supervisory management was removed in order to build team autonomy, closer engagement with customers and control over day-to-day working life. Such participatory forms of work organisation are highly trust-based and, in the case of Tegral, stemmed directly from partnership culture and the practice of gainsharing.

A highly developed example of the nurturing relationship between representative participation and participative teamworking comes from a surprising source. *Kaiser Permanente* (KP) is the biggest non-profit health care organisation in the US. KP has received a great deal of attention amongst European health services for its high standards and cost effectiveness, particularly in the integration of primary and acute services. Less widely reported is the high level of trade union and employee involvement that underpins these achievements, driving the introduction of multidisciplinary teamworking and other service innovations.

KP's *Labor Management Partnership* (LMP) involving managers, workers and physicians is the largest and most comprehensive agreement of its kind. The LMP was formed in 1997 after years of labour turmoil within Kaiser Permanente combined with growing competitive pressures in the sector. Two years earlier, 26 local unions representing KP workers had joined together in the *Coalition of Kaiser Permanente Unions* to coordinate bargaining strategy more effectively. Kaiser Permanente and the Union Coalition created the LMP as a means of transforming their relationship and the organisation as a whole. Today it covers more than 92,000 union employees, including some 20,000 managers and 16,000 physicians across nine US States and Washington DC.

Partnership in KP goes far beyond traditional industrial relations. On a day-to-day basis partnership means that workers, managers and physicians engage in joint decision making and a problem-solving process based on common interests. KP's Value Compass, originally formulated by the LMP to set the direction for improving organisational performance by focusing on subscribing members of the public and patients. The Value Compass is now driving the Corporate Agenda, based on the concept of the balanced score card to maximise performance and so create value:

Kaiser Permanente
"Value is with the workers"

The Value Compass

Workplace social dialogue at KP takes place at three interdependent levels: the *strategic and policy level* provides a platform for whole systems change and continuous improvement, the *meso level* is the locus for union representation and management in the day-to-day operation of the business, and the *microsystems* level comprises *Unit Based Teams* (UBTs) as the basic building block.

Unit Based Teams were introduced in 2005 following extensive discussion in the LMP and provide the platform for performance improvement across Kaiser Permanente. More than 90,000 employees now work in 34,000 unit-based teams. A team includes all the participants in a natural work unit or department, including supervisors, union stewards and staff members, physicians, dentists and managers. The team supports the regional business strategy and goals for performance, service quality, efficiency and growth. Because teams increase consistency and standardisation of treatment, they also improve care. A dramatic reduction in sepsis has been attributed to the introduction of UBTs, as has the success of the design and implementation of the integrated IT electronic patient record system.

At UBT level there is an expectation that everyone will contribute to building the vision for the future direction of the business. Unit Based Teams tap the creativity, skills and experience of their members in a process that consistently engages frontline workers in improving performance. The LMP ensures the quality of dialogue and participation at team level through a system of *Inclusion Control and Openness*. Unions credit the arrangement not only with improving patient care and satisfaction, but in making Kaiser Permanente a better place to work.

The significance of KP for this study is that it demonstrates the way in which workplace social dialogue can permeate the whole organisation even in a context where partnership is somewhat antithetical to the national system of industrial relations. Representative partnership in the form of the LMP acts as both the stimulant and guardian of direct participation at the frontline with demonstrable benefits for organisational performance, staff and patients.

An example from the healthcare sector in Europe demonstrates that *regional* social dialogue can play a comparable role in driving direct participation, in this case involving significant service redesign and restructuring. At *Guastalla Hospital* in Italy, an agreement signed by management in the Reggio Emilia Local Area Health Authority, by the trade union confederations Cgil, Cisl and Uil, and by the doctors' unions led to a partnership-based process of service appraisal and redesign in order to achieve a better and more efficient service, as well as improved job satisfaction and working conditions. Highly participative change methods such as Search Conferences and inclusive task groups enabled the knowledge and experience of staff at all levels to be engaged in the redesign of work organisation and the reduction of hierarchical and professional demarcations. As a result, high involvement work practices emerged which achieved integrated patient pathways as well as enhanced cooperation and mutual learning. Quality of care and patient satisfaction improved while lead-times and inefficiency were reduced (Telljohann 2010, p. 2).

Tegral, Kaiser Permanente and Guastalla Hospital each illustrate the potential role of formal structures from partnership forums to improvement groups in instigating, resourcing and sustaining direct employee participation. However Table 1 also drew attention to the importance of informal processes at both strategic and task levels. The following example from the vehicle components sector in Flanders illustrates the interaction of the formal and informal. *Tower Automotive* underwent dramatic transformation since a period of severe crisis in 2008/2009. Edwin Van Vlierberghe joined Tower in 2009, the eighth plant leader in 8 years. His priority was to break with precedent and become visible on the shopfloor, creating opportunities for employee dialogue. Edwin invited the plant's trade unions to discuss the financial situation, sharing information openly to enable them to reach their own conclusions about the need for redundancies. He worked with employees and unions to find creative solutions to the crisis, including functional flexibility and temporary outplacements to neighbouring companies until demand returned.

Edwin's management of the crisis earned considerable respect amongst employees and unions, and opened new, trust-based approaches to communication and dialogue. He has gradually transformed organisational culture, retraining line managers from a top-down approach to one in which their role is to empower and engage employees. Closing the gap between management and frontline workers' perceptions and experience is a key component in this culture change. Managers are encouraged and resourced to "think as an operator"; frontline employees are asked to reflect on the types of management behaviours that would enable them to work more effectively. Where necessary he has not hesitated to remove those managers unable to make the transition. Edwin's willingness to drive this transformation, and his consistency of approach, clearly lies at the heart of its success.

Edwin's underlying goal has been to create an organisation in which quality, improvement and innovation are everyone's concern, improving company performance through job enrichment. Frontline employees are as much responsible for driving improvement as they are for performing their functional tasks. Critically Towers' approach recognises that spaces for productive reflection and dialogue have to be built into the everyday working life of each employee and that these cannot be confined to occasional participation in formal structures.

One UK company has made strides in this direction with a remarkable absence of formal structures and procedures. The *Lindum Group* is a fascinating case involving transformation from a traditional construction company to a diverse and entrepreneurial organisation. In the early nineties Lindum was not a high performing company. According to one long serving manager the dominant management style "was about control really . . . it was hands on from the top management-wise". However these top managers "couldn't see everything and couldn't control everything . . . things went wrong because the staff didn't really have the authority or the empowerment to do anything about it."

When David took over from his father as Chair in the early 1990s he was determined to do things differently, and to create an environment where employees can thrive and be creative. Lindum has consistently appeared in the *100 Best Companies to Work for* list over several years. Senior management attributes this to a dramatic culture shift achieved by changing the leadership approach to empower employees. This shift included a transformation of the leadership structure, an increase in stakeholder involvement through employee share ownership and an equal profit-related bonus for all employees. Lindum has grown by enabling and resourcing its employees' talents and creativity.

Lindum is remarkably free of formal rules, protocols or procedures: the emphasis is on "what works". One of David's early tasks was to remove the separate operating companies and bring them under one Executive Board in order to reduce complexity and bureaucracy. Under the old structure the 14 different boards had given frontline employees little opportunity to come forward with their own ideas. Although the Executive Board is a tightly bound team, the different trading divisions pursue their own direction with limited central co-ordination. Meetings throughout the company also tend to be relatively informal, ad hoc and inclusive.

On the other hand, informal dialogue and consultation is widespread. One rule which the company does try to enforce is that "the best argument should win no matter who makes it", whether addressing factors that shape the strategy and culture of the organisation as a whole or those that shape the ways in which employees engage with colleagues and work tasks. According to Warren Glover, Lindum's General Manager, "this is more than words; this means managers can't just insist on pushing through an idea without being able to justify it, and all employees have a voice."

Lindum recognises that innovative organisations are those which provide opportunities for employees at all levels to exercise imagination and creativity, and to use the full range of their knowledge and "know how". Employees are actively encouraged and resourced to identify potential service and process innovations. For example the manager responsible for maintaining the company's construction plant realised that there was a potential market if existing resources could be expanded to service heavy goods trucks and emergency vehicles. He was given training and support to develop a business plan and subsequently established a new trading division within Lindum.

The company is prepared to take risks and to look on failure as a learning and development opportunity. Individuals or teams are not "punished" in such circumstances because this would only serve to reduce creativity and the impetus to innovate. Warren Glover is clear about the benefits of such a culture: "that's over 440 pairs of eyes looking out for new market opportunities, new parcels of land or cost saving ideas". The business has diversified into several new markets based on employee generated ideas and initiatives and now has 12 trading divisions including construction, joint venture commercial property, house building, plant, joinery and maintenance within East Anglia and the East Midlands.

7 Reflections on the Cases

These cases only begin to describe the diversity of workplace social dialogue contexts and practices that exist in Europe. The cases add weight to our argument that workplace social dialogue cannot only be understood in terms of formal, rights-based structures. Rather it can exist in less tangible ways and that it embraces both strategic and task-based decision making.

Table 2 Tegral, Kaiser Permanente and Guastalla Hospital

Forms of social dialogue

Strategic Decisions

	1	2	
Formal	Clear rules Tangible outcomes Bounded areas	Ad hoc communication Informal routes Spontaneous forms	Informal
	3	4	
	Direct forums Improvement groups Defined areas Clear goals	Active process of involvement Difficult to measure Intangible Loosely defined	

Task-Based Decisions

Tegral, Kaiser Permanente and Guastalla add direct insight into the question that lies at the heart of this paper. Both cases demonstrate that representative workplace social dialogue can stimulate and shape the development of participative work practices where there is shared understanding of the need to drive management-union partnership beyond the confines of traditional industrial relations. In terms of Table 2, these three cases demonstrate a clear connection between Boxes 1 and 3, but also lead to the less tangible culture changes represented by Box 4. The arrows are two-way because representative partnership both shapes and is shaped by direct participation.

The Tower case places much greater emphasis on the informal side of the table. Formal structures were in place at Tower including a works council and team-based production systems, but Edwin realised that dialogue and culture change at the informal level were required to build the reflexivity and creative solutions required at both task-based and strategic levels if breakthroughs were to be achieved. His starting point was therefore to create spaces for informal dialogue with trade union and employee representatives as a means of transforming formal practices. Again the two-way arrows suggest the existence of mutually reinforcing practices (Table 3).

Lindum presents a very different case: formality is largely absent yet dialogue is rich, pervasive and intended to be inclusive within the informal sphere, an evolving bridge between the strategic concerns of senior management and the tacit knowledge of employees (Table 4).

Each case demonstrates in different ways how diverse forms of workplace social dialogue (formal/informal; strategic/task-based) combine in mutually reinforcing ways when knowledge sharing and the co-production of innovation and improvement become the bridge between direct and indirect forms of participation.

Table 3 Tower Automotive

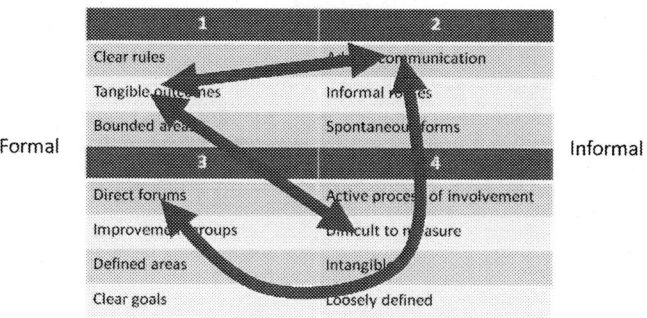

Table 4 The Lindum Group

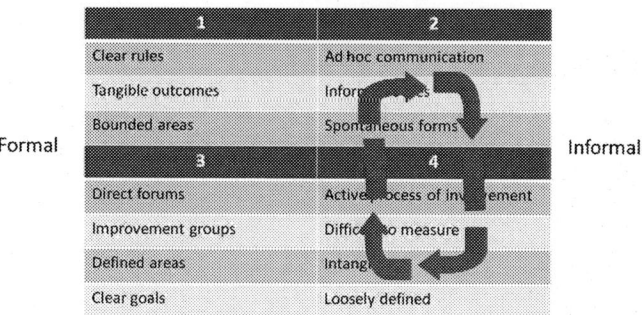

8 Conclusion

The concept and practice of productive reflection demonstrate the social nature of workplace innovation in two ways. Productive reflection, lying at the heart of workplace innovation, is an inherently social process which bridges formal and informal dialogue between different actors in the workplace. Secondly the win-win outcomes uniquely achieved through the participative nature of workplace innovation lead to profound social outcomes including enhanced health, active ageing, social cohesion and wealth creation. This is why the workplace should be at the heart of the EU's social innovation agenda.

References

Ackers, P., Marchington, M., Wilkinson, A., & Dundon, T. (2005). Partnership and voice, with or without trade unions: Changing UK management approaches to organisational participation. In M. Stuart & M. Martinez Lucio (Eds.), *Partnership and modernisation in employment relations*. London: Routledge.

Applebaum, E., & Batt, R. (1994). *The new American workforce: Transforming work systems in the United States*. Ithica: Cornell ILR Press.

Bacon, N., & Storey, J. (2000). New employee relations strategies in Britain: Towards individualism or partnership. *British Journal of Industrial Relations, 38*(3), 407–427.

Batt, R., & Applebaum, E. (1995). Worker participation in diverse settings: Does the form affect the outcome, and if so, who benefits? (CAHRS Working Paper #95-06). Ithaca: Cornell University, School of Industrial and Labor Relations, Center for Advanced Human Resource Studies. Available at: http://digitalcommons.ilr.cornell.edu/cahrswp/196.

Beaumont, P. B., & Hunter, L. C. (2005). *Making consultation work: The importance of process*. London: CIPD.

Bessant, J., Adams, R., & Phelps, R. (2006). Innovation management measurement: A review. *International Journal of Management Reviews, 8*(1), 21–47.

Boud, D., Cressey, P., & Docherty, P. (2006). *Productive reflection at work*. London: Routledge.

Boxall, P., & Purcell, J. (2003). *Strategy and human resource management*. Basingstoke: Palgrave Macmillan.

Bryson, A. (2001). The foundation of 'partnership'? Union effects on employee trust in management. *National Institute Economic Review, 176*, 191.

Bryson, A., Forth, J., & Kirby, S. (2005). High involvement management practices, trade union representation and workplace performance in Britain. *Scottish Journal of Political Economy, 52*, 451–491.

CBI/TUC. (2001). *The UK productivity challenge*. Report of the Best Practice and Productivity Working Party.

Danford, A., Richardson, M., Stewart, P., Tailby, S., & Upchurch, M. (2005). Workplace partnership and employee voice in the UK: Comparative case studies of union strategy and worker experience. *Economic and Industrial Democracy, 26*, 593.

European Foundation for the Improvement of Living and Working Conditions. (1997). *EPOC: Direct participation in organisational change. First results of establishment survey*. Dublin: European Foundation.

Fernie, S., & Metcalf, D. (1995). Participation, contingent pay, representation and workplace performance: Evidence from Great Britain. *British Journal of Industrial Relations, 33*, 379–415. *39*, 919–969.

Guest, D. (2000). Human resource management and industrial relations. In J. Storey (Ed.), *Critical perspectives on human resource management* (3rd ed.). London: Routledge.

Guest, D., & Peccei, R. (1998). *The partnership company*. London: Involvement and Participation Association.

Guest, D., & Peccei, R. (2001). Partnership at work: Mutuality and the balance of advantage. *British Journal of Industrial Relations, 39*(2), 207–236.

Huselid, M. A. (1995). The impact of human resource management practices on turnover, productivity, and corporate financial performance. *Academy of Management Journal, 38*, 635–672.

Huselid, M. A., Jackson, S. E., & Schuler, R. S. (1997). Technical and strategic human resource management effectiveness as determinants of firm performance. *Academy of Management Journal, 40*(1), 171–188.

Ichniowski, C., Kochan, T., Levine, D., Olson, C., & Strauss, G. (1996). What works at work: Overview and assessment. *Industrial Relations, 35*(3), 299–333.

IPA. (1997). *Towards industrial partnership: New ways of working in British companies*. London: Involvement & Participation Association.

Kark, R., & Carmeli, A. (2008). Alive and creating: The mediating role of vitality and aliveness in the relationship between psychological safety and creative work involvement. *Journal of Organizational Behaviour*. Available at: www.interscience.wiley.com.

Kessler, I., & Purcell, J. (1995). Individualism in theory and practice. In P. Edwards (Ed.), *Industrial relations: Theory and practice in Britain*. Oxford: Blackwell.

Kim, J., MacDuffie, J. P., & Pil, F. K. (2010). Employee voice and organizational performance: Team versus representative influence. *Human Relations, 63*, 371.

Knell, J. (2001). *The quiet birth of the free worker*. London: The Industrial Society.

Lado, A. A., & Wilson, M. C. (1994). Human resource systems and sustained competitive advantage: A competency-based perspective. *Academy of Management Review, 19*(4), 699–727.

Martinez Lucio, M., & Stuart, M. (2002). Assessing partnership: The prospects for, and challenges of, modernisation. *Employee Relations, 24*(3), 395–573.

Oxenbridge, S., & Brown, W. (2004). Achieving a new equilibrium? The stability of cooperative employer-union relationships. *Industrial Relations Journal, 35*(5), 388–402.

Pass, S. (2008). *Working in partnership: what does the academic research tell us?* London: Department of Health.

Purcell, J., Kinnie, N. J., Hutchinson, S., Rayton, B., & Swart, J. (2003). *Understanding the people and performance link: Unlocking the black box*. London: CIPD.

Rousseau, D. (1995). *Psychological contracts in organisations*. Thousand Oaks: Sage.

Teague, P. (2005). What is enterprise partnership? *Organization, 12*, 567.

Telljohann, V. (2010). Employee-driven innovation in the context of Italian industrial relations: The case of a public hospital. *Transfer, 16*, 2.

Totterdill, P., & Sharpe, A. (1999). *An evaluation of the new work organisation in Ireland programme*. Dublin: Irish Productivity Centre.

Totterdill, P., Dhondt, S., & Milsome, S. (2002). Partners at work?. A report to Europe's policy makers and social partners. The Work Institute, Nottingham (The Hi-Res Study, available at www.ukwon.net).

WERS (1998). Workplace employee relations survey: First findings. London: Department of Trade & Industry. Available at: http://www.berr.gov.uk/whatwedo/employment/research-evaluation/wers-98/index.html.

Wilkinson, A., Dundon, T., Marchington, M., & Ackers, P. (2004). Changing patterns of employee voice: Case studies from the UK and Republic of Ireland. *Journal of Industrial Relations (JIR), 46*, 298.

Social Innovation of Work and Employment

Frank Pot, Steven Dhondt, and Peter Oeij

Abstract Social innovation of work and employment are prerequisites to achieve the EU2020 objectives of smart, sustainable and inclusive growth. It covers labour market innovation on societal level and workplace innovation on organisational level. This paper focuses on the latter. Workplace innovations are social both in their ends (quality of working life, well-being and development of talents together with organisational performance) and in their means (employee participation and empowerment). Complementary to technological innovations they regard innovations in social aspects of organisations such as work organisation, HRM and work relations. Workplace innovation – or innovative workplaces as it is sometimes called – deserves to be better incorporated in EU policies, as also has been recommended by the European Economic and Social Committee and the OECD. Some countries have experienced the benefits of national campaigns already.

1 Urgency

European economies are facing a period of economic crisis and there is a political urgency for continuous innovation and growth in productivity in order to realise sustainable growth and welfare provision within the European Union (EU). To achieve this aim, it is not sufficient just to introduce new technologies and seek competitive advantage by means of cutting costs. It will require the full utilisation of the potential workforce and creation of flexible work organisations. Recently, a number of European countries (e.g. Finland, Germany, Ireland, UK, Belgium, and The Netherlands) have started national programmes or initiatives to meet these

---

F. Pot (✉)
Radboud University, Nijmegen, Netherlands
e-mail: f.pot@fm.ru.nl

S. Dhondt • P. Oeij
TNO Work and Employment, Hoofddorp, Netherlands

challenges. These programmes are launched under the heading of 'Social Innovation' or 'Workplace Innovation' (Totterdill et al. 2009; Pot et al. forthcoming).

Why have these programmes come into existence, already before the financial and economic crises? There are four main reasons for the emerging attention for workplace development. The first one is the need to enhance labour productivity to maintain our level of welfare and social security in the near future with fewer people in the workforce due to the ageing population. The second reason is the need to develop and utilise the skills and competences of the potential workforce to increase added value as part of a competitive and knowledge-based economy. The third reason is that private and public work organisations can only fully benefit from technological innovation if it is embedded in workplace innovation (making technology work by means of proper organisation). The fourth reason is that workplace innovation itself appears to be more important for innovation success than technological innovation does. Research by the Erasmus University/Rotterdam School of Management in industrial sectors shows that technological innovation accounts for 25 % of success in radical innovation, whereas non-technological innovation, or social innovation – as it is called in the Netherlands – accounts for 75 %. The success of incremental innovation can be based for 50 % on each technological and non-technological innovation (Volberda et al. 2006).

2 Workplace Innovation

Social innovation is usually defined as ways of societal renewal in a broad sense with reference to societal issues ranging from social inequality to environmental pollution (e.g. Caulier-Grice et al. 2010; Howaldt and Schwarz 2010). It refers to socio-economic topics of various kinds. This paper, however, will focus on social innovation of work and employment. A distinction is made between societal level (labour market innovations and related social security and education issues) and organisational level (Table 1). The term used for renewal on organisational level is *workplace innovation*. Since no uniform definition of workplace innovation is at hand, the following work definition is proposed: *workplace innovations are strategically induced and participatory adopted changes in an organisation's practice of managing, organising and deploying human and non-human resources that lead to simultaneously improved organisational performance and improved quality of working life* (Eeckelaert et al. 2012). In this definition economic and social goals are combined. Other concepts cover more or less the same topics: 'innovative workplaces', 'sustainable work systems', 'high involvement workplaces' etc. In the concept of 'high performance workplaces' the objective of quality of working life is not always covered and the concept of 'non-technological innovation' focuses on organisational innovation, new business and marketing models without paying attention to quality of working life. The concept 'new world of work' refers in particular to mobile workplaces, flexible working times, advanced ICT and management by results.

Table 1 Social innovation of work and employment

Elements	Labour market innovation	Workplace innovation
Needs	Increased labour productivity, development of competences, flexible organisation, innovative capacity	Ibid
Societal challenges	Global competition, knowledge economy, decreasing/ageing workforce, technology gap	Ibid
Values	Sustainable, smart and inclusive growth	Competitiveness and performance, development of talents, quality of working life
Process dimensions	New forms of collaboration with social partners, governments and research institutions, and industrial relations on national and sector level	Participation of stakeholders, trust
Levels of action	European, national, regional and sector	Public and private organisations, sector, region
Content dimensions	(National/European) Policy measures on employment and flexicurity as active labour market and social protection policy and competencies and training (ESF), promotion of workplace innovation (Flagship Initiatives) and Social Innovation Europe	Organisational measures on work organisation, labour relations and network relations (e.g. The combination of organisational innovation, ergonomics, development of competences, employment relations within the organisation)

Workplace innovation includes aspects of management (absorption of external knowledge), flexible organisation, working smarter, continuous development of skills and competences, networking between organisations and the modernisation of labour relations (including human resource management) and industrial relations (Totterdill et al. 2009; Totterdill 2010; Pot 2011). Workplace innovation is regarded as complementary and conditional to technological innovation.

In recent economic recession times 'reduced working hours' (instead of laying off employees) and 'flexible working times', with the government making up some of the employees' lost income, was a social innovation of the labour market. In countries such as Germany and the Netherlands it helped to avoid mass layoffs and to keep skilled work groups together. The available time besides work was sometimes used for extra training or occupational safety and health management.

3 Evidence

Evaluation research has been carried out in some countries and we would like to share some results with you. Interesting data have been collected about the results of the *Finnish Workplace Development Programme* – concerning 'work, organisational and management practices' (WOM) – in 470 projects in the years 1996–2005. Management and staff representatives and experts of 409 projects in different sectors and of different sizes made a self-assessment. Performance was measured by labour productivity, quality of goods and services, quality of operations, flexible customer service and smoothness of operations. Quality of working life (QWL) covered team-like working methods, cooperation between management and staff, social relationships in the workplace, development of vocational skills and mental well-being. In a cluster analysis, three groups were distinguished: the best group (achieving better performance and better QWL) with 152 projects, the worst group (poor or no impact for both factors) with 31 projects, and a group with the remaining projects. In the best group, employment was increased significantly more than in the worst one. The most striking difference between the best group and the worst one was that in the best group the staff played a role in initiating the project more often, employee participation was stronger and internal collaboration was better than in the worst group (Ramstad 2009).

In another investigation, a representative sample of 398 manufacturing firms with more than 50 employees in Finland in 2005, it was found that innovation practices such as performance-based pay, flexible job design and employee involvement, developing employee skills and labour-management cooperation are positively correlated to firm productivity. However, not all specific interventions had a significant effect. Profit-sharing and consultative committees seem to matter more than individual incentive systems, teams, job rotation and formal training strategy (Jones et al. 2008).

Finally – concerning Finland – a survey among 5,270 employees confirmed the expected positive effects of workplace development on quality of working life but the research did not cover performance outcomes (Kalmi and Kauhanen 2008).

In *Germany* there have been no systematic evaluations so far. One exception is the management survey of AOK (an insurer) among 212 partner companies. A wide variety of issues were paid attention to in these companies (both in production sectors and in trade and services), ranging from physical workload (91.5 % of production companies; 80 % of trade and services) to sickness absenteeism, ergonomics, work organisation, safety, style of leadership, up to stress management (30.8 % production; 50.5 % trade and services) (Bonitz et al. 2007). Performance results as assessed by management were substantial (Fig. 1).

Further analysis shows that higher productivity goes hand in hand with better communication and higher employability, resulting from both a decrease in absenteeism and an increase in social and vocational competences (Bonitz et al. 2007, p. 34).

In an important report on 'high performance work systems' (HPWS) in *Ireland*, employee well-being was only measured by employee turnover. Nevertheless, the conclusions of this investigation among 132 medium to large companies in the manufacturing and services industries are relevant. The results of HPWS confirm that "strategic human resources management practices are clearly associated with business performance outcomes, including labour productivity, innovation levels, and employee well-being. The more novel findings relate to the discovery that other factors, including diversity and equality systems, and workplace partner systems,

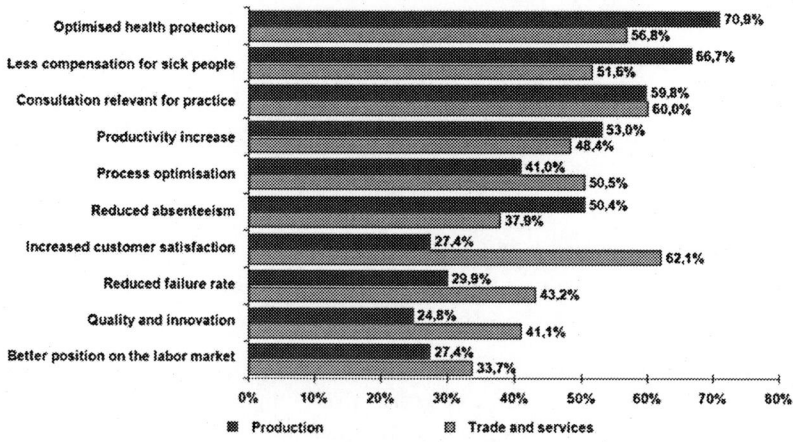

Fig. 1 Performance effects as assessed by management (Bonitz et al. 2007, p. 23)

Table 2 Working smarter and performance

Performance criterion	% change in performance last 2 years	
	SMEs without working smarter	SMEs with working smarter
Company results	2	18
Company turnover	7	15
Productivity	5	14
Employment	6	11

Economic Institute for SMEs. Source: Hauw et al. 2009

are positively and synergistically associated with significantly higher levels of labour productivity, workforce innovation, and reduced employee turnover (Flood et al. 2008, p. 10)."

In *the Netherlands* research by the *Economic Institute for SMEs* in 2008 in 650 Dutch SMEs indicated that companies with workplace development projects achieve higher productivity and financial results compared to companies that do not implement this kind of projects. However, the outcomes regarding quality of working life have not been measured except for employment that in most cases had increased (Hauw et al. 2009) (Table 2).

The *Erasmus Competition and Innovation Monitor* of the Erasmus University Rotterdam – edition 2010 – included 932 Dutch companies of different sizes in different private business sectors. The broad concept of social innovation of the ECIM covers dynamic management, flexible organisation, working smarter and external cooperation. Compared to non-social innovative companies the social innovative companies perform better regarding increase in turnover, profit and market share, and regarding innovation, productivity, new clients and reputation. Between 2008 and 2009 the number of social innovative forms had increased with 5.2 %. Between 2009 and 2010 the increase was 12.8 % (Volberda et al. 2010) (Table 3).

Table 3 Social innovation and performance

Performance	Performance social innovative versus not social innovative organisations
Increase in turnover	16 % higher
Increase in profits	13 % higher
Innovation	31 % higher
Productivity	21 % higher
New clients	17 % higher
Reputation	12 % higher
Contented employees	12 % higher

Erasmus Competition and Innovation Monitor 2010. Source: Volberda et al. 2010

In the *Netherlands Employers Work Survey* (edition 2008) the Netherlands Organisation for Applied Scientific Research (TNO) includes four aspects in social innovation: strategic orientation, product-market improvement, working flexibly and organising more smartly. In different sectors, 3.468 employers with ten or more employees filled in the questionnaire. Organisational performance was measured as a combination of an increase in turnover, profit and labour productivity during the last 2 years. This combined performance was significantly better in organisations with more social innovation. This is also the case for the four different aspects of social innovation (Oeij et al. 2011). The employers in innovative companies were more contented with the terms of employment and HR practices in their organisations, compared to those in non-innovative organisations (Oeij et al. 2010).

Summarizing, recent research on national level indicates that through workplace innovation positive effects regarding organisational performance can be expected. Simultaneous improvement in quality of working life and productivity is possible, in particular in projects with strong employee participation. This conforms with previous research on European level (Eurofound 2005; Totterdill et al. 2002).

4 Organisational Performance and Quality of Working Life

Workplace innovation does not cover the whole range of occupational safety and health (OSH) topics, but it does include low stress risks, high job autonomy, lower physical workload, continuous development of competences, better labour relations (Pot and Koningsveld 2009; Ramstad 2009; Westgaard and Winkel 2011; Oeij et al. 2011). This can be called 'quality of working life' (QWL) and its effect on individual level is well-being. There is a need for more research to develop this association. The systematic review of Westgaard and Winkel (2011) is the first to give an overview of the possible relationship between workplace innovation and OSH topics. The rationalisation strategy, High Performance Work System (HPWS), was associated with the highest fraction of positive studies. Worker participation, resonant management style, information, support, group autonomy and procedural justice were modifiers with favourable influence on OSH outcomes. The main advantage of this assumption is that it might help companies to not solely see QWL as a cost factor, but also as a strategic benefit. In the Community Strategy for OSH 2007–2012 'improving quality and productivity at work' are mentioned. However, productivity in this document relates primarily to the costs of absenteeism.

How can the theoretical coherence of QWL, innovation and performance be understood? Individual and group performance is not directly the result of employee satisfaction or motivation, but through the involvement and commitment of workers' representation, HRM practices and work organisation (Judge et al. 2001; Taris et al. 2008). For instance, organisational commitment can be brought about by an organisational design that provides job autonomy, possibilities of consulting others, learning opportunities etc. (Karasek and Theorell 1990). These are exactly the same measures that are recommended to reduce psychological stress risks as a way of 'prevention at the source' (Pot et al. 1994; Cox et al. 2000). People do not suffer from severe strain because of problems and disturbances in their work, but because they are not able to solve these (De Sitter et al. 1997). Such problems reveal discrepancies, for example, between quantitative job demands and available time or staff, between qualitative job demands and education or training, between problems and disturbances on the one hand, and support from supervisors and colleagues on the other hand, between complexity of the job and control capacity (De Sitter et al. 1997).

Such reasoning has found a theoretical home in the so-called 'job demand – control model'. This model argues that – to understand performance – a proper work organisation is more important than satisfaction (Karasek and Theorell 1990). 'High demands and high control' provides opportunities for learning, whereas 'high demands and low control' is a stress risk and stress inhibits learning. Design and implementation of active jobs (high demands, control/autonomy and support) is an important sub dimension of workplace innovation. A recent review of 83 studies between 1998 and 2007 shows that there is almost always a positive effect on general psychological well-being where the sample size of the study was sufficient to calculate effect. For effects to job-related well-being (job satisfaction and emotional exhaustion) there was consistent evidence in cross-sectional studies, but support rates were lower in longitudinal data (Häusser et al. 2010) (Table 3).

The relationship between work organisation and learning opportunities can be extended further. In much research, control is only measured by job autonomy (freedom of action within a specific job). Job autonomy makes it possible to learn how to do the job better. This could be called 'internal control capacity,' which is related to 'single loop learning': doing things better (Argyris and Schön 1978). Without job autonomy an employee can solve problems only in a standardised manner, without really learning anything new. Another question however is 'are we doing the right things': 'double-loop learning'? This requires for the worker control of another kind, which could be called 'external control capacity' (participation in decision making, consultation on the shop floor, co-determination) as is elaborated in 'modern socio-technology' (De Sitter et al. 1997; Kira and Eijnatten 2008), the 'action regulation theory' (Hacker 2003) and in theories of the 'learning organisation' (Senge 1990), 'high road organisations' (Totterdill et al. 2002, 2009), 'the flexible firm' (Oeij et al. 2006; Goudswaard et al. 2009) and the 'innovative firm' (Sabel 2006).

The same kind of reasoning concerning autonomy, learning and control holds for ergonomic design of workplaces. This serves not only as the objective of the reduction of physical workload, prevention of musculoskeletal diseases (allowing better postures and movements; reducing lifting) and health improvement (physical exercise), but also that of enhancing productivity (easier and faster handling and processing; better lay-out). In particular if the design and implementation processes are characterized by a participatory approach (Koningsveld et al. 2005; Vink et al. 2006; Koningsveld 2008).

In this sense, workplace innovation is directed at both improved organisational performance and improved QWL. Workplace innovation serves both economic goals, namely performance and productivity (as is the case with non-technological innovation), and social goals (talent development and well-being).

5 Different Meanings of 'Social' and Disputable Contradictions

Some conceptual confusion is caused by the different meanings of 'social'. One meaning refers to political objectives such as 'good for people', either on individual or on societal level (empowerment, health, well-being), opposed to business innovation or economic innovation. A second meaning refers to intervention domains, complementary to technological innovation, such as institutional arrangements, behaviours, work organisation, HRM and work relations. A third meaning refers to change agents: civil society, social entrepreneurs, employees, opposed to public authorities and management.

So, sometimes innovations are not considered to be social innovations if they are primarily focussed on business targets or if they are initiated by public authorities or management. However, the contradictions concerning agents and objectives are not tenable. When we look at the first EU pilot project social innovation on 'active and healthy ageing' it becomes clear immediately that public authorities, technology industry, pharmaceutical industry, commercial and not-for-profit (health)care institutions, patients associations, families and neighbourhoods have to participate and collaborate in finding solutions. Looking at work and employment on societal level, employment policies by the EU, member states and social partners need to become social innovative to achieve inclusive growth. Workplace innovation is needed to achieve smart and sustainable growth through 'working smarter' and competence development for 'sustainable employability'. Of course it is possible to initiate non-technological innovation only for business targets, without any concern for competence development and/or quality of working life. We would not call that workplace innovation or social innovation at work.

6 Workplace Innovation Not Yet Clearly Defined in EU Policy

Within the context of European policy, social innovation is conceived as a broad topic, as it is a means to combat both social and societal challenges such as the financial and economic crisis, unemployment, participation, social cohesion, climate change and innovation, productivity and growth through societal innovation. 'Social innovation refers to new responses to pressing social demands, by means which affect the process of social interactions. Social innovations are characterised by the production of a social return and the creation of new social relationships or partnerships which involve the end users and thereby make policies more effective' (European Commission 2010a). A study on social innovation by the Social Innovation eXchange (SIX) and the Young Foundation (Caulier-Grice et al. 2010, pp. 17–18) provides another definition of social innovations as being: '…social both in their ends and in their means. Specifically, we define social innovations as new ideas (products, services and models) that simultaneously meet social needs (more effectively than alternatives) *and* create new social relationships or collaborations. In other words they are innovations that are both good for society *and* enhance society's capacity to act'. The European Commission has embraced this definition (European Commission 2010a, p. 2), arguing that just as stimulating innovation, entrepreneurship and the knowledge society was at the core of the Lisbon strategy for growth and jobs, social innovation should now be part of a new strategy to reach sustainable growth in the EU.

Unfortunately workplace innovation programmes have been overlooked in these documents, not taking into account EU's own history. Looking at the European policy on workplace innovation at the end of last century we find the Commission's initiative to prepare a 'Green Paper on Partnership for a new Organisation of Work' (European Commission 1997). This paper was a first attempt to organise the field of work organisation as a separate policy goal. In the framework of that paper, Totterdill et al. (2002) investigated 100 cases in six countries and developed the concept of 'the high road of organisational innovation'. This so-called 'high road of organisational innovation' aims at sustainable innovation by employee involvement and a high quality of working life. The alternative for this strategy is characterised in this study as 'mainly oriented at cutting costs'. The authors also list several benefits of the high road, which could be measured: productivity, quality of products, and costs. Less tangible effects were: knowledge, innovation, technological efficacy, and quality of working life (Totterdill et al. 2002).

The relation between work organisation, competence development, QWL and social innovation has recently been mentioned in the draft guidelines for the employment policies (European Commission 2010b) and in the accompanying document for the Flagship Initiative Innovation Union (European Commission 2010c). At the launch event of Social Innovation Europe (SIE), initiated by DG Enterprise and Industry, on 16/17 March 2011 a workshop on Workplace Innovation was organised (Dhondt et al. 2011) as well as at Challenge Social Innovation in Vienna on 19–21 September 2011. In other words, it is observed that Europe seems at the brink of uniting the concepts of social innovation and workplace innovation. We give some more examples to support this optimistic view.

In the draft 'Guidelines for the employment policies of the Member States' we find the following text in proposed guideline 7: "Work-life balance policies with the provision of affordable care and innovation in work organisation should be geared to raising employment rates, particularly among youth, older workers and women, in particular to retain highly-skilled women in scientific and technical fields. Member States should also remove barriers to labour market entry for newcomers, support self-employment and job creation in areas including green employment and care and promote social innovation" (European Commission, 2010b, p. 8). Guideline 8 is mainly on developing a skilled workforce: "Investment in human resource development, up-skilling and participation in lifelong learning schemes should be promoted through joint financial contributions from governments, individuals and employers" (European Commission 2010b, p. 9). Unfortunately 'promoting job quality' is only mentioned in the title of this guideline 8. Finally, some additional texts have been proposed by the Employment Committee on the Employment Guidelines, including these citations: "Together with the social partners, adequate attention should also be paid to internal flexicurity at the workplace" and "The quality of jobs and employment conditions should be addressed." (Council of the European Union 2010, p. 2).

In 2007, an ESF-programme (DG EMPL) focused on a more flexible labour market. One of the main areas proposed for investment was the 'design and dissemination of innovative and productive methods of work organisation'. The European Social Fund (ESF) invests in social innovation: more than €2 billion in institutional capacity building; another €2 billion in mutual learning between the Member States "and a further €1 billion is spent on innovative activities related to new forms of work organisation, better use of employees' skills and resources, productivity improvement, new approaches to lifelong learning and new ways of combating unemployment through entrepreneurship. Overall, however, activity levels are sub-critical and most authorities involved in social innovation activities recognise the need for experimentation and 'scaling-up'" (European Commission 2010c, p. 67).

The European Parliament, in its Resolution of 12 May 2011 on Innovation Union "stresses that social innovation provides an opportunity for citizens, in any role, to enhance their working and life environment and thus could help strengthen the European social model."

Social partners at European level also discussed the issue of workplace innovation. The European Economic and Social Committee stressed in an own opinion initiative that "The idea that quality and social innovations implemented in the workplace have a major impact on business success must be actively promoted" (EESC 2007). In its recent own-initiative opinion "The EESC believes that although the concept of the 'innovative workplace' is not mentioned in the Commission document, it is at the heart of the Europe 2020 strategy, as it is one of the key prerequisites for the success of this strategy, and therefore recommends that the 'innovative workplace' concept should be incorporated into the strategy" and "Workplace innovation is used to try and sustainably improve the productivity of organisations, while improving the quality of working life" (EESC 2011, pp. 1 and 4).

There is also support for workplace innovation in another important and recent international document, 'The OECD innovation strategy', which is the culmination of a 3-year, multi-disciplinary and multi-stakeholder effort. The OECD emphasises that 'empowering people to innovate' and 'fostering innovative workplaces' is important for creativity, innovation and productivity. Although these topics are subject of firms' decisions, "governments may be able to shape national institutions to support higher levels of employee learning and training in the workplace" (OECD 2010a, pp. 74–80). The relation between types of work organisation and organisational learning to foster innovative workplaces is further elaborated by the OECD and partners, making use of the data of the European Working Conditions Survey of Eurofound, Dublin (OECD 2010b).

A recent literature study on social innovation even states that a paradigm shift in innovation is becoming manifest: as economic and technological innovation are proving to be insufficient in effectively combating broad societal issues, it is necessary to turn to social innovation, including the renewal of workplaces (Howaldt and Schwarz 2010).

7 EU Support for Workplace Innovation Needed

In conclusion, one can say that, despite the use of broad concepts of social innovation in many of the EU policy documents and related studies, it can be discerned that the road is paved for workplace innovation as well.

However, public and private organisations do not easily implement workplace innovation for the following reasons. There is only little research on the claim of a win-win situation. Quite a number of managers wait for others to find out how it works or prefer short-term results instead of long-term innovativeness. A lot of managers are not equipped for participatory approaches and/or are afraid to share power with their employees. Trust is a difficult asset to develop and to maintain. So, if we leave workplace innovation to the initiative of the market, we can only expect workplace innovation in a limited number of organisations with visionary governors and strong works councils. The majority of interventions will be just cost reduction strategies. EU and national campaigns are needed to support workplace innovation, in particular in those countries where there is little experience. The research that is available clearly shows the possibility of convergence of organisational performance and quality of working life which is a prerequisite to achieve the EU2020 objectives of smart, sustainable and inclusive growth. Recently (summer 2012) the Directorate General Enterprise and Industry of the European Commission adopted the concept of 'workplace innovation' and published a call for "a European Learning Network for Workplace Innovation".

References

Argyris, C., & Schön, D. (1978). *Organisational learning*. Massachusetts: Addison-Wesley.

Bonitz, D., Eberle, G., & Lück, P. (2007). *Wirtschaftlicher Nutzen von betrieblicher Gesundheitsförderung aus der Sicht von Unternehmen*. Bonn: AOK-Bundesverband.

Caulier-Grice, J., Kahn, L., Mulgan, G., Pulford, L., & Vasconcelos, D. (2010). Study on social innovation. *Social Innovation Exchange* (SIX)/Young Foundation.

Council of the European Union. (2010). Proposal for a Council Decision on guidelines for the employment policies of the Member States. Part II of the Europe 2020 Integrated Guidelines. Opinion of the Employment Committee, Brussels, 21 May 2010, Inter institutional File 2010/0115(NLE).

Cox, T., Griffiths, A., & Rial-González, E. (2000). *Research on work-related stress*. Luxemburg: European Agency on Safety and Health at Work.

De Sitter, L. U., Hertog, J. F., & Dankbaar, B. (1997). From complex organisations with simple jobs to simple organisations with complex jobs. *Human Relations, 50*(5), 497–534.

Dhondt, S., Gramberen, M. V., Keuken, F., Pot, F., Totterdill, P., & Vaas, F. (2011). *Workplace innovation, Social Innovation Europe launch event*. Nottingham: UKWON.

Eeckelaert, L., Dhondt, S., Oeij, P., Pot, F., Nicolescu, G. I., Webster, J., & Elsler, D. (2012). *Review of workplace innovation and its relation with occupational safety and health*. Bilbao: European Agency for Safety and Health at Work.

Eurofound. (2005). *New forms of work organisation. Can Europe realise its potential? Results of a survey of direct participation in Europe*. Dublin: Eurofound.

European Commission. (1997). *Green paper on partnership for a new organisation of work*. Luxembourg: Office for Official Publications of the European Communities.

European Commission. (2010a). *Social innovation as part of the Europe 2020 strategy*. Brussels: Bureau of European Policy Advisers.

European Commission. (2010b). Proposal for a council decision on guidelines for the employment policies of the member states. Part II of the Europe 2020 Integrated Guidelines, Brussels: COM92010) 193/3.

European Commission. (2010c). Accompanying document to the Europe 2020 Flagship Initiative Innovation Union, Brussels: Commission staff working document, COM(2010)546/SEC (2010)1161.

European Economic and Social Committee. (2007). Promoting sustainable productivity in the European workplace, Brussels (SOC/266).

European Economic and Social Committee. (2011). Innovative workplaces as a source of productivity and quality jobs, Brussels (SC/034).

Flood, P. C., Guthrie, J. P., & Liu, W. (2008). *New models of high performance work systems*. Dublin: National Centre for Partnership & Performance.

Goudswaard, A., Oeij, P., Brugman, T., & De Jong, T. (2009). *Good practice guide to internal flexibility policies in companies*. Dublin: European Foundation for the Improvement of Living and Working Conditions.

Hacker, W. (2003). Action regulation theory: A practical tool for the design of modern work. *European Journal of Work and Organisational Psychology, 12*(2), 105–130.

Häusser, J. A., Mojzisch, A., Niesel, M., & Schulz-Hardt, S. (2010). Ten years on: A review of recent research on the Job Demand-Control (−Support) model and psychological well-being. *Work and Stress, 24*(1), 1–35.

Howaldt, J., & Schwarz, M. (2010). *Social innovation: Concepts, research fields and international trends*. Dortmund: Sozialforschungsstelle Dortmund, ZWE der TU-Dortmund.

Jones, D. C., Kalmi, P., Kato, T., & Mäkinen, M. (2008). *The effects of human resource management practices on firm productivity – Preliminary evidence from Finland*. Helsinki: The Research Institute of the Finnish Economy.

Judge, T. A., Thoresen, C. J., Bono, J. E., & Patton, G. K. (2001). The job satisfaction – Job performance relationship: A qualitative and quantitative review. *Psychological Bulletin, 127*, 376–407.

Kalmi, P., & Kauhanen, A. (2008). Workplace innovations and employee outcomes: Evidence from Finland. *Industrial Relations, 47*(3), 430–459.

Karasek, R. A., & Theorell, T. (1990). *Healthy work: Stress, productivity and the reconstruction of working life*. New York: Basic Books.

Kira, M., & van Eijnatten, M. (2008). Socially sustainable work organizations: A chaordic systems approach. *Systems Research and Behavioral Sciences, 25*, 743–756.

Koningsveld, E. A. P. (2008). Factors of competitive advances through ergonomics interventions. In L. I. Sznelwar, F. L. Mascia, & U. B. Montedo (Eds.), *Human factors in organisational design and management* (pp. 265–270). Santa Monica: IEA Press.

Koningsveld, E. A. P., Dul, J., van Rhijn, J. W., & Vink, P. (2005). Enhancing the impact of ergonomic interventions. *Ergonomics, 48*(5), 559–580.

OECD. (2010a). The OECD innovation strategy: Getting a head start on tomorrow. Paris: OECD Publishing. www.oecd.org/innovation/strategy

OECD. (2010b). Innovative workplaces. Making better use of skills within organisations. Paris: OECD Publishing. http://dx.doi.org/9789264095687-en

Oeij, P., Dhondt, S., & Wiezer, N. (2006). Conditions for low stress-risk jobs: Europe's case. *European Journal of Social Quality, 6*(2), 81–108.

Oeij, P., Dorenbosch, L., Klein Hesselink, J., & Vaas, F. (2010). *Slimmer werken en sociale innovatie (Working smarter and social innovation)*. Den Haag: Boom Lemma.

Oeij, P., Dhondt, S., & Korver, T. (2011). Social innovation, workplace innovation and social quality. *International Journal of Social Quality, 1*(2), 38–49.

Pot, F. D. (2011). Workplace innovation for better jobs and performance. *International Journal of Productivity and Performance Management, 60*(4), 404–415.

Pot, F. D., & Koningsveld, E. A. P. (2009). Quality of working life and organizational performance – Two sides of the same coin? *Scandinavian Journal of Work, Environment and Health, 35*(6), 421–428.

Pot, F. D., Peeters, M., Vaas, F., & Dhondt, S. (1994). Assessment of stress risks and learning opportunities in the work organization. *European Work and Organisational Psychologist, 4*(1), 21–37.

Pot, F. et al. (forthcoming). Workplace innovation in the Netherlands. In I. Houtman (Ed.), *Quality of working life in the Netherlands*, vol 2, Hoofddorp: TNO.

Ramstad, E. (2009). Promoting performance and the quality of working life simultaneously. *Internal Journal of Productivity and Performance Management, 58*(5), 423–436.

Sabel, C. F. (2006). A real-time revolution in routines. In C. Heckscher & P. Adler (Eds.), *The firm as a collaborative community* (pp. 106–156). Oxford: Oxford University Press.

Senge, P. (1990). *The fifth discipline*. New York: Doubleday.

Taris, T. W., Schreurs, P. J. G., Eikmans, K. J. L., & van Riet, P. (2008). Werkkenmerken, welzijn en organisatieprestatie: een toets van de happy-productive worker hypothese op organisatieniveau. (Work characteristics, well-being and organisational performance: A test of the happy-productive worker hypothesis on organisation level). *Gedrag & Organisatie, 21*(1), 3–18.

Totterdill, P. (2010). Workplace innovation. Europe 2020's missing dimension. Report of a workshop hosted by DG Employment, Social Affairs and Equal Opportunities, 23 June 2010. Nottingham: UKWON.

Totterdill, P., Dhondt, S., & Milsome, S. (2002). *Partners at work? A report to Europe's policymakers and social partners*. Nottingham: The Work Institute.

Totterdill, P., Exton, O., Exton, R., & Sherrin, J. (2009). *Workplace innovation policies in European countries*. Nottingham: UKWON.

van der Hauw, P. A., Pasaribu, M. N., & van der Zeijden, P. T. (2009). *Slimmer werken: gebruik, mogelijkheden en opbrengsten in de praktijk (Working smarter: application, opportunities and proceeds in practice)*. Zoetermeer: EIM.

Vink, P., Koningsveld, E. A. P., & Molenbroek, J. F. (2006). Positive outcomes of participatory ergonomics in terms of greater comfort and higher productivity. *Applied Ergonomics, 37* (2006), 537–546.

Volberda, H. W., Van den Bosch, F. A. J., & Jansen, J. J. P. (2006). *Slim managen & innovatief organiseren (managing smartly and organising innovatively)*. Rotterdam: Eiffel.

Volberda, H., et al. (2010). *Sociale innovatie: nu nog beter! (Social innovation, today even better!)*. Rotterdam: INSCOPE.

Westgaard, R. H., & Winkel, J. (2011). Occupational musculoskeletal and mental health: Significance of rationalization and opportunities to create sustainable production systems – A systematic review. *Applied Ergonomics, 42*(2), 261–296.

Part VI
Social Innovation, Open Innovation and Social Media

Challenges at the Intersection of Social Media and Social Innovation: A Manifesto

Christoph Kaletka, Karolin Eva Kappler, Bastian Pelka, and Richard Ruiz de Querol

Abstract Inspired by recent critical social and economic developments – and their most visible eruptions in the Arab world, Spain and Greece – which demonstrate that there is a relatively low barrier of entrance for individuals and groups to adopt social media for virtually any shared purpose, objective or cause, a "manifesto" has been written by a group of transdisciplinary researchers, activists and practitioners from the fields of ICT and social movements.

It promotes the possibility of using social media as a platform to effectively support the processes of social innovation, overcoming its limitations of speed and scale to become an alternative to currently established institutional mechanisms. Such social innovations comprise all new strategies, concepts, ideas and organizations that meet current social needs and strengthen civil society.

Further, the present paper proposes a framework for research into the elements of socio-technical architectures capable of sustaining large scale social innovations enabled by the availability of social media, considering the "paradigm shift of communication" in a knowledge society and describing key challenges of social innovation initiatives. In this context, the objective of the Manifesto on Social Media for Social Innovation is to propose actions oriented to extract the best of the potential synergies among those two concepts of social innovation and social media.

C. Kaletka (✉) • B. Pelka
Social Research Centre at Dortmund University of Technology, Dortmund, Germany
e-mail: kaletka@sfs-dortmund.de

K.E. Kappler • R.R. de Querol
Barcelona Media Foundation, Barcelona, Spain

1 Introduction

Social media, an umbrella term designating a constellation of internet platforms allowing users to publish, share, comment, distribute and remix all types of digital content, are causing significant changes in the way the internet is used and perceived. The most popular platforms, including social networks like Facebook, content sharing sites such as YouTube, collaboration sites such as the Wikipedia and new communication channels such as the micro-blogging site Twitter, are among the internet platforms with the largest absolute number of users (Comscore 2011). Most significantly, the amount of time spent by the average user on those social media sites is much larger than time spent on traditional sites such as Google or Yahoo! (Nielsen 2011). It therefore seems plausible to foresee that social media will have a lasting and significant effect both in the functionalities of the internet platforms and in the practices of the users accessing them, similar to the impact that the World Wide Web had during the 1990s. (Berners-Lee 1999).

In parallel, social innovation is also becoming an attractive concept for both public authorities and the so-called social entrepreneurs. As there is growing evidence that social innovation can bring about tangible results (Goldsmith 2010), it is receiving increased attention from public agencies (Bepa 2010; SIX 2010; White House 2010) as well as from academia (Phills et al. 2008; Howaldt and Schwarz 2010), the private sector (Hunt 2009) and even business magazines (Baker 2009). One of the reasons for the surge of interest in social innovation seems to hinge on the expectation that the contribution from social entrepreneurs can bring about a transformation and an increase in productivity in the public sector similar to the one that many businesses experienced from the mid 1990s. Nevertheless, those expectations are moderated by the evidence that social innovation has a problem of "speed and scale" (The Economist 2010).

Overcoming this problem might just be a matter of time. As demonstrated by economic analysis (Solow 1987; Brynjolfsson 1993; Castells 1999: chap. 2), it took several decades for business investments in information technologies to result in measurable increases in productivity. In fact, the process of organisational rearrangement towards the so-called network economy (Castells 1999) is still fully underway in sectors such as music and content publishing. Something similar could happen regarding the full exploitation of the capabilities of information technologies to help social innovation to gain greater speed and scale, although taking place at a different pace in the diverse categories of social innovation (Bepa 2010). Some locally oriented practices, such as the 'social innovation camp',[1] are already highly intensive in their use of technology. But tackling the challenges of the large scale, systemic changes needed to solve today's most pressing social problems (Touraine 2010; Morin 2011) will inevitably take some more time.

Addressing the prospect of the uses of social media to foster social innovation requires a proper sociological approach to both the processes of innovation

---

[1] http://www.sicamp.org/global/

(Howaldt and Schwarz 2010) and of social appropriation of technology (Tuomi 2002). Innovation, even technological innovation, is as much about creating new meanings as it is about creating novel material artefacts (Tuomi 2002, p. 13). As meaning is constructed in society through the process of communicative action (Castells 2009, p. 12), mediated by whichever communication mechanisms are available at a given time, social media can be expected to become increasingly relevant.

2 Framing the Manifesto: Social Media for Social Innovation

In order to frame the Manifesto, we start from the current economic and political situation, characterized and dominated by an acute and prolonged economic and financial crisis, social and civil uprisings in both Arab and European countries and an expanding social movement unified by its "indignation". Citizens, political and economic leaders start to understand that new governance models are needed to face the present situation. Social innovation and social media might help to find bottom-up, participative, innovative and new solutions.

2.1 What Are Social Innovations?

Howaldt and Schwarz (Howaldt and Schwarz 2010, p. 21) define social innovations with a reference to Schumpeter:

> A social innovation is a new combination and/or new configuration of social practices in certain areas of action or social contexts prompted by certain actors or constellations of actors in an intentional targeted manner with the goal of better satisfying or answering needs and problems than is possible on the basis of established practices. An innovation is therefore social to the extent that it, conveyed by the market or 'non/without profit', is socially accepted and diffused widely throughout society or in certain societal sub-areas, transformed depending on circumstances and ultimately institutionalized as new social practice or made routine.

With this definition Howaldt and Schwarz do not only distinguish a social innovation from technological innovations (that are "tangible", in comparison to "intangible" social innovations) but also from social inventions and social change. Social inventions are intended, new and social, but not necessarily used. And social change is not intended, it "happens". With this scientific understanding, we also deny that there is a normative layer of social innovations. Our scientific perspective is the adoption of an innovation by society. While the manifesto itself is a political type of text which naturally has to consider its claims and approaches as "good" or socially desirable, this distinction is very important in transdisciplinary cooperation, especially if the disciplines involved are not only scientific ones. So in framing the manifesto, we will not define "good" social innovations, but can only indicate which innovations as social practices could be useful because of their potential to contribute to a *common goal* (see Chap. 3.2).

Here, as Howaldt and Schwarz (Howaldt and Schwarz 2010, p. 3) say, the "preparedness of society to adopt new solutions for needs and challenges comes into play. (...) Social values, ideologies, institutions, power imbalances, other disparities, and – last but not least – prevailing patterns of innovations have an effect on the success of different kinds of innovation ('path dependency')." One important factor of preparedness is the extent of use of social media in a society. Social media, obviously, are dependent on an active involvement of a broad and interconnected public (Kaletka and Pelka 2010, p. 152). In recent years while the use of the internet and social media has increased tremendously worldwide, the socio-demographic characteristics of the internet users have also changed; users more and more represent the overall population. Setting this as a background, we can say that social media have the potential to give birth to social innovations. Its problem – not only with or within social media – seems to be the issue of "speed and scale" (The Economist 2010). This is the anchor for the manifesto: It aims at describing pathways for speed and scale of social innovations through social media.

2.2 Empowerment Through Social Media

In this context of a growing need of and expectation from social innovations, the manifesto formulates the requirements and options we currently see to initiate social innovation processes supported and accelerated by social media. This vision contrasts the current hype around the latter which mainly is concerned with its use for leisure and entertainment and the opportunities thereby generated for the marketing and advertisement industries, the "attention industry" (Globalwebindex 2011).

Our understanding of social media and their impact on society goes far beyond that: We see a new communication pattern raised by social media with the potential to better empower individuals to participate in different processes in modern society. This entails the replacement of top-down, linear processes and "finished products" by "never finished products" created and evolved incrementally through bottom-up, collaborative, distributed processes. This development is in line with the change from an industrial to a knowledge society as well as with the decentralisation of knowledge and content production processes taking place in a variety of social fields; although its consequences and implications have not been analytically analysed yet.

Communication mechanisms are one of the threads in the fabric of societies. The new communication and coordination possibilities through social media are and could further be used for a societal evolution going much beyond the economics of leisure and consumption. The paradigm shift of communication challenges multiple layers of the knowledge society. The four most striking ones are:

1. *Change of labour.* The shift from an industrial to a knowledge society goes hand in glove with a shift in forms of labour and management, which means: the way people work and the way organizations are managed and generate potential innovations. The way social media support cooperation between individuals and foster the production of user-generated content shows analogies to cooperation strategies in knowledge based labour processes. The potential of social media – not seen as a technology, but as a new communication paradigm – seems underexploited in labour processes.
2. *Political participation.* The availability of social media, which enables many new options for online interaction and content creation for all kinds of users, has already severely influenced both horizontal and vertical political communication processes. The "horizontal" level addresses new or accelerated coordination potential among political interest groups, with the extensive use of social media by Greek and Spanish youth movements of 2011 as the most prominent and recent example. "Vertical" communication takes place between citizens and interest groups with public authorities. Here, the impact of social media becomes visible in the substantial research effort which is being organized in the USA to address national political priorities (Pirolli et al. 2010). Its objective is to create new socio-technical architectures for the online public spaces that allow citizenship at large to contribute to vital community and national projects. Similarly in Europe, the European Commission has declared the objective to "empower citizens and business by eGovernment services *designed around users' needs and developed in collaboration with third parties* [...]" (European Commission 2010a).
3. *eInclusion.* Quite strongly linked to the field of political participation is the question of participation. E-inclusion is, on the one hand, an approach to overcome the "digital divide" of society and to support *digital* inclusion. Social media, even if quite simple to use, are still means of ICT and demand basic ICT skills and access to ICT and internet. So called "digitally excluded persons" either lack ICT access or competences or motivation. The potential of social media for e-inclusion is high, if social media are embedded in supporting social structures that these target groups will need to make full profit of social media as e-inclusion means (Kluzer and Rissola 2009; Kaletka et al. 2011). On the other hand, e-inclusion is also a concept and political approach to support *social* integration by making use of ICT. In this sense, e-inclusion is the use of ICT to overcome social and economic disadvantages and exclusion, especially of already disadvantaged people, being a central aim of the Digital Agenda for Europe (European Commission 2010c).
4. *Education and training.* Education has long since discovered the potential of user-driven learning approaches. Modern learning environments deny "teaching" in the sense of mediating knowledge but place the learner in the centre of the learning process. This shift from "teaching" to "learning" came along with pedagogical approaches and technological environments that enable learners to find their own way of acquiring needed knowledge, skills and competences. Social media show analogies to this approach: They also put the learner in the

middle of the process and offer him the instruments of navigating through learning content. The potential of social media for education and training seems underexploited by far (Pelka 2010).

The increasingly shared view of local and global risks and the necessity of new and innovative governance models is confirmed by the European Commission, stating that there is a need "to move towards a more open model of design, production and delivery of online services, taking advantage of the possibility offered by collaboration between citizens, entrepreneurs and civil society" (European Commission 2010a). Even then, the writing of a manifesto seems to be still necessary in order to emphasize the need of the merging of the social and technological aspects in an effective process. Therefore, the Manifesto starts from the assumption that communication mechanisms and especially the social interactions enabled by the new and social media are one of the threads in the fabric of societies. In this context, one of the main research questions is how to improve the success of social innovation initiatives by supporting collaboration among the disparate players who must work together to bring these projects to bear. While the importance of establishing networked collaboration for successful innovations has been demonstrated across a variety of sectors (Dubini and Aldrich 2002; Jenssen 2001), we still do not know how best to support this process in the social arena. Nevertheless, a first review of existing literature and theories (Ruiz De Querol and Kappler 2011) shows that the widespread availability of 'social computing' mechanisms can have a significant impact fostering "bottom-up" networks of innovation and collaboration that incorporate a wide array of diverse parties, including social entrepreneurs, communities, not-for- and for-profit organizations, and government agencies.

In spite of the relevance of horizontal communication, it has been demonstrated that there exists a number of limitations and risks of applying the current generation of Web 2.0 tools to the often simplistic cliché expectations about the "wisdom of the crowds" and similar metaphors (Sunstein 2006, 2007).

Aside from the current hype around social media, it seems to be clear that "effective Technology Mediated Social Participation (TMSP) designs" are needed that "improve usability and sociability to better engage people with diverse motivations, experiences, perspectives, skill and knowledge and to create the conditions for citizens to participate, connect and undertake constructive action" (Pirolli et al. 2010). According to Castells, "the greater the autonomy of the communicating subjects vis-à-vis the controllers of societal communication nodes, the higher the chances for the introduction of messages challenging dominant values and interests in communication networks" (Castells 2009, p. 413). These new socio-technological architectures of the online public space can be crucial in order to change the existing power relations. In this sense, the potentials of social media represent a paradigm shift in the way people communicate and work.

3 A Socio-technical Framework for Social Media and Social Innovation

3.1 Basic Challenges

It would be naive to foresee that social innovation would overcome barriers of speed and scale just by throwing in social media. Not only should one not expect to solve social problems with algorithms (McQuillan 2011); technology by itself does not solve social problems either. We should not forget, for example, that besides a transformation of the technological base of society the industrial revolution entailed at least equally radical ideological, political and organisational transformations (Polanyi 2002). On the same footing, the worldwide expansion of the internet can only be fully understood in the framework of the process of globalisation (Castells 1999; Tuomi 2002). Social change does not happen when society adopts new technologies – it happens when society adopts new behaviours.

With this in mind, one can note that the many definitions of social innovation (for example Bepa 2010; Howaldt and Schwarz 2010; Phills et al. 2008) have all in common the attempt to deal with a phenomenon which does not fit and does not want to be fitted into a dichotomous world of the 'market' and the 'state'. This suggests using the work of scholars such as Elinor Ostrom as a starting point in looking for the coupling of social media and social innovation. The following statement of Ostrom's (2009) Nobel Prize lecture is readily applicable to social innovation:

"*Designing institutions* to force (or nudge) entirely self-interested individuals to achieve better outcomes has been the major goal posited by policy analysts for governments to accomplish for much of the past century. Extensive empirical research leads me to argue that instead, a core goal of public policy should be to *facilitate the development of institutions* that bring out the best in humans. We need to ask how diverse polycentric institutions help or hinder innovativeness, learning, adapting, trustworthiness, levels of cooperation of participants, and the achievement of more effective, equitable and sustainable outcomes at multiple scales". (Ostrom 2009 (emphasis added)).

Ostrom's research helped to identify design principles for bottom-up organisations to be sustainable over time, as well as rules for individual behaviour inside those organisations. Communication and information sharing among the participants are elements of these principles and behaviours, as well as a substrate for the build-up (or the loss) of trust and other key elements. It seems therefore worthwhile to explore how to best blend those design principles and rules with the communicative capacities of the currently available social media or with those of other platforms yet to be developed.

The shortcomings of early attempts to bind social media and social innovation are evident, for instance, in a recent call from the European Commission to open a dialogue about the desirable characteristics of platforms for "collective awareness and actions" (Madelin 2011). The call emanates from the vision that "individuals can save the planet if they are given the opportunity to act socially, based on trusted information [...] Such an extended awareness can be enabled by ICT technologies". The proposed objective would be to deploy "social innovation platforms for sustainability aware lifestyles and for collective action" that would support "innovative environmentally aware, bottom-up processes and practices to share knowledge, to achieve changes in lifestyle, production and consumption patterns, and eventually to set up more participatory democratic processes" (Madelin 2011).

It is obvious that the nature of the envisaged social and collective action seems pretty much limited to sharing knowledge and generating 'awareness', while achieving more participatory democratic processes is left out to be handled 'eventually'. This rings a tone of 'libertarian paternalism' (Thaler and Sunstein 2008) where the framing of the problem and the affordable choices are defined and set up in a pre-established top-down matter. The contrast with the spirit of Ostrom's quote above is quite evident.

3.2 A Layered Socio-Technical Architecture

In the light of the above, we propose to consider a socio-technical architecture with three basic components:

- A top layer encompassing the overall design principles and rules of governance of communities involved in social innovation, including those affecting the other layers underneath. The transposition of Ostrom's results to contexts of social innovation, including the evidence that there is not a universal all-encompassing governance scheme applicable to all kind of contexts and issues, could be a starting point. When the context where innovation takes place is closely connected to a larger social-ecological system, these governance activities might be themselves organised in multiple nested layers.
- An intermediate level which would include the rules and practices regarding the social creation and sharing of content supported by the technical infrastructure, including crucial issues such as that of the management of online identity, reputation and trust, as well as of the mechanisms ensuring transparency and accountability of content, among others. Ostrom's research also indicates the relevance of allowing the individuals in a community to take part in making and modifying its rules. Therefore, mechanisms for effective online deliberation and resolution of conflicts should also be included.
- The bottom level would comprise the design principles and governance rules of the technical infrastructure required for social media communication. Separate consideration should be given, on the one hand, to the design, implementation and management of the software implementing the functionalities required by the two levels above and, on the other hand, to the provision and management of the hardware and communications infrastructure (Fuster 2010).

One can easily establish indicative parallelisms between this framework and those at work in success cases such as those of the invention of the internet (Abbate 2000), the development of open source (Tuomi 2002, Weber 2004) and that of Wikipedia (Fuster 2010).

Fleshing out this framework and filling out the missing details will require specific research which is way beyond the objective of this paper. A manifesto proposing a set of research questions and a call for action regarding them is motivated by these arguments.

4 The Manifesto on Social Media for Social Innovation

This Manifesto was compiled by a group of transdisciplinary researchers, activists and practitioners from the fields of ICT and social movements. They came together in a workshop of the 5th International Conference on Weblogs and Social Media (ICWSM-11), held on the 21 July in Barcelona. The Manifesto was composed in order to address researchers in social sciences and internet technologies, people and organizations interested in the applications of social media for social innovation and institutions potentially interested in supporting researchers and practitioners to further social innovation through social media. The following ideas were leading the discussions in the workshop.

4.1 Motivation

Based on the above, the joint scenario for social innovation and social media could be summarized as following:

1. There is an increasingly widespread agreement that the economic and social reference models that have worked during the last decades are not sustainable any more.
2. The financial crisis demonstrates that many current socio-technical systems need to be redesigned and redeployed, not merely readjusted. A similar conclusion can be reached about other relevant societal issues.
3. Social innovation is proving to be a sensible alternative to some of the traditional government-led institutional frameworks for addressing social issues and concerns. Nevertheless, many conventional, top-down, public policies do not yet take enough into account the potential benefits of social innovations.
4. Social innovations can and will be a key ingredient to the solution of new and existing societal problems; but it needs improvements in speed and scale.
5. Social media or other forms of technology-mediated social participation (TMSP) can provide platforms and tools supporting social innovation to grow more effective and at a larger scale.
6. Existing social media tools will need to be adapted or redesigned for a TMSP directed to social innovation.

4.2 Objectives

In this context, the objective of the Manifesto on Social Media for Social Innovation is to propose actions oriented to extract the best of the potential synergies among those two concepts. The Manifesto puts forward a frame of principles and intentions that, if widely shared, will help fighting the limitations of speed and scale that need to be overcome for social media to become an alternative to currently established institutional mechanisms.

In order to accomplish social media evolving towards a support as effective as possible for the growth of consolidation of social innovation worldwide, the technologically innovative communities and the socially innovative communities should establish a close and interdisciplinary collaboration towards the shared goal of more sustainable societies, emphasizing the social components and processes of social media-platforms.

4.3 Proposed Actions

The Manifesto proposes a set of actions, mainly focused on the research needs detected and described previously. The main task of the Manifesto is the promotion (within FP7, "Horizon 2020" and elsewhere) of research and discussions about policies and practices that would enable valuable social innovation initiatives to acquire speed and scale comparable to those of successful businesses and organizations, as well as the promotion of research and development of social media technological platforms which in their provisioning, interface design, functionalities and management are most suitable for the needs of social innovation. Based on these research initiatives and development, the objective is to launch prototype socio-technological architectures and platforms in order to test their functionality in large scale social experiments.

Furthermore, the Manifesto proposes to promote awareness and training programmes for social innovators and entrepreneurs to reinforce their management skills as well as their ability to effectively use social media to support their ventures.

Third, we suggest more research on the needs and resources of people using – and people not using – social media. If social media are supposed to become a discourse platform for political participation, education, e-inclusion or the world of labour, society has to give the chance of participation to all citizens. Social media – even though very simple – still are means of ICT that not all citizens can handle. But a society can not exclude parts of its citizens from a discourse platform. Therefore, the needs, resources and restrictions, especially from disadvantaged persons, have to be identified and mechanisms, support structures and technologies have to be developed to include these parts of society. It is our conviction that it is necessary to offer social support structures on top of ICT-tools to these target groups in order to avoid their exclusion (Kluzer and Rissola 2009; Kaletka et al. 2011).

The Manifesto envisions a future where social innovations evolve with enough speed and acquire enough scale to become alternatives to existing public and private organizations, locally as well as globally. In this context, we have limited the scope of the Manifesto to the European context and developed countries, at least in its initial state, but – considering its international support group, including representatives of non-European countries, and the global need for social innovations – it is planned to open the Manifesto to other partners, i.e. non-European and underdeveloped regions, and related issues, such as questions of e-inclusion and e-participation.

Annex: Social Media for Social Innovation: A Manifesto Draft

Because...

- There is an increasingly widespread agreement that the economic and social reference models that worked well during the last decades are not sustainable.
- The financial crisis demonstrates that many current socio-technical systems need to be redesigned and redeployed, not merely readjusted. A similar conclusion can be reached about other relevant societal issues.
- Social Innovation is proving to be a sensible alternative to some of the traditional government-led institutional frameworks for addressing social issues and concerns.
- Social Media provide socio-technical platforms that can be used to empower individuals and groups to pursue many valuable causes through Social Innovation.

We Envision a Future Where...

- Social innovations evolve with enough speed and acquire enough scale to become alternatives to existing public and private organizations, locally as well as globally.
- Social Media, in parallel to its current orientation towards leisure and consumption, evolves towards a support as effective as possible for the growth of consolidation of Social Innovation worldwide.
- The technology innovative communities and the social innovative communities collaborate towards the shared goal of more sustainable societies.

In Order to Accomplish this, We Will...

- Promote (within FP7 and FP8 and elsewhere) research and discussions about policies and practices that would enable valuable social innovation initiatives to acquire speed and scale comparable to those of successful businesses.
- Promote (within FP7 and FP8 and elsewhere) research and development of social media technological platforms which in their provisioning, interface design, functionalities and management are most suitable for the needs of social innovation.
- Promote awareness and training programs for social innovators and entrepreneurs to reinforce their management skills as well as their ability to effectively use social media to support their ventures.
- Use Social Media to nucleate a support group that will further develop these initiatives.
- Seek and obtain support for the above from socially responsible businesses as well as from socially responsible public administrations. Use Social Media widely in order to develop our cause and obtain increased support.

We Address this Manifesto to...

Researchers in Social Sciences and Internet technologies; People and organizations interested in the applications of Social Media for Social Innovation; Institutions potentially interested in supporting researchers and practitioners to further Social Innovation through Social Media.

Context

Most of the current hype around Social Media turns around its use for leisure and entertainment and the opportunities thereby generated for the marketing and advertisement industries, the 'attention industry'.

While those applications are and will be relevant indeed, they only touch the surface of the 'social' potential of Social Media. Communication mechanisms are one of the threads in the fabric of societies. The new communication and coordination possibilities afforded by Social Media could be used for a societal evolution going much beyond the economics of leisure and consumption.

In this context, the objective of this Manifesto on Social Media for Social Innovation is to propose actions oriented to extract the best of the potential synergies among those two concepts. The Manifesto puts forward a frame of principles and intentions that, if widely shared, would help fighting the limitations of speed and scale that need to be overcome for Social Media to become an alternative to currently established institutional mechanisms.

A first version of the Manifesto emerged from the workshop on Social Innovation and Social Media (SISoM) which took place during the 5th International Conference on Weblogs and Social Media (ICWSM-11) in Barcelona.

We intend to present a final version of the Manifesto on Social Media for Social Innovation at the event *Challenge Social Innovation – Innovating innovation by research – 100 years after Schumpeter* that will take place in September in Vienna. In the meanwhile, we'll seek further input and feedback from interested persons and parties.

Research Questions

An initial, tentative set of research questions to be explored would include the following:

RQ1. Which are the characteristics of the outstanding policy questions which would make them more amenable to be helped by social innovation?

RQ2. What is the current perception by policy makers of the potential of social innovation to address outstanding social and policy problems? Which are the social and policy challenges? Which are the technological challenges?

RQ3. Which are the conceptual stages of policy making and/or implementation in which social innovations could potentially have greater impact? (e.g. identification of problems and issues, policy design, modeling and simulation, implementation, management, ...)

RQ4. Which are the functional primitives of Social Media that would be potentially most relevant for fostering social innovations in the public policy domain? What would be the requirements? How can the performance of currently available platforms, tools and services be measured and compared to those requirements?

RQ5. How can the results of the research of Elinor Ostrom and others regarding the rules and conditions that allow bottom-up organizations to succeed be potentially translated to social scenarios in which social media technologies would be widely available?

RQ6. Which modeling strategies and tools would be best suited to model the potential impact of social media on policy design, evaluation and implementation? (e.g. increased user feedback, distributed coordination and management among others).

RQ7. What would be the functional and performance requirements of a Social Media Toolbox that would be useful for policy practitioners to best exploit the potential of social innovation?

Support Issues

At this stage, previous to its presentation in its final version at the Vienna Conference, we are not yet asking for any kind of commitment in support of the Manifesto.

Contributions and suggestions are of course most welcome. But they will not be taken as neither implicit nor explicit support.

Communication Issues

We will use and promote the Twitter hashtag #SISoM in order to communicate progress and updates on the Manifesto.

Who Are We

This first draft of the Manifesto is being promoted by a network of researchers and practitioners working at the intersection of social and technological development. It is known that many of the most relevant innovations happen at the boundaries between disciplines and knowledge domains. We believe that this is much needed in order to generate new solutions to pressing existing problems. We will join our expertise and resources to make it happen.

References

Abbate, J. (2000). *Inventing the internet*. Cambridge, MA: MIT Press.
Baker, S. (2009). A bull market in social entrepreneurs. *Business Week*, 10 June 2009.
BEPA. (2010). Empowering people, driving change: Social innovation in the European Union, Bureau of European Policy Advisors. Accessible online (Download: http://ec.europa.eu/bepa/pdf/publications_pdf/social_innovation.pdf. Aug 2011).
Berners-Lee, T. (1999). *Weaving the web*. New York: Harper Business.
Brynjolfsson, E. (1993). The productivity paradox of information technology. *Communications of the ACM, 36*(12), 66–77.
Castells, M. (1999). *The rise of the network society*. Oxford: Blackwell.
Castells, M. (2009). *Communication power*. Oxford: Oxford University Press.
Comscore. (2011). comScore Media Matrix Ranks Top 50 U.S. Web Properties for June 2011, press release. (Download: www.comscore.com. Aug 2011).
Ruiz de Querol, R., & Kappler, K. (2011). Challenges at the intersection of social media and social innovation, challenge social innovation, Vienna, September 19.
Dubini, P., & Aldrich, H. (2002). Personal and extended networks are central to the entrepreneurial process. In N. F. Krueger (Ed.), *Entrepreneurship: Critical perspectives on business and management* (pp. 217–228). London: Routledge.
European Commission. (2010a). The European eGovernment Action Plan 2011–2015, COM (2010) 743, December.
European Commission. (2010c). *A digital agenda for Europe*, Brussels.
Fuster, M. (2010). Governance of online creation communities: Provision of infrastructure for the building of digital commons. PhD thesis, European University Institute.

Globalwebindex. (2011). Annual Report 2011: Welcome to Social Entertainment. (Download: http://www.slideshare.net/Tomtrendstream/welcome-to-social-entertainment-annual-report-2011. August 2010).

Goldsmith, S. (2010). *The power of social innovation*. San Francisco: Jossey-Bass.

Howaldt, J., & Schwarz, M. (2010). Social innovation: Concepts, research fields and international trends. In K. Henning, & F. Hees. (Eds.), *Studies for innovation in a modern working environment – international monitoring* (Vol. 5). Aachen: Eigenverlag (Download from: http://www.sfs-dortmund.de/odb/Repository/Publication/Doc%5C1289%5CIMO_Trendstudie_Howaldt_Schwarz_englische_Version.pdf. Accessed 09 June 2011).

Hunt, T. (2009). Ethical banks cash in after trouble on the high street, The Guardian Green Living Blog, April 20 (Download: http://www.guardian.co.uk/environment/ethicallivingblog/2009/apr/17/ethical-money-ethical-living, August 2011).

Jenssen, J. I. (2001). Social networks, resources, and entrepreneurship. *The International Journal of Entrepreneurship and Innovation, 2*(2), 103–109.

Kaletka, C., & Pelka, B. (2010). Web 2.0 zwischen technischer und sozialer Innovation – Anschluss an die medientheoretische Debatte. In J. Howaldt & H. Jacobsen (Eds.), *Soziale Innovation. Auf dem Weg zu einem postindustriellen Innovationsparadigma* (pp. 143–161). Wiesbaden: VS Verlag.

Kaletka, C., Kopp, R., & Pelka, B. (2011). Social media revisited. User generated content as a social innovation. Proceedings of ICWSM 2011 – international AAAI conference on weblogs and social media, SISoM-11, pp. 17–19.

Kluzer, S., & Rissola, G. (2009). E-inclusion policies and initiatives in support of employability of migrants and ethnic minorities in Europe. *Information Technologies and International Development, 5*(2), 67–76.

Madelin, R. (2011). Platforms for Collective Awareness and Action, DG Information Society (Download: http://ec.europa.eu/information_society/activities/collectiveawareness/index_en.htm, August 2011).

McQuillan, D. (2011). Social Innovation Hacktivism, ICWSM 2011 – SISoM-11 Workshop (Download: http://www.slideshare.net/internetartizans/social-innovation-hacktivism, August 2011).

Morin, E. (2011). *La Voie: Pour l'avenir de l'humanité*. Paris: Fayard.

Nielsen. (2011) June 2010: Top Online Sites and Brands in the U.S., NielsenWire (Download: http://blog.nielsen.com/nielsenwire/online_mobile/. Date Aug 2011).

Ostrom, E. (2009). Beyond markets and states: Polycentric governance of complex economic systems, 2009 Nobel Prize address. (Download: http://www.nobelprize.org/nobel_prizes/economics/laureates/2009/ostrom-lecture.html. Aug 2011).

Pelka, B. (2010). Die Potenziale des Web 2.0 bei der Unterstützung von Lernprozessen. In Medien und Erziehung, Zeitschrift für Medienpädagogik, 54. Jahrgang, 4/2010/2010, pp. 58–62.

Phills, J. A., Deiglmeier, K., & Miller, D. T. (2008). Rediscovering Social Innovation. *Stanford Social Innovation Review, 6*(4), 34–43

Pirolli, P., Preece, J., & Shneiderman, M. B. (2010). Cyberinfrastructure for social action on national priorities. *IEEE Computer Magazine, 43*(11), 20–21

Polanyi, K. (2002). *The great transformation: The political and economic origins of our time*. Boston: Beacon Press.

SIX. (2010). Study on Social Innovation, Social Innovation eXchange (SIX) and the Young Foundation for the Bureau of European Policy Advisors at the European Commission. (Download: http://essesummerschool.files.wordpress.com/2011/06/six-study-on-social-innovation.pdf. August 2011).

Solow, R. (1987). We'd better watch out. *New York Times Book Review*, July 12, 36.

Sunstein, C. R. (2006). *Infotopia*. Oxford: Oxford University Press.

Sunstein, C. R. (2007). *Republic.com 2.0: Revenge of the blogs*. Princeton: Princeton University Press.

Thaler, R. H., & Sunstein, C. R. (2008). *Nudge: Improving decisions about health, wealth and happiness*. New York: Penguin.
The Economist. (2010). Let's hear those ideas, August 12 (Download: http://www.economist.com/node/16789766. August 2011).
Touraine, A. (2010). *Après la crise*. Paris: Seuil.
Tuomi, I. (2002). *Networks of innovation: Change and meaning in the age of internet*. Oxford: Oxford University Press.
Weber, S. (2004). *The Success of Open Source*. Cambridge: Harvard University Press.
White House. (2010). Blog of the White House Office of Social Innovation and Civic Participation. (Download: http://www.whitehouse.gov/administration/eop/sicp. Date Aug 2011).

Coordination and Motivation of Customer Contribution as Social Innovation: The Case of Crytek

Daniel Kahnert, Raphael Menez, and Birgit Blättel-Mink

Abstract While research on social innovation develops the idea of opening up innovation processes towards society, the economic concepts of "open innovation" and "user innovation" focus on the implications for companies, customers and users of such processes. In order to find out how companies coordinate open resp. user innovation, and why users actively support companies in innovating, a case study of a German company developing computer games (Crytek) has been carried out. Adopting the theoretical facets of user innovation to this case, among others game designers and community managers of Crytek have been surveyed as well as "modders", users who are deeply involved in generating new products. The following main results can be reported: (1) in terms of user motivation, intrinsic, social as well as extrinsic motives have a role. Extrinsic motives of the modders correlate clearly with the intentions of Crytek itself, in that it every now and then recruits its employees out of this group.

1 Introduction

Research on "social innovation" aims to overcome the techno-centric view on innovations predominant in the debates of most disciplines during the last decades. The techno-centric view on innovations overlooks the relevance of social action in innovation processes and therefore social innovations themselves (Howaldt and Jacobsen 2010; Howaldt and Schwarz 2010; Rammert 2010). Social innovations differ from technological innovations by focusing on social practices and social structures instead of technical artefacts. A social innovation is a reconfiguration of social practice in a certain field or context done by certain actors or constellation

---

D. Kahnert (✉) • R. Menez • B. Blättel-Mink
University of Frankfurt, Frankfurt, Germany
e-mail: kahnert@soz.uni-frankfurt.de

of actors with the goal of solving needs or problems in a better way than it was or could be done on the basis of known and established practices and structures (Howaldt and Schwarz 2010: 89).

Social innovations diffuse by gaining social acceptance in society or in some areas of society and being transformed into routines or social norms (Howaldt and Schwarz 2010: 89/90). Social as well as technical innovations can be preconditions or contributing factors for social change, without being the same thing: While social innovations are the outcome of intended actions, social change is either precondition, part or outcome of social innovations, which intend to lead social change strategically and to alternate social practice on micro-, meso- or macro level of society (Howaldt and Schwarz 2012: 55).

While research on the concept of social innovation is firmly linked to the idea of an opening up of innovation processes towards society and diffusion of innovative practices within society (Howaldt et al. 2011), the concepts of "open innovation"[1] (Chesbrough 2003; Chesbrough et al. 2006) and especially "user innovation"[2] (e.g. von Hippel 2005; Baldwin and von Hippel 2010) discuss exactly such social innovation processes and the implications for companies, customers and users. Realizing that the Schumpeterian idea of a single entrepreneur, innovating by recombining own resources and selling full products on a market is outdated; "open innovation" is regarded as a paradigm that allows to model the innovation process as open for many different actors to participate in networks of collaboration and creation aiming towards the development of new ideas and commercializing them: [...] *innovators rarely innovate alone. They tend to band together in teams and coalitions based on 'swift trust', nested in communities of practice and embedded in a dense network of interactions* (Laursen and Salter 2006: 132). "Open innovation" conceptualizes innovation processes as not ending at the borders of a firm or their R&D labs but implementing actors as innovators, idea generators or concept developers, regardless of their institutional background (Möslein and Neyer 2009: 86). "User innovation" concentrates on a specific type of actors as part of an open innovation process: the users and customers who also initiate innovation processes and the creation of ideas, concepts and solutions on their own or, in communities open collaborative innovation (Piller 2005). The openness of the innovation process in the "user innovation" concept refers to the open access to relevant information related to it (Baldwin and von Hippel 2010).

In the next part of this article we will provide some basic theoretical considerations for the understanding of the phenomenon of open innovation. Then we will present an empirical case study which illustrates how an open innovation process with users can be re-conceptualized as a social innovation.

---

[1] Current state of research e.g. in R&D Management (Volume 39, Issue 4 and Volume 40, Issue 3), International Journal of Technology Management (Volume 52, Issue 3/4) and Technovation (Volume 31, Issue 1).

[2] For a systematic overview on user innovation see Bogers et al. (2010).

2 Theoretical Frame

A new and innovative way of satisfying needs and solving problems is being established through processes of open innovation. As Piller and Ihl (2009) state, in order to stay profitable in a dramatically changing economy, companies have to be able to involve users and customers into the value creation process. Numerous studies have shown that innovations by users have had huge impact in several industries: semiconductors (von Hippel 1988), American high-tech industries (Danneels 2002), software sector (Urban and von Hippel 1988; Franke and von Hippel 2003) and consumer goods (Lüthje 2004; Tietz et al. 2005). It could be shown that user innovation is highly relevant and users tend to innovate on a large scale. While the fun and extreme sports sector was the first to provide solid data, showing that 10 % (Lüthje 2004); almost 20 % (Lüthje et al. 2005) or up to 40 % of the users innovate (Franke and Shah 2003), today huge representative studies support these findings (Von Hippel et al. 2010). This proves the empirical evidence of open innovation in modern societies and economics.

In open innovation concepts the distinction between need information and solution information plays a weighty role: In the closed innovation process it is the company having the solution information and the customers having the need information. Need information contains information about what needs, wishes and desires a user has towards the usage of a product. Solution information contains information about possibilities to satisfy the articulated needs. This includes information on the solution itself or the way to get to the solution. One of the main goals of a company is to obtain the need information of the customers, which is usually done by marketing research. Based on solution information and problem solving capabilities a company has to offer, an in-house innovation process brings up a product aimed to satisfy the identified needs of the customers. In open innovation processes need information, solution information and problem solving capabilities are brought together in a much more flexible way. The roles of the participants are not predefined as it is the case in closed innovation processes. It is assumed that users as well as firms can have solution information relevant to needs that occur. This defines a major change in the way customers or users are looked upon by companies. Being rather passive recipients of new products developed by companies in the old model, in the new model they can be large contributors to an innovation or even the only contributors to an innovation independent from any company (Baldwin and von Hippel 2010).

The classic dyadic relation between a company as innovator and producer and customers as consumers is no longer the only way these two parties interact. This is what we clearly identify as a social innovation: the contribution to innovation processes and value creation by users and customers, which is diffusing into many societal fields, and how companies conceive and conceptualize this as a strategic managerial approach of value creation. In an open innovation process with users resp. customers we identify two main trends that to a large extent contribute to what we consider a social innovation in terms of a new social practice to satisfy needs or solve problems, the *first* being user communities especially online-communities, the *second* being toolkits. We will present in what way these two trends are founding a new practice of collaboration between companies and customers.

2.1 Communities

In research on open innovation (Bogers et al. 2010; Piller and Ihl 2009; West and Bogers 2011) user communities (Franke and Shah 2003) are identified as a possible strategy for companies to integrate user contributions into the value creation of the firm. *[...] firms are organizing the process of customer innovation. Firms are building capabilities and infrastructures that allow customers to perform activities in their innovation process* (Piller and Ihl 2009: 17). Research on user communities shows that they are organized according to the basic principles of commons-based peer production (Benkler 2006; Reichwald and Piller 2009). This means that a large number of users collaborates in a shared and open value or knowledge creation process working on divided and self selected tasks. The tasks are modular in terms of being split into several different elements and they are granular in terms of being split into small pieces, which can easily be put together to a whole. Other relevant insights into collaboration and motivation of users in innovation processes and into forms of governance and meritocratic structures of communities are provided by Benkler (2006); Lerner and Tirole (2002); Lakhani and von Hippel (2003); von Krogh et al. (2003); Shah (2006); O'Mahony and Ferraro (2007).

The phenomenon of users offering instead of protecting their ideas and their know-how and sharing them not only with other users but also with manufacturers is also of great importance for research on open innovation with users and is covered by the concept of free revealing (Harhoff et al. 2003). The practice of free revealing has to be considered as substantial for user-based innovation.

Today exists a rather differentiated understanding of internet communities, how they function and what their role in the user-based innovation process can be. Communities are either understood as firm-independent (von Hippel 2007; Franke and Shah 2003), community-founded (West and O'Mahony 2005), firm-sponsored (West and O'Mahony 2008) or firm-hosted (Jeppesen and Frederiksen 2006; Wiertz and de Ruyter 2007). Firm-independent communities are able to protect their ideas from unwanted access by companies (O'Mahony 2003); as a consequence companies develop strategies to get their hands on those valuable sources of knowledge and ideas. Dahlander and Wallin (2006) have shown that companies employ staff to be active members and developers in e.g. open source software communities to interfere with or affect the way such a project develops. This firm-sponsoring method may lead to a situation where a company gains control over the community (West and O'Mahony 2008). From a company's perspective the question arises whether and under which conditions it is viable to open up the innovation process for communities. Boudreau and Lakhani (2009: 69) showed that *communities are useful when an innovation problem involves cumulative knowledge, continually building on past advances. Markets are effective when an innovation problem is best solved by broad experimentation. In general, communities are more oriented toward the intrinsic motivations of external innovators (the desire to be a part of some larger cause, for instance), whereas markets tend to reward extrinsic motivations (such as through financial compensation).*

Communities are an important factor for open innovation as social innovation, because they intentionally establish new ways for multiple actors to communicate and cooperate, to exchange knowledge, create ideas and solve problems.

2.2 Toolkits and Motivation

Toolkits for user innovation and design (von Hippel 2001; von Hippel and Katz 2002; Franke and von Hippel 2003) have been the subject of many studies, and today a good understanding of them is established. Toolkits are defined as ... *development environment which enables customers to transfer their needs iteratively to a concrete solution – often without coming into personal contact with the manufacturer. The manufacturer provides users with an interaction platform where they can produce a solution according to their needs using the toolkit's available solution space* (Piller and Ihl 2009: 25). Solutions space defines how much room there is at a specific aspect, level or stage of an innovation to be filled with input from the toolkit users. As the solution space that shall be offered by a toolkit can be flexibly scaled, they can be used for plenteous different innovation tasks to access the user's knowledge.

Studies have come over the fact that a significant shortening of the innovation and production process can be achieved with the use of toolkits (von Hippel and Katz 2002) and that they have benefits for the users as well: contentment of users rises by using toolkits because they can (a) implement their own personal preferences into customized products; (b) identify more with a product because of a feeling of *I made it myself* (Franke et al. 2010) and (c) have fun using toolkits (Franke and Schreier 2010). The innovation process can be shortened because the phase of testing and improving a product or prototype does not have to be organized in a form of iterating and exchange of most likely insufficient information between testers, developers and producers. Toolkits can provide exchange of more detailed information about needs and solutions by users in a standardized setting easy to implement in a new product development (NPD). By that, transaction costs of information transfer can be lowered for all sides and a better fit to market and fit to customer is more likely. Companies also benefit from the use of toolkits by raising the customers' willingness to pay for a product and strengthening their identification with a brand (Franke and von Hippel 2003; Franke and Piller 2004). As von Hippel and Katz (2002): 822 point out toolkits shift *need-related product development tasks to users*. Users benefit from that by getting a chance to create a design based on ideas of what they anticipate to satisfy their needs. Via toolkits they can also identify design flaws and even find solutions correcting them, if the toolkit prides a solution space big enough for such tasks. Users can create designs according to their own personal needs and transfer these designs to a producer in a way that does not cost them too much effort. Those designs can in fact be produced as well. That greatly raises the probability to get final, accessible product which satisfies users' needs much better than any standardized product, built without users' participation.

Toolkits establish an interface for users and customers to transfer detailed information to a company and vice versa. They establish a new way of collaboration between them. We therefore consider toolkits as a main factor for open innovation as social innovation.

The question why users contribute to innovation processes, what their motivations are, has been the subject of numerous studies. Six plausible types of motives have been identified (also look at Bogers et al. 2010):

1. *Sticky Information*[3] (von Hippel 1994)
2. *Benefits of using the innovation* (von Hippel 1988, 2005)
3. *Pro*fit by selling the innovation (Shah and Tripsas 2007; Haefliger et al. 2010)
4. *Enjoying problem solving* (Lüthje 2004; Antikainen et al. 2010)
5. *Career concerns* (Holmström 1999; Lerner and Tirole 2002)
6. *Reputation among peers and firm recognition* (Jeppesen and Frederiksen 2006)

After having presented the relevant theoretical preliminary considerations for the understanding of innovation practices with users and customers we will now present the findings of an empirical study from the computer games sector with *Crytek*.

3 Crytek: Open Innovation and Collaboration with Users of the Modding Community

The Crytek company, located in Frankfurt/Main (Germany), with about 600 employees in 2011 is one of the largest German developers of computer games and considered to be one of the innovation leaders worldwide. The web-based collaboration between Crytek and their customers and users differentiates three types of target markets, where each is approached and later integrated in a different way (see Fig. 1): The *casual gamers* constitute the largest group of 'normal' computer game players. They are the classic paying customers and are approached

---

[3] "We define the stickiness of a given unit of information in a given instance as the incremental expenditure required to transfer that unit of information to a specified locus in a form usable by a given information seeker. When this cost is low, information stickiness is low; when it is high, stickiness is high" (von Hippel 1994: 430).

Fig. 1 Crytek-related communities and toolkits

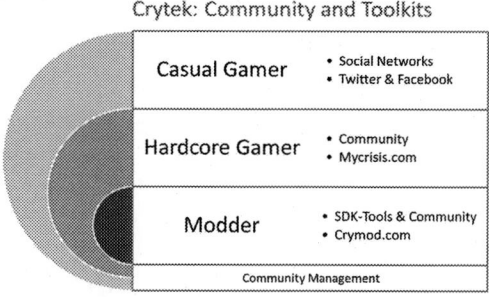

through conventional marketing strategies using editorials in pertinent magazines and/or the use of social networks such as Facebook and Twitter. *Hardcore gamers* have been involved in the company for many years, have formed a loyal fan community, know all the Crytek games inside out, because they play them multiple times, each time under different conditions (e.g. different levels, different equipment, single or multiplayer mode). The latter group of customers is particularly important for quality control as well as feedback and has their own separate community on the mycrisis.com platform. Finally, the *modders* are gamers who have the special status of distinguished experts with distinct qualifications that enable them to modify the games. They are able to modify the software in such a way that the flow of the game, the graphics or individual elements of the game are changed. Such modifications, called "mods", are then distributed to the gamers and made available at no cost over the web (Jeppesen 2004; Postigo 2007). Crytek offers this target group an exclusive platform on crymod.com. There, the modders can not only develop their mods and make them available to the community of gamers, the platform is also used to coordinate and facilitate the entire exchange among the modders themselves, between the modders and the company as well as between the entire international modding community. In addition, Crytek supplies special toolkits to the modders that allow them to modify individual games. Such Software Development Kits (SDK)[4] are essentially a light version of the tools that the developers employed at Crytek are using to program and design the games.

3.1 Customer Perspective

All of the 195 modders responding the online questionnaire are male. 61 % are between 15 and 19 years old[5], many are still attending school (47 %), 30 % have a

---

[4] A software development kit (SDK or "devkit") is typically a set of development tools that allows the creation of applications for a certain software package, software framework, hardware platform, computer system, video game console, operating system, or similar platform http://en.wikipedia.org/wiki/Software_Development_Kit.

[5] The youngest of the modders at crymod.com is now 12 years old but started modding 2 years ago. Because of his unusually young age and because of his special talent, he is already "well known" in the community.

Fig. 2 Motivation Index

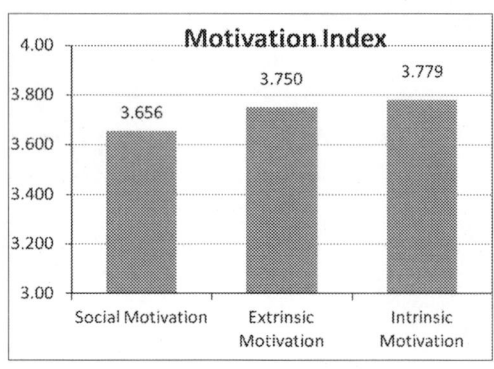

high school diploma. 77 % of the responding modders come from countries other than Germany. 42 % live in Europe, 24 % in North America. Concerning the question as to why modders agree to contribute voluntarily to the improvement, development or remodeling of the computer games and make the modifications available to the community free of charge, it has been observed that three types of motives played a major role. Figure 2 shows that intrinsic, extrinsic and social motivation are estimated almost equally on a rather high level.[6]

Items with highest agreement investigating social motives were: to receive help from others (87.4 %) and to help other modders (77 %); followed by the possibility to pursue interesting discussions (80 %). Top items investigating intrinsic motives were: Creativity (93 %) and creative design (91 %), the experience of achievement (90 %). In terms of extrinsic motives almost 70 % of the respondents agreed with the statement that they plan to apply their modding capabilities in their professional career. The respondents also want to use their modding experiences to increase their technical know how and abilities (90 %). In response to the question of which type of competencies are most enhanced by modding, the respondents primarily mentioned aspects of team-building. The items reaching the highest level of agreement were: learning to accept criticism (85 %), to be able to voice constructive criticism (81 %) and the ability to work in teams (81 %).

The results allow a surprising conclusion: The responding modders who perform their modding activity in their free time do so not only because modding is an end in itself. They do so with the intention to improve their social and technical competencies in order to apply the acquired skills in a professional context in the future.[7] For many modders, full-time employment at Crytek seems to be a very

---

[6] The motivation index was generated on the basis of 13 to 16 items, explored with a scale of five. Tests of reliability of the indices showed a high Cronbachs Alpha of 0.741 for intrinsic motives, 0.834 for extrinsic motives and 0.842 for social motives.

[7] Initial multivariate analyses point in this direction: An explorative factor analysis to structure the data identified six factors with a total explained variance of 70 %. The largest factors are loading on performance (leadership, teamwork, sense of responsibility and discipline) as well as on technical competence (editing, image processing and removal of bugs).

desirable option, as two respondents expressed[8]: *I am able to learn more on modding/programming, and may even get a future job at Crytek or other great developers.* and *I want to work for Crytek in the future. Learning their tools in and out seems like the best way to accomplish this.*

3.2 Company Perspective

Indeed, the five semi-structured interviews with selected experts at Crytek supported the fact that the career aspirations of the modders would not remain dreams but rather represent a quite realistic career path. Recruiting personnel from the community of modders is common practice at Crytek - presently, about 30–40 former members of the modding community hold positions at Crytek: *...that we frequently get people from the modding community has the simple reason that they do such a good job, they are so professional, that we say: 'They are good enough'. We should not waste such talent and therefore, we take them on. Meanwhile, we have about 30 or 40 people from the modding community, of course, accumulated after all those years, starting with Far Cry and so on and now they work at Crytek worldwide, in all our studios (Cry1).* The clear advantage for Crytek is the fact that the modders are already trained even though they have not worked in the company yet and have acquired their competencies and abilities independently through the community: *It's a natural byproduct of running a site such as Crymod.com. It benefits us and it benefits them, when we have guys sitting on our forum who have been using our product for 3–4 years. A lot of the times it is beneficial for us, it saves us time training people up on our engine. It is very beneficial for us to get these guys on board, as soon as possible. They really have a good idea of what our engine does, what Crytek is, what our games are. These guys really understand our community and our products inside and out (Cry2)* (see Fig. 3).

The idea of creating a modding portal at Crytek came up during the development of the first game, Far Cry. It was an idea born out of hardship, because game development took up all the resources and Crytek no longer had the capacity to make the most out of their game engine. Therefore, input from the crowd was appreciated. *But somehow, we had the feeling that we should be doing something in the direction of modding, because even at this early time, we had such a powerful engine and we knew we could bring out so much more with this. We don't have the time to do that, because we are working on Far Cry but we can give the tools and all that stuff to the community and see what they come up with...and then we realized: Wow; this is really unbelievable, the type of stuff that people are able to produce (Cry1).* As the expert interviews reveal, Crytek employees benefit particularly from all the suggestions and ideas the modding community provides. Direct copying or a one-to-one takeover of an artefact created by a modder, however, is not acceptable

---

[8] Open response to the question: "Why did you decide to join the Crymod community?".

Fig. 3 Collaboration between Crytek and the modders

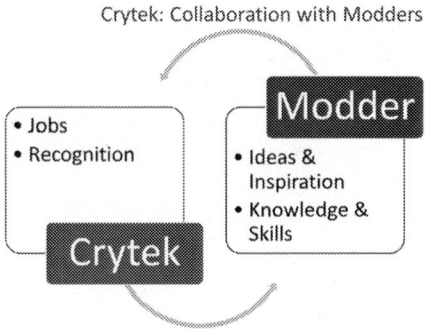

– instead the modder in question will be recruited and integrated into the team: *...but copying directly, no, something like that would never happen. If anything, we would hire the person. If someone were to create the mod of the century right now and it would be the best idea ever available in a game, I believe, this person would be here faster than he could [blink] (Cry3).*

In the interview the game designer explains the reasons why direct copying is not an option. It is related to his work ethic: *...one-to-one takeover is not possible because there is always the problem that one wants to achieve something. I would feel very uneasy, if I were to copy something from somebody else, well, because it would simply not be mine. For me, personally that would not work and I certainly know quite a few people who think the same way, because, you know, many want to show off, want to prove themselves and they want to be able to put their name on something* (Cry3).

Instead, there are many ways in which something can be developed together with the community: be it a patch or bug fix that is developed cooperatively, the exchange of ideas and further developments at community meetings or competitions and challenges that are issued by Crytek to solve particular problems or to implement certain ideas. *...for example, we developed a patch for Far Cry together with the community. That means we got the most talented artists from the community together and said 'Ok, this and that is our wish-list. Do you feel like working with us on this and then publishing the complete community patch?' And that was the first collaboration of Crytek and the community for such a general patch (Cry1).*

It was apparent during the interviews that the experts' identification with the community was quite high and that there was a sense of connectedness and mutual esteem on both sides: *And if you talk directly with the people, you can see immediately how strong the emotions are, how they are all hot for the whole thing and this is absolutely great for us, just watching, because without them this entire community would not work. Really, it is that simple...the fan-sites and so on are, all these people are so unbelievably important and that's why we try and invite then as often as possible and start such events (Cry1).* This connectedness is not only celebrated at certain events but is part of everyday life in the Crytek community. Every Crytek employee has a forum account and can communicate with the users and modders in the different communities. Some employees even switch roles, become free-time modders and join a modding team after work. One of these modding teams received the award for "Mod of the year 2009".[9] *"That was truly sensational! We had hoped for it, we had wished for it, but when it really happened it was awesome. ModDB is the No. 1 modding site for the whole of the modding scene and we had been nominated! I say "we" because this is our community and we feel part of it. ... Later on we recruited two of the modders. They simply were that good. So we said: "Join us and work for us"" (Cry1).* In order to keep the interaction between Crytek and the community working as fast and as smoothly as possible, Crytek engages community managers, who are often recruited directly from the community. Community managers see themselves as speakers for the community within the company and as a link between the company and the active web users.

The impact of the modding community for Crytek is based on the fact that this is where the true hard core of self-motivated and very competent users is located. This type of user has the status of a highly specialized expert and on a social level identifies strongly with the company. So much so that the company can eliminate certain common market risks when incorporating external knowledge or recruiting external experts by using the route over the community.

4 Conclusion

The case study has revealed a new species of customers: the modders, self-motivated and often sharing the work on modifications of computer games in highly complex team structures be it by providing changes to the game concept, the game design or the game construction. Modders combine several roles and generate artefacts of content in a hybrid process between production, distribution and consumption. Here, modders have the status of experts and for companies such as Crytek they can transmit information concerning their needs as well as the solution to those needs. Modders are particularly valued for their ability to develop new ideas or applications using the tools provided by Crytek in a new and creative way and thereby extending the solution space offered by the CryENGINE. The relationship between Crytek and the modders has been described as one of open innovation and collaboration with users. The company and the members of the community collaborate in developing modifications on existing products and innovations using the help of web 2.0 technology and SDK tools. This has an effect on the creation of value for the company, since the company receives information from the community about needs and problems as well as information concerning the solution to exactly those needs and problems. Therefore, the scope of possible solutions

---

[9] In 2009 both the "Editor's Choice" and the "Gamer's Choice" awards went to the Crysis-Mod "MechWarrior: Living Legends" (http://www.mechlivinglegends.net).

provided by the CryENGINE can continuously be extended. Users benefit from this collaboration by being enabled to transfer *their* needs and solutions to the company at low cost and thus actively take part in the development process of the game. An additional result concerns the recruitment of personnel. Modders active in the community are extrinsically motivated in regard to their professional aspirations and through modding, they acquire important skills, especially technical and social competencies. These competencies match the requirements of skills and abilities of the workforce at Crytek. Thus, Crytek not only benefits from the ideas of the modders, the company also follows the strategy to recruit talent from the community and integrates them into the team in order to profit from their expert knowledge and creativity.

Whether this process of open and user innovation as a social innovation will diffuse among the sector of online gaming and among other branches as well will have to be explored by further research.

References

Antikainen, M., Mäkipää, M., & Ahonen, M. (2010). Motivating and supporting collaboration in open innovation. *European Journal of Innovation Management, 13*(1), 100–119.
Baldwin, C., & von Hippel, E. (2010). Modeling a paradigm shift: From producer innovation to user and open collaborative innovation. MIT Sloan School Of Management Working Paper No. 4764-09. Cambridge: MIT.
Benkler, Y. (2006). *The wealth of networks: How social production transforms markets and freedom*. Yale: Yale University Press.
Bogers, M., Afuah, A., & Bastian, B. (2010). Users as innovators: A review, critique and future research directions. *Journal of Management, 36*(4), 857–875.
Boudreau, K. J., & Lakhani, K. R. (2009). How to manage outside innovation. *MIT Sloan Management Review, 50*(4), 69–76.
Chesbrough, H. (2003). *Open innovation: The new imperative for creating and profiting from technology*. New York: Harvard Business School Press.
Chesbrough, H., Vanhaverbeke, W., & West, J. (Eds.). (2006). *Open innovation: Researching a new paradigm*. Oxford: Oxford University Press.
Dahlander, L., & Wallin, M. W. (2006). A man on the inside: Unlocking communities as complementary assets. *Research Policy, 35*, 1243–1259.
Danneels, E. (2002). The dynamics of product innovation and firm competences. *Strategic Management Journal, 23*(12), 1095–1121.
Franke, N., & Piller, F. (2004). Value creation by toolkits for user innovation and design: The case of the watch market. *Journal of Product Innovation Management, 21*(6), 401–415.
Franke, N., & Schreier, M. (2010). Why customers value mass-customized products: The importance of process effort and enjoyment. *Journal of Product Innovation Management, 27*(7), 1020–1031.
Franke, N., Schreier, M., & Kaiser, U. (2010). The "I designed it myself" effect in mass customization. *Management Science, 56*(1), 125–140.
Franke, N., & Shah, S. K. (2003). How communities support innovative activities: an exploration of assistance and sharing among end-users. *Research Policy, 32*(1), 157–178.
Franke, N., & von Hippel, E. (2003). Satisfying heterogeneous user needs via innovation toolkits: The case of Apache security software. *Research Policy, 32*(7), 1199–1215.

Haefliger, S., Jäger, P., & von Krogh, G. (2010). Under the radar: Industry entry by user entrepreneurs. *Research Policy, 39*(9), 198–1213.

Harhoff, D., Henkel, J., & von Hippel, E. (2003). Profiting from voluntary information spillovers: How users benefit by freely revealing their innovations. *Research Policy, 32*(10), 1753–1769.

Holmström, B. (1999). Managerial incentive problems: a dynamic perspective. *Review of Economic Studies, 66*(1), 169–182.

Howaldt, J. (2010). Stand und Perspektiven der sozialwissenschaftlichen Innovationsforschung. In J. Howaldt & M. Schwarz (Eds.), *"Soziale Innovation" im Fokus. Skizze eines gesellschaftstheoretisch inspirierten Forschungskonzepts* (pp. 13–33). Bielefeld: Transcript Verlag.

Howaldt, J., Jacobsen, H. (Eds.). (2010). *Soziale Innovation. Auf dem Weg zu einem postindustriellen Innovationsparadigma*. Wiesbaden: VS Verlag.

Howaldt, J., Schwarz, M. (Eds.). (2010). *"Soziale Innovation" im Fokus. Skizze eines gesellschaftstheoretisch inspirierten Forschungskonzepts*. Bielefeld: Transcript Verlag.

Howaldt, J., Kopp, R., Beerheide, E. (Eds.) (2011). *Innovationsmanagement 2.0. Handlungsorientierte Einführung und praxisbasierte Impulse*. Wiesbaden: Gabler Verlag.

Jeppesen, L. B. (2004). Profiting from innovative user communities: How firms organize the production of user modifications in the computer games industry, IVS/CBS working papers 2004-03. Department of Industrial Economics and Strategy, Copenhagen Business School.

Jeppesen, L. B., & Frederiksen, L. (2006). Why do users contribute to firm-hosted user communities? *Organization Science, 17*(1), 45–63.

Lakhani, K. R., & von Hippel, E. (2003). How open source software works: "Free" user-to-user assistance. *Research Policy, 32*(6), 923–943.

Laursen, K., & Salter, A. J. (2006). Open for innovation: the role of openness in explaining innovation performance among UK manufacturing firms. *Strategic Management Journal, 27*(2), 131–150.

Lerner, J., & Tirole, J. (2002). Some simple economics of open source. *Journal of Industrial Economics, 50*(2), 197–234.

Lüthje, C. (2004). Characteristics of innovating users in a consumer goods field: An empirical study of sport-related product consumers. *Technovation, 24*(9), 683–695.

Lüthje, C., Herstatt, C., & von Hippel, E. (2005). User-innovators and "local" information: The case of mountain biking. *Research Policy, 34*(6), 951–965.

Möslein, K. M., & Neyer, A. (2009). Open Innovation. Grundlagen, Herausforderungen, Spannungsfelder. In A. Zerfaß & K. Möslein (Eds.), *Kommunikation als Erfolgsfaktor im Innovationsmanagement* (pp. 85–103). Gabler: Strategien im Zeitalter der Open Innovation, Wiesbaden.

O'Mahony, S. (2003). Guarding the commons: How community managed software projects protect their work. *Research Policy, 32*(7), 1179–1198.

O'Mahony, S., & Ferraro, F. (2007). The emergence of governance in an open source community. *Academy of Management Journal, 50*(5), 1079–1106.

Piller, F., & Ihl, C. (2009). Open innovation with customers – foundations, competences and international trends, http://www.internationalmonitoring.com/fileadmin/Downloads/Trendstudien/Piller-Ihl_Open_Innovation_with_Customers.pdf.

Piller, F. (2005). User Innovation: Der Kunde als Initiator und Beteiligter im Innovationsprozess. Working-Paper, www.downloads.mass-customization.de/pil2005-1.pdf.

Postigo, H. (2007). Of mods and modders. Chasing down the value of fan-based digital game modifications. *Games and Culture, 2*(4), 300–313.

Rammert, W. (2010). Die Innovationen der Gesellschaft. In J. Howaldt & H. Jacobsen (Eds.), *Soziale Innovation. Auf dem Weg zu einem postindustriellen Innovationsparadigma* (pp. 21–51). Wiesbaden: VS Verlag

Reichwald, R., & Piller, F. (2009). *Interaktive Wertschöpfung Open innovation, individualisierung und neue Formen der Arbeitsteilung*. Wiesbaden: Gabler.

Shah, S. K. (2006). Motivation, governance, and the viability of hybrid forms in open source software development. *Management Science, 52*(7), 1000–1014.

Shah, S. K., & Tripsas, M. (2007). The accidental entrepreneur: The emergent and collective process of user entrepreneurship. *Strategic Entrepreneurship Journal, 1*(1), 123–140.

Tietz, R., Morrison, P. D., Lüthje, C., & Herstatt, C. (2005). The process of user-innovation: A case study in a consumer goods setting. *International Journal of Product Development Management, 2*(4), 321–338.

Urban, G. L., & von Hippel, E. (1988). Lead user analyses for the development of new industrial products. *Management Science, 34*(5), 569–82.

von Hippel, E. (1988). *The sources of innovation*. New York: Oxford University Press.

von Hippel, E. (1994). Sticky information and the locus of problem solving: Implications for innovation. *Management Science, 40*(4), 429–439.

von Hippel, E. (2001). Perspective: User toolkits for innovation. *Journal of Product Innovation Management, 18*(4), 247–257.

von Hippel, E. (2005). *Democratizing innovation*. Cambridge: MIT Press.

von Hippel, E. (2007). Horizontal innovation networks: By and for users. *Industrial and Corporate Change, 16*(2), 293–315.

Von Hippel, E., de Jong, J. P. J., & Flowers, S. (2010). Comparing business and household sector innovation in consumer products: Findings from a representative study in the UK. http://papers.ssrn.com/sol3/papers.cfm?abstract_id=1683503.

von Hippel, E., & Katz, R. (2002). Shifting innovation to users via toolkits. *Management Science, 48*(7), 821–833.

von Krogh, G., Spaeth, S., & Lakhani, K. R. (2003). Community, joining, and specialization in open source software innovation: A case study. *Research Policy, 32*(7), 1217–1241.

West, J., & Bogers, M. (2011). Profiting from external innovation: A review of research on open innovation. Paper presented at the 9th international open and user innovation workshop in Vienna, 4–6 July 2011.

West, J., & O'Mahony, S. (2008). The role of participation architecture in growing sponsored open source communities. *Industry & Innovation, 15*(2), 145–168.

West, J., & O'Mahony, S. (2005). Contrasting community building in sponsored and community founded open source projects, faculty publications, Paper 2, http://scholarworks.sjsu.edu/org_mgmt_pub/2.

Wiertz, C., & de Ruyter, K. (2007). Beyond the call of duty: Why customers contribute to firm-hosted commercial online communities. *Organization Studies, 28*(3), 347–376.

Part VII
Measuring Social Innovation

Measuring Social Innovation and Monitoring Progress of EU Policies

Werner Wobbe

Abstract The current European Commission policies are guided by the "Europe 2020" strategy paper under which the "Innovation Union" forms one of the mayor policy flagship initiatives for the years to come. These policies are led by the Commissioner of Research and Innovation. The Innovation Union document understands innovation in a much broader sense than it was traditionally the case with seeing innovation as a technology-based process. This recent policy consensus includes social innovation as an integral part of the Innovation Union Flagship Initiative and the documents foresee a monitoring of innovation in order to control the progress made by innovative actions at European Union and at Member State level.

Measuring innovation and in particular social innovation is quite a new and challenging approach in methodological and practical terms. Therefore, the author reflects on the feasibility of measuring progress caused by social innovations and on pre-conditions to monitoring policy impact in relation to social innovations at international level.

Currently, innovation monitoring chiefly is applied with an economic focus although social data base developments have been funded by the European Commission research and development programmes over years. The paper presents selected EU research activities as well as the method and policy relevance of two innovation monitoring approaches targeting the economic dimension in the EU: the Innovation Union Scoreboard (IUS) and the Community Innovation Survey (CIS). The approaches shed some light on how monitoring instruments of social innovation may be developed.

European Commission, Directorate General Research and Innovation. The views expressed are purely those of the writer and may not in any circumstances be regarded as stating an official position of the European Commission.

W. Wobbe (✉)
European Commission, Brussels, Belgium
e-mail: werner.wobbe@ec.europa.eu

The paper concludes that a high obstacle to monitoring social innovation is its proliferation of targets in various policy fields. Therefore, the notion of social innovations may be blurred too much in the current policy debate in order to be instrumental for measurement. Consensus needs to be reached on the point of view if either targets of specific policies (innovation, security, health, social, environment, transport, etc.) shall be monitored to which social innovation is instrumental, or if social innovation is a subject in its own to be monitored.

1 Social Innovation Could Address a Range of Policy Targets

The concept of social innovation has recently been recognised by the Barroso II Commission (2010–2014) expressed by its lead policy document "Europe 2020" (European Commission 2010a). Social innovation is seen as an instrument to help reaching headline targets of smart, sustainable, and inclusive growth by fostering innovation as a cornerstone of the European research funding policies. The Innovation Union Initiative (European Commission 2010b) – one of the seven flagship initiatives – recognises a broad concept of innovation, including social and societal dimensions like business models, design, marketing, services, public sector involvement, and stakeholder relationships. In this view, it abandons the innovation notion restricted to science and technology. Contrary to this, it gives a notion to social innovation that applies to a range of sectors in economy and society. However, the broad understanding of social innovation creates obstacles of conceptualising the approach and tailoring the analytical tools to better target dimensions of monitoring.

In addition, social innovation should be instrumental to support the European Union headline targets which are:

- 75 % employment rate (% of 20–64 year population)
- 3 % investment in R&D (% of EU GDP); new innovation indicator to be developed
- 20 % reduction in greenhouse gas emissions (30 % conditional offer); 20 % share of renewable in final energy consumption; move towards 20 % increase in energy efficiency
- School drop-out reduction rates to less than 10 %; at least 40 % of 30–34-year-olds to complete tertiary education or equivalent
- Lift at least 20 million people out of the risk of poverty and exclusion

The headline targets address a broad range of policies like employment, science and technology, environment, energy, education, social policies, etc. Social innovation would be an instrument achieving the headline targets. While headline targets might be monitored easily, the monitoring of social innovation in relation to the headline targets is complicated and requires a bulk of reflection and research.

Given the case we restrict social innovation in support to the objectives of the Innovation Union Flagship Initiative and we mainly look at competitiveness-relevant indicators and policies, e.g. structural change, adaptation of industry to climate change, skills, business environment and SME policy – to aiming at the "social" improvement of economic framework conditions – even these innovations with limited targets pose fundamental methodological and practical challenges. Questions that emerge are:

- In how far is measuring feasible as a base for the monitoring of innovation of international developments?
- Are indicators the right approach: how complex and multidimensional should they become or should a single indicator be the way forward?
- How comprehensive are current approaches and is improvement required?

In order to enlarge the range of questions to monitoring of social innovation questions may emerge like the following ones:

- What are the differences in monitoring social innovation in contrast to economic monitoring?
- Is the concept and focus of social innovation clearly enough spelled out in order to specify indicators?

This paper will take into account the latest review on assessment activities of social innovations carried out for the Social Innovation Europe Initiative (SIE) on a draft road-map proposal for an effective assessment of social innovation. As social innovations are linked to a broad range of policies the paper will restrict itself and focus on socio-economic aspects of research and innovation policies. It will review business-oriented innovation monitoring instruments which are most developed. The focus shall serve to conclude on the conditions under which a social innovation monitoring could be established. It therefore would contribute to advance the scientific conceptualisation of social innovation and to stimulate research on innovation.

After having reviewed current assessment approaches of social innovation the paper selects two socio-economic innovation monitoring approaches that illuminate the problematic of innovation monitoring. From that basis it tries to shed light on the problematic of a social innovation monitoring which is broader in scope. The approaches selected are the

- Community Innovation Survey (CIS) and the
- Innovation Union Scoreboard (IUS)

The CIS is a survey-based approach contrary to the IUS which is based on indicators. These approaches are the two major methodologies in the European Union to monitor socio-economic dimensions of innovations.

2 Assessment Activities of Social Innovation in Europe

In March 2011 a "Social Innovation Europe Initiative (SIE)" was launched by the European Commission (European Commission 2011a) in Brussels. In this context a consortium led by "Social Innovation eXchange (SIX)" prepared an overview and review on assessment approaches. This overview includes a roadmap to improve the metrics and assessments needed for policy-making as well as for performance management of social innovation (Caulier-Grice et al. 2010; Leighton and Wood 2010; Murray et al. 2011; Reeder and O'Sullivan 2011).

The SIX study differentiates between the metrics for policy-making and the metrics for performance management of social innovations.

The *policy-making metrics* should support decisions. For that purpose assessments of the policy project progress, the ability to make progress by social innovation projects to be funded, as well as the assessment of impact, outcomes and efficiency of social innovations is required. Metrics which are related to that kind of assessment have been developed in the OECD Oslo Manual (OECD/Statistical Office 2005) or have been applied by the Innovation Union Scoreboard – IUS (European Commission 2010c), the EU eco-innovation scoreboard (European commission 2011b), Measuring public innovation in the Nordic countries – MEPIN (Bloch 2011), and the National Endowment for Science Technology and the Arts – NESTA (NESTA 2007).

Metrics for the performance management shall aim at inputs, outputs and outcomes according to the study. "An organization uses the inputs (staff, buildings, equipment and so on) to produce a set of outputs (products and services), which then influence the results for individuals and society (for example, a less polluted environment, or a deeper set of skills and knowledge). For example, in health, inputs include doctors, nurses and scanning equipment; these produce outputs such as diagnoses, medical treatments and operations; and these in turn affect the outcomes of longer life expectancy and quality of life. A key challenge is to measure the outputs and the change in outcomes associated with a given social innovation on a consistent and understandable basis." (Reeder and O'Sullivan 2011: 18f) Methodological approaches to value or to measure social innovations could be detected by the Bell-Mason stage-gate approach (Bell Mason Group 2012), the EFQM Excellence Model of the European Foundation for Quality management (EFQM 2012), the Bilan Sociétal and the CJDES – social reporting and impact assessment tool (CJDES 2012) and the ESF Community of Practice on Result Based Management (ESF 2009).

All of the approaches mentioned try to value or measure mainly inputs and outputs and to a lesser extent they measure outcomes of different kinds of social innovation. The mentioned approaches all intend to monitor performance. Each metrics is particularly adapted to the specific case. In this sense each of the mentioned study may give inspiration to approach a new case to be assessed. However, the approaches are distant from offering a general formula.

The SIX study concludes on a lack of robust and comparable metrics and assumes that this fact poses a significant barrier to developing the field of social innovation because practitioners, policy makers, investors, funders and other stakeholders require effective approaches to evaluate the outcomes of social innovations. Only if metrics would reveal the scale of improvement to outcomes of social innovations and if metrics could provide clarity on performance of activities the support for social innovations would grow and social innovation would be more viable. Developing metrics for social innovation would be an essential way to draw attention to effective methods and models within the field of social innovation. Unfortunately indices and metrics for innovation in the social field were underdeveloped compared to metrics for measuring innovation in other fields (Reeder and O'Sullivan 2011: 34). Therefore, development work on concepts and methods like benchmarking, metrics, and indicators is required as well as data collection, its analysis, and its assessment. By this development work, monitoring in support of learning, best practice exchange and fostering the dissemination of successful cases of social innovations would benefit the overall approach.

The SIE initiative therefore suggests a road map (Reeder and O'Sullivan 2011: 34–36) starting in 2011 and targeting the year 2021 in three stages. The activities should select the public sector. Stage one should immediately improve and enlarge the Community Innovation Survey in order to get data on social innovation performance for social enterprises and non-profit bodies within sectors of welfare to work, education and health. The next stage would aim at developing a database of methods and tools in order to monitor and assess social innovation in the public and private sectors and in the civil society in the next Framework Programme for Research and Innovation "Horizon 2020". Different funding areas for ideas, prototypes and pilots, for the implementation and dissemination of social innovation activities and projects should be established. Eventually, in the last stage the metric approach and learning activities are to be established for a wider dissemination.

3 European Research Projects and Social Data Base Development

Innovation and social innovation is a research subject that has a long tradition in research funding of the European Union and the European Commission in its Research Framework Programmes. The current one, FP7, by the "Socio-economic Sciences and Humanities (SSH)" programme supports more than 30 research initiatives in the field of innovation and the knowledge and service economy. It has supported basic material for the development of social innovation monitoring like social databases, labour markets and indicators like the European Social Survey, data on work and welfare, on education policies, lifelong learning, kinship and social security, young people, living conditions, occupations and health. And it also deals with intergenerational care regimes, demographic, crime, organisational changes, migration and integration statistics, as well as gender issues.

A selection of projects is displayed in Box 1 (European Commission 2010d).

After having presented an overview on current assessment approaches of social innovation the paper now selects two socio-economic innovation monitoring approaches that shed more light in greater detail to the problematic of innovation monitoring before concluding on conditions for social innovation monitoring.

Box 1: Projects in the Field of Innovation and Knowledge Economy (Project Acronym/Title of the Project)

AEGIS Advancing knowledge-intensive entrepreneurship and innovation for growth and social well-being in Europe

COINVEST Competitiveness, innovation and intangible investment in Europe

DEMETER Development of methods and tools for evaluation of research

EERQI European educational research quality indicators

FINESS Financial systems, efficiency and stimulation of sustainable growth

FINNOV Finance, innovation and growth: changing patterns and policy implications

FRIDA Fostering innovation and development through anchors and networks

GLOBINN The changing nature of internationalization of innovation in Europe: impact on firms and the implications for innovation policy in the EU

GRASP Growth and sustainability policies for Europe

IAREG Intangible assets and regional economic growth

INDICSER Indicators for evaluating international performance in service sectors

INGINEUS Impact of networks, globalisation, and their interaction with EU strategies

INNODRIVE Intangible capital and innovations: drivers of growth and location in the EU

INNOS&T Innovative S&T indicators combining patent data and surveys: empirical models and policy analyses

SCIFI-GLOW Science, innovation, firms and markets in a globalized world

SELUSI Social entrepreneurs as "lead users" for service innovation

SERVICEGAP The impact of service sector innovation and internationalisation on growth and productivity

SERVPPIN The contribution of public and private services to European growth and welfare, and the role of public-private innovation networks

VICO Financing entrepreneurial ventures in Europe: impact on innovation, employment growth, and competitiveness

WALQING Work and life quality in new and growing jobs

WIOD World input–output database: construction and applications

WORKABLE Making capabilities work

4 Community Innovation Statistics and Community Innovation Survey (CIS)

EUROSTAT monitors progress of enterprise innovation activity in Europe since more than a decade editing the Community Innovation Statistics which is based on an enterprise survey. Data are collected on a 4-yearly basis. The first pilot of the survey was carried out in 1993 and CIS 2008 was the latest survey published before in 2012 a new one will be issued.

The Community Innovation Statistics are collected by the European Statistical Office and represent a central data source for measuring innovation in Europe. According to EUROSTAT, the data give basic information of the enterprise, product and process innovation, innovation activity and expenditure, effects of innovation, innovation co-operation, public finding of innovation, source of information for innovation, and patents. The Community Innovation Statistics are produced in all Member States of the European Union, EU candidate countries and the three remaining EFTA countries.

CIS has broadened its innovation definition over the years by including organisational issues. The definition is as follows: *Innovation activities include the acquisition of machinery, equipment, software and licences; engineering and development work, training, marketing and R&D when they are specifically undertaken in order to develop and/or implement a product or process innovation.*

Although the latest 2008 questionnaire was improved to meet the third revision (2005) of the Oslo Manual, the question on innovation expenditures is still limited to product and process innovation in order to maintain continuity with earlier versions. The improvement was achieved by giving greater weight to organisational and marketing innovation. However, fewer questions are asked of organisational and marketing innovation than for product and process innovation.

CIS provides by its construction a broad overview on enterprise-related innovations and how these enterprises are distributed in Europe as the following Fig. 1 shows.

5 The Innovation Union Scoreboard (IUS)

The Innovation Union Scoreboard aims at country comparisons and the innovative capability of a whole country instead of seeing a country as a collection of enterprises and its individual innovation capability. The overall ambition of the Innovation Union Scoreboard is to inform policy discussions at national and EU level, by tracking progress in innovation performance within and outside the EU over time. The IUS is based on the previous European Innovation Scoreboard

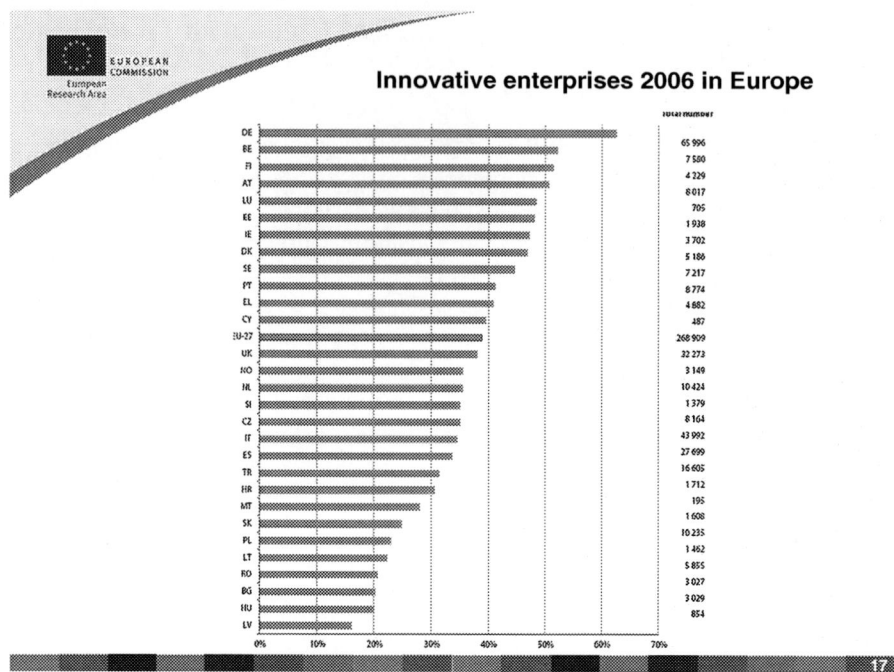

Fig. 1 Innovative enterprises 2006 in Europe

(EIS).[1] The modifications are targeted to monitor better the implementation of the Europe 2020 Innovation Union flagship. They allow assessing the relative strengths and weaknesses of the EU27 Member State research and innovation systems.

As Fig. 2 shows, the methodology of the IUS identifies the performance of different classes of innovative capabilities of countries. The Innovation Union Scoreboard IUS as already its predecessor EIS identifies four performance groupings which are "innovation leaders", "innovation followers", "moderate innovators" and "modest innovators". The performance of the different grouping is striking: innovation leader performance is 20 % or more above that of the EU27 while modest innovators are below 50 % of that of the EU27. Detailed analysis of the performance in innovative activities in different dimensions allows insight into weaknesses and strengths of whole countries or country groupings and allows targeting and improving innovative activities.

---

[1] Nineteen of the previous 29 indicators have been carried over from last year's edition, of which 12 indicators have not been changed, 2 indicators have been merged, and 5 indicators have been partly changed by using broader or narrower definitions or different denominators. The IUS 2010 includes innovation indicators and trend analyses for the EU27 Member States, as well as for Croatia, Iceland, the Former Yugoslav Republic of Macedonia, Norway, Serbia, Switzerland and Turkey. It also includes comparisons based on a more reduced set of indicators between the EU27, the US, Japan and the BRIC (Brazil, Russia, India and China) countries.

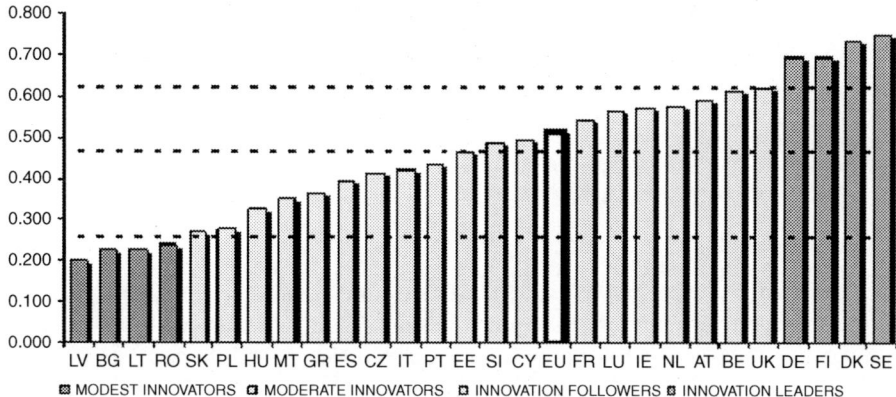

Fig. 2 EU Member States' innovation performance. Average performance is measured using a composite indicator building on data for 24 indicators going from a lowest possible performance of 0 to a maximum possible performance of 1. Average performance in 2010 reflects performance in 2008/2009 due to a lag in data availability.

The scoreboard is released annually. From 2007 on, four consecutive editions have been published. In this relatively short time span, it appears to emerge a steady convergence, where less innovative Member States have been growing faster than the more innovative Member States on average. This convergence process however seems to be slowing down. While the moderate and modest innovators clearly catch up to the higher performance level of both the innovation leaders and innovation followers, there is no convergence between the different Member States within these two lower performance groups. Convergence between the Member States does take place within the innovation leaders grouping and in particular within those of the innovation followers. However, the impact of the financial crisis and of how the different actors like enterprises or public authorities in Member States cope with the crisis has to be seen in the longer run. In any case, the instrument allows concluding on the behaviour of different actors.

The indicators used by the Innovation Union Scoreboard are taken from statistics of Eurostat and other internationally recognised sources as available at the time of analysis. International sources have been used wherever possible in order to improve comparability between countries (Hollanders and Tarantola 2010).

The IUS is differentiated into 25 indicators grouped into eight innovation dimensions and three main classes of indicators. The high levels of aggregation – the eight innovation dimensions – already allow a differentiated picture and analysis of country group comparison.

Enablers

1. Humans resources
2. Attractive research system
3. Finance and support

Firm activities

4. Firm investment
5. Linkages and entrepreneurship
6. Intellectual assets

Outputs

7. Innovators
8. Economic output

The Enablers capture the main drivers of innovation performance external to the firm and differentiate between three innovation dimensions. The "human resources" dimension includes three indicators and measures the availability of a high-skilled and educated workforce. The new "open, excellent and attractive research systems" dimension includes three indicators and measures the international competitiveness of the science base. The "finance and support" dimension includes two indicators and measures the availability of finance for innovation projects and the support of governments for research and innovation activities.

Firm activities capture the innovation efforts at the level of the firm and differentiate between three innovation dimensions. The "firm investments" dimension includes two indicators of both R&D and non-R&D investments that firms make in order to generate innovations. The "linkages and entrepreneurship" dimension includes three indicators and measures entrepreneurial efforts and collaboration efforts among innovating firms and also with the public sector. The "intellectual assets" dimension captures different forms of Intellectual Property Rights generated as a throughput in the innovation process.

Outputs indicate the effects of firms' innovation activities and differentiate between two innovation dimensions. The "innovators" dimension includes three indicators and measures the number of firms that have introduced innovations onto the market or within their organisations, covering both technological and non-technological innovations and the presence of high-growth firms. The indicator on innovative high-growth firms anticipates the new EU2020 headline indicator, which will be identified by the end of 2012. The Economic effects dimension includes five indicators and captures the economic success of innovation in employment, exports and sales due to innovation activities (Fig. 3).

The spider web presentation on innovation performance shows at a glance how advanced the four groups of countries are in the eight dimensions of innovation. In particular it indicates the differences between innovation leaders and modest innovators by dimension. While human resources are a relatively strong asset for modest innovators, linkages and entrepreneurship are particularly weak features.

In order to give a fully-fledged overview how the innovation dimensions are broken down into indicators they are spelled out in detail. The 25 innovation indicators grouped in three levels of analysis are listed in Box 2.

The exhaustive list as well as its hierarchical grouping may inspire researchers to reflect on how a monitoring of social innovation may be constructed. However, a hierarchical grouping in main types, dimensions and eventually indicators requires

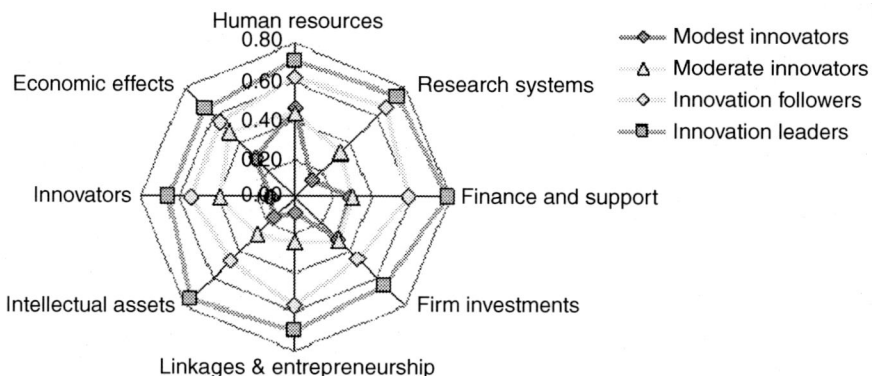

Fig. 3 Country groups: innovation performance per dimension

a concept that allows an orientation for types, dimensions and indicators to be developed for a social innovation monitoring. As the discussion of the conference demonstrates, a consensus has not emerged yet. Therefore, intellectual work on the construction of a monitoring instrument and its methodology might be invited to be taken up.

Box 2: Innovation Indicators
1. Enablers

   1.1. Human resources

   1.1.1. New doctorate graduates (ISCED 6) per 1,000 population aged 25–34
   1.1.2. Percentage population aged 30–34 having completed tertiary education
   1.1.3. Percentage youth aged 20–24 having attained at least upper secondary level education

   1.2. Open, excellent and attractive research systems

   1.2.1. International scientific co-publications per million population
   1.2.2. Scientific publications among the top 10 % most cited publications worldwide as % of total scientific publications of the country
   1.2.3. Non-EU doctorate students as a % of all doctorate students

   1.3. Finance and support

   1.3.1. Public R&D expenditures as % of GDP
   1.3.2. Venture capital (early stage, expansion and replacement) as % of GDP

   (continued)

2. Firm activities

   2.1. Firm investments

      2.1.1. Business R&D expenditures as % of GDP
      2.1.2. Non-R&D innovation expenditures as % of turnover

   2.2. Linkages and entrepreneurship

      2.2.1. SMEs innovating in-house as % of SMEs
      2.2.2. Innovative SMEs collaborating with others as % of SMEs
      2.2.3. Public-private co-publications per million population

   2.3. Intellectual assets

      2.3.1. PCT patents applications per billion GDP (in PPS€)
      2.3.2. PCT patent applications in societal challenges per billion GDP (in PPS€) (climate change mitigation; health)
      2.3.3. Community trademarks per billion GDP (in PPS€)
      2.3.4. Community designs per billion GDP (in PPS€)

3. Outputs

   3.1. Innovators

      3.1.1. SMEs introducing product or process innovations as % of SMEs
      3.1.2. SMEs introducing marketing or organisational innovations as % of SMEs
      3.1.3. High-growth innovative firms

   3.2. Economic

      3.2.1. Employment in knowledge-intensive activities (manufacturing and services) as % of total employment
      3.2.2. Medium and high-tech product exports as % total product exports
      3.2.3. Knowledge-intensive services exports as % total service exports
      3.2.4. Sales of new to market and new to firm innovations as % of turnover
      3.2.5. License and patent revenues from abroad as % of GDP

6 Conclusion

The Europe 2020 Innovation Union Flagship Initiative document commits the Commission Services to monitor innovation processes and to develop a new innovation headline indicator that focuses on output and impact as well as on ensuring international comparability. In this context, the current Commission monitoring activities are based on indicators of economic dimensions. The new innovation headline indicator probably will be based on the share of fast-growing, innovative companies in the economy which would allow to benchmark against main trading partners.

We may conclude that the current innovation monitoring focuses on productive forces in the Member States and on economic dimensions either by enterprise surveys or by socio-economic indicators. A monitoring of social innovations may target social dimensions inside and outside social policies. The challenge would be reaching other policies than social policies mentioned in the Europe 2020 headline targets. For example, social innovations also touch economic dimensions like those in the economic non-market economies or those activities governed by the public sector related to employment and learning or those the civil society contributes by economic added value to the society. These economic dimensions in social innovation would be worthwhile to be explored in greater detail.

An exploratory document on social innovation established by the Commission Services – BEPA (Hubert 2010) revealed the systemic and multi-faceted character of social innovation for policy. Also, social innovation and economic growth are intertwined. For analytical and operational monitoring reasons they should be discerned. The conference "Challenge Social Innovation" made no systematic assessment of the multi-faceted character of social innovation. Therefore, further discussion and research would be required in order to advance a concept on monitoring of social innovation.

The SIE study detected a lack of robust and comparable metrics as a barrier in developing the field of social innovation because metrics would reveal the scale of improvement to outcomes of social innovations and metrics could provide clarity on performance of activities. The idea of developing metrics for social innovation has to be supported, as it would draw attention to effective methods and models to be applied within the field of social innovation. Indices and metrics for innovation in the social field are underdeveloped compared to metrics for measuring innovation in the economic area. Therefore, development work on concepts, methods, metrics, and indicators is required to support the dissemination of successful social innovations.

In this respect, dimensions of social innovations need to be discerned in order to advance a concept of monitoring the effects of social innovations in sectors of human activities. For example, a relatively simple indicator for good living would be a "happiness indicator" carried out by interview surveys – or even online interviews – insofar answers of questionnaires could be compared internationally and avoid cultural biases. Contrary to this, a hard indicator for an active and self-determined society would be the extent of voluntary work for example.

Recently, an interesting approach has been established by the OECD's "Better life index" (OECD 2012). It uses online voting establishing international comparative rankings of the composite of what is called better life and which is clearly associated with the social dimension. Satisfaction and individual online judgement on dimensions of housing, income, jobs, work-life balance, community, education, environment, governance, health, life satisfaction, and safety discern as well as establish the composite of the social construct "better life".

The comparison of the two economic innovation monitoring approaches (CIS and IUS) in view of reflecting on the feasibility of monitoring and establishing social innovation indicators hints to the fact that obstacles will be met due to a lack of basic definitions of the multi-faceted dimensions in social innovation.

Research and innovation policies will be geared to the so-called Grand Societal Challenges to come in the next years. Social innovation should find a place in this context. The notion of Grand Societal Challenges embodies research and innovation in the fields of health, demographic changes, well-being, food security, sustainable agriculture and bio-economy, secure, clean and efficient energy, smart green and integrated transport, environment, climate action and resource efficiency, and inclusive, innovative and secure European societies by which social policies are concerned. If social innovation would find a place in that context, for each of the different policies missions and objectives have to be defined as well as which forms of social innovations would contribute in order to elaborate metrics and indicators for monitoring the objectives. For all of the Grand Societal Challenges probably lead indicators could be developed and a reflection may be launched on how indicators for specific forms of social innovation could be developed.

The conference has revealed that social innovation is associated with a bundle of policy dimensions and that social innovation could be instrumental to progress on various policy targets. Leaving aside the instrumental character of social innovation for policies social innovations may deserve to be monitored in its own rights as an achievement for a better life.

7 Online International Innovation Monitoring Data Sources

From a point of view of research and innovation monitoring, online services of the European Commission constitute a solid framework on socio-economic monitoring instruments. These are the "Innovation Scoreboard" established by ProInno and the "Community Innovation Survey" established by EUROSTAT as well as the "EU Industrial R&D Investment Scoreboard". The EC research department offers an additional analytic source: The "Innovation Union Competitiveness Report" which is issued bi-annually and which had a predecessor, the "Science, Technology and Competitiveness Key Figures". Although none of these monitoring instruments is focussed on social innovation they may indicate the direction into which a social innovation monitoring may be developed.

- **European Innovation Scoreboard 2010**
  http://www.proinno-europe.eu/inno-metrics/page/innovation-union-scoreboard-2010
- **EUROSTAT: Community Innovation Survey – CIS**
  http://epp.eurostat.ec.europa.eu/cache/ITY_SDDS/en/inn_esms.htm
  Science, Technology and Competitiveness Key Figures
  http://ec.europa.eu/research/era/pdf/key-figures-report2008-2009_en.pdf

- **DG RTD Innovation Union Competitiveness Report**
  http://ec.europa.eu/research/innovation-union/index_en.cfm?section=competitiveness-report&year=2011
- **EU Industrial R&D Investment Scoreboard**
  http://iri.jrc.ec.europa.eu/research/scoreboard_2010.htm
- **OECD Better life index**
  http://www.oecdbetterlifeindex.org/

References

Bell Mason Group. (2012). The Bell Mason Framework. http://www.bellmasongroup.com/framework/.

Bloch, C. (2011). Measuring public innovation in the Nordic countries (MEPIN). http://nordicinnovation.org/Global/_Publications/Reports/2011/201102_MEPIN_report_web.pdf.

Caulier-Grice, J., Kahn, L., Mulgan, G., Pulford, L., Vasconcelos, D. (2010). Study on social innovation. A paper presented for the Bureau of European Policy Advisors.

CJDES – Centre des jeunes, des dirigeantes, des acteurs, de l'economie sociale 2012, Bilan Social. http://www.cjdes.org/1093-BILAN_SOCIETAL.

EFQM – European forum for quality management. (2012). The EFQM excellence model. http://www.efqm.org/en/tabid/132/default.aspx.

ESF – Agentschap Vlaanderen vzw. (2009). RBM self-assessment tool. http://www.coprbm.eu/?q=node/428.

European Commission. (2010a). EUROPE 2020. A strategy for smart, sustainable and inclusive growth. COM(2010) 2020 final. http://eur-lex.europa.eu/LexUriServ/LexUriServ.do?uri=COM:2010:2020:FIN:EN:PDF.

European Commission. (2010b). Europe 2020 Flagship initiative: Innovation union, SEC(2010) 1161. http://ec.europa.eu/research/innovation-union/pdf/innovation-union-communication_en.pdf#view=fit&pagemode=none.

European Commission. (2010c). Innovation union scoreboard (IUS) 2010. The innovation union's performance scoreboard for research and innovation. http://ec.europa.eu/enterprise/policies/innovation/files/ius/ius-2010_en.pdf.

European Commission. (2010d). Innovation: Creating knowledge and jobs. Insights from European research in socio-economic sciences. ftp://ftp.cordis.europa.eu/pub/fp7/ssh/docs/creating-knowledge-jobs_en.pdf.

European Commission. (2011a). DG enterprise and industry conference report – Social innovation Europe launches in Brussels: The innovation union moves forward. http://ec.europa.eu/enterprise/policies/innovation/policy/social-innovation/social-inno-event_en.htm.

European Commission. (2011b). The eco-innovation observatory. The Eco-Innovation scoreboard. http://www.ecoinnovation.eu/index.php?option=com_content&view=article&id=2&Itemid=34.

Hollanders, H., & Tarantola, S. (2010). Innovation union scoreboard 2010 – Methodology report Seville. http://ec.europa.eu/research/innovation-union/pdf/innovation-union-communication_en.pdf.

Hubert, A. (2010). Empowering people, driving change: Social innovation in the European union, Working paper, Brussels.

Leighton, D., & Wood, C. (2010). Measuring social value: the gap between policy and practice. Demos. www.demos.co.uk/files/Measuring_social_value_-_web.pdf?1278410043.

Murray, R., Caulier-Grice, J., & Mulgan, G. (2010). The open book of social innovation, national endowment for science, technology and the arts. www.nesta.org.uk/library/documents/Social_Innovator_020310.pdf.

NESTA. (2007). Hidden innovation – How innovation happens in six 'low innovation' sectors, research report. http://www.nesta.org.uk/library/documents/Nesta%20Report%20HiD%20Innov%20final.pdf.
OECD: Statistical Office of the European Communities. (2005). *Oslo manual: Guidelines for collecting and interpreting innovation data, the measurement of scientific and technological activities* (3rd ed.). Paris: OECD Publishing.
Reeder, N., & O'Sullivan, C. (2011). Strengthening social innovation in Europe: Road-map for effective assessment, a paper prepared for the social innovation Europe initiative.

How to Measure the Intangibles? Towards a System of Indicators (S.A.V.E.) for the Measurement of the Performance of Social Enterprises

Andrea Bassi

Abstract The paper presents the results of a research project the principal aim of which has been to elaborate and test a measurement tool for non-profit organisations (NPOs) called SAVE (Social Added Value Evaluation) operating in the welfare area (social and health services). The basic idea is to select a sample of 12 NPOs (six organisations of volunteers and six social cooperatives) dealing with services for disabled people, elderly, physical impaired, mental illness, youth, families with problems, etc., and to carry out an in-depth sociological analysis, using the case study model of social and organisational inquiry. NPOs are regarded as special organisations because they have a triple bottom line: an economic one, a social one (volunteers, workers, users, clients, etc.) and an environmental one (local community), reflecting their various stakeholders. Our hypothesis is that NPOs are characterized by two main features: the capacity to produce relational goods and their ability in generating social capital in the community.

> We will never find a purpose for our nation nor for our personal satisfaction in the mere search for economic well-being, in endlessly amassing terrestrial goods.
> We cannot measure the national spirit on the basis of the Dow-Jones, nor can we measure the achievements of our country on the basis of the gross domestic product (GDP).
> Our gross national product counts air pollution and cigarette advertising, and ambulances to clear our highways of carnage.
> It counts special locks for our doors and the jails for those who break them. It counts napalm and the cost of a nuclear warhead, and armored cars for police who fight riots in our streets. It counts Whitman's rifle and Speck's knife, and the television programmes which glorify violence in order to sell toys to our children.
> Yet the gross national product does not allow for the health of our children, the quality of their education, or the joy of their play. **It does not include the beauty of our poetry or the strength of our marriages**; the intelligence of our public debate or the integrity of our public officials.
> It measures neither our wit nor our courage; neither our wisdom nor our learning; neither our compassion nor our devotion to our country; it measures everything, in short,

---

A. Bassi (✉)
University of Bologna, Bologna, Italy
e-mail: andrea.bassi7@unibo.it

except that which makes life worthwhile. And it tells us everything about America except why we are proud that we are Americans.

It measures everything, in short, except that which makes life worthwhile. And it tells us everything about America except why we are proud that we are Americans."
Speech by Robert Kennedy, 18 March 1968, University of Kansas.

1 Introduction

The economic and financial crisis of 2008 opens a series of challenges to the theoretical framework predominating in the last 30 years in Western democracies: the so called neo-liberalism (Hertz 2002; Klein 2007; Patel 2009). Indeed, after the so called glorious 30 (1945–1975), a period characterized by the development and the implementation of the Welfare State in the majority of the western world following the Keynesian economic theories of broad intervention of the public sector in the realm of economy (Bassi and Colozzi 2003), during the following three decades the 1980s, the 1990s and the first decade of 2000, the leading economic approach has been the neo-liberal doctrine. During this period the key words were deregulation, liberalization, free-market economy, globalization.

But something very unexpected and with dramatic consequences happened in 2008 that even the Harvard Business Review started to question the sustainability of the current model of production and distribution of wealth. In an article published in January–February 2011 Porter and Kramer ask themselves "how to reinvent capitalism" (Porter and Kramer 2011) and recognize that "the legitimacy of business has fallen to levels not seen in recent history" (Ivi, p. 4). As the authors state the ultimate cause of the problem lies in a narrow and outdated approach to value creation:

> They [the companies] continue to view value creation narrowly, optimizing short-term financial performance in a bubble while missing the most important customer needs and ignoring the broader influences that determine their longer-term success (Ivi, p. 4).

At the Department of Sociology of the Bologna University, a research team has been analysing the transformations of western societies and in particular focuses on the evolution of the civil society sphere for more than 30 years. The main topics of research have been the role of non-profit voluntary organisations in the social and health services local delivery systems, the trends in civic participation, the structure of social capital creation (and destruction) (Colozzi 2006), the production of relational goods, the transformations of third sector organisations in the social policy field.

Following this long running path of research in the years 2008–2009, a sub-unit of research carried on a research programme called "The social added value of the Third Sector: how to measure the production of relational goods" (Bassi 2011). This article illustrates the main results of this empirical, experimental inquiry aimed at analysing the capacity of non-profit organisations working in the field of welfare services to produce *relational goods* and to create *social capital* in the community they are embedded in.

We defined these two capacities as "the specific *social added value* (SAV)" that the not-for-profit organisations (NPO) provide for the society as a whole (Rey Garcia 2008). Since the majority of goods that a NPO working in the welfare sector produces are personal service (health, education, social) and since the content of such a good is by definition "intangible" (Kendall and Knapp 2000), the main problem we faced was to find a set of indicators in order to 'measure' the intangible, meaning the proper, specific contribution of NPO to the society (at micro, meso and macro levels of analysis).

The logic scheme of research follows three main steps: (a) the definition of social added value; (b) the selection of units of analysis: the NPOs; (c) the sector of activity: the field of personal social services.

The first semantic knot requires three main phases: (1) the definition of the concept of *value* (use value, exchange value and link value), (2) the definition of the property of *added* of a value, (3) the definition of the quality of *social* of a value (different from economic value, political value, cultural value, etc.) (Nef 2009).

After defining the theoretical approach (see Sect. 1 below) and the research plan (see Sect. 2 below) the next step consisted in conceiving the tools for the information gathering. These have requested three main phases: (a) the spotting of the dimensions of analysis (internal relationships, task environment relationships, external relationships); (b) the specification of the sub-dimensions (governance; management; operational level); (c) definition of indicators for each dimension and sub-dimension.

The first dimension takes into account the quality and quantity of the relationships that occur inside the organisational boundaries. There are four main kinds of stakeholders involved in this dimension: members, human resources (workers and volunteers), managers (CEO's) and the president (Head of the board of trustees).

The second dimension (task environment) deals with the production process meaning the delivery of personal services. Here we found the relationships workers/users (or clients) and as its main issue the quality of this interaction process.

The third and final dimension concerns (the quality and quantity of) the relationships that the NPO builds with a plurality of stakeholders (external) in the community (territory, area) where it works: public administration bodies, private firms, other NPO's, local community actors.

For each dimension we elaborated a set of indicators and then we transformed these indicators into questions and items (see Sect. 3 below). Section 3 presents some of the indices we calculated from the data collected during the empirical research on the 12 case studies realized: six with social enterprises, i.e. social co-operatives, and six with associations, i.e. organisations of volunteers.

In the conclusive paragraph we try to synthesize the main results of our inquiry and to present some new possible tracks of in-depth examination for future empirical research and theoretical reflection.

2 Definition of Social Added Value

2.1 On the Concept of Value

In early stages of their development the social sciences are deeply concerned with the concept of value. Both sociology (Weber, Durkheim, Simmel) and economics (Marx, Pareto, Schumpeter) put the concept of value at the core of the analysis of the new society that was growing at the time (nineteenth century and first half of twentieth century). It is only after the Second World War that the two disciplines separated their methods and tools of inquiry and *value* (singular) became the object of study of the economics whereas the world of *values* (plural) became the main topic of sociology and anthropology.

This idea that there is a unique (objective) value that can be used as a unit of measurement of the economic (monetary) value of things and goods, is inherently wrong because it separates the two inner constitutive properties of value: to be at the same time "a positive quality of an object or state of fact" and "a measure of a physical size". The two dimensions that we can call the "subjective one" (judgment) and the "objective one" (measurement), are inseparable and constitute the semantic spectrum of the meaning of value (Westall 2009). So there is not such a thing like a quiet, objective world of *value* (Mulgan 2010) meaning the sphere of society where it is possible do apply "objective" units of measurement to the things and objects that are exchanged, to be studied by the economics, and on the other side the messy world of *values* where different points of view about what is good or bad are confronting themselves, to be studied by sociology and anthropology.

We can conclude on this point saying that the two conceptual dimensions of value: (a) "a positive quality considered in abstract as an element of reference for a judgment" and (b) the "measure of a physical size; the state assumed by a variable" (Zingarelli 2012) are embedded in the meaning of value(s) and cannot be separated. This epistemological break and the following separation of the two main disciplines of the social sciences has been one of the main causes of the fallacy of these sciences in reading the evolution of our post-modern societies.

Following this approach it is not surprising to discover that the prevailing definition of value has been the economic one. Indeed, looking at the literature we find two main typologies of value: the use value and the exchange value:

(a) Use value (intrinsic): it refers to the capacity of a good to satisfy, directly and immediately, a need;
(b) Value of exchange (market value): it is the value of a good based on its place in the exchange system of goods.

And there is no doubt about the fact that the last 30 years have shown a predominance of the second term over the first one.

Against this mainstream line of thought, in the mid-1980s in France a group of social scientists founded the Mauss (Mouvement Anti-Utilitarist dans les Sciences Sociales), from the name of the famous anthropologist Marcel Mauss. This group of

Table 1 Types of value

		Point of reference of the relationship	
		Things	Persons
Value base of	Intrinsic	Use value (Needs)	–
The good	Extrinsic	Exchange value (Desires)	Link/bond value (Feelings)

scholars and researchers found out that there is a third type of value in our society that they named the "link (tie, bond) value" (Godbout 1992). It has the following two characteristics:

(a) Unlike the 'use value', it refers not to a property or a characteristic of a good but it assumes meaning only inside a network (circuit) of relations, of references of meaning.
(b) And unlike the 'value of exchange', it refers not to a relationship among things (price) but to a relation between persons involved in the exchange (gratuitousness, emotional value, time) (Table 1).

What we try to argue is that in our societies there is a lack in the production of this kind of value which is fundamental for building an inclusive, cohesive, equal society. During the years of the development of the welfare states (after the Second World War) there has been a prevalence of the 'use value' creation and distribution via the state. There is no doubt that the following 30 years have shown a predominance of the "exchange value" creation via the market. The financial crisis of 2008 put in question this model of wealth creation and distribution. There is space for a third sphere of society: the civil society actors, non-profit organisations, voluntary associations, local groups of mutual and self-help that typically are the main producers of "link value(s)", such as trust, reciprocity, responsibility, care, etc. (Table 2).

There is no doubt that we need to change the concepts (Weltanschauung) with which we see the world but we do also need to change the way we measure what is a positive achievement for society and what is not. In this search of a new conceptual framework we need to redefine what we mean by the word *added*.

2.2 The Concept of Added *Value*

Similar to what happened with the concept of value even for the meaning of "added" the late modernity operates a semantic contraction. Nowadays with added we mean "more" as opposite to "less"; we indicate growth, an augmentation in quantitative terms of the "exchange value" of a good (price).

This conflation of the meaning of "added" with the concept of "growth" obviously had consequences for its measurement with quantitative aspects being preferred to qualitative ones. This happened at both the micro and macro level, as

Table 2 Typology of Italian non-profit organisations by 'value creation' and 'value distribution' functions

		Value distribution		
		Members	Non-members	Both
Value	Members	Members associations	Organisations of volunteers	Social co-operatives-Type B
Creation	Non-members		Corporations	Foundations
	Both		Small and medium enterprises	Social co-operatives-Type A

shown by the crisis of the GNP as a unit of measurement of the wealth of a country (Stiglitz et al. 2009). We should recognize that the last 30 years have shown an increasing separation of the GNP from the improvement of the quality of life in western countries (Latouche 2004).

In the present study we adopt a definition of 'added value' that goes beyond a simplistic economic dimension towards a more complex and multi-dimensional approach:

> The *economic definition* of *added value* is the increase of value that a good receives by the effect of manufacturing and transformations, directed to make it saleable; it is obtained by the subtraction from the production value of the cost of the raw material utilized to produce it. In other words, *added value* is obtained by the difference between the output value (price) of an economic actor and the input value (cost, fee) necessary for the production of the output. Therefore, it can be measured with a subtraction: output-input-added value. It expresses the "value increase that a good or service undergoes because of production processes which transform it into a thing usable by a third part" (Enciclopedia dell'Economia 2001).

While the economic definition stays on the quantitative side, our more complex and multi-dimensional approach or

> *Sociological definition* conceives added value as the result of a transformation process of a good or service in *qualitative* terms, meaning with reference to a perceived quality of a service by the user beneficiary.
>
> What the NPO's produce has an added value if, and only if, it has a different value for, is perceived as different by those who are the beneficiaries of the service compared to what they can get if the service was produced by public administration agencies or for-profit enterprises. For us, 'added' does not mean *more than* something else but different *from* something else and *for somebody*

2.3 The Concept of Social *Added Value*

Obviously there are many quantitative and qualitative increments in value (exactly value added) which an organisation, and a third sector organisation in particular, can effectively produce for society in general. In order to examine this subject more closely, we will use T. Parsons' (1951) "four functions scheme" (AGIL) to indicate the components of the *general system of action* (see Fig. 1). In principle, it is possible to identify at least four principal declinations of added value that an

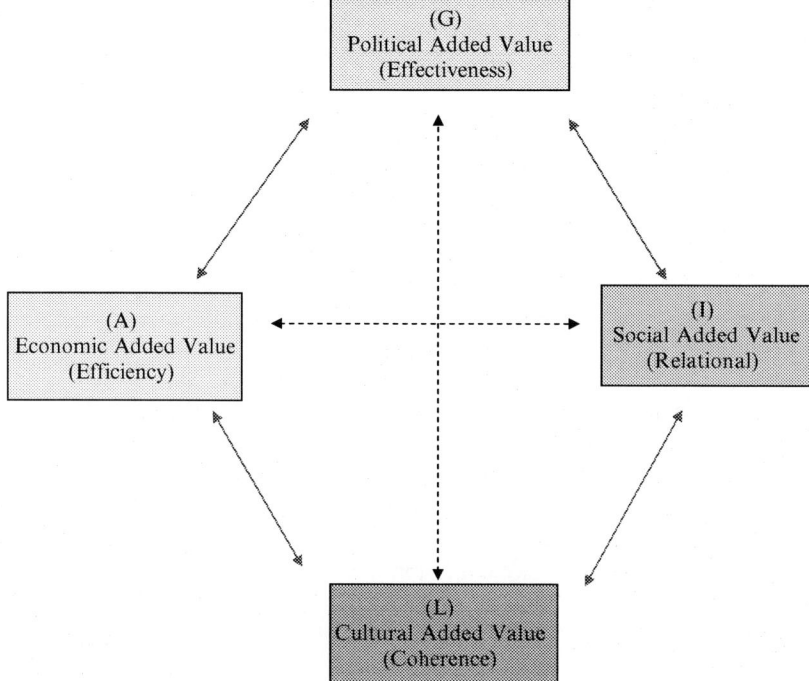

Fig. 1 Four types of added value produced by an organisation

organisation, in our case a third sector organisation (TSO) can bring to society in general (macro level), to the local community (meso level), and to the people who work in it or who benefit from its services (micro level) (see Fig. 1).

In the first place, we find the EAV (Economic Added Value), which is a contribution in terms of augmentation (or non-consumption) of the material, economic and financial wealth (investment, savings) which a TSO produces through their specific activity. For example, in occupational terms, it is important to note not merely the number of jobs "created" but rather the quality (dignity) of the occupational positions. Other important occupational factors include the compatibility of the rhythms of life and the rhythms of work, differences in salaries offered (with the highest not more than two or three times higher than the lowest), the training offered to qualified professionals, etc.

In the second place, we can identify the *PAV* (Political Added Value) which comes from the capacity of a TSO (or a network, committee or delegation) to influence the political agenda (in this case also at the macro, meso and micro levels) to bring debate, arguments, questions and problems into the political arena, which, without the TSO's contribution, the political system would not have dealt with. There is also the contribution in terms of the achievement of planned objectives and of the TSO's capacity to respond to social problems.

In the third place, there is the *SAV* (Social Added Value), in other words, the specific contribution of a TSO in terms of the production of relational goods (internal relational dimension) and creation of social capital (external relational dimension).

Finally, we have the *CAV* (Cultural Added Value) which is the specific contribution a TSO makes in the diffusion of values (equity, tolerance, solidarity, mutuality) coherent with its own mission in the surrounding community.

At this point we may investigate the **TAV** (Total/Societal Added Value) of a third sector organisation for society (territorial community in which it operates) which is made up (resultant) of different added values which said TSO creates (or not) through its activities in various *relational spheres*: economic, political, societal, and cultural. The result is the following formula:

$$Total/Societal\ Added\ Value\ (TAV) = EAV + PAV + SAV + CAV$$

In summary, the specific contribution of the third sector (non-profit sector) is to *produce a sense of responsibility* towards the public (for people/citizens), a number of *relational goods*[1] (or collective goods, or meritorious goods) (for organisations and the local territorial systems); and, in the end, a solid amount of *social capital*[2] (for the complex social systems or the vast community). As a consequence, the principal differences between the non-profit sector, the profit sector, and the public sector, from the point of view of production, are not so much in *what* is produced but rather mainly in *how* to produce, and above all *with* and *for* whom they produce.

---

[1] The definition of *relational good* is adopted from the Italian sociologist Pierpaolo Donati, and it has been developed in a scientific research program of more than 30 years. It refers to a good or service that holds the following characteristics: (a) it is a good where the production, distribution and consuming require the involvement of both the producer and the user; (b) it is a good that can be enjoyed only by and through the social relation; (c) the quality of the good is embedded in the social relation. The relational good differs both from the public and the private goods. See: Donati P. (a cura di) 1996, pp. 37–39.

[2] On the concept of social capital there is nowadays a wide bibliography. For a review of the principal approaches and an original version of the concept see Donati 2007; Donati and Tronca 2008; Colozzi 2005. These are some of the main definitions around which the scientific debate did develop.

Pierre Bourdieu (1980, 1986): "[social capital is] the sum of resources, actual or virtual, that accrue to an individual or a group by virtue of possessing a durable network of more or less institutionalized relationships of mutual acquaintance and recognition."

James Coleman (1988, 1990): "Social capital is defined by its function. It is not a single entity, but a variety of different entities having two characteristics in common: They all consist of some aspect of social structure, and they facilitate certain actions of individuals who are within the structure. Like other forms of capital, social capital is productive, making possible the achievement of certain ends that would not be attainable in its absence."

Robert Putnam (1993, 1995, 1995a): "social capital ... refers to features of social organisation, such as trust, norms, and networks, that can improve the efficiency of society by facilitating coordinated actions."

Given that the specific object of the present work is to discuss the social added value (SAV), in the following pages we must limit our analysis exclusively to this component of the four possible added values which the TSOs can produce/create for society.

3 The Research Plan

The research team coordinated by Andrea Bassi, operated under the scientific supervision of Prof Colozzi and worked for 2 years (2008–2009). The research project has been organised in seven phases.

During the *first phase* we analysed the national and international literature (books, journals, reviews, grey material) in the field of non-profit organisations, third sector, civil society, social policy, welfare systems, social programme evaluation, social impact, organisational performance. In particular, we utilized the key words: social capital, relational (or shared) goods, social value, added value, shared value, social impact. Based on this material we elaborated our operative definition of "social added value" for the non-profit organisations (see paragraph 1).

The *second phase* was dedicated to the construction of our data collection tool. It was a very complex work, due to the fact that there is not yet a shared definition of "social added value" in the scientific community. So we decided to adopt an experimental research design in order to test the validity of our data collection tool.

We drew up a semi-structured questionnaire with many "open questions", in order to allow the interviewees to express themselves in a more discursive way detailing their points of view on the topics exposed. We identified 36 main questions (with some sub-questions) organised in three sections:

A] – Internal relationships (Quest. A1–A17)
B] – External relationships (Quest. B1–B7)
C] – Structural organisational data and trends (Dom. C1–C12)

The *first* section includes questions aimed to find out the capacity of the NPO to produce "relational goods". The 17 questions of this section have been divided into three main areas:

A1 – Governance [Assembly, Council (Board), President (Head of the Board)];
A2 – Relationships among the staff (CEO, paid staff, volunteers, members)
A3 – Relationship with the beneficiaries of the organisation activities (staff, users/ clients, members)

The *second* section deals with the capacity of NPO to generate social capital in the community. The questions included in this section aimed to gather information about the wideness of the network of relationships the organisation is involved in (number of relationships, typology of organisations and institutions the NPO is related with, intensity and strategic importance of the relationship, level of trust).

Table 3 Typology and geographical area of the NPOs

	Forlì 120.000	Parma (200.000)	Total
Organisations of volunteers	3	3	6
Social co-operatives	3	3	6
Total	6	6	12

The *third* section includes several classical questions about the structural characteristics of an organisation (budget, human resources, income, etc.) and some questions concerning medium-period trends (3/5 years). The aim is to gather information that can offer a broader picture of the 'organisation's health status'. The trends are related to: incomes/earnings, loss/profit, membership, staff, volunteers, turn-over. The data of this section are a benchmark for the data collected in the other two sections. Our hypothesis is to verify, if there is a significant relationship between the "quality of the relationships" the NPO establishes with internal and external stakeholders (social added value produced) and the structural trends (organisational soundness).

During the *third phase* we identified our *unit* of research. We chose the non-profit organisations working in the field of personal services (education, health and social services). We decided to focus our inquiry on four types of organisations: organisations of volunteer (Italian law 266/91), social co-operatives (Italian law 381/91), associations (Italian law 383/00), in particular "family associations", and self-help mutual-help groups. The research team I coordinated carried out the case studies related to the first two typologies above mentioned: organisations of volunteers and social co-operatives. As our territorial area where to realize the empirical field research, we chose the social-health districts of two municipalities in the Emilia Romagna Region (north-east of Italy), the social-health district of Forlì and the social-health district of Parma. We selected 12 NPOs, six for each territorial area. The selection process was carried out through the collaboration of two umbrella organisations. For the organisation of volunteers we asked the two CSVs (Service Centers for Volunteering; Art. 15 Italian Law 266/91) of Forlì and Parma to give us a list of about 20 (10 + 10) organisations that, based on their judgment, where more "innovative". Then we extrapolated randomly six organisations (3 + 3) out of this list. As far as the social co-operatives are concerned we followed a similar method. We asked the two Federations of Social Co-operatives (Federsolidarietà) at the provincial level (Forlì and Parma) to give us a list of about 20 (10 + 10) social co-ops that where more "innovative". Then we randomly extracted six organisations (3 + 3) out of this list (see Table 3).

The *fourth phase* was dedicated to discussing with leaders of local NPOs the content of the questionnaire. We realized two focus groups, one in each territory, during which we presented the research topic and goals as well as the tools we elaborated, and asked them for comments, critics, suggestions, etc. The information that came out of the focus groups was utilized to modify the phrasing of some questions and the position of some other questions in the questionnaire structure.

During the *fifth* phase we conducted the empirical inquiry (field data gathering). For each of the 12 organisations, at least three visits were paid to their headquarters.

During the first visit the interviewer met the President, the CEOs, the members of the Board and informed them about the documentation he needed. During the second visit he gathered the documents and spoke with administrative employees. During the third visit he observed the daily life activities of the organisation in a specific service area (child care, home care for the elderly, etc.), in order to get an overall impression of the "organisational climate".

The *sixth* phase was characterized by the activity of "codifying the data". During this process we came to a rewriting of the questions included in the questionnaire moving from a majority of "open ended" questions to a large number of "closed" ones. We were able to produce a second version of our research tool.

The *seventh* and final phase was occupied by the analysis of the data and the construction of indicators (see paragraphs 3.1 and 3.2).

4 The Social Added Value Evaluation (SAVE) System

For the elaboration of the tool for measuring the social added value we carried out a bibliographic search both at national and international level. What emerges is a clear picture that the field is covered more by working papers, reports, and grey material published by institutions working in the field (charities, foundations, think tanks, networks of practitioners, etc.) than scientific institutions and academic bodies.

Our impression is that we are still at an initial phase of analysis and elaboration of tools (Barman 2007) for the measurement of the social impact, social performance and social outcomes of the NPOs.

In the Italian scientific community the most systematic research programme on the evaluation of the quality of services in the field of welfare is the work of Giovanni Bertin and his équipe of research. Following the logical-methodological scheme of Bertin and his team (2008), we identified for each of our two main criteria of creating social added value, i.e. the capacity of producing "relational goods" and the ability to generate "social capital" the dimensions, the sub-dimensions and the 'observable elements' (see Fig. 2) (Table 4).

As it is clear from the above scheme (see also Fig. 3), the capacity to produce relational goods has been defined as the degree of "internal relational capacity" of an NPO. It consists of the frequency of relationships among the internal stakeholders and the "intensity" (strategic importance) of these relationships. As far as the second criterion is concerned, this has been defined as the degree of "external relational capacity" of NPO. It consists of the frequency of relationships with the external stakeholders and the "intensity" (strategic importance) of these relationships. We identified four dimensions of analysis (see Fig. 4) and four types of stakeholders involved (see Fig. 5).

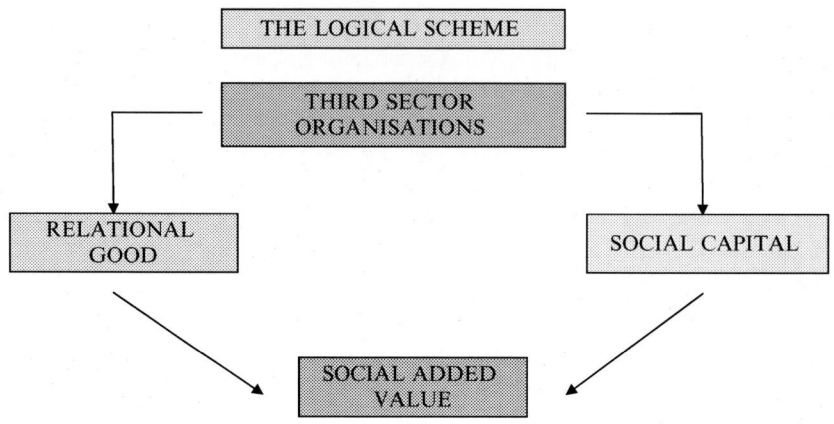

Fig. 2 Logical scheme

Table 4 Logical framework of SAVE

Criterion	Dimension	Sub Dimension	Observable elements
Capacity to produce	Internal relationality (quest. a3–a17)	'Quantity of internal relations'	President CEO Workers/volunteers Members Beneficiaries
Relational goods		Quality of internal relations	Formal/informal; intensity; strategic importance;
Capacity to create social capital in the local community	External relationality (quest. b1–b7)	Quantity of external relations	Public Admin. Corporation Other NPOs Local Community intensity; strategic importance;
		Quality of external relations	

4.1 Indicators of Internal "Relational Capacity"

From the data analysis it was possible to extract 13 indices of internal relational capacity.

4.1.1 A] Index of Relational Governance

The first index tries to measure the degree in which the members of the NPO participate in the decision making process. It has been constructed from the aggregation of four variables coming from questions A3/A3bis (one variable) and question A4 (three variables).

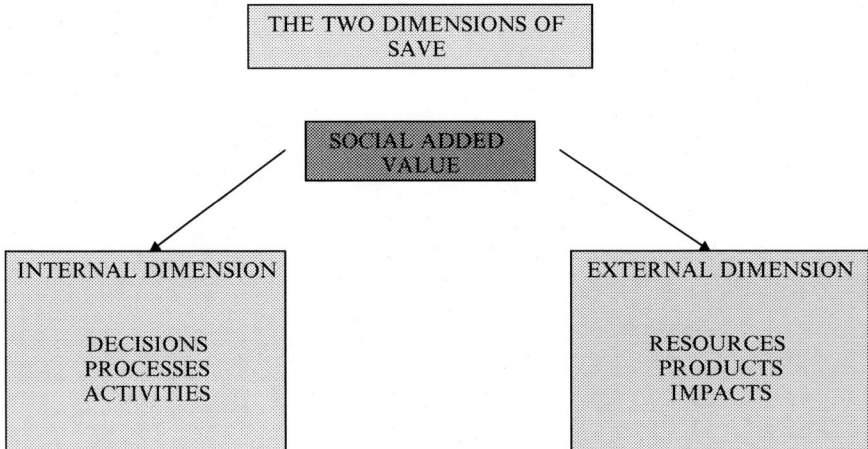

Fig. 3 Two dimensions of the S.A.V.E. tool

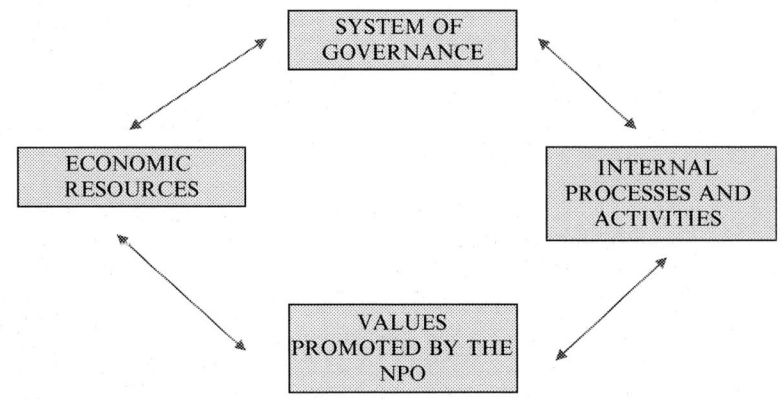

Fig. 4 The four dimensions of analysis

Questions A3 and A3bis produce a variable with four states of affairs: (1) 2 yearly assemblies; (2) More yearly assemblies; (3) Council of directors or council of directors open to the members; (4) commissions/working groups. These states move in a scale that goes from a minimum to a maximum level of participation.

Question A4 produces three variables with four states of affairs each ((1) none, (2) narrow, (3) moderate, (4) high). It aims to measure the "real capacities" of the members to influence three key aspects of the decision making process: the election of the President; the election of the Council members; the political strategic decisions.

To each item was assigned a value based on the different weight of each of them on the indicator "degree of internal democracy". This indicator has been calculated in relation to the level of participation of the members: 2–4–6–8 for the first

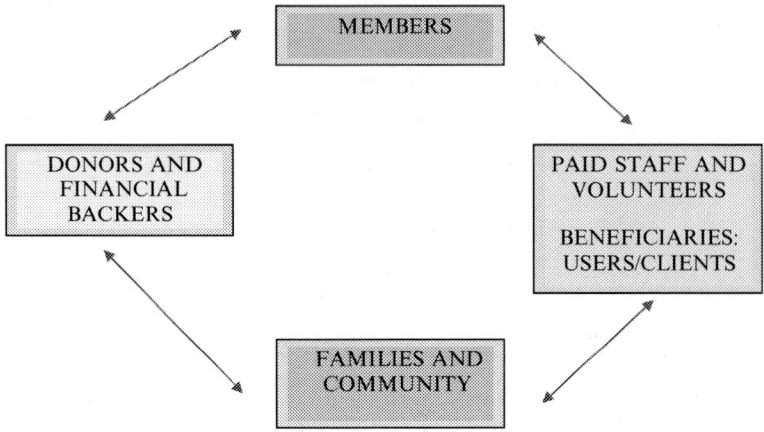

Fig. 5 The four types of stakeholders

variable and 0–2–4–6 for the other three variables. Summing the four variables up, we got a score between 2 and 26.

Then we divided the score in four classes of the same width (size) (first score 2–8) (second score 9–14) (third score 15–20) (fourth score 21–26), in this way we obtain a synthetic index with the following values: (1) low, (2) moderate, (3) good, (4) high.

4.1.2 B] Index of Internal Relationships

The second group of indicators includes four indices aiming to measure the degree of internal relationships in the NPO, meaning the quantity and quality of relationships among their internal stakeholders. These indicators emerge from the elaboration of the answers to questions A7_1–A12_2 .

This conceptual nucleus is the core of the first section of the questionnaire consisting of six pairs of questions, the first of which aimed to measure the frequency of the relationship ((1) absent; (2) occasional not programmed; (3) irregular programmed; (4) frequent programmed). The second question (open) aimed to find out the significance of the relationship. The latter has been codified in two variables measuring: the "degree of formalization" and the "degree of importance" of the relationships for the NPO.

The questions deal with:

(a) The relationships between the President and others internal stakeholders (three questions: President-Management (CEO); President-workers/volunteers; President-members);
(b) The relationships between the Management and others internal stakeholders (two questions: CEO-workers/volunteers; CEO-members);
(c) The relationships between the workers/volunteers and members (one question).

The first group of questions produce the index "Political internal relational capacity", the second the index "Managerial internal relational capacity", and the third the index "Operational internal relational capacity". Each of them has been constructed dividing the total score in four classes of the same width (size): (1) low, (2) moderate, (3) good, (4) high.

Using the same criteria we calculated an index of "Total internal relational capacity".

Moreover, we have a set of questions aimed to find out: (a) the ways through which the NPO controls the quality of the services delivered; (b) the locus where the NPO analyses its activities and the future strategies; (c) the topics around which the users/clients are involved. Each of these questions gives rise to a specific index.

4.1.3 C] Index of Relational Evaluation

The first index named "relational evaluation" detects the degree of closedness/openness of the NPO towards the beneficiaries of its services.

Question A13 gives rise to three dummy variables (yes/no) indicating each the presence/absence of a specific form of evaluation/control: (a): through direct meetings with users and families; (b) through analysis of data collected by workers/volunteers; (c) by a questionnaire of user satisfaction. Using a logical framework the three options were crossed giving rise to a variable with five states: (1) low, (2) moderate, (3) good, (4) high, (5) very high.

The hypothesis we follow is that there is a growing level of openness of the NPO moving from b (data collected by workers/volunteers) to c (user satisfaction questionnaire) to the first one (direct meetings) considered as the most intense. The scores have been assigned based on the presence of one, two or all three possibilities and on their specific combination.

4.1.4 D] Index of Relational Strategic Capacity

The second index named "relational strategic capacity" detects the degree of closedness/openness of the NPO in analysing its activity and its future development perspectives with respect to a plurality of internal stakeholders (council, members, volunteers) and external stakeholders (users, families, local community, citizens).

Question A14 gives rise to four dummy variables (yes/no) indicating each the presence/absence of a specific form of strategy debate: (a) council of directors; (b) general assembly of members/volunteers; (c) general assembly open to users and families; (d) public assembly open to the local community. Using a logical framework the four options were crossed giving rise to a variable with four states: (1) low, (2) moderate, (3) good, (4) high.

The hypothesis we follow is that there is a growing level of openness of the NPO moving from the first operational mode to the last one. The scores have been assigned based on the presence/absence of the above mentioned operational mode.

4.1.5 E] Index of User Involvement

The third index named "user involvement" detects the degree of closedness/openness of the NPO in the process of service delivery, with respect to the beneficiaries (users/clients).

Question A15 gives rise to three dummy variables (yes/no) indicating each the presence/absence of a specific form of user involvement: (a) in the phase of planning the service; (b) in the phase of delivering the service; (c) in the phase of evaluating the service. Using a logical framework the three options have been crossed giving rise to a variable with five states: (1) low, (2) moderate, (3) good, (4) High, (5) very high.

The hypothesis we follow is that there is a growing level of openness of the NPO moving from the last operational mode to the first one and to the second one. The scores have been assigned based on the presence of one, two or all three possibilities and on their specific combination.

4.1.6 F] Index of Relational Training

Going further, there is a group of questions dealing with training policy adopted by NPOs. Many authors affirm that the training is one of the strategic policies for social enterprises. Moreover, training can be seen as a motivational incentive for workers that show higher levels of satisfaction on the job than those working in private business and public administration with equally high or even slightly lower salaries. We take into consideration three aspects of the training process: (a) the target groups; (b) the topics; and the operational modes of the training activities.

F.1] Index of the Degree of "Relational Capacity" of the Training Process

As far as the target group of training activity is concerned our hypothesis is that there is a growing level of openness of the NPO in relation to the typology of participants. We found the following possibilities: (a) only NPO workers; (b) only NPO volunteers; (c) both; (d) with other NPO workers; (e) with public administration workers; (f) with both. The scores have been assigned based on the presence of one, two or more possibilities and on their specific combinations (2–5–7–10).

F.2] Index of the 'Technical Level' of the Training

The second variable deals with the subjects of the training activities. It identifies four kinds of subjects and gives a value to each of them following a scale that reflects their capacity to promote the level of "relational capacity" inside the NPO: *low* for technical-professional topics; *medium-low* for motivational topics, *medium-high* for ethical-value topics and *high* for the relational topics. The scores have been assigned based on the combination of the topics (2–5–8).

F.3] Index of the "Relational Capacity" of the Operational Mode of Training Course Delivery

Question A16bis deals with the operational mode of training activities. We found the following possibilities: (a) promoted and organised by NPO; (b) promoted by NPO but organised by public administration (PA); (c) (a) promoted and organised by PA.

The question was aimed to find out the capacity of NPO to plan and work together with others, to build collaborations. The scores have been assigned along a continuum from a low level of collaboration capacity to a high level (2–4–6).

Summing up the scores of the three variables (2–10; 2–8; 2–6) we elaborated an index named "relational training". Then we divided the score in four classes of the same width (size), this way obtaining a synthetic index with the following values: (1) low, (2) moderate, (3) good, (4) high.

4.1.7 G] Index of the Level of Sociability

Finally, the last indicator of this section, concerning the "internal relational capacity", deals with the "level of sociability" (or "informal relational capacity" or "internal social capital") existing among the NPO stakeholders.

Question A17 aimed to find out if there were social events (dinners, parties, travels, etc.) among the organisation members and others stakeholders, and how many.

The answers were placed on a scale from a minimum level of openness to a maximum level: (a) only workers (paid staff and volunteers); (b) workers and beneficiaries (users/clients); (c) workers, beneficiaries and donors; (d) workers, beneficiaries, donors and families and community members. The scores have been assigned following the combinations along the continuum (2–5–8).

In synthesis, from the data we collected it is possible to extrapolate the following picture (see Table 5):

As we can see the majority of the indices show positive values. Only three indices have a low score: A] internal democracy, D] index of relational strategic capacity (level of involvement of external stakeholders), E] index of user involvement.

In our opinion this is a first not trivial result of our research, meaning to be able to indicate three operational aspects of weakness. Three areas on which to intervene in order to increase the level of internal "relational capacity" of the NPOs analysed. With the aim to ameliorate their capacity to produce relational goods, that means lastly to increase the quality of the services delivered.

Table 5 Mean index scores of internal "relational capacity"

Index	Mean
[A] Index of internal democracy (scale 1–4)	1.58**
[B.1] Index of political internal "relational capacity" (scale 1–4)	3.00
[B.2] Index of managerial internal "relational capacity" (scale 1–4)	3.00
[B.3] Index of operational internal "relational capacity" (scale 1–4)	3.08
[B] Index of total internal "relational capacity" (scale 1–4)	3.16
[C] MONITOR – Index of relational evaluation (scale 1–5)	3.50
[D] STRATEGY – Index of relational strategic capacity (scale 1–4)	1.66**
[E] USERS – Index of user involvement (scale 1–5)	2.33**
[F.1] TRAINING TARGET – Index of the degree of "relational capacity" of the training process (scale 2–10)	7.00
[F.2] TRAiNING TOPIC – Index of the "technical level" of the training (scale 2–8)	5.75
[F.3] TRAINING PARTNER – Index of the "relational capacity" of the operational mode of training course delivery (scale 2–6)	5.33
[F] TRAINING – Relational training (scale 1–4)	3.08
[G] SOCIALIZE – Index of the level of sociability (scale 2–8)	7.00

** Negative value (below the mean)

What emerges from our inquire is the necessity to set up policies able to:

- Foster the members participation in the decision-making process;
- Foster the external stakeholders participation in the definition of the future strategies;
- Foster the users/clients involvement in the services delivering process.

4.2 External Relational Capacity

As far as the external relational capacity of the NPO is concerned the questionnaire contains several questions aimed to find out the extent and the importance of the network of relationships the organisation is involved.

The table below shows the frequencies of the answers to four questions regarding the presence/absence of relationships [B1], the quality of the relationships [B2], trends on trust [B4], and the origin of the relationship [B3] (Table 6).

As it emerges clearly from the table below, the NPOs show a wide network of relationships (Bassi 2010) with the others actors of the political, economic and social environment where they operate.

On the first place we found the relationships with the Public Administration. In particular all the 12 NPOs included in the survey indicate that they have relationships with the Municipality and with the Local Health Unit.

Less developed appear to be the relationships with the private for profit sphere. On the other side very diffuse are the relationships with other third sector organisations, such as Foundations and Social Co-operatives.

Table 6 The networks of external relationships of NPOs

	Presence of relationships	Mean intensity/ importance (scale 2–10)	Mean of trust (scale 1–5)	Willingness to start the relationship
Municipality	12	8.6	3.27	12
Province	7	4.2	3.00	5
Local Health Unit	12	6.6	3.55	12
Region	7	2.7	2.88	7
Other Pub. Adm.	7	4.5	3.33	6
Private firms	12	5.7	3.55	12
Assoc. of economic categories	6	2.5	3.17	5
Chamber of commerce	0	–	–	–
Other private	1	–	–	1
organisations of volunteers	11	6.9	3.90	7
Associations	8	2.3	3.29	7
Social co-operatives	12	7.5	4.09	11
Foundations	12	5.5	3.27	12
Other NPOs	5	4.6	3.60	5
Parish	10	5.8	3.67	3
Families	11	7.9	4.00	7
Other community	10	6.3	3.89	8

Quite good is also the level of involvement with the local community (civil society), indeed almost all the NPOs analysed affirm to have relationships with families, parishes, and other community actors.

We found a deeper differentiation looking at the data concerning the "level of intensity" of the relationship. The index construction has been illustrated in paragraph 3.1.

Following this indicator, the institutions and actors that play a strategic role for the NPOs are: the municipality (score 8.6, on a scale 2–10); the families (score 7.9), other social co-operatives (score 7.5), organisations of volunteers (score 6.9), the local Health Unit (score 6.6), and other actors of the local community (score 6.3). It is noticeable that the private for-profit firms and the foundations register lower scores (5.7 and 5.5).

A third element of analysis is given by the number of organisations/institutions/actors with which the NPOs have relationships. This data give us a picture of the network extension (Bassi 2012).

One NPO out of four declares to have relationships with all the public administration agencies included in the questionnaire (high network extension); one out of three reports relations with four agencies; and the same number says to be related with three agencies.

Concerning the relationship with other NPOs, our data show the following picture: one organisation out of four declares to be in touch with all the NPOs included in the question, half of them say with four actors and another fourth with three actors.

The network of relationships with the private for profit firms is narrow. Half of the NPOs included in the survey have relationships with at least one private organisation, and another half with a maximum of two.

Finally the network of relationships with the actors of their local community appears to be wide. Three fourths of the NPOs affirm to be connected with all the subjects included in the question.

Another variable that we take into consideration is the level of trust the NPOs show towards the other organisations. The question asks if after the relationship the level of trust remained the same, increased or decreased. Our data reveal that only for the other NPOs the level of trust increased. The maximum score is with social co-operatives (4.09), followed by families (4.00), by organisations of volunteers (3.90) and other actors of the community (3.89).

As far as the public administration agencies and the private for profit firms are concerned, the levels of trust usually remain the same or decrease during the relationship.

The last variable analysed deals with the origin of the relationship. We asked if the relationship was activated voluntarily by the NPOs or if it emerged casually during the organisation action. As you can see the NPOs were pro-active towards the municipality, the local health unit, the private for-profit enterprises and the foundations, while the relationships with the actors of the local community and the other NPOs origin by chance during the NPOs everyday activities.

The last three questions of the section concerning the "external relationships" play a key role in the collection of information about the capacity of NPO to generate social capital in the community. These questions give rise to three dummy variables (yes/no) indicating each the presence/absence of the specific capacity.

4.2.1 H] Capacity to Generate Associations

The first one is aimed to detect the organisation's capacity to gemmate other third sector actors (with different levels of formal/informal constitution): social co-operatives, associations, community organisations, informal groups.

	A.V.	%
Yes	5	45.5
No	6	54.5
Total	11	100

This is a very key dimension in our research's theoretical framework. Indeed it is a sign of the fact that the NPO is not merely focused on service delivery functions but pushes out in a pro-active way towards the local community in which it is embedded.

4.2.2 I] Degree of Openness/Closure Towards the Community

A similar argument can be applied to the second question of this section dealing with the capacity of the NPO to organise initiatives (conferences, workshops, meetings, fairs) not only for its members, staff, volunteers, donors, etc. but for a wider public (local community).

	A.V.	%
Yes	10	90.9
No	1	9.1
Total	11	100

This activity is placed in a lower degree than the previous one, in relation to the capacity of the NPO to generate social capital in the community, but nevertheless it detects a propensity to go beyond the organisational boundaries and to characterise itself as a social enterprise open to the community.

4.2.3 L] Quality of Planning and Projects Achieving

The third question is intended to obtain information about the NPO capacity in planning and realizing the projects. It asked if a project, an activities, a service of the NPO has been adopted by others NPOs or agencies of the public administration, because of its innovative or excellence properties.

	A.V.	%
Yes	10	90.9
No	1	9.1
Total	11	100

Also this one is a very key dimension in our research's theoretical framework concerning the attempt of measuring the capacity of the NPO to generate social capital.

4.2.4 M] Index of Relational Innovation

The data obtained by the above mentioned questions were merged in a synthetic index named "index of relational innovation". The new variable shows three values: (1) Low (only one of the three activities), (2) Medium (two activities), (3) High (three activities).

	A.V.	%
Low	0	0
Medium	8	72.7
High	3	27.3
Total	11	100

As mentioned in the introduction, the theoretical objective of this research programme has been to elaborate and to test a tool for the detection of the *social added value* of Italian NPOs working in the field of personal services (education, health and social services).

After an in-depth analysis of the existing literature we drew up a first draft of the tool and we discussed it in two focus groups with leaders and practitioners of Italian NPOs. This gave rise to a second draft that was tested in 12 case studies with six social co-operatives and six organisations of volunteers.

The collected data were codified and analysed by the research team. This allowed us to elaborate a second version (2.0) of our tool, adding several significant changes in the questions phrasing and wording, and eliminating some questions that have shown to be not related to our research topic.

The new version of the tool is mainly (almost uniquely) composed of closed questions whereas the first one contained several open questions. In this sense, we think that the final result of our research project has been a positive one. Now in the next years we would like to apply the tool to a wide sample of Italian NPOs in order to test its validity and eventually to improve it.

5 Conclusions: Are the Social Enterprises (Nyssens 2006) Really Different?

The question underlying our research programme has been the following one: "Are the NPOs really different from others kinds of organisations (private firm and public administration agencies)?" and in an affirmative case "In what are they different"? In other words: "Is it possible to find a 'distinctive characteristic', a 'specificity' of NPOs in the field of personal services that make them different"? This question calls upon the possibility to delineate a system of indicators able to grasp (measure) this specificity (or distinctiveness), a benchmarking to compare the NPOs' performance (at micro, meso and macro levels).

In the *first* place, we tried to define this distinctive characteristic in qualitative terms and not only in quantitative terms, as the literature usually does. The theoretical framework focus was not on 'what' the NPOs do but on 'how' they operate, that is to say if they were 'qualitatively different'. We identified two dimensions along which to detect the degree of presence (or absence) of such a distinctiveness: (a) the capacity of the NPOs to produce "relational goods", and (b) the capacity to generate "social capital" in the community around them. These two capacities determine the level of social added value the NPO produces for the society as a whole (see Fig. 6).

The significance of our research programme is testified by the diffuse and high dissatisfaction among NPO leaders, managers, practitioners, public decision makers and the scientific community, with the actual system of evaluation of NPO performance and social impact (Bassi and Colozzi 2009). This is a key

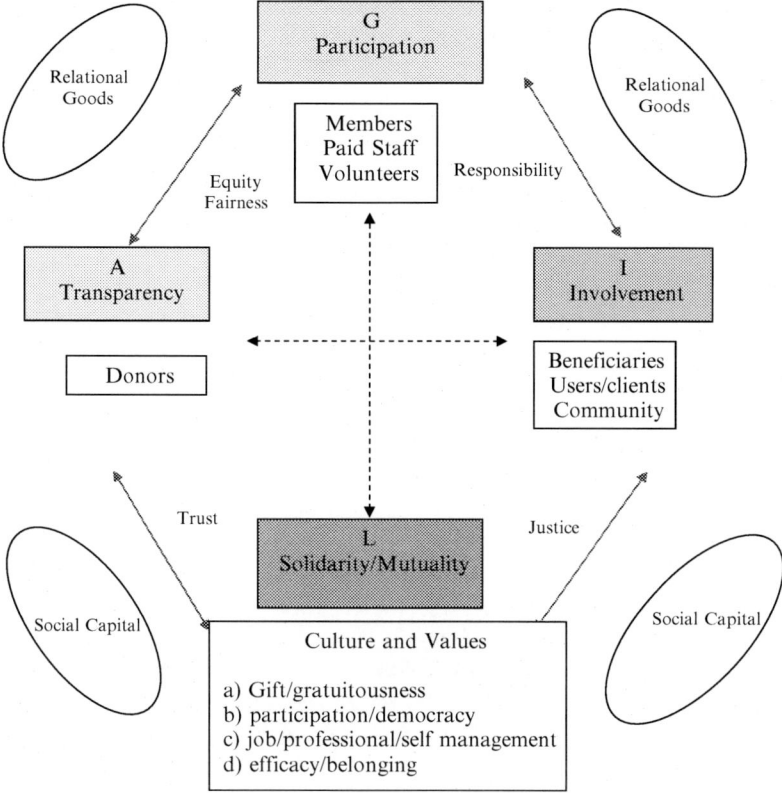

Fig. 6 Internal operational dimensions of NPOs

point in determining the quality of the welfare system in western democracies, because the actual *systems of certification* (ISO 9001 and similar) are widely used by the national, regional and local governments as guidelines for their policy of "accreditation" of social, health and education services, all of them sectors where NPOs are significant players in the service delivery system.

The *second* step in the research project development was the in-depth study of the concept of *social added value*, in order to come to an operational definition. We analysed the different typologies of value that organisations (the NPOs, too) can produce and what we found were four main categories: economic value, political value, social value, cultural value. The aggregation (not the sum) of these four values comes to determine the *total/societal added value* that an organisation (NPO too) contributes to the society as a whole.

The *third* step of our theoretical track has consisted in the assumption that the specificity of NPOs is to produce the third type of value, i.e. social value, since the first type, economic value, is proper to private for-profit firms, the second, the political value, is the core of the political system (political parties, government, public administration), and the fourth, the cultural value, is proper of several social institutions such as religious ones, churches, ideological movements, etc. It is important to recognize that in a complex society all types of organisations produce all kinds of value, but each of them is defined by its distinctive value production.

Fourthly, we identified the concepts, the dimensions and the indicators able to find out an operative definition of the concept of social added value. We detected the organisational internal and external elements (both at the structure and process level), capable to measure the level of production of relational goods and of generation of social capital by an NPO. This allowed us to develop a data collection tool, in a *pilot version*, and to test it during an empirical research with 12 case studies.

As a result of a thorough phase of textual analysis of the qualitative data collected (interviews), which have been written out and codified, we were able to develop several indicators of the capacity of social added value creation by the NPOs. We were also able to elaborate a second version (2.0) of our tool, adding several significant changes in the questions phrasing and wording, and eliminating some questions that have shown not to be related to our research topic.

At the end of our research project we can say that we succeeded in elaborating a refined version of the S.A.V.E. *tool*. There is no doubt that the tool still needs more piloting and to be tested in wider experimental surveys.

But, as clearly emerged during the focus groups with non-profit leaders, we received plenty of feedback that we are in the right pathway toward the setting-up of a measuring instrument able to grasp the *specificity* and *distinctiveness* of this particular type of organisation, namely the non-profit organisations (third sector, civil society, social enterprise, social co-operatives, associations, etc.) in post-modern societies.

References

Barman, E. (2007). *What is the bottom line for nonprofit organization? A history of measurement in the British Voluntary Sector.* In Voluntas, no. 2/2007, London.
Bassi, A., & Colozzi, I. (2009). Leaders of nonprofit (third sector) organizations in Italy: Cultures of three types of organizations. *International Leadership Journal*, *1*(3/4), Spring/Summer 2009.
Bassi, A. (2010). La mosaïque coopérative. Stratégies de réseaux de la coopération sociale à ravenne, in Xabier Itcaina (sous la direction de), La politique du lien, Les nouvelles dynamiques territoriales de l'économie sociale et solidaire, aux Presse Universitaire de Rennes, pp. 109–126.
Bassi, A. (2011). The social added value of third sector organizations. *EMES conferences selected papers series*. ECSP-R11-28. http://www.emes.net/index.php?id=538.
Bassi, A. (2012). Another brick in the wall. Housing policy as a means to social integration: the role of nonprofit organizations. A case study in the municipality of Ravenna-Italy, in Juan-Luis Klein (sous la direction de), Pour une nouvelle mondialisation: le défi d'innover, Presses de l'Université du Québec (Social Innovation Séries), Montréal, Canada.
Bertin, G., Sonda, G., & Palutan, C. (2008). Definire e valutare la qualità nelle imprese sociali. Percorso metodologico e strumenti di analisi, Quaderni di RESTORE no. 6, Trento, 2008.
Bourdieu, P. (1980). Le Capital Social: note provisoires. In Acte de la recherche en sciences sociales, no. 3.

Bourdieu, P. (1986). The forms of capital. In J. G. Richardson (Ed.), *Handbook of theory and research for the sociology of education*. New York: Greenwood Press.
Coleman, J. (1988). Social capital in the creation of human capital. *American Journal of Sociology*, 94, 95–120.
Coleman, J. (1990). *Foundation of social theory*. Cambridge: Harvard University Press.
Colozzi, I. (2005). Cosa sono i beni relazionali: un confronto fra approcci economici e approccio sociologico. *Sociologia, 2*, 13–20.
Colozzi, I. (2006). Terzo settore e valutazione di qualità. *Misurare la produzione di beni relazionali. Lavoro Sociale, 6*(3), 411–419.
Colozzi, I., & Bassi, A. (2003). *Da terzo settore a imprese sociali*. Carocci Faber: Introduzione all'analisi delle organizzazioni non profit.
Donati, P. (1996). Che cos'è il terzo settore: cultura, normatività, organizzazione, ruolo societario. In P. Donati (Ed.), *Sociologia del Terzo settore*. Roma: NIS-La Nuova Italia Scientifica.
Donati, P. (1997). L'analisi sociologica del terzo settore: introdurre la distinzione relazionale terzo settore/privato sociale. In G. Rossi (Ed.), *Terzo settore, stato e mercato nella trasformazione delle politiche sociali in Europa*. Milano: Franco Angeli.
Donati, P. (2007). L'approccio relazionale al capitale sociale. In P. Donati (Ed.), *Il capitale sociale. L'approccio relazionale, numero monografico della rivista "Sociologia e Politiche Sociali"* (10th ed., Vol. 1). Milano: Franco Angeli.
Donati, P. (2008). Introduzione. Il capitale sociale come qualità della società civile. In P. Donati & L. Tronca (Eds.), *Il capitale sociale degli italiani*. Milano: Franco Angeli.
Durkheim, E. (1911). Giudizi di valore e giudizi di realtà. In E. Durkheim, Sociologia e Filosofia (a cura di) Bouclé C. (1924).
Enciclopedia dell'Economia (2001). Milano: Garzanti.
Godbout, J. T. (1992). *L'Esprit du don*. Paris: Edition La Découverte.
Hertz, N. (2002). *The silent takeover. Global capitalism and the death of democracy*. London: Arrow.
Hertz, N. (2006). *I.O.U. The debt threat and why we must defuse it*. London: Harper Perennial.
Kendall, J., & Knapp, M. (2000). Measuring the performance of voluntary organizations. *Public Management Review, 2*(1), 105–132.
Klein, N. (2007). *The shock doctrine: The rise of disaster capitalism*. New York: Picador.
Latouche, S. (2004). Survivre au développement. De la décolonisation de l'imaginaire économique à la construction d'une société alternative, Vol. II Petit traité de la décroissance sereine, Editions Mille et une Nuits, Paris.
Mulgan, G. (2010). Measuring social value. *Stanford Social Innovation Review*, Summer *8*(3), 38–43.
Nef-New Economic Foundation. (2009). *A bit rich: Calculating the real value to society of different professions*, Nef, London.
Nyssens, M. (Ed.). (2006). *Social enterprise – At the crossroads of market public policies and civil society*. London/New York: Routledge.
Patel, R. (2009). *The value of nothing. How to reshape market society and redefine democracy*. London: Portobello.
Parsons, T. (1951). *The social system*. New York: Free Press.
Porter, M. E., & Kramer, M. R. (2011). Creating shared value. How to reinvent capitalism and unleash a wave of innovation and growth. *Harvard Business Review*, January–February 2011, *89*, 2–17.
Putnam, R. (1993). Making democracy work. Princeton: Princeton University Press. Trad. It., La tradizione civica nelle regioni Italiane, Mondadori, Milano.
Putnam, R. (1993a). The Prosperous community: Social capital and public life. *The American Prospect, 4*(13), 1–11.
Putnam, R. (1995). Bowling alone: America's declining social capital. *Journal of Democracy, 6*, 65–78.

Putnam, R. (1995a). The strange disappearance of civic America. *The American Prospect, 28*(4), 664–683.
Rey Garcia, M. (2008). Evaluating the organizational performance and social impact of third sector organizations: A new functional realm of nonprofit marketing. Paper presented at the 8th International Conference of ISTR (Working Papers Volume. www.istr.org).
Stiglitz, J., Sen, A., & Fitoussi, J.-P. (2009). Report by the commission on the measurement of economic performance and social progress, Paris.
Weber, M. (1995). *Economia e Società* (Vol. I). Milano: Edizioni di Comunità.
Westall, A. (2009). Value and the third sector. Working paper on ideas for future research. Third Sector Research Centre, Working paper 25.
Zingarelli, N. (2012). *lo Zingarelli 2012, Vocabolario della lingua italiana*. Bologna: Zanichelli.

Part VIII
Social Innovation and the Social Sciences

Social Innovation and Action Research

Bjørn Gustavsen

Abstract The ability to perform innovation is dependent upon the way in which the relevant actors are organized. This becomes of particular importance when emphasis is on experience-based innovation, on the ability of the wider social context to support innovation, and on the need to create innovation that can meet the demand for social responsibility. This contribution traces the development of a research tradition where the point of departure was research-driven experiments with alternative forms of work organization but which has become subject to a communicative turn as well as a turn towards change that can involve many actors simultaneously. In its present shape the tradition emerges as a distributive set of activities with the idea of democratic dialogue as the core and a strong emphasis on notions like networks and regions. This research tradition has played a major role in establishing Scandinavia as the leading area for "learning organization" in Europe. The article concludes by discussing some of the challenges facing "bottom-up" change in working life today: the increasing dominance of centrally managed systems thinking, a possible reduction in influence from the labor market parties and an associated breakdown of the strong links between the local and the central and, third, difficulties associated with integrating and giving a society level profile to a pattern of distributive research.

1 Introduction

Although it has always been reason to assume that the ability of people to innovate is dependent upon the organizational context in which they exist, it was during the 1960s that the relationship between organization and innovation became subject to broader social science analyses, i.e. Burns and Stalker (1961). The link to action

---

B. Gustavsen (✉)
Work Research Institute, Oslo, Norway
e-mail: bjoern.gustavsen@afi.no

research emerged through a series of field experiments with autonomous forms of work organization, where the promotion of learning in work was a major theme. With its point of origin in the UK and Norway (Emery and Thorsrud 1976), the idea of doing research-driven field experiments around the notion of learning in work spread, during the 1970s, to a number of other countries, such as Denmark (Agersnap 1973), Sweden (Sandberg 1982), Germany (Fricke 1975), Holland (Beinum and Vliest 1979), Italy (Butera 1975), the US (Duckles et al. 1977) and more.

The major experiment in Norway occurred in a process plant where a traditional specialized organization, based on three separate hierarchies for, respectively, the factory, the control room, and maintenance, was replaced by autonomous shift groups, where each group covered all the functions. Initially giving rise to much conflict, this experiment was successively forgotten among the local actors. By the 1990s, however, international competition, in combination with a loss of national advantages, such as cheap energy, forced forth a strong wave of rationalization and change. While the actors did not want to turn back to the specific organizational solutions of the 1960s, they wanted to maintain, and further develop, the kind of labor-management co-operation that had been a major prerequisite for the experiments of the 1960s. Contact, although sporadic, had been maintained with the research group responsible for the original experiment, and this group was now called in to help promote new and more intensive forms of collaboration (Qvale 2011). The first step in the new process was to set up a forum for experience exchange between representatives from management and unions from all the major process plants located in the area (the area – called Grenland – has the largest assembly of process plants in Scandinavia). As the co-operation between the plants intensified, there emerged a need to strengthen the internal processes within each plant, so as to avoid "the network perspective" overrunning internal processes. In the third phase, the participating plants agreed to explore co-operation around issues like maintenance, moving on from there to look into possible joint products and services for external sale. The next step was to include local suppliers in the co-operation. The most major step occurred, however, when regional political and administrative actors were pulled in, providing the platform for a joint regional development policy with initiatives that span from improved work processes to the establishment of a new R&D laboratory through the merger and reconstruction of the quality control departments that used to exist in all the process plants. Included are also initiatives to improve on roads and harbors. Today, the region appears, in spite of the shut-down of three of the major plants, as a highly successful region, with more people employed than ever before. In addition to a continuous synthetization of experiences, research has designed and organized the substantial and complex series of encounters needed to get this machinery on its feet (Qvale 2011).

While this case is unique in terms of the length of the co-operation between research and industry, it is not unique in terms of activity pattern. Beginning in the 1980s, there has been a continuous development of projects where the main point is to bring formerly separate actors together, or improve on existing relationships, to create new processes of communication (Gustavsen 1992). Haga (2007) reports, for instance, from a project where two factories that had co-existed along the banks of a Norwegian fjord for close to a 100 years but never collaborated, were able to start working together, one of the benefits being that waste products from one factory could be used as raw materials for the other. Johnstad (2007) describes the role of research as participant in a process where a former munitions factory was made subject to a process of fission, leading to the establishment of about 30 new companies, with an additional 30 local suppliers. Even when splitting up, the local actors did not want to lose the advantages inherent in being an environment of some size with a substantial industrial competence, and wanted to develop new and network oriented forms of co-operation. One of the results has been the creation of a substantial automobile supply industry. Eriksson et al. (2011) describes how a local university college in Sweden set itself up as an innovation engine in its own region, with a particular emphasis on health care technology, one of the outcomes being a system for safe and easy entrance for health workers to client homes. Ekman and Ahlberg (2011) describe the new demands on co-operation between different categories of health personnel needed to make real the notion of "patient centered care", and some of the innovations to emerge from efforts to meet these demands. Kantola et al. (2011) present a project within the tourist trade in a region in Finland where the main point is to make a substantial number of small enterprises work together, not only in terms of short term practical co-operation, but also in terms of the establishment of a regional identity. The case shows, among other things, how companies as small as consisting of one person can become partners in a development under the orchestration of a regional university college. We can, in a sense, talk about a "wave of development" focusing on expanding co-operation and communication but with much variance and fluid boundaries towards movements that must be seen as based on other ideas .

2 Characteristics

What are the more specific characteristics of the role of research in this kind of development? The characteristics must be seen in the light of some general points concerning innovation: First, the need to consider not only science as an important source of innovation but also the experiences and learning among those concerned (see for instance Asheim 2011). Second, the recognition that innovation often demands an interplay between a number of actors as much as the brilliant thoughts of the exceptional individual, a recognition that has given rise to the notion of "innovation system" (Lundvall 1992; Asheim 2011).

The social sciences generally do not create "technological solutions" in terms of services/products that can function more or less as technology. The contributions of the social sciences must primarily be understood within the framework of the notion of the innovation system as such. What social science can do is help construct the social relationships needed for an innovative process of interaction to occur. While each social science contribution within this kind of context is unique, it is seldom unique in a general, abstract sense.

The need to apply an innovation system perspective is strengthened by two further points: First, while specific forms of innovation can be generated by project groups or similar relatively small units of organization, the existence and success of such units are often dependent upon their wider context. This wider context can be more or less supportive of innovation, and for this reason the promotion of "innovative environments" has become a core issue. In Europe "the region" is often in focus in this context (Asheim and Gertler 2005). Second, in the wake of the finance crisis, the issue of "socially responsible innovation" has entered the scene in full force (Gustavsen 2011). While the "new financial products" that triggered the crisis can be seen as innovations, they were not beneficial to the broader society. The point is, consequently, not only to promote innovation but to promote innovation that can benefit a broad range of actors and society in general. This demands, in turn, that innovation occurs within a context with elements of a broadly framed democratic process.

In sum, the need to promote practice- and learning based forms of innovation, the need to create innovation supportive environments, and the need to make innovation subject to criteria of social responsibility, all demand that many actors are brought into the picture, linked to each other and enabled to develop joint discourses. This creates, in turn, major challenges of organization.

Over the years, "challenges of organization" have been met in different ways. One belief is that everyday experience among everyday actors is all that is needed. Another belief is that "rational technology" automatically reflects itself in "rational organization". If it is thought that some kind of special competence is called for, it has often been in terms of modest inputs, for instance the hiring of one "human resources consultant" to co-ordinate some hundreds of engineers. The problem with such assumptions is that they are not completely faulty. Organization is, after all, an everyday topic for people in everyday situations; otherwise they would not survive for long. In most practical situations it is not possible to set aside large resources for handling issues of organization, and so on. If we believe, however, that "knowledge" can play a role in this sphere, as in all other spheres of life, we need to develop a role for research that does, on the one hand, contribute something that would otherwise not have been there without the skills and competences of people in general being lost.

Since communication and dialogue are well established topics in "theoretical discourse" (cfr. for instance Buber 1970; Bohm 1996; Habermas 1981–1984) we can easily substantiate a claim for the relevance of research-based knowledge about communication. It was, however, not a theoretical "paradigm shift" that initiated "the communicative turn" in Scandinavian work research but new agreements on workplace development made by the labor market parties in Sweden and Norway in the early 1980s. These agreements did not hold forth specific forms of work organization as better than others; what they did was to emphasize the need for the parties locally to consider issues like work organization, collaboration and leadership, and take steps towards improvement. What the agreements actually did, were first and foremost to call for new "local discourses".

When research was asked to help implementing these agreements (Gustavsen 1992), this was the perspective that had to be placed in focus. To some extent the labor market parties attacked this problem themselves. Being accustomed to negotiations between representatives, over quantifiable issues, in an adversarial atmosphere, the labor market parties wanted discourses on local development to follow another pattern. To achieve this, they simply reversed the traditional criteria, to open up for patterns of communication characterized by participation from all concerned, openness towards all kinds of questions, and a co-operative rather than an adversarial atmosphere. This was the raw material on which research set to work.

The task facing research was to work out a more complete set of criteria for the kind of discourse called for by the agreements. This was done through research acting as participant in and organizer of, the kind of events that were called for by the agreements. This triggered a process of events and reflections that over some years generated a set of more specific perspectives on what came to be called "democratic dialogue", along with a series of design criteria for the organization of a kind of event called "the dialogue conference" (Gustavsen and Engelstad 1986). The criteria that eventually came to remain on the list after the process of trial and error were those that seemed able to move the process forwards:

In addition to the ordinary perspectives on dialogue, such as the need to listen to each other, help each other, and generally to treat each other as equal partners, a set of concerns more specifically relating to workplace dialogues were introduced:

First, an approach to how to bring in all concerned. On an abstract level, the issue of who is concerned can give rise to endless discussions. For this reason it was decided to define all concerned as all the people working in those enterprises that were given support under the agreements, and instead let the issue of who would ultimately be concerned be settled stepwise as a part of the process to unfold. As shown by the Grenland case (above), a start in a plant could end in a region. The point was to let this emerge out of practical concerns rather than in-advance theoretical considerations. Second, work experience should be the point of departure. On an arena that is to be seen as democratic, access for all concerned is not enough; the joint agenda must be made up of issues that can be discussed by all. Third, all participants must act on the same arena. When designing a conference, the practical point is that all actors who want to share the dialogue must participate. This may look trivial, but in working life it is quite common for actors to want to participate by written declaration, by proxy, and similar. Fourth, it must be possible for all present to develop an understanding of the issues under discussion. This does not mean that only simple "everyday" issues can be taken up, but that the introduction of other issues takes place over time, as the capacity of the dialogue and the competence of the participants are growing. Fifth, the legitimacy of an argument must be settled on the basis of its content, not its source. Nobody has an in-advance legitimacy over and beyond that of the others. Sixth, the participants should be able to tolerate and handle an increasing degree of difference of opinion. One danger linked to the historically given patterns of co-operation in Scandinavian working life, is that the co-operation attains its own value in such a way that the participants are not willing to put it at risk. Unless the participants can launch increasingly more radical arguments and proposals, the dialogue will hardly be innovative. Seventh: the dialogue should continuously generate agreements on joint practical action. Unless such agreements are generated, and ensuing practical steps taken, a dialogue in a workplace development context is pointless. The demand for agreement does not mean that all divergent perspectives and interests among the participants are to be merged. What is called for are practical agreements on things the local parties will do together; what motives and interests hide "behind" these agreements are up to the parties themselves. Eighth: The conference itself should generate a plan concerning who is to do what in the first period after the conference.

Along with the dialogue criteria there was also a development of criteria for the design of conferences. Some examples: There should be no introductory speeches or other forms of talks. The conference should go directly into a working mode involving all participants. Time is a scarce resource and has to be not only treated with respect but also shared equally between the participants. All time frames are to be unconditionally observed. The participants themselves perform all tasks of chairmanship, reporting etc., on the basis of rotation. The topics of a conference can vary, but the first conference in a process of development should focus on four main issues: future challenges, problems that need to be handled to overcome the challenges, ideas of relevance in this context and, finally, action program. The themes may be seen as trivial, but they are easily recognized as important by the participants, and function better in terms of triggering discourse than more complex and "advanced" themes. Groups constitute the main arena for discussion. It is only within groups of up to 10 persons that participants not accustomed to speaking in assemblies will be able to develop communicative competence in a discussion. The groups can be put together in different ways; common are to use homogenous groups in the first round (groups where all participants have the same kind of role in their respective organizations); diagonal groups (where, say, management in one department face workers from another) in the second, freely composed groups in the ideas session and, finally, groups made up of those who need to work together after the conference. The group discussions are to not be referred, but each group must tell the plenary what conclusions it has reached. The reports are not subject to broad discussion. The referee as well as the chairman are elected by the group. The reports constitute the backbone of a conference report that functions as the platform for the first round of a development process. The ideal number of participants in a conference of this kind is around 40. Then there will be a reasonable number of people present and possibilities for a cross-fertilization of relationships and ideas, at the same time as the number of groups can be limited to four. Since the demand also is that "all concerned" should take part, 40 is sometimes too few. Conferences can, if so needed, be organized with as much as 100 participants, and it is possible to run several conferences in parallel, with some general meeting points. There are also other ways in which to meet the demand for participation from all concerned (Engelstad 1996). Duration can vary, but it is hardly possible to draw the benefits of this kind of encounter with a duration of less than one full working day, preferably from lunch to lunch, leaving an evening for social purposes.

One reason why dialogue criteria and the design of encounters have been presented in some degree of detail is to demonstrate how this kind of research works. Rather than focusing on the abstract, hidden, or "deep" aspects of dialogue, focus is on what to do in actual practice, the guiding principle being "what works". It may be a triviality but the one who wants to influence practical events needs practical solutions.

The use of dialogue conferences mushroomed during the 1980s, in particular in Norway, where as much as 600 enterprises may have participated in one version or other of the dialogue conference (Gustavsen 1993), but to some extent also in Sweden (Naschold 1993). Although the idea of dialogue conference was met with enthusiasm among many local labor market parties the ability to generate long term development processes was limited, in particular in the beginning. As the criteria for dialogue and design successively came to cover more ground, the ability of the conferences to generate further activity grew. Towards the end of the decade the number of projects and project supportive activities showed an upward curve, while the use of conferences went down (Gustavsen 1993).

As the continuous project work started to take over as the prime driving force, the notion of democratic dialogue and its expression in the notion of dialogue conference has changed. The criteria of the dialogue conference have more and more come to function as reference points to be implemented in a number of different contexts, but also in a differentiated way. Johnsen (2011) reports, for instance, the case of the transformation of the patterns of communication in a process plant, away from the limited, adversarial kind of communication characterizing traditional negotiations, and to a pattern characterized by close co-operation on a number of different arenas. To create this transformation took several years and a number of initiatives, ranging from dialogue conferences via different forms of meetings, inquiries of various forms, to a joint study tour to another enterprise. The breakthrough cannot be linked unequivocally to one of the measures but must rather be seen in the light of the overall impact of the whole package. In all the initiatives the criteria of a "pure" dialogue conference were applied but generally mixed with other ingredients. A number of new types of arenas have emerged, such as on the spot meetings between those concerned to handle acute problems (Claussen 2003); dialogically structured frameworks for discussing "best practices" (Arnkil and Spangar 2011); arenas for "network reflection" (Gausdal 2008) and many more. Pålshaugen (2001a) has explored the potential of direct intervention in ongoing workplace discourses without establishing any new arenas at all. Given the magnitude of units, bodies, and arenas dedicated to the task of creating change, several concepts have appeared for the purpose of providing an overall name for them all; the most widely used are "learning network" (Alasoini et al. 2011) and "development organization" (Pålshaugen 2001b). Given this process of differentiation, the original dialogue conference emerges, in spite of its pragmatic origin, as an "ideal type", to find expression in many different forms and contexts. It is also important to note that even though "the dialogue conference" appears as the most idealized expression of the communicative turn in working life, a successful development presupposes much more than one conference or even a sequence of conferences. A long term development will go through different phases with different demands as activities and supportive structures are concerned.

3 Impact

While most action research – and other forms as well – is built on the notion of making – or finding – an exceptional case, presenting it to the world in terms of a theoretical interpretation, and hoping that "the world will listen", the kind of research indicated above does not assume that the world is willing to listen, nor to read. The assumption is, instead, that broad change will have to emerge from nodes of new practices through processes where new actors link to the nodes, making them grow. Research is organized in such a way that it can help initiate a number of nodes, thereby enabling a number of processes to emerge (Gustavsen 2007b). Each process is characterized by a blend of general and local elements. How well does this strategy work?

No country – the Scandinavian ones not excepted – has a working life research that enables us to unequivocally identify what working life looks like nor what forces lie behind. What can be done is to combine different indicators that all have their shortcomings but where some kind of a general picture can be made. In this context, only a couple of such indicators can be mentioned:

Since Finland as well as Norway have explicitly structured general programs to promote workplace development based on democratic forms of communication, there are central data bases. Projects largely following the pattern indicated above covers, in Finland, at the moment, about 300 000 workplaces; the corresponding program in Norway – administered by the national research council – has about 1,100 user enterprises. There are, however, many versions of the pattern, as well as fluid boundaries between this pattern and other patterns. Denmark and Sweden are lacking explicit programs at the moment, but a number of developments along the same lines are reported. While these figures are far from modest, they nonetheless identify limited slices of working life, roughly about 10 % of the total labor market. Furthermore, information centrally available does not necessarily tell all that much about the more specific nature of each local development. On the other hand: the present emphasis on democratic forms of communication has, in all likelihood, to some extent spread to the rest of working life. Of interest in this context are the work organization surveys performed regularly by the European Foundation for the Improvement of Living and Working Conditions. Using criteria like variation, control and freedom in the work role, the surveys can be used to develop some perspectives on learning in work and, through this, on the potential for innovation. Lorenz and Lundvall (2011) identify, on the basis of the relationship between demand for learning and freedom to learn, four main patterns: "Learning organization", characterized by (relatively) high scores on both; "lean organization" characterized by high on learning, low on freedom, "Taylorism", characterized by low on both, and "traditional" characterized by a non-reflective relationship to such issues as freedom and learning in work. All forms are present in all societies; the differences pertain to degree. On top as learning organization is concerned are, however, the Scandinavian countries: Denmark, Finland, Norway and Sweden. The Scandinavian countries belong, furthermore, to the countries that show a (relatively) high score on income per capita. If we combine income and learning in work, the Scandinavian countries constitute a group of their own, followed closely, however, by countries like Switzerland and Holland. Major industrial societies like the UK and Germany seem to show more of the "lean" pattern, while southern Europe is more strongly characterized by traditionalism (for a more thorough analysis, see Lorenz and Lundvall 2011).

Learning organization as defined through criteria for job design is not fully identical to learning organization as defined through criteria of communication. That there is a high degree of interaction is, however, substantiated by a number of research projects as well as by common sense. Most of the criteria for freedom and discretion in the job – such as influence over working conditions – can be made real only through communication. The task-oriented criteria for freedom – or autonomy – in work originally worked out by "the socio-technical school" (Herbst 1962) are not to be abandoned, but they need to be supplemented by criteria emanating from the idea of democratic communication.

It is obviously not possible for research to claim to be "the cause" of the Scandinavian picture. Most interpreters see the Scandinavian pattern in the light of the more general co-operation between the labor market parties and between these parties on the one hand and the government on the other. This co-operation is, however, not abstract. Rather, it finds its expression in specific acts and measures; measures to promote learning in work being no exception. There are grounds for claiming that research that can help promote learning in concrete, practical terms has been, and is, a major element. There have, generally, been more initiatives aiming at promoting learning in work in Scandinavia than elsewhere in Europe, and more use of research in this context (Gustavsen 2007a). Scandinavian programs seem, furthermore, more oriented towards the creation of open learning situations than what is generally the case in Europe, where more emphasis is placed on the implementation of pre-specified socio-technical patterns (Alasoini 2011). There is, furthermore, little doubt that research has not only been an executive body for the labor market parties and other central institutions, but has in itself exerted a major impact on what learning has occurred among these institutions.

4 Challenges

The processes described, however briefly, above, have a "bottom-up" character. They emanate from a number of local environments, each process being strongly influenced by the specific characteristics of this environment. Stepwise, as the processes grow in number, scope and impact, there emerge linking points on higher levels, for instance the region, but also the nation. "The Scandinavian model" of interplay between micro-, meso- and macro levels was largely worked out before the 1980s. The last three decades have generally been characterized by minor adjustments. The major exception is Norway, where the very large oil and gas incomes have made it possible for the central political actors to continuously expand their activities into the regional, local and civil spheres. Some years ago most of the health services were transferred from local-regional ownership and administration, to state administration. The impacts of this reform are unclear. There is, however, much to indicate that while the performances that can be controlled through mechanical measures on high levels of administration are improved, those that depend on a high local learning capacity and an ability to create those finely tuned relationships between the people concerned needed to make real concepts like patient centered care (Ekman and Ahlberg 2011) are suffering. Under present conditions as steering systems are concerned (data-based systems, economism, New Public Management, evidence based policy and other evaluation schemes) there seems to emerge a real threat along the line characterized by Habermas (1971) as the colonization of the life world by the systems world.

A major element in the kind of development described above is the orientation and co-operation of the labor market parties. Its importance does not lie only in the point that the unions and the employer organizations represent the actors in working life, but also in the rather close and direct relationships that exist between top and bottom as both parties are concerned. The labor market parties centrally have to keep a very careful track of what goes on among the membership and in this way provide a strong link between top and bottom. This link has provided the main balancing mechanism between the central political sphere and the civil sphere as working life is concerned. During the 1960s and 1970s there emerged a union membership dissatisfaction with the overall progress of the labor movement on the political as well as the local levels, in particular in Sweden. The major Swedish union confederations initially negotiated with the employer confederations about change; but when negotiations did not provide the desired results, they turned to the social-democratic governments and demanded legislation. Two of the main results were the Co-determination Act, expanding the rights of the unions to demand information and negotiation in various contexts, such as rationalization measures, and the establishment of wage earners funds, demanding that the companies put some of their profits into shares to be administered by funds with politically appointed steering bodies (Meidner 1978). While it turned out to be possible for the employers to agree with the unions on how to handle the Co-Determination Act, a similar agreement was impossible as the wage earners funds were concerned. After a short period they were abandoned, but in the meantime the employers had decided to put co-operation on workplace issues in the freezer. Stepwise, this was accompanied by the deconstruction of the various institutions that had been established over the years to handle the myriad of issues emanating from co-operation in working life. The process reached its end point when the present conservative government entered office in 2006, and closed the National Institute for Working Life; the result of a series of mergers and closures that started in the middle 1990s.

A strategy for change consisting of a number of processes emanating from different local environments implies that the associated research starts out with a high degree of differentiation. Unless the processes can eventually be linked, seen in the light of each other, and be argued to constitute "one wave of change" they will lack visibility on the national scene. For this reason, a distributive approach to change is critically dependent upon a successive link-up between the different units of change. This is one of the main reasons why much of the efforts to promote learning in work in Scandinavia have been organized in the form of "programs" that can function as umbrellas and linking mechanisms for a number of projects. Although we face, again, a picture characterized by much variation, it is a clear impression that this integration is lagging behind. Under the pressure of "conventional academism" the research groups put much emphasis on constructing theories at the expense of clarifying and reporting results. In constructing theory there is a tendency to link up to many different schools of thought, resulting in an exceedingly complex conceptual landscape that can only with difficulties be communicated not only outside the programs but even between the groups within each program. What is intended to be "one movement" easily looks, from a distance, like scattered projects occurring at many different institutions under different headings. From a research policy angle this is not a particularly beneficial situation.

The expansion of systems thinking, the breakdown of the links between top and bottom and the lack of research integration, are trends. They can be observed, together with their consequences. Up to now they constitute challenges, not absolute hindrances. A major advantage is that they do not occur everywhere simultaneously, but tend to spread out over countries as well as over time. The historically given close relationship between the Scandinavian countries generally makes it possible to move on in some contexts when it becomes impossible in other contexts. Looking at the period from the 1970s, Sweden was for a long time the leading country as initiatives to promote learning in work was concerned. Workplace projects occurred on a substantial scale, institutions to support the development were established not only in numbers but also in size, one example being the Work Life Fund that spent, in the period 1990–1995 about 10 billion SEK (one billion Euros) to create 25000 projects covering half of working life (Gustavsen et al. 1996). When problems started to pile up in Sweden, Norway and Finland took over as workplace development programs were concerned (Gustavsen 2007a), and so on. It is not necessary to handle all problems in all places at the same time. What is called for is progress in some places that can be used to re-create development in other places.

While "the Scandinavian scene" may be seen as providing fruitful conditions for approaching contemporary challenges, the problems again grow if we assume that these challenges are not peculiar to Scandinavia. It is the fact that working life has attracted much attention in Scandinavia, that the labor market parties have been active, and that measures to promote learning have been many as well as differentiated; that makes it possible to draw the kind of picture of an overall situation done above. But is it unique to Scandinavia? A pattern where many different research groups work with a number of different local research and development projects, with modest links between them, under conditions where the visibility of each project is limited, impacts unclear and, in addition, often overrun by the effects of central policies, seems to be the picture in large parts of Europe. It can be argued that what we face is nothing less than the future of social research as an actor with responsibility for the promotion of a better world.

The discourses on this span far beyond those on "action research". In fact, it can be argued that the emphasis on "large theories" built not only on "small cases", but often few of them as well, is a characteristic also of action research. Even action research generally needs to shift its focus, from demonstrating theories to creating change (Gustavsen 2003). Change is not "exceptional cases" but actually the opposite; a number of cases that all evolve in the same direction, at the same time as they represent something new. Such movements call for integration, co-operation and an orientation towards what is achieved. In a review of Gergen's most recent book – "Relational Being" (Gergen 2009; Gustavsen 2010) – this author had occasion to wholeheartedly agree with Gergen, but at the same time to argue that the greatest need at the moment is not for being told once more that we live our life in relationships, but for specific research approaches that can reflect "the relational" in the ways in which we, as researchers, relate not only to our project partners but to our own research community as well.

References

Agersnap, F. (1973). Samarbejdsforsøg I jernindustrien. København: Foreningen af Verkstedfunktionærer i Danmark/Centralorganisationen af Metalarbejdere i Danmark/Sammensludningen af Arbejdsgivere indenfor jern-og metalindustrien i Danmark.

Alasoini, T. (2011). Strategies to promote workplace innovation: A comparative analysis of nine national and regional approaches. In M. Ekman, B. Gustavsen, B. T. Asheim, & Ø. Pålshaugen (Eds.), *Learning regional innovation: Scandinavian models* (pp. 253–273). London: MacMillan-Palgrave.

Arnkil, R., & Spangar, T. (2011). Open and integrated peer-learning spaces in municipal development. In T. Alasoini, M. Lahtonen, N. Rouhaininen, C. Sweins, K. Hulkko-Nyman, & T. Spangar (Eds.), *Linking theory and practice. Learning networks at the service of workplace innovation. Tykes report 75* (pp. 144–165). Helsinki: Tekes.

Asheim, B. T. (2011). Learning, organization and participation: Nordic experiences in a global context with a focus on innovation systems and work organization. In M. Ekman, B. Gustavsen, B. T. Asheim, & Ø. Pålshaugen (Eds.), *Learning regional innovation: Scandinavian models* (pp. 15–49). London: MacMillan-Palgrave.

Asheim, B. T., & Gertler, M. S. (2005). The geography of innovation: Regional innovation systems. In J. Fagerberg, D. Mowery, & R. Nelson (Eds.), *The Oxford handbook of innovation* (pp. 291–317). Oxford: Oxford University Press.

van Beinum, H., & van der Vliest, R. (1979). QWL developments in Holland: An overview. In: The international council for the quality of working life (Eds.), *Working on the quality of working life* (pp 93–110). Nijhoff: Leiden.

Bohm, D. (1996). *On dialogue*. New York: Routledge.

Buber, M. (1970). *I and thou*. New York: Scribner.

Burns, T., & Stalker, G. M. (1961). *The management of innovation*. London: Tavistock Publications.

Butera, F. (1975). Environmental factors in job and organization design: The case of Olivetti. In L. E. Davis & A. Cherns (Eds.), *The quality of working life* (Vol. 2, pp. 166–200). New York: The Free Press.

Claussen, T. (2003). Participation and enterprise networks within a regional context: Examples from south-west Norway. In W. Fricke & P. Totterdill (Eds.), *Action research in workplace innovation and regional development* (pp. 83–102). Amsterdam: John Benjamins.

Duckles, M. M., Duckels, R., & Maccoby, M. (1977). Process of change at Bolivar. *The Journal of Applied Behavioral Science, 13*(3), 387–399.

Ekman, M., & Ahlberg, B. M. (2011). Incremental innovations in organizational performance in health care. In M. Ekman, B. Gustavsen, B. T. Asheim, & Ø. Pålshaugen (Eds.), *Learning regional innovation: Scandinavian models* (pp. 104–119). London: MacMillan-Palgrave.

Emery, F. E., & Thorsrud, E. (1976). *Democracy at work*. Leiden: Nijhoff.

Engelstad, P. H. (1996). The development organization as communicative instrumentation. In S. Toulmin & B. Gustavsen (Eds.), *Beyond theory. Changing organizations through participation* (pp. 89–118). Amsterdam: John Benjamins.

Eriksson, H., Haga, T., & Hofmaier, B. (2011). The initiation and organization of regional innovation processes. In M. Ekman, B. Gustavsen, B. T. Asheim, & Ø. Pålshaugen (Eds.), *Learning regional innovation: Scandinavian models* (pp. 150–169). London: MacMillan-Palgrave.

Fricke, W. (1975). *Arbeitsorganisation und Qualifikation*. Bonn: Schriftenreihe des Forschungsinstitut der Friedrich Ebert Stiftung, Neue Gesellschaft.

Gausdal, A. (2008). Developing regional communities of practice by network reflection: The case of the Norwegian electronics industry. *Entrepreneurship and Regional Development, 20*, 209–235.

Gergen, K. J. (2009). *Relational being: Beyond self and community*. Oxford: Oxford University Press.

Gustavsen, B. (1992). *Dialogue and development*. Assen: van Gorcum.

Gustavsen, B. (1993). Creating productive structures: The role of research and development. In F. Naschold, B. Gustavsen, R. Cole, & H. van Beinum (Eds.), *Constructing the new industrial society* (pp. 133–168). Assen: van Gorcum.

Gustavsen, B. (2003). Action research and the problem of the single case. *Concepts and Transformations, 8*(1), 97–103.

Gustavsen, B. (2007a). Work organization and "the Scandinavian model". *Economic and Industrial Democracy, 28*(4), 650–671.

Gustavsen, B. (2007b). Research responses to practical challenges: What can action research do? *International Journal of Action Research, 3*(1–2), 93–111.

Gustavsen, B. (2010). Review of K. J. Gergen: Relational being: Beyond self and community. *International Journal of Action Research, 6*(1), 139–146.

Gustavsen, B. (2011). Innovation, participation and "constructivist society". In M. Ekman, B. Gustavsen, B. T. Asheim, & Ø. Pålshaugen (Eds.), *Learning regional innovation: Scandinavian models* (pp. 1–14). London: MacMillan-Palgrave.

Gustavsen, B., & Engelstad, P. H. (1986). The design of conferences and the evolving role of democratic dialogue in changing working life. *Human Relations, 39*(2), 101–116.

Gustavsen, B., Hofmaier, B., Ekman-Philips, M., & Wikman, A. (1996). *Concept driven development and the organization of the process of change*. Amsterdam: John Benjamins.

Habermas, J. (1971). *Knowledge and human interest*. New York: Beacon.

Habermas, J. (1981–1984). Theorie des Kommunikativen Handelns (English translation). *The theory of communicative action* (1984). Boston: MIT Press.

Haga, T. (2007). The role of development facilitators in company innovation in Norway. In B. Gustavsen, B. Nyhan, & R. Ennals (Eds.), *Learning together for local innovation. Promoting learning regions. CEDEFOP Reference series 68* (pp. 66–77). Luxembourg: Office for Official Publications of the European Communities.

Herbst, P. G. (1962). *Autonomous group functioning and exploration in behavior theory and measurement*. London: Tavistock Publications.

Johnsen, H. C. G. (2011). Discourse and change in organizations. In M. Ekman, B. Gustavsen, B. T. Asheim, & Ø. Pålshaugen (Eds.), *Learning regional innovation: Scandinavian models* (pp. 93–103). London: MacMillan-Palgrave.

Johnstad, T. (2007). Raufoss: From a learning company to a learning region. In B. Gustavsen, B. Nyhan, & R. Ennals (Eds.), *Learning together for local innovation. Promoting learning regions. CEDEFOP reference series 68* (pp. 102–110). Luxembourg: Office for Official Publications of the European Communities.

Kantola, T., Lassila, S., Mäntylä, H., Ayvari, A., Kalliokoski, S., Ritalahti, J., Sipila, A., & Saisalon-Soininen, T. (2011). Shared learning spaces as enablers in regional development. In M. Ekman, B. Gustavsen, B. T. Asheim, & Ø. Pålshaugen (Eds.), *Learning regional innovation: Scandinavian models* (pp. 206–225). London: MacMillan-Palgrave.

Lorenz, E., & Lundvall, B. Å. (2011). The organization of work and systems of labour market regulation and social protection: A comparison of the EU-15. In M. Ekman, B. Gustavsen, B. T. Asheim, & Ø. Pålshaugen (Eds.), *Learning regional innovation: Scandinavian models* (pp. 50–69). London: MacMillan-Palgrave.

Lundvall, B. Å. (Ed.). (1992). *National systems of innovation*. London: Pinter.

Meidner, R. (1978). *Employee investment funds: an approach to collective capital formation*. London: Allen and Unwin.

Naschold, F. (1993). Organization development: National programmes in the context of international competition. In F. Naschold, B. Gustavsen, R. Cole, & H. van Beinum (Eds.), *Creating the new industrial society* (pp. 3–105). Assen: van Gorcum.

Pålshaugen, Ø. (2001a). The use of words: Improving enterprises by improving their conversations. In P. Reason & H. Bradbury (Eds.), *Handbook of action research: participative inquiry and practice* (1st ed., pp. 163–180). London: Sage Publications.

Pålshaugen, Ø. (2001b). The competitive advantage of development organizations. *Concepts and Transformations, 5*(2), 237–255.

Qvale, T. U. (2011). Participative democracy and the diffusion of organizational innovations. In M. Ekman, B. Gustavsen, B. T. Asheim, & Ø. Pålshaugen (Eds.), *Learning regional innovation: Scandinavian models* (pp. 187–205). London: MacMillan-Palgrave.

Sandberg, T. (1982). *Work organization and autonomous groups*. Lund: Gleerup.

Towards Advancing Understanding of Social Innovation

Anne de Bruin

Abstract This paper advances understanding of social innovation on two fronts. First it reflects on the role and responsibility of researchers in advancing social innovation and traces the purpose and activities of the New Zealand Social Innovation and Entrepreneurship Research Centre to illustrate how academic institutes might catalyze social innovation. Second, it highlights parallel discourses following either more micro- or macro-level leanings. At the micro level, accompanying a growing literature on social entrepreneurship is an embedded discussion on social innovation linked to innovations by social entrepreneurs. More overarching research centres on broad processes of innovation, implications of a new innovation paradigm and social innovations concerning societal issues. Bringing these two research streams closer and bridging dichotomous micro-macro perspectives, is necessary for a holistic view of innovation that recognizes social innovation as a crucial facet of innovation systems.

1 Introduction

Now more than ever before, social innovation has a crucial role to play in society. It can help developed and developing economies cope with the fall-out of the worst financial crisis experienced since the Great Depression. It can make a vital contribution toward addressing significant global challenges including poverty, climate change and sustainable development as well as more national and local level challenges such as unemployment and crime in communities (European Union/ The Young Foundation 2010). The development of social innovation is therefore an urgent task-'one of the most urgent there is' (Mulgan et al. 2007a: 7). Knowledge

---

A. de Bruin (✉)
New Zealand Social Innovation and Entrepreneurship Research Centre, Massey University School of Economics and Finance, Albany Campus, Auckland, New Zealand
e-mail: a.m.debruin@massey.ac.nz

and research on social innovation unfortunately is in its infancy and policy and debate that acknowledges social innovation is embryonic. While it is widely acknowledged that innovation is crucial to economic performance, there is a lopsided focus on technical innovation with relatively little account of social innovation despite its historical, common, and constant presence. Raising awareness that social innovation is an integral facet of any innovation system especially in an era where a new innovation paradigm is taking hold (Howaldt and Schwarz 2010), and mitigating the glaring knowledge gap on social innovation is vital.

This paper seeks to advance understanding and raise awareness of social innovation on two fronts. First, it elaborates on the New Zealand (NZ) experience of social innovation and the role, activities and research agenda of the New Zealand Social Innovation and Entrepreneurship Research Centre (SIERC) and provides concluding comment on the role of researchers. This first discussion is also premised on the beliefs that building the community of like-minded scholars and other interested stakeholders is vital, and that dissemination of country-based social innovation insights is invaluable to growing the field of social innovation. Second, it briefly discusses dichotomous macro and micro strands of the social innovation discourse and a suggestion on how the macro-micro divide might be bridged is made. The paper concludes with comments especially on 'responsible reciprocity' and higher obligations of social science researchers in the field and the need for building a critical mass of interdisciplinary oriented scholars and other like-minded individuals and organisations dedicated to advancing a holistic innovation perspective that incorporates social innovation.

2 New Zealand Insights

NZ, a Pacific Island country with a small population of around 4.4 million is known for the creativity and ingenuity of its people-'Kiwi ingenuity' (Bridges and Downs 2000). NZ has a long tradition of social innovation (though the term social innovation itself is relatively new). For example, the women's suffrage movement in NZ led by Kate Sheppard, resulted in NZ becoming the first country to give women the right to vote in parliamentary elections in 1893. NZ was the trail-blazer. In democracies like Britain and the United States women were granted the right to vote only after the First World War. Leadership in women's suffrage was central to creating NZ 's image as a pioneering 'social laboratory' (Ministry for Culture and Heritage n.d.). A contemporary example of social innovation is in the area of restorative justice. In an attempt to stem the tide of recurring offending by Maori[1] and catalyzed by the establishment of the Restorative Justice Trust in 1999 in Auckland, traditional Maori Restorative Justice is now being revitalized as an alternative to the mainstream criminal justice system. Although forms of restorative

---

[1] *Maori are the indigenous people of NZ.*

justice have been practiced in different cultures over the years, the NZ lead has the model beginning to spread to other communities overseas. Restorative justice schemes also illustrate that a recycling and revitalization process of innovative social practices can take place.

While there are several examples of pioneering social innovation in NZ and there is emphasis on the national system of innovation; until recently social innovation rarely enters the picture in the research and policy discourse. Innovation in science and technology takes pride of place (OECD 2007; Smith 2006). Albeit a small policy advance has been evidenced with establishment in 2010 of the *Quality Services and Innovation Fund*, a 4 year fund to encourage community services to work closely together and develop new innovative ways to improve the efficiency of services and support to children, young people and families; a drastic change in innovation focus to include social innovation is long overdue.

Research, especially in the social sciences, has an important role and responsibility to enhance understanding of *all* facets and forms of innovation. Recent heightened awareness of the importance of social innovation especially in academic circles has seen a corresponding rise in the number of consultancy and research centers devoted to this area (Howaldt and Schwarz 2010). The NZ Social Innovation and Entrepreneurship Research Centre (SIERC), launched in October 2010, is among the latest. It recognises the critical need for more scholarly research on social innovation and entrepreneurship to address social and environmental needs and problems, which in turn must connect with and feed into all stakeholders, including practitioners, policy makers and philanthropists, who could use, benefit and fund this research. It is the only university based research center in NZ, specifically devoted to a social innovation and entrepreneurship research agenda. Its Mission has a straightforward focus: 'To be a centre of research excellence dedicated to advancing social innovation and entrepreneurship in New Zealand and internationally'. Its objectives include more NZ specific foci: 'To become the pre-eminent research centre and knowledge hub for social innovation and entrepreneurship in New Zealand; In association with Government-central, regional and local; professional, business and community groups, to contribute toward social innovation in New Zealand.' Other objectives also emphasize the role of research collaborations and partnerships in building social innovation knowledge: 'To undertake collaborative research within Massey University and with other national and international research groupings' and education and student related aspects also feature as objectives (http://sierc.massey.ac.nz/).

Interdisciplinary research is a core value of SIERC and research associates and external research affiliates are from across the Social Science and Humanities disciplines. Research associates are from all three Massey University campuses and represent a range of disciplines, including economics, management, sociology, accountancy, banking and religious studies. External affiliates are non-Massey University researchers from New Zealand and overseas and are invited to affiliate to the Centre due to their special research expertise and scholarly activities, which are closely aligned to its general mission, a particular research project, or research focus, and/or to their ongoing research collaborations with associates of the Centre.

They are integral to widening the research capability of SIERC, thereby contributing to the fulfillment of its vision of research excellence. External affiliates include Jürgen Howaldt, Director, Sozialforschungsstelle Dortmund, University of Dortmund, Germany and Jill Kickul, Director, Stewart Satter Program in Social Entrepreneurship, New York University, USA.

SIERC's emblem, Harakeke (Phormium tenax) or NZ flax is different from the European variety of flax, has deep meaning for Maori and is a resilient plant used in traditional Maori weaving. It symbolizes the concerted effort and resilience necessary for social innovation and change; the collaborative research approach and partnerships embodied in SIERC; and commitment to entwining research excellence with knowledge advancement in a real world context. In the short time since its launch, SIERC has instituted several initiatives designed to disseminate and grow knowledge in the field. It commenced the 2011 Massey University Albany Campus Innovation Lecture Series-public lectures by internationally reputed speakers on the themes of innovation, entrepreneurship and its social dimension. SIERC's Director Anne de Bruin and external affiliate Eleanor Shaw are co-editing a Special Issue of the *International Small Business Journal* (ISBJ) on the theme 'Social Innovation and Social Entrepreneurship: Extending Theory, Integrating Practice' with the Call for Papers closing in March 2012. The inaugural Massey University Social Innovation and Entrepreneurship Conference, with the same theme was convened by SIERC and held from 1–3 December 2011. It is illustrative of the catalytic role academic institutes can play in advancing the field through the creation of forums for interdisciplinary, like-minded scholars and community stakeholders to share insights and exchange knowledge. The conference brought together the full range of social innovation and entrepreneurship stakeholders to share insights, exchange knowledge and engage in an inclusive dialogue in order to 'extend theory, integrate practice'. With timely publication and availability without charge, from the SIERC website, SIERC hopes to continue the dialogue on social innovation and entrepreneurship through rapid availability and fluid dissemination of the conference proceedings (de Bruin and Stangl 2011).

In addition to being a catalyst of research sharing and dissemination, SIERC driven research is also being undertaken. An ongoing study aims at identification of success factors of social innovation in NZ using interviews and case-study. Preliminary findings highlight effective leadership as important for success and scaleability. There is however, no 'one size fits all'. Transformational leadership, particularly of founders, may be associated with start-up and early funding phase of an organisation formed to address a social need. As an organisation matures, ongoing innovations while remaining closely bound to core values, might become more widely dispersed within the organization, and leadership style could change to being directed to developing and supporting innovation in practice across the organization. Encouragement given to develop creative thinking in others and support for the resulting innovations implemented, results in capacity building in the organization as in the Problem Gambling Foundation New Zealand, an international leader in the field of problem gambling (de Bruin 2011). Leadership style and influences vary too. For example, Philip Patston, founder of Diversityworks, a small trust working to address issues in the disability sector, appears to work within a model that enables and promotes individual agency in a hybrid organisation combining profit and not-for-profit goals. By contrast a collective vision and goals model drives Nuku Rapana who is a social entrepreneur and president of the Pukapuka[2] Island Community in NZ. Success was located for him, in meeting collective goals, and was therefore determined largely from within the community. As a small community within the wider Pasifika[3] network, they had to work out their own ways of meeting these goals that had cultural integrity, which was vital to their wellbeing as a community (de Bruin 2011).

Another key finding concerned the difficulties of measuring social innovation and social impact. For example, difficulties and inadequacies of measuring success in financial terms, and the lack of measures to quantify more important, but less tangibly measurable goals like confidence and morale within the community were highlighted by an interviewee. Another spoke about the need to capture stories for what they can tell about the impact the work has on lives. These stories, which are considered as 'soft measurements', are actually trying to capture the essence of the work done-the 'hard' part of the work. The connections made are what actually facilitate change and empowerment for those who receive the service, and for the most part, hard measures do not capture this effectively (de Bruin 2011).

Social innovation has a strong historical presence (European Commission 2010; Phills et al. 2008). Faith-based organisations for instance have a long history of involvement in social service provision. They are now, however, adapting to new needs in communities and society in innovative ways. This was highlighted during the course of the study. Major Roberts of the Salvation Army, described a philosophy underlying change in his organisation as 'to be in the gap. ... we did have a really extensive aged care component up to a few years ago. . . .when we evaluated, we were no longer providing a gap service. We were providing a service that other people could equally provide and so there was no need for us to be there ... we did pull out of it'. He described a new focus aimed at serving the needs of the elderly where the organisation acted as a volunteer broker by 'linking up need with the person who can meet that need' (de Bruin 2011).

Stephen Goldsmith's 'civic entrepreneur', is an appealing concept to label social entrepreneurs who catalyze and scale social innovation through their ability to build partnerships and navigate the choppy seas of bureaucracy. Civic entrepreneurs can be public servants and elected officials, venture capitalists, philanthropists, faith-based providers, engaged citizens and business leaders promoting new notions of corporate social responsibility. 'Civic entrepreneurship represents both the spirit of change and the spirit of community' (Goldsmith et al. 2010: 6) which entrepreneurial communities resolute on enhancing the quality of life must foster. The presence of civic entrepreneurship in Auckland, NZ, was yet another finding. The former

---

[2] *Pukapuka is in the Northern Cook Islands.*
[3] *Term used for people living in NZ who identify with the Pacific Islands because of their ancestry and heritage.*

North Shore City Council programmes of youth engagement in civic processes are a good example. These emerged as a response to significant problems involving youth in the late 1990s and early 2000s, e.g. disorder, drunkenness and crime associated with large parties at the weekends. This prompted the Council to become more responsive to the needs of youth and seek to engage them in civic life. Converse Youth Forums and Youth Council, were initiatives used to encourage youth to be involved in their community, give voice to their concerns, encourage action to provide their own solutions to perceived problems and to support development of leadership skills. The ongoing processes of Converse Youth Forums and Youth Councils sustained a conversation between youth and the elected local government members. While youth councils are not new and have been around since the early twentieth century, e.g. they were utilised by Nazis to recruit youth into the movement, they illustrate how existing ideas can be renewed in different contexts and for different purposes, as with their adaptation to mitigate locally-based youth-related problems in Auckland.

SIERC's future research agenda plans include a focus on younger people. Youth are the future of a productive knowledge society. Disengaged, unemployed and less productive youth are not only a loss to nations and society, but can be the cause of social problems and unrest. Although NZ's unemployment rate is much lower than the OECD average, NZ's proportion of youth unemployment to total unemployment is higher than any other OECD country. Forty-five percent of NZ's total unemployed are youth (Boven et al. 2011). Social innovation for younger people and also by younger people in NZ, will therefore be a valuable area of research that SIERC will engage with in the future.

Collaboration with overseas researchers, especially enabled by SIERC's external research affiliate network, to undertake comparative research will also be a vital part of SIERC's future research. Thus for example, SIERC will link with the Centre for Charitable Giving and Philanthropy (CGAP) in the UK, to research entrepreneurial philanthropy. Similarly, a comparative study of ecopreneurship in the small scale alternative energy sector between NZ and Sweden, will be driven by collaboration.

3 Bridging the Social Innovation-Social Entrepreneurship Discourse Divide

The shift from an industrial society to a knowledge and service economy, business co-creation of value with customers and engagement with users (Fora 2009), and 'collaborative creativity' with users as the originators of new products (Leadbeater 2010), are key contributors to dramatic change in the processes and structure of innovation. Additionally, businesses are finding new opportunity in global and political challenges and are engaging in 'corporate social innovation' (Fora 2009).

We have moved to a new era of innovation characterized by multiple actors. The call for recognition of a new innovation paradigm (Howaldt and Schwarz 2010) that includes social innovation as an integral and independent facet of innovation is gaining momentum. This discourse on the nature of innovation in general, and the role and importance of social innovation is often an overarching one. It is a more macro level discussion that also encompasses examination of new social practices, behaviors, institutions, customs and mores that are elements of social change.

A parallel discourse is taking place on the nature of social entrepreneurship and activities of social entrepreneurs. This discussion is mainly enveloped as part of the general research agenda on entrepreneurship. As with the field of social innovation, understanding of social entrepreneurship is in its infancy. There is neither consensus on the meaning of the term social entrepreneurship nor the boundaries of the field (Nicholls 2010; Perrini 2006, Short et al. 2009). Social entrepreneurship sits at a fuzzy intersection with entrepreneurship, innovation, social need and change. Research and discourse on social entrepreneurship is conducted at a more micro level. Studies often seek to differentiate social entrepreneurs from their commercial counterparts and engage with the opportunity development strategies and practices of social entrepreneurs themselves (cf. Corner and Ho 2010; di Domenico et al. 2010; Robb-Post et al. 2010). Social innovation is an embedded rather than a dedicated strand of this social entrepreneurship discussion and is linked to innovations by social entrepreneurs.

In order to advance the field of social innovation, the social entrepreneurship research field with its corollary micro discussion of social innovation, must link better with the broader macro perspectives of the general social innovation discourse. The differing strands must be bridged. One critical bridge could be through finding common definitional threads.

Currently, there is lack of a universally accepted definition of social innovation and ambiguity surrounds the term. For example, Howaldt and Schwarz emphasize novel social practices in their definition: 'A social innovation is a new combination and/or new configuration of social practices in certain areas of action or social contexts prompted by certain actors or constellations of actors in an intentional targeted manner with the goal of better satisfying or answering needs and problems than is possible on the basis of established practices.' (2010: 21). By contrast, the social problem-solution aspect is the focus of definition provided by Phills et al. who define social innovation as 'A novel solution to a social problem that is more effective, efficient, sustainable or just than existing solutions and for which the value created accrues primarily to society as a whole rather private individuals' (2008: 36). Similarly, the working definition of the LEED Forum on Social Innovations (OECD 2000) emphasizes that social innovation 'seeks new answers to social problems'. Meeting social needs is the angle that Mulgan et al. (2007b: 9) prefer when they define 'social innovations as the development and implementation of new ideas (products, services and models) to meet social needs.' This absence of definitional consensus is however, not unexpected for a new field of study and given the complexity of social innovation.

As in the field of social innovation, there is no consensus definition of social entrepreneurship. A lack of definitional consensus is, however, not surprising since social entrepreneurship is a new sub-area of entrepreneurship research, and a universally accepted definition even of entrepreneurship is yet to emerge. Nevertheless there is consensus that opportunity recognition, pursuit and development lies at the heart of entrepreneurship and entrepreneurial activity (cf. Ardichvili et al. 2003; Shane and Venkataraman 2000). The centrality of opportunity is recognized in the social entrepreneurship definition of Zahra et al. who highlight, 'Social entrepreneurship encompasses the activities and processes undertaken to discover, define, and exploit opportunities in order to enhance social wealth by creating new ventures or managing existing organizations in an innovative manner' (Zahra et al. 2008: 118). It is worthwhile also to note that this definition places innovation at the core of opportunity identification and exploitation.

In order to connect definitional strands, I point out that the opportunity discovery and development process, may be conceived in terms of finding and developing solutions to problems (Nickerson and Zenger 2004; Shane 2003) and "the situations representing opportunities" may be related to "problem-solution pairings" (Hsieh et al. 2007: 1256; de Bruin and Ferrante 2011). Aligning with the definitions of Phills et al. (2008) and the LEED Forum cited above which conceives social innovation in terms of novel solutions to social problems, the dots are now joined to move to an integrating definitional strand. The social problem-solution-opportunity perspective provides an example of a bridge that can link the more macro-oriented social innovation arena with the micro focused social entrepreneurship field. Further bridges need to be conceived to simultaneously advance knowledge in both fields.

4 Concluding Comments

Researchers, particularly in the social sciences, can play a key role in advancing social innovation. Research centres and institutes such as New Zealand's new interdisciplinary SIERC and other more established institutes such as Zentrum für Soziale Innovation, Vienna, through their activities can build and disseminate knowledge in the field. They can bring together like-minded scholars and other stakeholders to catalyze the awareness and *"preparedness of society* to adopt new solutions for needs and challenges" (Hochgerner 2010: Preface). Only with a critical mass of like-minded researchers and protagonists of social innovation can the lopsided perspective on innovation, which unduly emphasizes technical innovation, be changed to a holistic and inclusive standpoint on innovation.

Social science researchers can serve a useful purpose both by playing a robust research-backed active advisory role to governments, supra-national organisations such as the European Commission, social needs oriented enterprises and foundations and/or acting as Gramscian 'organic intellectuals'[4] albeit not in the pure Gramscian sense (Gramsci 1971). When Gramsci was writing his *Prison Notebooks* (1971) from 1929 to 1935 he was also interested in ideological hegemony as it applied at the time. Associates of SIERC do not see themselves as hegemonic intellectuals nor counter-hegemonic intellectuals but as University academics mindful of their 'critic and conscience of society' responsibilities which is a statutory obligation for NZ universities (de Bruin et al. 2010; NZ Government 1989). With social innovation and entrepreneurship, including innovative nonprofit and voluntary sector activities and public sector innovation in meeting social needs, already of vital importance and continuing to accelerate in significance in contemporary society, Gramscian organic intellectuals must play a crucial role in advancing theory and practice of the field. They must work not as leaders but in partnership with other stakeholders to support social innovation and social and environmental change movements.

Institutes such as SIERC can also undertake research and dissemination of country experiences of social innovation. National and regional research is valuable because successful social innovations can be conveyed and adapted to new contexts. Comparative research can also be undertaken. Institute driven groupings can contribute to satisfying the need for robust and collaborative research to mitigate the wide knowledge gap in the area; can increase awareness of the importance of social innovation for addressing socio-environmental challenges, supporting economic, social and cultural development and employment growth and contributing to positive institutional change.

In their presentation on conducting social entrepreneurship research de Bruin and Kickul (2011) questioned if there can really be an end to the research. They raise the issue of what they term 'responsible reciprocity' and higher obligations of the social entrepreneurship researcher. They believe that where possible the researcher and the research process should contribute to the development of organizations and social enterprises that have been studied through feedback of findings. It is the role of social entrepreneurship researchers to develop practical and meaningful implications through their work and assessment that can assist social entrepreneurs in driving long-term systematic change for broader social, political, and economic wellbeing. As discussed in Mair and Martí (2006), the study of social entrepreneurship creates the opportunity to integrate, challenge, and debate traditional entrepreneurship assumptions in an effort to develop a cogent and unifying paradigm (de Bruin and Kickul 2011). In similar vein, researchers in the field of social innovation too have higher obligations, can act as Gramscian organic intellectuals, and their study and advocacy of social innovation can supplement and complement the current mainstream technical innovation perspective to provide a holistic and inclusive innovation paradigm.

---

[4] *Gramsci's words provide the best explanation of the 'organic intellectual': 'Every social group, coming into existence on the original terrain of an essential function in the world of economic production creates together with itself, organically,* one *or more strata of intellectuals which give it homogeneity and an awareness of its own function not only in the economic but also in the social and political fields' (1971: 5). Furthermore 'all men are intellectuals . . . but not all men have in society the function of intellectuals (1971: 9).*

References

Ardichvili, A., Cardozo, R., & Ray, S. (2003). A theory of entrepreneurial opportunity identification and development. *Journal of Business Venturing, 18*(1), 105–123.

Boven, R., Harland, C., & Grace, L. (2011). More ladders, fewer snakes: two proposals to reduce youth disadvantage. The New Zealand Institute, Discussion Paper 2011/1.

Bridges, J., & Downs, D. (2000). *No. 8 Wire–The Best of Kiwi Ingenuity*. Auckland: Hodder Moa Beckett.

Corner, P. D., & Ho, M. (2010). How opportunities develop in social entrepreneurship. *Entrepreneurship Theory and Practice, 34*(4), 635–659.

de Bruin, A. (2011). Social innovation. *Business and Economy in Auckland 2011*. Auckland Council, pp. 19–21.

de Bruin, A., & Stangl, L. (Eds.) (2011). Proceedings of the Massey University social innovation and entrepreneurship conference: Extending theory, integrating practice. http://sierc.massey.ac.nz/conference/proceedings/.

de Bruin, A., & Kickul, J. (2011). Conducting social entrepreneurship research: beginning, middle, end? Presentation at the Samoa conference II, National University of Samoa, July 4–8, 2011.

de Bruin, A., & Ferrante, F. (2011). Bounded opportunity: A knowledge-based approach to opportunity recognition and development. *Entrepreneurship Research Journal, 1*(4), 2. doi:10.2202/2157–5665.1018.

de Bruin, A., Fabrizi, S., Lee, L., & Lippert, S. (2010). Not for loss: Insights on building a community asset. Paper presented at the 7th annual Satter conference on social entrepreneurs, November 3–5, New York University.

Di Domenico, M., Haugh, H., & Tracey, P. (2010). Social bricolage: Theorizing social value creation in social enterprises. *Entrepreneurship Theory and Practice, 34*(4), 681–703.

European Commission–Enterprise and Industry (2010). This is European Social Innovation, Belgium, European Union.

European Union/The Young Foundation. (2010). Study on social innovation. A paper prepared by the Social Innovation EXchange (SIX) and the Young Foundation for the Bureau of European Policy Advisors.

FORA (2009). New nature of innovation. Report to the OECD. Copenhagen. Download from: New Nature of Innovation http://www.newnatureofinnovation.org/full_report.pdf. Accessed 11 August 2011.

Goldsmith, S., Georges, G., & Burke, T. G. (2010). *The power of social innovation: How civic entrepreneurs ignite community networks for good*. San Francisco: Jossey-Bass.

Gramsci, A. (1971). Selections from the Prison Notebooks, (editor and trans: Q. Hoare and G. Nowell-Smith). London: Lawrence and Wishart.

Hochgerner, J. (2010). Preface: Considering the social relevance of innovation. In Howaldt, J., & Schwarz, M. (Eds.), *Social innovation: Concepts, research fields and international trends*. IMA/ZLW & IfU, IMO International Monitoring (Vol 5).

Howaldt, J., & Schwarz, M. (2010). Social innovation: Concepts, research fields and international trends. IMA/ZLW & IfU, IMO International Monitoring (Vol 5).

Hsieh, C., Nickerson, J., & Zenger, T. (2007). Opportunity discovery, problem solving and a theory of the entrepreneurial firm. *Journal of Management Studies, 44*(7), 1255–1277.

Leadbeater, C. (2010). On innovation. http://www.ted.com/talks/charles_leadbeater_on_innovation.html.

Mair, J., & Martí, I. (2006). Social entrepreneurship research: A source of explanation, prediction, and delight. *Journal of World Business, 41*(1), 36–44.

Ministry for Culture and Heritage no date. New Zealand women and the vote. URL: http://www.nzhistory.net.nz/politics/womens-suffrage. Accessed 6 Sep 2011.

Mulgan, G., Tucker, S., Ali, R., & Sanders, B. (2007a). Social Innovation: What it is, why it matters and how it can be accelerated, The Young Foundation. Skoll Centre for Social Entrepreneuship Working Paper.

Mulgan, G., Ali, R., Halkett, R., & Sanders, B. (2007b). In and out of sync. The challenge of growing social innovations. Research report, London. The Young Foundation. http://www.youngfoundation.org/files/images/In_and_Out_of_Sync_Final.pdf.

New Zealand Government. (1989). Education Act 1989 No. 80 (as at 01 February 2011), Public Act of Parliament.

Nicholls, A. (2010). The legitimacy of social entrepreneurship: Reflexive isomorphism in a pre-paradigmatic field. *Entrepreneurship Theory and Practice, 34*(4), 611–633.

Nickerson, J., & Zenger, T. (2004). A knowledge-based theory of governance choice: The problem solving approach. *Organization Science, 15*(6), 617–632.

OECD. (2000). LEED Forum on Social Innovation. http://www.oecd.org/document/21/0,3746,en_2649_34417_44255253_1_1_1_1,00.html.

OECD. (2007). *OECD reviews of innovation policy: New Zealand*. Paris: OECD.

Perrini, F. (2006). Social entrepreneurship domain: setting boundaries. In F. Perrini (Ed.), *The new social entrepreneurship: What awaits social entrepreneurial ventures?* Northampton: Edward Elgar.

Phills, J. A., Deiglmeier, K., & Miller, D. T. (2008). Rediscovering social innovation. *Stanford Social Innovation Review, 6*(4), 34–43.

Robb-Post, C., Stamp, J. A., Carsrud, A. L., & Reynolds, P. D. (2010). Social ventures from a resource-based perspective: An exploratory study assessing global Ashoka fellows. *Entrepreneurship Theory and Practice, 34*, 661–680.

Shane, S. (2003). *The individual-opportunity nexus approach to entrepreneurship*. Aldershot: Edward Elgar.

Short, J., Moss, T., & Lumpkin, G. (2009). Research in social entrepreneurship: Past contributions and future opportunities. *Strategic Entrepreneurship Journal, 3*, 161–194.

Shane, S. & Venkataraman, S. (2000). The promise of entrepreneurship as a field of research. *Academy of Management Review, 25*, 217–226.

Smith, K. (2006). Public policy framework for the New Zealand innovation system. Ministry of Economic Development Working Paper, 06/06.

Zahra, S., Rawhouser, H., Nachiket, B., Neubaum, D., & Hayton, J. (2008). Globalization of social entrepreneurship opportunities. *Strategic Entrepreneurship Journal, 2*, 117–131.

Final Observations

Hans-Werner Franz, Josef Hochgerner, and Jürgen Howaldt

The book does not need concluding remarks. Born from the wealth of research and experience of its authors in the unlimited fields of social innovation, we, the editors, can only try to safeguard that nothing from its rich and imaginative generation process is lost. It is for this reason that we want to make one step back in order to look ahead.

Generated through the process of preparation and the vivid and dense congregation of social innovation minds during the Challenge Social Innovation Conference in Vienna from September 2011, along with this book and along with 17 further contributions published in the ZSI Discussion Papers (www.zsi.at/dp), we have succeeded in collecting, structuring and editing the Vienna Declaration, as an immediate output and key result of the conference. It was conceived as a service to research and innovation policy experts from the European Commission, OECD and UNESCO as well as from national research policy institutions who needed a vote of the scientific community on social innovation gathered in Vienna on what this convention of scholars deemed necessary to be dealt with in the research agendas to come next.

As the Declaration, accessible via the conference website (www.socialinnovation2011.eu), points out, "in light of the increasing importance of social innovation, the conference looked at the theoretical concepts, areas of empirical research, concepts and developments in the field of social innovation. What is required here is to redraw boundaries (both in terms of differences as well as overlaps and interactions) between business innovations and new technologies, on the one hand, and social innovations on the other hand. Increasingly, innovation blossoms where sectors, systems and concepts converge."

H.-W. Franz (✉) • J. Howaldt
Social Research Centre, Dortmund University of Technology, Dortmund, Germany
e-mail: Franz@sfs-dortmund.de; howaldt@sfs-dortmund.de

J. Hochgerner
Centre for Social Innovation, Linke Wienzeile 246, 1150 Vienna, Austria
e-mail: hochgerner@zsi.at

The Vienna Declaration explicitly refers to the social and societal challenges which the European Commission has put forward in its Europe 2020 Strategy:

"In response to major societal challenges the Europe 2020 strategy sets measurable targets such as Employment of 75 % of the workforce, investment of 3 % of the EU GDP in Research, Development and Innovation (RDI), adapting to the challenges of Climate Change (20 % less greenhouse gas emissions, 20 % increase in energy efficiency, 20 % of energy from renewable resources), reducing school drop-out rates below 10 % and enabling 40 % of age cohorts to complete third level Education, and reducing the number of people in or at risk of Poverty and Social Exclusion by 20 million.

The fulfilment of such specified targets will require novel technologies and economic measures, yet, to an unprecedented extent, also social innovations. The necessary co-ordination of scientific as well as practical activities in the wide domains of employment, RDI, climate change, education, and social inclusion will be impossible without major changes in social practices in the domains of business, the civil society, and the state. The tracks of international research on innovation demonstrate that the technology-oriented paradigm – shaped by the industrial society – does not cover the broad range of innovations indispensable in the transition from an industrial to a knowledge and services-based society: Such fundamental societal changes require the inclusion of social innovations in a paradigm shift of the innovation system.

The new innovation paradigm is essentially characterised by the opening of the innovation process to society. Alongside companies, universities and research institutes, citizens and customers become relevant actors of innovation processes. Terms and concepts such as open innovation, user-led innovation, customer integration and innovation networks reflect aspects of this development. Innovation becomes a general social phenomenon and increasingly influences all walks of life.

Further innovations in technology and business are imperative; yet in order to reap their full potential, and at the same time creating social development that is beneficial to cultures as inclusive as diverse, social innovations will make the difference: There is a lot of evidence that social innovation will become of growing importance not only with regard to social integration and equal opportunities but also with regard to preserving and expanding the innovative capacity of companies and society as a whole.

The most urgent and important innovations in the twenty-first century will take place in the social field. This opens up the necessity as well as possibilities for Social Sciences and Humanities to find new roles and relevance by generating knowledge applicable to new dynamics and structures of contemporary and future societies."

How did we produce this Declaration? The 14 thematic sessions of the conference were asked to suggest up to four topics from their thematic area which they considered to be the most urgent and relevant ones in research on social innovation. The plenary sessions of the 350 participants of the conference then voted on the 56 suggestions, prioritizing the 14 headlines which are the core of the Declaration. As the Declaration itself stresses, these topics "do not represent the completion of the process of determining research issues. In fact, the whole operation was built on being courageous enough to start the process of getting there, while at the same time remaining modest enough to know that this is just a beginning. The Vienna Declaration shall be read, commented and considered as a starting point to specify crucial research topics in Social Sciences and Humanities, aiming at the identification, development and implementation of the most needed social innovations of the twenty-first century."

The results of the debates and the voting procedures can be summarised under two headings:

1. Overall scientific advancement required to meet expectations and developments in social innovation practices

    - Elaboration on the particular features of the concept and clarification of definitions
    - Embedding the concept of social innovation in a comprehensive theory of innovation
    - Development of coherent methodologies to identify and measure social innovations

2. Prioritised research topics

    - The potential of social innovation in the social economy, civil society, business firms, and the state
    - Multi-level governance and receptivity of governments to social innovations
    - The role of social processes in varied collaboration formats and organisational structures in business innovation
    - The relationship between service innovations and social innovations
    - Workplace innovations for smarter and better working
    - Value creation by social innovations and measuring different sorts of value
    - Monitoring, assessment, and measurement of social resources for innovation and of social impact of technology
    - Approaches and competencies of social sciences to actively contribute to the practical implementation of social innovations
    - The distinctive contributions of Humanities-based knowledge and methods of enquiry (time: history; ideas and concepts: philosophies and worldviews; communication: linguistics . . .) to social innovations
    - Establish a multi-national evidence-base of promising practices for inclusion and integration
    - Conditions of participation and self-management in social innovations aimed at overcoming poverty and pauperisation
    - Indicators of short-term and long-term effects of the educational system on quality of life, well-being, innovativeness
    - Lifelong learning, work and intergenerational solidarity as components of socially engaged ageing
    - Opportunities and risks of social media for enabling large scale and systemic social innovations

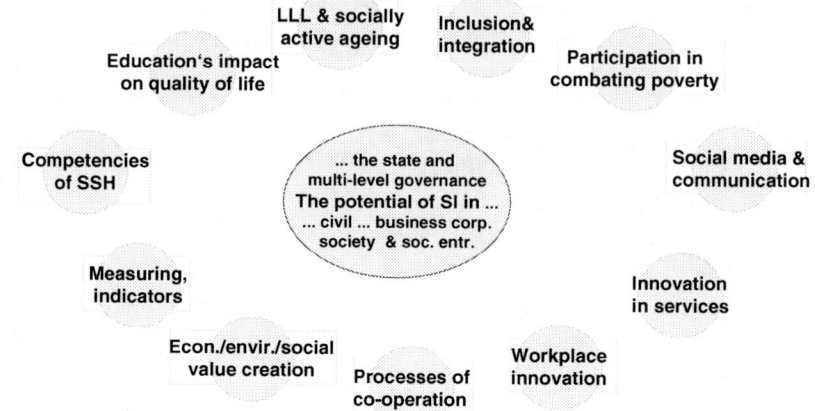

Fig. 1 Topical research areas in brief overview

In a graphic illustration, combining a few of the topics in the central focus point highlighting the potentials of social innovation, the topics prioritised may be briefly depicted like planets in a solar system around the central issue of applying social innovations systematically in all societal sectors. Each of these 'planets' needs research and development, and further 'planets' need to be discovered (cf. Fig. 1).

There are three main ways to build on the results of the conference captured in the Vienna Declaration:

1. Suggested input to include social innovation topics in research programmes
   The core intention of the conference was to establish for the first time a large international convention of researchers concerned with social innovation, reaching out to all continents. Accordingly, the great majority of the 350 participants were scholars and researchers from the wide realms of Social Sciences and Humanities across Europe and the world. Thus scientific background and manifold research competencies are reflected in all research topics proposed, and discernible degrees of agreement expressed in the 14 prioritised topics.
   The topics on this list received support by the majority. They may therefore be considered a strong vote by the respective scientific community to address such issues in processes of drafting future research programmes in Social Sciences and Humanities. This could become relevant on European as well as on national levels wherever social innovations should be analysed with a view to their context, initiation, implementation or impact.
   We hope the Vienna Declaration, follow-up statements and papers can assist and inspire future discussions of research programmes in FP7 and Horizon 2020, as well as activities under the Flagship Initiative Innovation Union of the Europe

2020 strategy, and other European, national or international measures concerning science, research and innovation.

Beyond the EU and its Member States, the Vienna Declaration also was brought to the attention of the OECD LEED Forum on Social Innovation and the Social Innovation Programme of UNESCO.

2. Scientific exchange among scholars

The full documentation of the making and results of the Vienna Declaration (all topics proposed during the conference, the voting process and scores, comments contributed and debates stimulated) remain available at the CSI website www.socialinnovation2011.eu. The forum is open for further provision of comments and dissemination through communication channels in science, the wider public, printed and digital media including Web 2.0. By and by continuing discussion and reflexion may create a repository of statements, thematic clusters, methodologies suggested and tested, as well as of research references, literature and statistical sources.

The conference organisers will serve as nodes in such communications, connecting participants and additional colleagues or institutes. Ultimately, stimulating discussions and collaboration across scientific disciplines, national and institutional borders shall facilitate trans-disciplinary research: Bridging of science and research on the one hand, and implementation and practice of social innovation on the other hand.

3. Community building in the framework of the European School of Social Innovation (ESSI)

The European School of Social Innovation, formally established (10 Oct. 2011) and based in Vienna, was launched in collaboration between researchers from the Centre for Social Innovation (ZSI) in Vienna and the Social Research Center (sfs) at the Technische Universität Dortmund. It is conceived as an international competence network, reaching out to European and global scholars and institutions involved in social innovation research, academic education and vocational training.

The School, comprising and co-ordinating activities in research and education, is not called a European School because it should be confined to European researchers, students and institutions. On the contrary, it will be open for intercontinental participation in research, courses and study programmes, yet with a specific focus on the conditions and sources of social innovations rooted in European social systems.

The debates during the conference and the selection of 14 prioritised research topics concerning social innovation clearly illustrated that until recently the area of social innovation has been virtually ignored as an independent phenomenon in socio-economic research on innovation, let alone research in humanities: Social innovation rarely appears as a specific and defined term with a clearly delineated scope. Mostly it is used as a sort of descriptive metaphor in the context of social and technical change. We have to admit that social innovation currently is a term that almost everybody likes, but a precise and broadly accepted definition is still missing.

The European School of Social Innovation shall help to correct this deficiency by bringing together an international research community, enabling increasingly prolific scientific cooperation, and advancing the development of a theoretically sound concept of social innovation. We see a growing number of renowned research institutes all around the world engaging in scientific research on social innovation. Many researchers from these institutes have been with us at the conference. Henceforth, much will depend on aligning competencies of Social Sciences and Humanities by joint efforts to analysing and lecturing on improved concepts, knowledge and research on social innovations.

Printed by Books on Demand, Germany